The
HIDDEN INNS
of
THE WEST COUNTRY

including
Dorset, Somerset, Devon
and Cornwall

Edited by
Barbara Vesey

© Travel Publishing Ltd.

ii

Published by:
Travel Publishing Ltd
7a Apollo House, Calleva Park
Aldermaston, Berks, RG7 8TN
ISBN 1-902-00748-4
© Travel Publishing Ltd

First Published: 2000

Regional Titles in the Hidden Inns Series:

West Country	Southeast England
South of England	Wales

Regional Titles in the Hidden Places Series:

Cambridgeshire & Lincolnshire	Channel Islands
Cheshire	Chilterns
Cornwall	Derbyshire
Devon	Dorset, Hants & Isle of Wight
Essex	Gloucestershire & Wiltshire
Heart of England	Hereford, Worcs & Shropshire
Highlands & Islands	Kent
Lake District & Cumbria	Lancashire
Norfolk	Northeast Yorkshire
Northumberland & Durham	North Wales
Nottinghamshire	Potteries
Somerset	South Wales
Suffolk	Surrey
Sussex	Thames Valley
Warwickshire & W Midlands	Yorkshire

National Titles in the Hidden Places Series:

England	Ireland
Scotland	Wales

Printing by: Ashford Press, Gosport
Maps by: © MAPS IN MINUTES ™ (2000)
Line Drawings: Rodney Peace
Editor: Barbara Vesey
Cover Design: Lines & Words, Aldermaston
Cover Photographs: The Fox Inn, Ansty, Dorset © Britain on View/Stockwave; The
Bell Inn, Bovey Tracey, Devon; The Admiral Benbow, Penzance,
Cornwall.

Foreword

The *Hidden Inns* series originates from the enthusiastic suggestions of readers of the popular *Hidden Places* guides. They want to be directed to traditional inns "off the beaten track" with atmosphere and character which are so much a part of our British heritage. But they also want information on the many places of interest and activities to be found in the vicinity of the inn.

The inns or pubs reviewed in the *Hidden Inns* may have been coaching inns but have invariably been a part of the history of the village or town in which they are located. All the inns included in this guide serve food and drink and many offer the visitor overnight accommodation. A full page is devoted to each inn which contains a line drawing of the inn, full name, address and telephone number, directions on how to get there, a full description of the inn and its facilities and a wide range of useful information such as opening hours, food served, accommodation provided, credit cards taken and details of entertainment. *Hidden Inns* guides however are not simply pub guides. They provide the reader with helpful information on the many places of interest to visit and activities to pursue in the area in which the inn is based. This ensures that your visit to the area will not only allow you to enjoy the atmosphere of the inn but also to take in the beautiful countryside which surrounds it.

The *Hidden Inns* guides have been expertly designed for ease of use. *The Hidden Inns of the West Country* is divided into 8 regionally based chapters, each of which is laid out in the same way. To identify your preferred geographical region refer to the contents page overleaf. To find a pub or inn simply use the index and locator map at the beginning of each chapter which refers you, via a page number reference, to a full page dedicated to the specific establishment. To find a place of interest again use the index and locator map found at the beginning of each chapter which will guide you to a descriptive summary of the area followed by details of each place of interest.

We do hope that you will get plenty of enjoyment from visiting the inns and places of interest contained in this guide. We are always interested in what our readers think of the inns or places covered (or not covered) in our guides so please do not hesitate to fill out the reader reaction forms. This is a vital way of helping us ensure that we maintain a high standard of entry and that we are providing the right sort of information for our readers. Finally if you are planning to visit any other corner of the British Isles we would like to refer you to the list of Hidden Inns and Hidden Places guides to be found at the rear of the book.

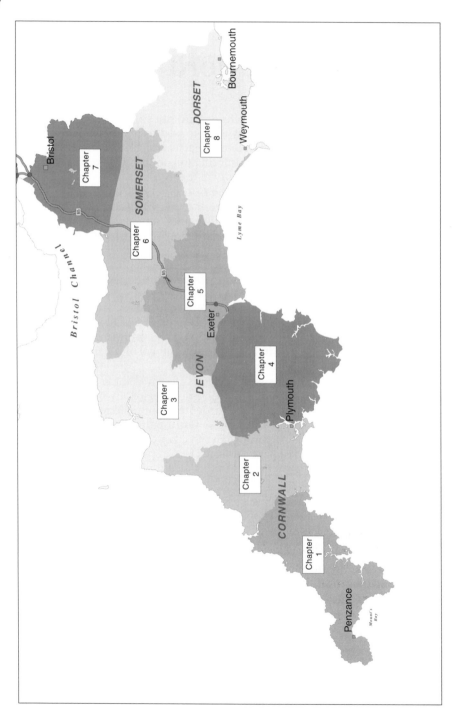

Contents

TITLE PAGE   *i*

FOREWORD   **iii**

CONTENTS   v

GEOGRAPHICAL AREAS:

    West Cornwall   1
    East Cornwall   41
    North Devon   73
    South Devon   97
    East Devon   137
    South and West Somerset   167
    North and East Somerset   197
    Dorset   231

INDEXES AND LISTS:

    Alphabetic List of Pubs and Inns   271
    Special Interest Lists of Pubs and Inns:
        With accommodation   275
        Opening all day   277
        Welcoming children   279
        Accepting credit cards   281
        With Garden, Patio or Terrace   284
        With occasional or regular live entertainment   287
        Where pets are welcome   289
        With a separate restaurant or dining area   290

    Index of Towns and Villages   293

ADDITIONAL INFORMATION:

    Reader Comment Forms   295
    Order Form   297

1 West Cornwall

PLACES OF INTEREST:

Bodmin   3
Charlestown   4
Come to Good   4
Creed   4
Falmouth   4
Godolphin Cross   5
Gweek   6
Hayle   6
Helford   6
Helston   7
Kestle Mill   7
Land's End   7
Lizard Peninsula   8
Mawnan Smith   8

Mevagissey   8
Newquay   9
Padstow   10
Penzance   10
Porthcurno   11
Redruth   11
St Agnes   12
St Austell   12
St Columb Major   13
St Ives   13
St Just in Roseland   15
St Michael's Mount   15
Truro   15
Washaway   16

PUBS AND INNS:

The Admiral Benbow, Penzance   17
The Angarrack Inn, Angarrack   18
The Barley Sheaf, Gorran Churchtown   19
The Blue Anchor Inn, Helston   20
The Boscawen Hotel, St Dennis   21
Cable Station Inn, Porthcurno   22
The Cornish Arms, St Blazey   23
The Crown Inn, St Ewe   24
The Farmers Arms, St Merryn   25
The Ferry Boat Inn, Helford Passage   26
The Fountain Inn, Newbridge   27
The George and Dragon, Bodmin   28

The Kings Arms, Paul   29
The Kings Arms, St Just   30
The Kings Arms, St Stephen   31
The London Inn, Padstow   32
The North Inn, Pendeen   33
The Pendarves Arms, Gwithian   34
The Queens Arms, St Just   35
The Royal Standard Inn, Gerrans   36
The Sawles Arms, Carthew   37
The Ship Inn, Polmear   38
The Ship Inn, Portloe   39
The Tolcarne Inn, Newlyn   40

The Hidden Inns of the West Country

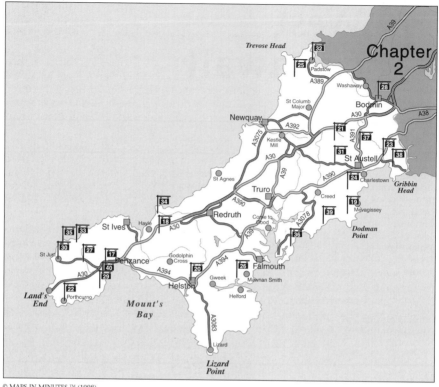

© MAPS IN MINUTES ™ (1998)

17 The Admiral Benbow, Penzance

18 The Angarrack Inn, Angarrack

19 The Barley Sheaf, Gorran Churchtown

20 The Blue Anchor Inn, Helston

21 The Boscawen Hotel, St Dennis

22 Cable Station Inn, Porthcurno

23 The Cornish Arms, St Blazey

24 The Crown Inn, St Ewe

25 The Farmers Arms, St Merryn

26 The Ferry Boat Inn, Helford Passage

27 The Fountain Inn, Newbridge

28 The George and Dragon, Bodmin

29 The Kings Arms, Paul

30 The Kings Arms, St Just

31 The Kings Arms, St Stephen

32 The London Inn, Padstow

33 The North Inn, Pendeen

34 The Pendarves Arms, Gwithian

35 The Queens Arms, St Just

36 The Royal Standard Inn, Gerrans

37 The Sawles Arms, Carthew

38 The Ship Inn, Polmear

39 The Ship Inn, Portloe

40 The Tolcarne Inn, Newlyn

Please note all cross references refer to page numbers

Fleets of trawlers, netters and crabbers, colourful harbours surrounded by pastel-washed houses, miles of fine sandy beaches and rugged cliffs - the towns and villages of north-western Cornwall offer visitors some of the most typically Cornish scenes and experiences. Narrow streets run down to bustling waterfronts, where fishing boats rub gunnels with cabin cruisers and yachts, and visitors can watch the ebb and flow of harbour life.

This region offers rugged coastlines, the beautiful towns and villages of the Fal Estuary, and some exceptionally pretty coastal communities. The Carrick Roads, a spectacular deep-water anchorage which is formed by the merging of seven river estuaries, is one of the many scenic highlights of the region, as is the famed Roseland Peninsula, the name given to the indented tongue of land which forms the eastern margin of the Fal Estuary.

This is a region of stunning gardens, and many stately homes. The legacy of Cornwall's seafaring heritage - of shipwrecks, booty and trawling - is also of course in abundance, in the shape of the many peaceful and secluded fishing villages that still exist.

Western Cornwall has for the most part a mild climate with the help of the warm flowing waters of the Gulf Stream. Legends abound in the area, with tales of shipwrecks, smugglers and exotic sea creatures. The great beauty and isolation of this wonderful part of the county has been an inspiration to many artists over the years - St Ives became an artists colony for the likes of Whistler, Sickert, Nicholson and Lanyon, and continues to attract many painters and other artists today.

The Cornish Riviera is characterised by small fishing harbours built in quiet natural coves. The home of Britain's surfing fraternity, both the seacoast and the inland countryside have much to offer those who enjoy the outdoor life. Lizard Point, the southernmost point of mainland Britain, is dotted with exquisite fishing villages and breathtaking scenery.

PLACES OF INTEREST

BODMIN

Bustling by day, yet quiet by night, the historic former county town of Bodmin lies midway between Cornwall's north and south coasts at the junction of two ancient cross-country trading routes.

For many centuries, traders between Wales, Ireland and northern France preferred the overland route between the Camel and Fowey estuaries to the hazardous sea journey around Land's End. **Castle Canyke** to the southeast of the town was built during the Iron Age to defend this important trade route, and a few centuries later the Romans erected a fort on a site above the River Camel to the west of the town, one of a string they built in the Southwest to defend strategic river crossings; the remains of a quadrilateral earthwork can still be made out today. The ancient cross-country route is now a waymarked footpath known as the Saints' Way.

Bodmin is also renowned for its holy wells - 11 in all. Some, such as **Eye Water Well**, are known for their restorative properties, and some, such as **St Guron's Well** opposite the church, for being ancient places of baptism. Bodmin was the only market town in Cornwall to be mentioned in the Domesday Book, and at one time it boasted its own mint and, later, the county assizes. However, the 19th century rise of Truro as Cornwall's cathedral city stripped Bodmin of its county town status. A number of impressive relics of its former glory

4

nevertheless remain, including the Tudor guildhall, the former court buildings, and the **Turret Clock** where former mayor, Nicholas Boyer, was hanged for his part in the Prayer Book Rebellion on 1549. Public executions were also held at Bodmin Gaol in Berrycombe Road, a once-feared place which now operates as an hotel and features a fascinating exhibition that takes in the former dungeons.

Bodmin also contains two first-rate museums: the **Town Museum** and the **Regimental Museum** (also known as the Duke of Cornwall' Light Infantry Museum), which is housed in the Duke of Cornwall's old headquarters. Turf Street leads up past Mount Folly to **The Beacon**, a scenic picnic area with a 140 foot obelisk at its summit which was built to commemorate the Victorian general, Sir Walter Raleigh Gilbert. One of Britain's earliest railways was opened in 1830 to link Bodmin with the Camel estuary at Wadebridge. In recent years the track has been reopened as a public cyclepath and walkway, **The Camel Trail**, which runs all the way from Boscarne Junction to Padstow.

CHARLESTOWN

Charlestown Harbour is a familiar location for TV programmes such as *Poldark* and *The Onedin Line*. Built in 1790 for the import of coal and export of china clay, this wonderful centre remains a Georgian time capsule, now providing permanent berth for square-riggers. The outstanding **Shipwreck and Heritage Centre** offers visitors a fascinating insight into the history of Chalestown and shipwrecks, housing the

Chalestown Harbour

largest general exhibition in the UK of artefacts recovered by divers. Animated scenes of village life, hundreds of photographs and prints, and the recovered valuables themselves - pewter plates, candlesticks, weapons, beads, gold and silver, among many others - make for a fascinating peek into the past.

COME TO GOOD

In this delightfully named hamlet the road between Carnon Downs and the King Harry Ferry passes a pretty cob and thatch building, the **Quaker Meeting House**, one of the oldest in the country. Built around 1710 when the Society of Friends was still outlawed, it is still in use to this day. Despite its pious-sounding name, the hamlet takes its name from the Cornish phrase Cwm-ty-quite, meaning 'house in the wooded combe'.

A mile east, the National Trust-owned **Trelissick Gardens** lie on either side of the B3289 as the road descends to the King Harry Ferry. These beautiful wooded gardens were laid out in their present form by the Copelands between 1937 and 1955 in the grounds of a 19th century neoclassical mansion (which is not open to visitors). Renowned for their collections of mature trees and flowering shrubs, which include magnolias, rhododendrons, azaleas and hydrangeas, the gardens are particularly lovely in early summer. Special features include a summer house with a Saxon cross and a Victorian water tower with a steep conical roof and 'squirrel' weather vane. A network of delightful woodland walks leads down to the banks of the Carrick Roads.

CREED

Just west of this charming small village is **Trewithen House**, an elegant Georgian manor house built early in the 18th century by the Hawkins family, in whose hands it remains today. The exceptionally beautiful 25 acre gardens were planted by George Johnson, an authority on Asiatic flowering shrubs, and contain a world-renowned collection of magnolias, camellias, azaleas and rhododendrons which are particularly spectacular in late spring.

The grounds of Trewithen House adjoin the **Probus Demonstration Gardens and Rural Studies Centre**, a seven-and-a-half acre area of permanent gardens devoted to the study of plants grown in different soils and climatic conditions.

FALMOUTH

Falmouth stands in a magnificent position at the entrance to the **Carrick Roads**, a spectacular deep-water anchorage which is formed by the merging of seven river estuaries. Although a settlement has existed here for many hundreds of years, it wasn't until the 17th century that the port was properly developed as a mail packet station which subsequently became the communications hub for the British Empire.

Three centuries before, Henry VIII built a pair of fortresses on either side of the estuary mouth to protect the strategically important deep-water anchorage from attack by forces loyal to the Catholic faith. **Pendennis Castle** on the western side is superbly sited on a 200 foot promontory overlooking the entrance to Carrick Roads. Its low circular keep has immensely thick walls and stands within a 16 sided enclosure;

Pendennis Castle

the outer curtain wall was added during Elizabethan times in response to the threat of a second Spanish Armada. One of the last Royalist strongholds to fall during the English Civil War, Pendennis only succumbed to the Parliamentarians following a grim siege lasting five months. The castle remained in use as a coastal defence station until the end of the Second World War and is now under the ownership of English Heritage. The spectacular viewpoint of **Pendennis Point** is also the location of the Maritime Rescue Centre, the operational headquarters which was opened in 1981 to coordinate all search and rescue operations around the British coastline.

That Falmouth was developed as a port at all was due to Sir Walter Raleigh, a man whose early vision was later realised by the influential local buccaneering family, the Killgrews. A monument to the family erected in 1737 can be seen in Grove Place, a short distance from the remains of their once-splendid Tudor man-

sion, **Arwenack House**. Falmouth's Royalist sympathies are demonstrated in the 17th century parish church which is dedicated to 'King Charles the Martyr'; much altered, it retains its curious rectangular tower and arcades with Ionic plaster capitals. Elsewhere in the town there are some handsome early 19th century buildings, including the **Falmouth Arts Centre** in Church Street, which began life as a Quaker institute 'to promote the useful arts', the synagogue in Vernon Place, and the Custom House with its fine colonnaded facade. A curious chimney near the Custom House was used for burning contraband tobacco and is still referred to as the 'King's Pipe'. The area around Custom House Quay has been made into a conservation area, the centrepiece of which is the tall-funnelled steam tug, the St Denys. This fascinating little ship forms part of **the Cornwall Maritime Museum**.

For those keen to explore the upper reaches of the Carrick Roads by boat, a variety of pleasure trips depart from the Prince of Wales pier, as do the cross-estuary passenger ferries to St Mawes and Flushing. The tree-lined square known as the 'Moor' can be found a short distance inland from the pier; on one side stands the town hall and art gallery, and on the other a steep flight of 111 steps known as Jacob's Ladder leads up to a Wesleyan chapel. An attractive sight throughout the summer months are the periodic races between Falmouth's old gaff-rigged working boats. These colourful competitions evolved from the traditional practice of racing out to newly-arrived sailing ships to tender for work. A number of these handsome working vessels, some of the last examples in the country still to operate under sail, are used for dredging oysters from the Helford estuary.

A lane to the southwest of Falmouth leads past the little-known **Penjerrick Gardens**, an attractive wild valley garden laid out by the Quaker Fox family which contains one of the largest magnolias in the country. Penjerrick is also famous for its hybrid rhododendrons, which were developed by the head gardener in the 19th century, and for its bamboos and tree ferns.

GODOLPHIN CROSS

The exceptional part-Tudor **Godolphin House**, featured in the Poldark series, can be found in the wooded lanes midway between this village

6

and Townshend. Part early 16th century with substantial Elizabethan and Carolean additions, this is the former home of the Earls of Godolphin, prominent Cornish entrepreneurs who amassed a fortune from their mining interests.

The unique north front was completed shortly after the English Civil War and incorporates an impressive seven-bay granite colonnade. The interior is noted for its splendid King's Room, fine Jacobean fireplaces, and a painting of the famous 'Godolphin Arabian', a stallion imported by the second Earl which is said to be one of the three from which all British thoroughbred horses are descended.

There is some excellent walking on nearby **Tregonning Hill**, a site littered with Bronze Age remains which also has an important place in industrial history, for it was here that William Cookworthy first discovered china clay, or kaolin, in the 1740's. An Admiralty signalling station was also established here during the Napoleonic Wars.

GWEEK

Gweek stands at the head of the westernmost branch of the **Helford River**. Although it is hard to imagine today, this was once a flourishing commercial port whose importance grew when the harbour at nearby Helston silted up in the 13th century. Gweek eventually suffered the same fate, and the cargo vessels of old have long since been replaced by small pleasure craft and sailing dinghies. In recent years, however, the port has undergone something of a rejuvenation with the opening of the **Quay Maritime Centre**, the largest collection of historic small craft in Cornwall. Another of Gweek's attractions is the **Cornish Seal Sanctuary**, which can be found a short distance from the village on the northern side of the creek. Injured seals and orphaned pups are brought here from all over the country for treatment and care before being returned to the wild; there is an underwater observatory which allows visitors to see the seals close to.

Just to the North of Gweek in the charming hamlet of **Torvan Cross** is the unusual location of a massive Bronze Age monolith known as the **Tolvan Holed Stone**. In the back garden of a cottage and standing 7 feet tall, this curious triangular stone is said to bring fertility to those who squeeze their naked bodies through

its 17 inch circular aperture.

HAYLE

Hayle was a major industrial port and engineering centre in the centuries leading up to the decline of the mining industry at the turn of the 20th century. The great Cornish inventor, Richard Trevithick, built an early version of the steam locomotive here in the early 1800s, and not long after one of the first railways in the world was constructed to carry tin and copper to Hayle Quay from Redruth. At the height of the industry in the 19th century, steam-powered engines built by the famous 'Harveys of Hayle' could be found in most of the mines in Cornwall. After more than a century of decline, plans have been drawn up to redevelop comprehensively the old port area.

Paradise Park can be found on the southern edge of Hayle. The park is a haven for rare and endangered birds, including the Cornish chough, a once-common inhabitant of the local cliffs which is now extinct in the county. (The striking red-billed bird is incorporated into the Cornish coat of arms.) Displays of eagles and other birds of prey in flight can be seen at certain times throughout the day.

HELFORD

During the summer, a passenger ferry operates between Helford Passage and the village of Helford on the southern bank. This picture-postcard village stands in one of the most lush and attractive settings in Cornwall, the secluded tree-line estuary of the **Helford River**. Once the haunt of smugglers, this deep series of tidal creeks is also rumoured to be the home of Morgawr, the legendary Helford monster. Since his first recorded sighting in 1926, he has been seen on a number of occasions and described as a 'hideous hump-backed creature with stumpy horns'. The village itself has a charming, relaxed atmosphere, with traffic being banned from the streets during the summer months.

The **Frenchman's Creek** immortalised by Daphne du Maurier in her novel of the same name lies half a mile to the west of Helford village. Although best seen by boat, land access to this beautiful wooded inlet can be made via the farm at Kestle, which is signposted off the road to **Manaccan**, another attractive village standing at the head of a tidal creek.

HELSTON

Helston is the westernmost of Cornwall's five medieval Stannary towns. During the early Middle Ages, streamed tin was brought here for assaying and taxing before being despatched throughout southern Britain and continental Europe. Although difficult to imagine today, this was a very busy port up until the 13th century, when a shingle bar formed across the mouth of the River Cober, preventing access to the sea. Goods were then transported to a new quay at Gweek, until further silting and a decline in tin extraction brought an end to the trade.

Helston's long and colourful history has left it with a legacy of interesting old buildings. The **Blue Anchor Inn**, a hostel for monks in the 15th century, can be found at the lower end of the main Coinagehall Street; further up, the part-16th century Angel Hotel is the former town house of the Godolphin family. In the 1750's, the Earl of Godolphin was responsible for rebuilding the parish **Church of St Michael** at the back of the town. The churchyard contains a memorial to Henry Trengrouse, the Helston man responsible for inventing the rocket-propelled safety line which saved so many lives around the British coast. Trengrouse devoted himself to developing the device after the frigate Anson ran aground on nearby **Loe Bar** in 1807, resulting in the unnecessary loss of 100 lives. An exhibit devoted to his life's work can be found in Helston's **Folk Museum**, a fascinating collection of historical artefacts which is housed in the old Butter Market.

Helston continues to be a market town, and on Mondays the main thoroughfare is lined with colourful market stalls. In Wendron Street there's a modest thatched cottage that was birthplace to 'Battling' Bob Fitzsimmons, who went on to become the world heavyweight boxing champion.

When the shingle bar formed across the mouth of the River Cober in the 13th century, the dammed river created the largest natural freshwater lake in the county. Lying a couple of miles southwest of Helston and once forming part of an estate belonging to the Rogers family, Loe Pool is now under the ownership of the National Trust. A delightful six-mile walk leads around the wooded fringes of the lake, although those less inclined to walk the full distance can take a shorter stroll through the woods on the western side. This tranquil body of water is a haven for seabirds and waterfowl, and is a paradise for ornithologists and picnickers.

On the southern approaches to Helston, the A3083 passes close to **Flambards**, a popular all-weather theme park set in attractive landscaped grounds and offering a variety of attractions, including an aero park, Victorian village, 'Britain in the Blitz' exhibition and an assortment of up-to-date fairground rides.

KESTLE MILL

The exceptionally attractive small Elizabethan manor house, **Trerice**, lies hidden in the lanes two miles northwest of Kestle Mill. Built in 1571 on the site of a medieval predecessor, it was the family home of the influential Arundell family for several centuries. The structure has a char-

Trerice House

acteristic E-shaped front and unusual carved gables, a possible Dutch influence, and stands within 14 acres of beautiful landscaped grounds. The interior is noted for its striking plasterwork ceilings, huge fireplaces and fine walnut furniture.

Most impressive is the great hall, with its delightful minstrels' gallery and remarkable window containing over 500 panes of glass, most of them original. An unusual small museum in one of the outbuildings is dedicated to the history of the lawnmower. The property is now under the ownership of the National Trust.

LAND'S END

Land's End is a curious mixture of natural spectacle and manmade indulgence. Here, the granite backbone of West Penwith succumbs to the Atlantic in a series of savage cliffs, reefs and sheer-sided islets, encompassing some awe-inspiring cliff scenery. On a clear day it is possi-

8

ble to see beyond the **Longships** (a mile and a half offshore) and the **Wolf Rock** (7 miles offshore) lighthouses to the Isles of Scilly, over 25 miles away to the southwest.

The Land's End site, mainland Britain's most westerly point, has long been in private hands and, over the years, various attempts have been made to create a visitor attraction worthy of this illustrious setting. The **'Land's End Experience'** heritage centre offers a range of impressive audio-visual presentations on the natural and maritime history of the area, which since Roman times has been known as the 'Seat of Storms'. There is also a hotel with magnificent sea views, and a number of children's attractions.

The Land's End airport is situated beside the B3306 to the northeast of Whitesand Bay; as well as a regular service to the Isles of Scilly, short flights can be taken which offer visitors a spectacular bird's-eye view of the surrounding coastline.

LIZARD PENINSULA

The rugged splendour of the Lizard Peninsula is a sight to be seen. Here the land rises onto Goonhilly Downs, an area of windswept granite and serpentine heathland which is littered with Bronze Age remains and some rather more up-to-the-minute human creations - the huge saucer aerials and satellite dishes of British Telecom's **Goonhilly Downs Earth Station**. A guided tour of the station can be taken during the summer months which incorporates an informative audiovisual presentation on the development of modern satellite communications.

As well as being of interest to the Bronze Age archeologist, the Lizard is of special interest to the botanist. The peninsula's moorland and cliffs are home to a number of rare wild plants, including the pink-flowering 'Cornish Heath', and a nature reserve has been established on **Predannack Downs** to preserve this valuable natural habitat. The rugged and undulating stretch of the **South West Coast Path** around the Lizard is among the most spectacular in Cornwall.

Lizard Point is the southernmost point on mainland Britain. Once the location of a coastal beacon, it was from here that the alarm was raised when the Spanish Armada was first sighted entering the western English Channel in 1588. The jagged fingers of serpentine and granite which project into the sea have long been a hazard for shipping, and as long ago as 1620, a lighthouse was erected on the headland to alert passing vessels of the danger. The original coal-fired warning light was erected by the notorious Killigrew family of Falmouth who were subsequently accused of trying to prevent shipwrecks on the Lizard so that vessels might founder nearer the Carrick Roads, where they held the appropriate rights of salvage. A more dependable lighthouse was established here in 1752, which was then taken over by **Trinity House** in 1790. Converted from coal to oil in 1815 and then to steam-driven electric power in 1878, it now has a tremendously powerful beam which can sometimes be seen from over 50 miles out at sea.

MAWNAN SMITH

Mawnan Smith is graced with three outstanding gardens: **Carwinion**, a 10 acre subtropical valley garden by the Helford River; **Glendurgan**, a secluded valley garden of great beauty leading down to the Helford estuary, created in the 1830's by Alfred Fox, and known for its magnificent tulip trees, magnolias, camellias, Giant's Stride and wonderful laurel maze; and **Trebah**, a superb ravine garden with rare trees and many exotics.

MEVAGISSEY

Once aptly known as Porthilly, Mevagissey was renamed in late medieval times after the Welsh and Irish saints Meva and Itha. The village is a renowned fishing port which was once an important centre of the pilchard industry. Each year during the 18th and 19th centuries, thousands of tons of this oily fish were landed here for salting, packing or processing into lamp oil.

Mevagissey Harbour

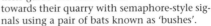

9

Some pilchards were exported to southern Europe, or supplied to the Royal Navy - to whose sailors they became known as 'Mevagissey Ducks'. The need to process the catch within easy reach of the harbour created a labyrinth of buildings separated by steeply sloping alleyways, some of which were so narrow that the baskets of fish sometimes had to be carried on poles between people walking one behind the other.

At one time up to 100 fishing luggers could be seen jostling for a berth in Mevagissey's picturesque harbour. Today, all but a handful of inshore fishing craft have gone but it remains the largest working fishing port in St Austell Bay.

There are a number of more modern indoor attractions, including a **World of Model Railways**, **Aquarium**, and a **Folk Museum** containing an interesting assortment of fishing and agricultural equipment.

NEWQUAY

A settlement since ancient times, evidence of an Iron Age coastal fort can be seen among the cliffs and caves of **Porth Island**, a detached outcrop which is connected to the mainland by an elegant suspended footbridge and which lies to the northeast of the centre of this popular seaside and surfing resort. In common with many Cornish coastal communities, Newquay

Porth Island from Newquay

was an important pilchard fishing centre in the centuries leading up to the industry's decline early in the 20th century. An original 'huer's' hut can still be seen on the headland to the west of the harbour; this was where a local man would keep a look-out for shoals of red pilchards and alert the fishing crews when one was

sighted close to shore by calling 'hevva' through a long loud-hailer. He would then guide the seine boats towards their quarry with semaphore-style signals using a pair of bats known as 'bushes'.

The town takes its name from the new harbour which was built in the 1830's by Joseph Treffry of Fowey for exporting china clay, a trade which continued for several decades until the purpose-built port facility was completed on the south coast at Par. The decline of Newquay as a

Newquay Harbour

port was tempered by the arrival of the railway in 1875, and before long train-loads of visitors were arriving to enjoy the town's extensive sandy beaches, scenic position and mild climate. Today Newquay is one of Cornwall's most popular and liveliest resorts. Over the years, a number of popular attractions have been constructed to satisfy tourist demand, including **Trenance Leisure Park** with its boating lake and miniature railway. **Newquay Zoo** is also in the park, and features a range of environments and habitats for the resident wildlife, including an African Plains enclosure and Tropical House. The **Sea Life Centre** is another of the town's interesting attractions, and **Tunnels Through Time** brings to life stories of bygone days in Cornwall's past, with over 70 life-size figures.

Towan Beach is one of a succession of fine beaches overlooked by the town, a good sheltered beach with a tidal paddling pool which is ideal for children, which can be found at the base of Porth Island. In recent decades Newquay has also acquired a reputation as one of the finest surfing centres in the British Isles. Throughout the year, thousands of keen surfers arrive in camper vans and the like to catch the waves of **Fistral Beach**, or to watch the increasing number of national and international surfing

10

competitions held here each season. Along with the cafes and giftshops, the streets of the town are lined with a refreshing variety of shops offering everything for the surfer, both for sale or hire. Another

Newquay Beach

colourful summer attraction involves Newquay's fleet of traditional pilot gigs, 30 foot rowing boats which race each other over a six-mile course in the bay.

PADSTOW

For many centuries, Padstow's sheltered position on the western side of the Camel estuary has made it a welcome haven for vessels seeking shelter from the perils of the north Cornish coast. However, the silting of the river in the 19th century created a new hazard for shipping, the evocatively named Doom Bar, which restricted entry to the estuary mouth and effectively spelled the end for the ancient settlement as a major port.

Once the ecclesiastical capital of Cornwall, the town's name is derived from St Petroc, the Irish missionary saint who landed here from Wales in the 6th century.

With its narrow alleyways and tightly packed slate-hung buildings, Padstow's old quarter retains much of its medieval character. The harbour still supports a sizable fishing fleet and is enhanced by the addition of floodgates which retain the sea water at low tide. The area around the old port contains a number of interesting old buildings, including the 15th century Merchants' Guild House on the north quay, and the 16th century Court House of Sir Walter Raleigh on the south quay; the latter was used by Sir Walter's agents for collecting Stannary taxes.

Today, Padstow's harbour and nearby shopping streets throng with visitors throughout the summer, some of whom arrive along the beautiful **Camel Cycle Path** which follows the course of the old railway line from Wadebridge; the long curved bridge which crosses the mouth of Little Petherick creek is one of its highlights. The Padstow Shipwreck Museum is also well worth a visit. Among the fine beaches in Padstow are those at St George's Well and Trevone Bay. The Camel Trail makes for excellent walking, and follows a former railway line.

PENZANCE

Penzance is the principal town of West Penwith, lying in the northwestern corner of **Mount's Bay**. For centuries, this was a remote market town which made its living from fishing, mining and smuggling. Along with nearby Newlyn and Mousehole, it was sacked by the Spanish in 1595, then at the end of the English Civil War it suffered a similar fate for being such a staunch supporter of the Royalist cause. However, the fortunes of the town were transformed by the arrival of the railway in 1859, a development which permitted the direct despatch of early flowers, vegetables and locally-caught fish to the urban centres of Britain, and which also allowed increasing numbers of holidaymakers to make the journey here easily. Today it is a bustling town and harbour, with Cornwall's only promenade.

The main, broad thoroughfare of Penzance, **Market Jew Street**, takes its name from the Cornish term for 'Thursday market'; it has a high stepped pavement on one side, and at its southwestern end there is a domed neoclassical **Market House** that was built in 1837. In front of this stands the statue of Penzance-born Humphry Davy, the 19th century scientists who is remembered for inventing the miners' safety lamp.

A number of interesting buildings are located in Chapel Street, a narrow thoroughfare which winds southwards from the Market House to the quay. The most unexpected of these is the **Egyptian House**, with its exotic 1830s facade, which has been restored by the Landmark Trust; the National Trust occupy the ground-floor shop. The **Maritime Museum** contains a unique collection of artefacts recovered from shipwrecks around the Cornish coast. Marie Branwell, the mother of the Bronte sisters, was brought up at No 25 Chapel Street, and at its lower end the early 19th century St Mary's Church stands on a ledge above the harbour and Customs House, a reassuring landmark for returning sailors.

Elsewhere in Penzance there is an interesting **Geological Museum** in Alverton Street, a good local history museum and an exhibition of paintings by the Newlyn School in **Penlee House Museum and Art Gallery**, and a striking collection of subtropical trees and flowers in **Morrab Gardens**. The **Aquarium and National Lighthouse Centre**, on the Quay, are also worth a look. The town is also a good stepping-off point for the ferry or helicopter to the Isles of Scilly.

PORTHCURNO

One of the most dramatic and atmospheric coves in West Penwith, Porthcurno lies to the west of the Logan Rock. Reached by way of the coastal path or along a narrow and tortuous approach from the B3315, its exquisite white sand beach shelves into a turquoise sea between cliffs of weather-beaten granite. A number of undersea cables, including one running beneath the Atlantic, come ashore here.

The justly famous **Minack Theatre** stands perched on the headland overlooking the cove. Based on ancient Greek amphitheatres, this superb open-air auditorium was created in the early 1930's by Rowena Cade. (It opened with an aptly chosen production of Shakespeare's The Tempest in 1932.) With its precariously positioned stage, rows of seating hewn from the rock, and azure backdrop of sea and sky, this must be one of the most spectacular theatre settings in the world. Performances take place from May through mid-September. Porthcurno

Minack Theatre

is also home to the fascinating **Museum of Wireless Telegraphy**.

REDRUTH

The southern approach to Redruth is dominated by the dramatic form of **Carn Brea** (pronounced Bray), a 738 foot granite prominence which is the site of the earliest known Neolithic settlement in southern Britain. The legendary home of a Cornish giant, many of the hill's features are dubbed with such names as Giant's hand, Giant's cradle, Giant's head, and even Giant's cups and saucers. (The last-named are natural rain-eroded hollows which over-imaginative Victorians thought had been made by bloodthirsty Druids.) The summit is crowned by an unprepossessing 90 foot monument dedi-

Cornish Engines, Rderuth

cated to Francis Basset de Dunstanville, a benevolent Georgian mine- and landowner who did much to improve the lot of poor labourers. Much more attractive is the small castle on the lower eastern summit, a part-medieval building which in its time has been used as a hunting lodge and is now a restaurant. More easily approached from the south, the whole site is strewn with fascinating industrial and archeological remains.

Once the bustling centre of the Cornish mining industry, Redruth and the neighbouring **Camborne** have administratively combined to form the largest urban centre of population in the county. In the mid-19th century, the surrounding area was the most intensely mined in the world, and the district is still littered with evidence of this lost era. In the 1850's, Cornwall had well over 300 mines, which together produced two-thirds of the world's copper and employed around 50,000 workers. However, most had to close in the first few decades of the 20th century, when the discovery of extensive mineral deposits in the Americas, South Africa and Australia rendered the local industry no longer economically viable.

The National Trust's **Norris Collection** of minerals can be seen here in the geological museum of the old Camborne School of Mines Museum and Art Gallery. Still one of the foremost institutes of mining technology, the School moved to these new premises in Redruth in the 1970s.

The home of Scots inventor William Murdock, who settled in the area at **Cross Street**, is open to the public. Murdock was responsible for such innovations as coal-gas lighting and the vacuum-powered tubes which were once a common feature in most department stores. Redruth also contains pockets of Victorian, Georgian and earlier buildings, particularly in **Churchtown** where there are some attractive old cottages, a Georgian church with a 15th century tower, and a lychgate whose unusually long coffin-rest was built to deal with the aftermath of mining disasters.

The B3300 to the northwest of Redruth leads past the **Tolgus Tin Mill**, an 18th century streaming mill where tin deposits were extracted from the river bed by a process of sifting and stamping. Nearby, at **Treskillard**, there is an interesting shire horse centre.

St Agnes

Once known as the source of the finest tin in Cornwall, the old mining community of St Agnes lies at the head of a steep valley. Despite being subjected to 200 years of mineral extraction, and almost 100 years of tourism, it still manages to retain its original character, especially around the narrow-spired parish church and nearby terrace of stepped miners' cottages which are known locally as the 'Stippy-Stappy'. The village is also renowned as the birthplace of the Georgian society painter, John Opie, and is known to thousands of readers of Winston Graham's Poldark novels as 'St Ann'. A good local museum can be found near the church, and there is also a popular leisure park to the south of the village which features a model of Cornwall in miniature and a number of themed areas, all set in seven acres of attractive landscaped grounds.

Trevaunance Cove near St Agnes is one of the best surfing beaches in Cornwall. A quay constructed here in the 18th century for loading tin ore survived here until it was washed away in a storm during the 1930s; its four predecessors having suffered a similar fate.

The surrounding landscape is littered with abandoned pump houses and mine shafts (walkers should keep to the paths): many of the mines, such as Wheal Kitty and Wheal Ellen, were named after female members of the mine-owning families, or, in the case of Wheal Freedom and Wheal Friendly, were given other romantic associations. One of the most photogenic of Cornwall's derelict pump houses stands on a narrow cliff platform 200 feet above **Chapel Porth**, a mile and a half west of St Agnes. Now under the ownership of the National Trust, Wheal Coates was in operation for 30 years between 1860 and 1890. A good circular walk from the car park at Chapel Porth also takes in St Agnes Head and St Agnes Beacon, a 628 foot peak which offers outstanding views

Disused Engine House, Chapel Porth

across Cornwall to Bodmin Moor in the east and St Ives in the west; it is said that over 30 church towers can be seen from here on a clear day.

St Austell

This sprawling former market and mining town was transformed in the second half of the 18th century when William Cookworthy discovered large deposits of china clay, or *kaolin*, here in 1755. Over the years, waste material from the clay pits has been piled into great conical spoil heaps which dominate the landscape to the north and west of the town. These bare bleached uplands are sometimes referred to as the 'Cornish Alps', although in recent years steps have been taken to landscape their surface and seed them with grass.

The narrow streets of old St Austell create an atmosphere more befitting a market town than a mining community. The central thoroughfares radiate from the parish church of the **Holy Trinity**, an imposing structure with a tall 15th century tower. Elsewhere in the town centre there are some notable old buildings, including the **Town Hall, Quaker Meeting House** and White Hart Hotel, as well as a good modern shopping precinct. Nearby, there's the **Mid-Cornwall Craft Centre** (at Biscovey), and the **Automobilia Motor Museum** at St Stephen.

The **Eden Project**, created from a Cornish clay pit 2 miles northeast of St Austell, is an ambitious and impressive project featuring a series of "biomes" - a collection of dome-shaped greenhouses with plants from all over the world in artificially controlled climates. This exciting horticultural centre will, on its completion, include the largest greenhouse in the world and is set amid acres of outstanding parkland. Visitors are invited to come see the work in progress (organised by Tim Smit, famed for his work on the Lost Gardens of Heligan, in Pentewan 3 miles south of St Austell) until November 2000; the gardens and greenhouses are expected to be completed by the Spring of 2001.

St Columb Major

Thankfully bypassed by the main road, the small town of St Columb Major was once considered as the location for Cornwall's cathedral (it lost out to Truro). The parish **Church of St Columba** is unusually large, with a four-tiered tower and a wide through-arch; inside there are some fine 16th and 17th century monumental brasses to the Arundell family. The church is adjoined to the south and east by handsome old residential buildings, creating something of the atmosphere of a cathedral close. The town is home to an annual music festival.

The Silver Ball Hotel marks one of the town's great sporting tradition, 'hurling the silver ball'. This rowdy medieval game is played twice a year - on Shrove Tuesday and on the Saturday 11 days later - and involved two teams of several hundred people (the 'townsmen' and the 'countrymen') who endeavour to carry a silver-painted ball made of apple wood through goals set two miles apart. Once a common pastime

throughout the county, this ancient Cornish game is now only practised here and, in a less rumbustious form, at St Ives. Such is the passion for the St Columb event that windows of houses and shops in the locality have to be boarded up for the occasion.

13

Two miles southeast of St Columb Major, the land rises to 700 feet above sea level on Castle Downs, site of the massive Iron Age hill fort known as **Castle-an-Dinas**, whose three earthwork ramparts enclose an area of over six acres. The climb to the gorse-covered summit is rewarded with panoramic views over the leafy Vale of Lanherne to the northwest, and towards the unearthly landscape of the china clap spoil heaps to the south.

To the South of St Columb Major and just off the main A30 lies **Screech Owl Sanctuary**.

St Ives

With its five sandy beaches, maze of narrow streets and picturesque harbour and headland, the attractive fishing and former mining centre of St Ives manages to retain a special atmosphere, despite being deluged with visitors throughout the summer. The settlement takes its name from the 6th century missionary saint, St Ia, who is said to have landed here having sailed across from Ireland on an ivy leaf. The

St Ives

14

15th century parish church near the harbour's shorter west pier bears her name. An impressive building with a soaring pinnacled tower, it contains an unusual granite font carved with stylised angels and lions. Another striking ecclesiastical building, a mariner's chapel, stands on St Ives Head, the promontory to the north of the harbour which is known locally as the 'Island'.

St Ives was one of Cornwall's most important pilchard fishing centres until the industry went into decline early in the 20th century. The town holds a record dating back to 1868 for the greatest number of fish caught in a single seine net. Once the pilchards were brought ashore, they were compressed to release fish oil before being salted and packed into barrels for despatch to southern Europe, where the Catholic stricture regarding not eating meat on Fridays guaranteed a steady demand. On catch days the streets of St Ives would stream with the oily residue of these plentiful fish, and the air would be filled with an appalling smell which would drive away all but the most determined outsiders. A local speciality, 'heavy', or hevva cake, was traditionally made for the seiners on their return with their catch.

Like many parts of western Cornwall, the surrounding valley was once rich in veins of tin, copper and other minerals, and indeed the building which now houses **St Ives Museum** began life as Wheal Dream copper mine. The town's labyrinth of narrow streets was once divided into two communities: 'Downalong', where the fishing families lived, and 'Upalong', which was inhabited by the mining community. There was much tension between the two, and fights would often break out between gangs of young rivals, a practice which ended with the closing of the mines and the steady reduction in the fishing fleet.

St Ives' decline as a mining and fishing centre has been offset by its rise as an artists' colony. The painter William Turner visited the town towards the end of his life, and both Whistler and Sickert are known to have been attracted here by the special quality of the light in west Cornwall. In the first half of the 20th century, Barbara Hepworth, Ben Nicholson and others began to convert the disused pilchard cellars and sail lofts around the harbour into artists' studios, and a 'St Ives School' was established which gained an international reputation. The town's artistic standing was also boosted by the

arrival in the 1920's of the potter Bernard Leach, who established a workshop at **Higher Stennack** (beside the B3306) which is still in operation.

One of the highlights of any stay in St Ives is a visit to the **Barbara Hepworth Sculpture Garden** and Museum in Barnoon Hill. After she died in a fire on the premises in 1975, the sculptor's living quarters, studio and garden were turned into a museum and gallery dedicated to her life and work. The garden is packed with a remarkable concentration of her work, and two particularly poignant features are the little summerhouse where she used to rest in the afternoons, and the workshop which has been left entirely untouched since her death. Barbara Hepworth's studio is now administered by the **Tate Gallery**, the London-based institution which has also opened a large-scale annexe in

Tate Gallery, St Ives

the town which is dedicated to the work of the St Ives School. An imposing white-painted building which uses Porthmeor Beach as a stunning backdrop, its architecture is thought by some to dwarf the quality of the work inside.

The narrow thoroughfares of St Ives contain an unusual number of museums and galleries. **Penwith Galleries** in Back Street West is a good place to see the work of the St Ives Society of Artists, a group founded by Sir Alfred Munnings. The **St Ives Museum** in Wheal Dream contains a unique collection of artefacts illustrating the natural, industrial and maritime history of the district, and includes a special feature on the exploits of John Knill. As a child, the writer Virginia Woolf spent most of her summers at Talland House overlooking St Ives Bay, from where it is possible to see the Godrevy lighthouse - the setting which provided the inspiration for her evocative and wonderful novel, *To the Lighthouse*.

15

A good way to travel to St Ives, especially in high summer when traffic congestion and parking can be a headache, is to park in **St Erth** or **Leland** and take the local train. The railway skirts St Ives Bay, with its five-mile long stretch of unbroken sand, and is widely regarded to be one of the loveliest coastal branch lines in Britain. The train also passes close to **Lelant Saltings**, a 500 acre tidal area at the mouth of the Hayle estuary which is now a RSPB bird sanctuary.

The eastern side of St Ives Bay is lined with one of the finest sandy beaches in Cornwall. A popular centre for windsurfing, various competitive events are staged here throughout the season, including breathtaking demonstrations of wave jumping.

St Just in Roseland

This enchanting hamlet has an exquisite part-13th century church which lies in one of the most superb setting in the country. Concealed in a steep wooded tidal creek and entered through a lychgate which is level with the top of the church tower, the churchyard contains a wonderful collection of trees and shrubs, including semi-tropical species such as the African fire bush and Chilean myrtle. Sadly, the church interior suffered a clumsy Victorian 'restoration', although the 15th century font and 16th century monumental brass survive. In 1733, a wealthy parishioner bequeathed 10 shillings (50 pence) a year to the vicar for dedicating a funeral sermon to him every 27th December.

St Michael's Mount

St Michael's Mount is a remarkable granite outcrop which rises dramatically from the waters of Mount's Bay. The steep-sided islet has been inhabited by human beings since prehistoric times, and it has been a place of religious pilgrimage since a party of fisherman saw a vision of St Michael on the seaward side of the rock in the 8th century. Three centuries later, Edward the Confessor founded a priory here which was granted to the Benedictine monks of Mont St Michel in Normandy, the island's even more spectacular cousin across the Chan-

St Michael's Mount

St Just in Roseland Church

nel. The monastery was fortified after the Dissolution in 1539, and later passed to the St Aubyn family who incorporated the old monastic buildings into a series of 18th and 19th century improvements to form the striking multi-layered structure we can see today. A direct descendant of the family, Lord St Levan, donated the 21 acre site to the National Trust in 1954.

Truro

This elegant small city has grown to become the administrative capital of Cornwall. Its site at the head of a branch of the Fal estuary has been occupied for thousands of years, but it wasn't until large-scale mineral extraction began in medieval times that the settlement took on any significance. One of the first Cornish

16

towns to be granted rites of Stannary, huge quantities of smelted tin or and other metals were brought here for weighing, taxing and shipping until the industry went into decline in the 17th century. By this time the estuary had also begun to silt up, allowing Falmouth to take over as the area's principal seaport. A number of picturesque alleyways or opes (pronounced opps) have survived from Truro's heyday as a port, many of which have colourful names such as Tippet's Backlet, Burton's Ope and Squeezeguts Alley.

An increase in metal prices during the 18th century led to a revival in Truro's fortunes; wealthy merchants and banks moved in, and the town became a centre for fashionable society with a reputation to rival Bath. This Georgian renaissance has left a distinctive mark on the town's architecture, particularly around **Pydar Street**, with its handsome Assembly Room and Theatre, Walsingham Place, and **Lemon Street**, one of the finest complete Georgian streets in the country. Also worth seeing are the indoor Pannier Market and the city hall in Boscawen Street.

A revival of the railway in 1859 confirmed Truro's status as a regional capital, and in 1877 it became a city in its own right when the diocese of Exeter was divided into two and Cornwall was granted its own bishop. Three years later, the foundation stone of Truro Cathedral, the first to be built in Britain since Wren's St Paul's, was laid by the future Edward VII, and over the next 30 years it was constructed to a design in Early English style by the architect John Loughborough Pearson. Finished locally-sourced granite and serpentine, this graceful three-spired structure incorporates the early 16th century south aisle of St Mary's church which originally occupied part of the site. The soaring 250 foot central spire can be seen for miles around and stands as a fitting centrepiece for this elegant and prosperous shopping and administrative centre. The **Royal Cornwall Museum and Art Gallery** is also worth a visit.

Those with an interest in gardening should make a point of finding **Bosvigo House** which lies just off the A390 Redruth road, three-quarters of a mile to the west of Truro city centre. This delightful series of walled herbaceous gardens is set around a handsome Georgian house (which is not open to the visitors); the grounds incorporate a woodland walk.

WASHAWAY

One of the loveliest country manor houses in the West Country can be found on the eastern side of the A389 Bodmin road. **Pencarrow House** lies hidden in a 50 acre wooded estate which encompasses an Iron Age encampment and a beautiful woodland garden with a lake, ice house, Victorian granite rockery, and American and Italianate gardens. The grounds also contain an internationally renowned collection of conifers and over 500 species of rhododendron. The interior of the Georgian house is furnished with some outstanding 18th century paintings, period furniture and china.

Admiral Benbow

17

46 Chapel Street,
Penzance,
Cornwall
Tel: 01736 363448
Fax: 01736 333574

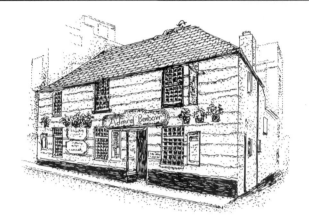

Directions:

From junction 31 on the M5 take the A30 past Bodmin to Penzance. The Admiral Benbow can be found in the centre of the town just a short distance from the harbour.

Found in the heart of Penzance, the **Admiral Benbow** inn is one of the town's oldest hostelries and the 17th century building is distinguished by the fascinating pilot light that stands high on the roof. An attractive white washed building that is bedecked with colourful hanging baskets and surrounded by flower filled tubs during the summer, this is certainly one place that is well worth visiting whilst exploring this ancient port. The interior of the inn, which was once the headquarters of the notorious Benbow pirates, is more reminiscent of a museum than a pub as there is a fabulous collection of nautical memorabilia found here. Many of the artefacts have been recovered from shipwrecks off the Cornish coast and the displays extend through out.

Mick, a local man with many years experience in the trade, is the landlord and, though he has only been here since 1999 he has certainly put the Admiral Benbow on the map. Surprisingly the main bar here, The Lady Hamilton, is found upstairs together with a games room, bar and cocktail lounge. Highly regarded for the excellent condition of the real ales there is also a well chosen wine list and both morning coffee and Cornish cream teas are served here. Food too is important and, in the Great Cabin Restaurant, there is a splendid à la carte menu from which to make a delicious choice, whilst, tasty and tempting bar meals and snacks are served in the rest of the inn. Naturally, fish is a speciality here and, along with the wonderful homecooked daily specials, there is sure to be something to tempt even the most jaded palate.

Opening Hours: Mon-Sun 11.00-15.00, 18.00-23.00

Food: Bar meals and snacks, À la carte

Credit Cards: Visa, Access, Delta, Switch

Facilities: Car parking close by, Children welcome

Entertainment: Themed evenings during the winter, Darts, Pool

Local Places of Interest/Activities: Beach, Trengwainton Gardens 2 miles, St Michael's Mount 4 miles, Carn Euny Ancient Village 4 miles, Land's End 8 miles, Walking, Cycling, Horse riding, Fishing, Swimming, Sailing

18   The Angarrack Inn

Angarrack,
near Hayle,
Cornwall TR27 5JB
Tel: 01736 752380

Directions:

From junction 31 on the M5 take the A30 round Bodmin to Camborne. Just after the town, turn left on to a minor road through Roseworthy and continue parallel to the A30 to Angarrack, where The Angarrack Inn lies in the centre of the village.

Found in the heart of the village, **The Angarrack Inn** is an attractive and distinctive black and white building with, in front of it, a large courtyard. An historic building, this was the home of Lottie Tregorran (1765-1753) who became known as the Robin Woman of Angarrack. The landlady of this inn until her death, according to letters found here during recent renovations, her story is one of tragedy. One day her son, Denzil, left on horseback and, whilst out, a robin startled his mount which reared up. Denzil was thrown to the ground, fatally fracturing his skull. Totally devastated by Denzil's death, Lottie vowed to kill all the robins in the area and she continued to throw poisoned scraps out into the courtyard right up to the time of her own death.

Today, The Angarrack Inn is managed by John and Lynda Watkins, an experienced couple who have worked hard to gain the excellent reputation which they now enjoy. A stylish and interesting establishment that is full of character and charm, not only is there an excellent choice of drinks, including three real ales, from the bar, but the inn is renowned for Lynda's splendid homecooked food. The standard menu is supplemented by a whole host of daily specials and, along with the tempting grills, Lynda's speciality are her delicious homemade pies. Children are welcome and the inn is becoming so popular now that bookings are needed throughout the weekend. Add to this the marvellous accommodation, where a good night's sleep is followed by a hearty breakfast, and The Angarrack Inn is certainly a place not to be missed.

Opening Hours: Mon-Sat 11.00-15.00, 18.00-23.00; Sun 12.00-15.00, 19.00-22.30

Food: Bar snacks and meals, À la carte

Credit Cards: None

Accommodation: 1 double room, 1 twin room, both en suite

Facilities: Patio garden, Car parking, Children welcome

Entertainment: Darts

Local Places of Interest/Activities: Beach 2 miles, Godolphin House 4 miles, St Ives 5 miles, St Michael's Mount 6 miles, Walking, Horse riding, Fishing, Sailing, Swimming, Bird watching, Golf

The Barley Sheaf 19

Gorran Churchtown,
near Mevagissey,
Cornwall PL26 6HN
Tel: 01726 843330
Fax: 01726 843330

Directions:

From junction 31 on the M5 take the A30 to Bodmin and continue along the road to the roundabout at the end of the dual carriageway. Turn left on to the A391 to St Austell and then continue along the B3273 to Mevagissey. Follow the signs to Gorran Churchtown and The Barley Sheaf lies in the village.

A splendid old stone built inn that stands at one end of a terrace of similarly styled buildings, **The Barley Sheaf** was built in 1837 by landowner, Mr Kendal, who had been barred from all the other local inns and so wanted his own - or so the local story goes! Fortunately, for today's visitors, it was built and this delightful place is certainly one that is sure to please everyone that walks through its centrally placed red front door. The interior too has obviously been cared for over the years and the real fires, Cornish slate floor and mass of photographs on the walls all add to the character of this lovely inn.

Landlord, Andrew Thomson, has been dispensing friendly hospitality from the inn since 1983 and he has certainly built up an enviable reputation for the high quality of his food and drink in that time - the popularity of The Barley Sheaf here is testament enough. Locally brewed real ales from Skinners and Sharp's join the large selection of drinks served from the bar whilst the mouthwatering menu of bar meals, snacks and specials provides a wide range of choice for those feeling peckish. Andrew is an experienced chef and so the dishes served here are not only of superb quality but also have a particular style and flair which is what makes a meal here so special. Whilst visitors can make use of both the dining room and the bar areas inside, the large beer garden is ideal for the summer. If too on visiting the inn it feels familiar, The Barley Sheaf has featured in several television programmes recently including *Strange but True* with Michael Aspel and *Wycliffe* the Cornish Detective.

Opening Hours: Mon-Sat 12.00-15.00, 18.00-23.00; Sun 12.00-22.30

Food: Bar meals and snacks, À la carte, Traditional Sunday lunch, Barbecues in summer

Credit Cards: Visa, Access, Delta

Facilities: Beer garden, Car parking, Disabled access to garden

Entertainment: Occasional live music, Skittles

Local Places of Interest/Activities: Beaches 1 mile, Dodman Point 2 miles, Lost Gardens of Heligan 3 miles, St Austell 6 miles, Walking, Fishing, Bird watching, Sailing

20   The Blue Anchor Inn

50 Coinagehall Street,
Helston,
Cornwall TR13 8EX
Tel: 01326 562821/565765
Fax: 01326 565765
Accommodation: 01326
569334

Directions:

From junction 31 on the M5
take the A30 round Bodmin to
Carland Cross. Turn left on to
the A39 towards Falmouth and,
near Penryn, turn right on to
the A394 to Helston. The Blue
Anchor Inn lies in the centre of
the town.

The Blue Anchor Inn dates back to the 15th Century when it was originally a monk's
rest home. After the dissolution of the monasteries it became a tavern brewing its own
uniquely flavoured beer, called "SPINGO", at the rear of the premises. This brewing
has continued to this day and people travel from all over the world to sample the
delights of this wonderful Inn largely untouched by time. From the front entrance the
bars and snugs are reached via a flagstone corridor, through the centre of the Inn. This
also leads on to the Brewery, Skittle Alley and Garden. The bars have low beamed
ceilings and an interesting array of paintings, lithographs and old posters.

The hosts Simon and Kim Stone have owned the Blue Anchor Inn since 1993 and
have done much to preserve its character. Kim is responsible for the tasty home cooked
dishes and Simon for the production of the world famous "SPINGO" ales. (Watch out!
they are a bit too easy to drink). A warm welcome is assured on visiting *"The Blue"*,
and please note there are no jukeboxes or gaming machines. Why? Because the customers in this local love to chat!

Next door to the Inn is No.52, a three story Edwardian town house that has been
painstakingly renovated to a superb standard, by Simon and Kim. This provides superior accommodation for even the most discerning guests.

Opening Hours: Mon-Sat 11.00-23.00; Sun
12.00-22.30

Food: Bar meals and snacks, Traditional
Sunday lunch - lunchtimes only 12.00-
15.00

Credit Cards: None

Accommodation: 2 double rooms, 2 twin
rooms, all en suite

Facilities: Car parking, Own brewery

Local Places of Interest/Activities: Coast
2 miles, Trelowarren House 4 miles,
Cornish Seal Sanctuary 4 miles, Lizard
Point 10 miles, Walking, Horse riding,
Fishing, Sailing, Bird watching, Golf

The Boscawen Hotel 21

Fore Street, St Dennis,
near St Austell,
Cornwall PL26 8AD
Tel: 01726 822275
Fax: 01726 822275

Directions:
From junction 31 on the M5 take the A30 to Bodmin. Continue overto the roundabout at Indian Queens and turn left on the B3279. The Boscawen Hotel lies 2 miles along this road.

An imposing stone building, the front of **The Boscawen Hotel** is softened in summer by numerous colourful, flower filled hanging baskets that add eyecatching detail to this roadside inn. Built in 1897 as a hotel, the inn was owned by EAH Boscawen, Lord Falmouth, which is, obviously, how its name came about. Despite its rather austere front façade, the interior of the inn is warm and inviting. Though much changed over the last 100 years or so, the three areas into which the ground floor has been divided still retain much of their charm and character. Everywhere is well decorated and comfortably furnished in a traditional manner and with many old prints and pictures hanging from the walls and a wood burning stove in winter, it has a very cosy atmosphere.

Coming here in the spring of 1999, landlord Ken Mason has worked hard to built up the reputation of the inn and put The Boscawen Hotel back on the map of Cornwall. Ably assisted by Duncan, the bar in this excellent free house serves a range of real ales along with a host of other beers, lagers, ciders and spirits so that everyone is assured of finding their favourite tipple here. Food too is an important part of life here and, as the chef, Ken provides a mouthwatering menu of dishes at both lunchtime and in the evening. From old favourites like the All day breakfast through to Sweet and sour chicken there is an interesting range from which to choose and, on Sunday lunchtimes, customers settle down to a lovely, traditional roast meal. To complete the list of excellent hospitality here, The Boscawen Hotel has a choice of guest rooms.

Opening Hours: Summer - Mon-Sat 11.00-23.00; Sun 12.00-22.30; Winter - Mon-Sat 11.00-15.00, 18.00-23.00; Sun 12.00-15.00, 19.00-22.30

Food: Bar snacks and meals, Traditional Sunday lunch (no food Monday)

Credit Cards: None

Accommodation: 4 double rooms

Facilities: Car parking

Entertainment: Live music Saturday evenings

Local Places of Interest/Activities: New Eden Project 4 miles, Wheal Martyn Museum 5 miles, St Austell 6 miles, Beaches 8 miles, Newquay 10 miles, Walking, Fishing, Sailing, Bird watching

22   Cable Station Inn

The Valley, Porthcurno,
St Levan, near Penzance,
Cornwall TR19 6JX
Tel: 01736 810479

Directions:

From junction 31 on the M5 take the A30 round Bodmin to Penzance. Follow the road towards Land's End and, at Catchall, turn left on to the B3283. After approximately 4 miles follow the signs for Porthcurno. The Cable Station Inn lies in the centre of the hamlet.

Just a short walk from the beach, the **Cable Station Inn** is an interestingly named place that stands opposite Porthcurno's Museum of Submarine Telegraphy. Found in the cliffs above the sandy beach of the bay and overlooked by the open air Minack Theatre, this was a communications centre during World War II from which crucial contact was maintained with all parts of the British Empire. The underground rooms house a fine collection of equipment that illustrates the development of communications from as early as 1870 and much of it remains in working order today. It is from this fascinating place that the splendid Cable Station Inn acquired its name and both are well worth a visit.

After holidaying in southwestern Cornwall for many years, Sandra and Mick Wilby moved to the area and they became landlords here in October 1998. A delightful, family run inn, the stylish interior is complemented by the attractive and rather continental patio garden that is surrounded by low walls and decorative wrought iron screens. Well known for serving excellent Cornish real ales, as well as lagers, cider and stout, Sandra and Mick, along with the rest of their family, have also put the inn back on the culinary map of south Cornwall. The extensive menu begins with a selection of all day breakfasts, covers light meals, such as burgers and sandwiches, and then goes on to a splendid array from the à la carte list. Add in the ever changing daily specials and there really is something for everyone here. Meanwhile, it is in the attractive old coach house next door to the inn that the comfortable accommodation can be found.

Opening Hours: Mon-Sat 11.00-23.00; Sun 12.00-22.30, supper hour licence until 24.00 Mon-Sat

Food: Bar meals and snacks, À la carte

Credit Cards: None

Accommodation: 1 double, 1 family room

Facilities: Patio garden, Car parking, Functions, Walkers' back packs transported, children and dogs welcome

Entertainment: Regular Karaoke, Antique fairs in summer, Occasional line dancing

Local Places of Interest/Activities: Museum of Submarine Telegraphy, Minack open air theatre, Beaches, Land's End 3 miles, Carn Euny Ancient Village 4 miles, Walking, Cycling, Horse riding, Fishing, Sailing, Bird watching

The Cornish Arms · 23

Church Street,
St Blazey,
Cornwall PL24 2NG
Tel/Fax: 01726 813001

Directions:

From junction 31 on the M5 take the A38 to Liskeard and then the A390 towards St Austell. St Blazey lies along this road, approximately 4 miles from Lostwithiel, and The Cornish Arms can be found in the village centre.

Dating back over 200 years, **The Cornish Arms** is a delightful old coaching inn that has a splendid columned doorway that would once have greeted weary travellers. A charming and attractive Georgian building, the stable block of the inn has been tastefully and sympathetically converted into top class accommodation and now The Cornish Arms can once again offer excellent hospitality. Landlord, Eddie Clements, a retired fireman, moved here from Worcester with his wife, son and daughter and, since their arrival neither they nor the inn has looked back but gone on from strength to strength.

Although the exterior of the inn is Georgian, the interior, following a recent refurbishment, is modern and the high ceilings give this open plan design a light and airy atmosphere. The quasi Art Deco style of decoration might sound out of place but the high standard of the workmanship makes it a great feature rather than a white elephant. In these interesting surroundings, customers can enjoy a wide selection of drinks from the bar including real ales and bottled beers whilst, in the pastel shades of the separate restaurant, diners can settle down to a delicious meal from the menu that ranges from succulent sandwiches and juicy steaks to all day breakfasts and 'dinner in a pudd'. This interesting and different approach to traditional English pub fare is as refreshing as the inn itself and no one visiting here will be surprised to know that The Cornish Arms is a very popular inn indeed.

Opening Hours: Mon-Sat 12.00-14.30, 18.00-23.00; Sun 12.00-2.30, 18.00-22.30

Food: Bar meals and snacks

Credit Cards: Visa, Access, Delta, Switch, Diners, Amex

Accommodation: 2 double rooms, 4 twin rooms, some en suite

Facilities: Car parking

Entertainment: Live music at weekends

Local Places of Interest/Activities: Eden Project 1 mile, Beach 1 mile, St Austell 3 miles, Wheal Martyn Museum 3 miles, Restormel Castle 5 miles, Lost Gardens of Heligon 7 miles, Walking, Cycling, Horse riding, Fishing, Sailing

Internet/Website:
www.eclements.freeserve.co.uk

24   The Crown Inn

Church Town,
St Ewe,
near St Austell,
Cornwall PL26 6EY
Tel: 01726 843322

Directions:

From junction 31 on the M5 take the A30 to Bodmin. Continue to the roundabout at the end of the dual carriageway and turn left on to the A391. From St Austell take the B3273 towards Mevagissey and, after passing Pentewan, turn right on to a minor road and The Crown Inn lies in the village.

Tucked away in the gentle Cornish countryside to the southwest of St Austell, **The Crown Inn** is a place that is well worth seeking out. An attractive and picturesque building, which dates from the 16th century, this was formerly a Methodist Meeting House which, surprisingly, then became an inn over 200 years ago. Looking more like a private residence than a public house, The Crown Inn's most distinguishing feature, from the outside, are its windows which, though unusual, are typical of other old buildings in the village. The interior is equally full of character and here little has changed over the years. The beamed ceilings and ancient fireplaces have all withstood the test of time and, along with the wealth of mementoes of long ago days all add to the olde worlde atmosphere here.

Although landlords Tim and Irene have only been here since September 1999 they have certainly made their mark. A Cornishman born and bred, Tim ensures that the real ales here are not only well kept but also reflect the local brews and there is also a brew here that goes by the worrying name of Daylight Robbery. However, what does bring people, from near and far, to this splendid inn is the delicious menu of essentially Cornish fayre that is prepared by our resident chef. The marvellous menu, that is supplemented by exciting daily specials, is a mouthwatering treat and will certainly make choosing a hard but rewarding decision.

Opening Hours: Winter - Mon-Sat 11.00-15.00, 18.00-23.00; Sun 12.00-15.00, 18.00-22.30. Summer - Mon-Sat 11.00-23.00; Sun 12.00-22.30

Food: Bar meals and snacks, À la carte

Credit Cards: Access, Visa, Mastercard

Facilities: Beer garden, Car parking opposite

Local Places of Interest/Activities: Lost Gardens of Heligan 1 mile, Beach 3 miles, Trewithen House 4 miles, St Austell 5 miles, Walking, Cycling, Horse riding, Fishing, Sailing, Bird watching

The Farmers Arms   25

St Merryn,
near Padstow,
Cornwall PL28 8NP
Tel: 01841 520303

Directions:

From junction 31 on the M5 take the A30 to Bodmin and then follow the A389 to Padstow. Leave the town on the B3276 towards Newquay and The Farmers Arms is a short drive along this road.

Found on the main road through this pleasant and picturesque Cornish village, **The Farmers Arms** is an attractive inn with a long frontage that blends in well with the other buildings of St Merryn. Originally three cottages, this smart, cream painted building became an inn in the 1870s and, although, time has march on since then, this is still an inn with traditional values. The interior too has kept much of its olde worlde charm and character and stepping inside is just like walking back in time. The ceilings are low and beamed, the walls are of exposed stone, the windows are small and there is a magnificent cast iron range as a feature in the main bar area. Dotted about the place, experienced landlords Graham and Sandra Eden have on display various old agricultural implements and there are some delightful pictures of by gone days in this area.

As this is a St Austell Brewery inn, visitors can be sure of finding an excellent choice of well kept ales here and, along with the guest ales, draught lagers, ciders and spirits, there is everyone's favourite tipple here. Food too is a key feature of The Farmers Arms and the menu, supplemented by the daily specials board, is a tempting range of carefully prepared sandwiches, burgers, grills, fish dishes and vegetarian options. The Sunday lunchtime carvery is very popular with both locals and visitors alike and the well chosen wine list will certainly provide the perfect drinking accompaniment. For visitors, The Farmers Arms also has superb accommodation, on a bed and breakfast basis, and, as they happily welcome children, the whole family can benefit from the delights of this inn.

Opening Hours: Summer - Mon-Sat 11.00-23.00; Sun 12.00-22.30: Winter - Mon-Sat 11.00-15.00, 18.00-23.00; Sun 12.00-15.00, 19.00-22.30

Food: Bar meals and snacks, Traditional Sunday lunch

Credit Cards: Visa, Access, Delta, Switch, Amex, Diners

Accommodation: 4 double ensuite rooms

Facilities: Patio garden, Car parking, Children welcome

Entertainment: Regular live music

Local Places of Interest/Activities: Beach 1 mile, Prideaux Place 2 miles, Padstow 2 miles, Camel Trail 4 miles, Walking, Cycling, Horse riding, Fishing, Sailing

26   The Ferry Boat Inn

Helford Passage,
near Falmouth,
Cornwall TR11 5LB
Tel: 01326 250625
Fax: 01326 250916

Directions:

From junction 31 on the M5 take the A30 and then the A39 to Truro. Continue along the A39, then the A394 to Helston. From the town take the A3083 towards Lizard and turn left on to the B3293. After approximately 2 miles turn off this road and follow the signs to Helford and The Ferry Boat Inn lies beside the river.

In a delightful waterfront location, overlooking the 500 year old ferry crossing of the River Helford, **The Ferry Boat Inn** is a wonderful 17th century inn that has been popular with boatmen for many, many years. In front of the inn is a spacious terrace, the perfect place to watch the activity on the river during long summer afternoons, although, if the weather is cool, the main bar also overlooks the Helford. Inside, this marvellous old building is full of character and charm with ship's lanterns, bells and ropes and even an old mast giving the place a very nautical theme. The design of the interior of this historic old inn is also one of The Ferry Boat Inn's special features and is worth a visit on its own. However, as the inn also has an enviable reputation for the fine food and drink served here a visit is rewarded in several ways.

A splendid selection of wines and spirits, lagers and beers are served from the bar which also include real ales from the local St Austell brewery. The superb dishes served here have also put The Ferry Boat Inn on the map and the menu, though simple, is a mouthwatering mix of freshly cut sandwiches, hot baguettes, grills and, the house speciality, fresh locally caught fish. A wonderful inn that is tucked away on the Cornish coast, The Ferry Boat Inn is always full of surprises.

Opening Hours: Mon-Sat 11.00-23.00; Sun 12.00-22.30

Food: Bar meals and snacks, À la carte

Credit Cards: Visa, Access, Delta, Switch, Amex, Diners

Facilities: Terraced garden, Car parking

Local Places of Interest/Activities: Coast and coastal walks, Trelowarren House 3 miles, Cornish Seal Sanctuary 4 miles, Lizard Point 9 miles, Walking, Golf, Horse riding, Fishing, Sailing

The Fountain Inn 27

Newbridge,
near Penzance,
Cornwall TR20 8QH
Tel: 01736 364075

Directions:

From junction 31 on the M5 take the A30 round Bodmin to Penzance. From the town take the A3071 towards St Just and The Fountain Inn lies approximately 2 miles along this road.

Found on the main road through the village, **The Fountain Inn** is a splendid old stone building, with a patio to the front, that dates back to the 16th century. Originally farm cottages, it first became an alehouse and then an inn but throughout these changes much of the building's character has remained. The interior is wonderfully atmospheric with exposed stone walls, ancient dark ceiling beams, flagstone floors and roaring log fires in winter. Upon some of the old beams is a greeting to visitors in the Cornish language whilst, from others, hang a collection of horse brasses and old mugs. All in all it is a very stylish step back in time to the days of smuggling and tin and copper mining.

Whether local or visitors to the area, everyone entering The Fountain Inn can be sure of a warm welcome from landlords Stephanie and Ian Shenton-Phelps. The couple both come from the Penzance area and they have, between them, an extensive knowledge of south Cornwall and are happy to help anyone plan their holiday or just point out the local features that are well worth seeing. Meanwhile, from the bar, Stephanie and Ian serve an excellent range of drinks, including two real ales from the St Austell brewery, and there is also a splendid menu of homecooked dishes that are prepared by Stephanie. Add to this the superb accommodation at this charming inn, which comes with a hearty breakfast, and The Fountain Inn is a place that certainly should not be overlooked.

Opening Hours: Summer - Mon-Sat 11.00-23.00; Sun 12.00-22.30: Winter - Mon-Sat 11.00-15.00, 18.00-23.00; Sun 12.00-15.00, 19.00-22.30 (No food Mon-Tue)

Food: Bar meals and snacks

Credit Cards: None

Accommodation: 2 double rooms all en suite

Facilities: Patio garden, Car parking

Entertainment: Celtic nights, Quiz nights

Local Places of Interest/Activities: Trengwainton 1 mile, Carn Euny Ancient Village 2 miles, Penzance 3 miles, Coast 4 miles, Land's End 7 miles, Walking, Horse riding, Fishing, Sailing, Bird watching

28 The George and Dragon

3 St Nicholas Street,
Bodmin,
Cornwall PL31 1ET
Tel: 01208 72514

Directions:

From junction 31 on the M5 take the A30 to Bodmin. The George and Dragon lies in the heart of the town, close to the preserved railway.

Found at the centre of this historic market town, the only such town in Cornwall to be mentioned in the Domesday Book, **The George and Dragon** can make its own claim to fame by being Bodmin's oldest pub. A splendid and imposing building, situated on one of the town's busy streets, the inn's black and white façade is livened up in summer by the addition of numerous flower filled hanging baskets. The interior is equally impressive as the old building's features, such as its beamed ceilings, have been blended well with the needs of a busy modern day town pub. In these stylish surroundings customers, both locals and visitors alike, can receive excellent Cornish hospitality from landords Dave and Dawn Bramall.

Whether eating and drinking in the inn's charming bar or outside in the sun trap beer garden, the choice and quality of the fare is assured. There are always three locally brewed real ales on tap, as well as all the usual drinks. The food too is excellent and freshly prepared and customers can choose from either the menu or the daily list of specials. Everything is here from sandwiches to steaks and children have their own special selection from which to choose. Finally, the guest rooms here share the same blend of old and new so that visitors can enjoy the luxury of today's facilities with the wonderful olde worlde surroundings of the inn.

Opening Hours: Mon-Sat 11.00-23.00; Sun 12.00-22.30

Food: Bar meals and snacks

Credit Cards: None

Accommodation: 3 double rooms

Facilities: Beer garden, Near by car park, Children welcome

Local Places of Interest/Activities: Bodmin and Wenford Railway, Bodmin Moor 1 mile, Lanhydrock 2 miles, Pencarrow 3 miles, Walking, Cycling, Horse riding, Fishing, Bird watching

The Kings Arms   29

Paul, near Penzance,
Cornwall TR19 6TZ
Tel: 01736 731224

Directions:

From junction 31 on the M5 take the A30 round Bodmin to Penzance. From the town take the B3315 and, after passing through Newlyn, turn left to Paul. The Kings Arms can be found opposite St Pol-de-Leon Church.

Found right in the heart of this small coastal village, **The Kings Arms** is an attractive inn that was converted from cottages that were built to house workers that were involved in the construction of the adjacent St Pol-de-Leon Church. With benches and tables outside and the front of the building bedecked in colourful hanging baskets, the courtyard in front of the inn is a particularly pleasant place to sit during the summer. Inside, the inn is equally delightful and, whilst the bar area has recently been refurbished, it has not lost any of its character or olde worlde charm. The flagstone floors have remained along with the painted coat of arms that decorates one of the walls. A warm and inviting inn, landlords Anthony and Penny Harvey have only been here since 1999 but they have lived in the area for many years. Anthony was born and bred in Paul and, before coming to The Kings Arms, he was a local dairy farmer for 42 years. The couples knowledge of the local area and its people is extensive and their love of west Cornwall enthusiastic.

The range of real ales, including local brews, and all the usual drinks ensures that everyone who visits the inn can enjoy their favourite tipple whilst the delicious and varied menu of tasty, homecooked dishes includes a variety of daily specials. However, The Kings Arms is well renowned in the area for their superb steaks that are a treat not to be missed. Add to this the excellent accommodation and the warm welcome that children receive and The Kings Arms is an inn that will make all the family happy.

Opening Hours: Winter - Mon-Sat 11.00-15.00, 18.00-23.00; Sun 12.00-15.00, 19.00-22.30: Summer - Mon-Sat 11.00-23.00; Sun 12.00-22.30

Food: Bar meals and snacks

Credit Cards: Visa, Mastercard, Switch, Delta

Accommodation: 3 doubles

Facilities: Patio garden, Car parking, Children welcome, dogs on leads welcome

Entertainment: Occasional live music throughout the year, Quiz nights in winter

Local Places of Interest/Activities: Coast ½ mile, Mousehole ½ mile, Newlyn 1 mile, Penzance 2 miles, Land's End 8 miles, Walking, Fishing, Sailing, Bird watching

30   The Kings Arms

5 Market Square,
St Just,
Cornwall TR19 7HF
Tel: 01736 788545

Directions:

From junction 31 on the M5 take the A30 round Bodmin to Penzance. From the town take the A3071 to St Just and The Kings Arms lies in the centre of the town.

Found at the heart of this old town that grew up on the proceeds of the local tin and copper mining industries, **The Kings Arms** is built of the same granite as many of the other houses and shops. Dating back to the 15th century, when it was originally built to house the workers involved in the construction of the church near by, this establishment has been an inn for over 300 years. Attractive and quaint inside, where the original beamed ceilings and fireplaces can still be seen, the inn is given an olde worlde feel by the mass of brass, copper and pottery jugs that hang from the beams. A colourful and unusual display, they make an interesting talking point although many of the inn's regular customers find that they need no prompting and the relaxed and friendly atmosphere here is plenty.

A popular town centre inn, landlords Alan and Janet McCall moved here in 1999 after having fallen in love with south Cornwall on holiday. As well as stocking all the usual beers, lagers, ciders and spirits, Alan intends to expand their range of real ales - it is just two at the moment - as soon as there is more room in the cellar. Though popular for its bar, The Kings Arms has an excellent reputation for the high quality of its cuisine. Taking the trouble to eat here is well worth while as the superb lunchtime and evening dishes are a treat that really should not be missed.

Opening Hours: Mon-Sat 11.00-23.00; Sun 12.00-22.30

Food: Bar meals and snacks

Credit Cards: All the major credit cards

Facilities: Street parking, Children welcome

Local Places of Interest/Activities: Carn Leskys 1 mile, Coast 2 miles, Levant Steam Engine 2 miles, Carn Euny Ancient Village 3 miles, Land's End 6 miles, Walking, Horse riding, Fishing, Bird watching, Sailing

The Kings Arms 31

6 Fore Street,
St Stephen,
near St Austell,
Cornwall PL26 7NN
Tel: 01726 822408

Directions:

From junction 31 on the M5 take the A30 to Bodmin. Continue to the roundabout at the end of the dual carriageway and turn left on to the A391. From St Austell take the A3058 towards Newquay and The Kings Arms lies some 4 miles along the road.

The Kings Arms is an attractive and solidly built stone pub that stands on the corner of St Stephen's main junction and so it is hard to miss. Originally built to house the workers who came here to work on the construction of the village church, this has been an alehouses for many years. Serving the needs of the local community and now those visitors who are lucky enough to discover it, The Kings Arms is now in the capable hands of landlords Ann and Harry Wilson. Although they have only been here a short while, since February 2000, they have certainly made the inn their own. The splendid olde worlde atmosphere is enhanced by the old prints of the village and the wealth of memorabilia that is on display but there is no disguising the building's many original features that remain: the black and ancient beams and the stone fireplaces.

Good, honest, homecooked food is very much the order of the day here and, in deed, it is served throughout the day. There is no permanent menu and the list of daily dishes that are prepared by Ann are displayed on the inn's blackboard. A wide variety of tastes and palates are catered for and it is easy to see why The Kings Arms is fast becoming one of the area's most popular places to eat. Add to this the excellent real ales, draught lagers, ciders and other usual drinks served from the bar, along with the top class accommodation, and The Kings Arms is a wonderful place to use as a holiday base.

Opening Hours: Mon-Sat 11.00-23.00; Sun 12.00-22.30

Food: Bar meals and snacks, À la carte

Credit Cards: None

Accommodation: 2 double room, 1 single room, all en suite

Facilities: Car parking

Local Places of Interest/Activities: St Austell 4 miles, Trewithen House 4 miles, Wheal Martyn Museum 5 miles, Lappa Valley Railway 7 miles, Beach 7 miles, Walking, Cycling, Horse riding, Fishing, Sailing, Bird watching

32   The London Inn

6-8 Lanadwell Street,
Padstow,
Cornwall PL28 8AN
Tel: 01841 532554

Directions:

From junction 31 on the M5 take the A30 to Bodmin and then the A389 through Wadebridge to Padstow. The London Inn lies in the centre of the town.

Found just two minutes walk from this ancient town's quaint quayside, **The London Inn** is a splendid old building that lies in the heart of Padstow down one of its many narrow roads. Obviously an ancient building that certainly appears older than its 300 years, the interesting and eyecatching timber and stone exterior construction is hard to pick out in the summer as the building is covered by a mass of hanging baskets that have, in the past, won landlords Ian and Suzie many awards. Inside, the inn is equally charming and has a real olde worlde atmosphere and, as well as the feature Cornish slate fireplace, there is, not surprisingly a strong nautical theme here.

An inviting inn where everyone is assured a warm welcome, Ian, who is Padstow born and bred, used to pick up the glasses here many years ago and, since he and Suzie took over in 1993, they have been helped by an excellent dedicated staff that includes several family members. The well stocked bar serves three superb real ales, including one known as HSD - High Speed Death - whilst the restaurant is always very popular too, particularly from Easter to mid September when it is advisable to book. Serving a well chosen menu of well prepared pub favourites, fish is, naturally, a house speciality and the fresh crab sandwiches are a superb lunchtime choice. The accommodation too is of the same high standard as the rest of the inn and, as well as including a hearty breakfast, guests also have the advantage of staying in such a wonderful old inn.

Opening Hours: Mon-Sat 11.00-23.00; Sun 12.00-22.30

Food: Bar meals and snacks, À la carte (no food Nov, Jan, Feb)

Credit Cards: None

Accommodation: 2 double rooms, 1 family room, all shared bathroom

Facilities: Use public car parks

Entertainment: Regular live folk music in summer

Local Places of Interest/Activities: Padstow Shipwreck Museum, Padstow Estuary, Prideaux Place 1 mile, Camel Trail 1 mile, Coast 2 miles, Walking, Cycling, Horse riding, Fishing, Bird watching, Sailing

The North Inn

33

The Square,
Pendeen,
near Penzance,
Cornwall TR19 7DN
Tel: 01736 788417
Fax: 01736 787504

Directions:

From junction 31 on the M5 take the A30 round Bodmin to Penzance. Take the A3071 towards St Just and, approximately 1 mile after Newbridge, turn right and follow the road to the junction with the B3306. Turn left and The North Inn lies along this road.

Dating back to the early 18th century, **The North Inn** is a splendid old building, covered in creeper, that lies in the centre of this attractive and peaceful village. However, things have not always been so quiet and relaxed here as this was once a busy tin mining village with miners coming here to work from places such as St Just. This is how the inn got its name - because Pendeen was known as the *North Country* or *"over north"*. Though the inn is still busy today, and certainly a regular haunt for many locals, there are no mines left open in the area and the visitors tend to arrive here whilst exploring the delights of the beautiful Cornish coast and to visit the Geevor Mine Heritage Centre.

Landlord John Coak and his brother Andrew are both local men and, along with Andrew's wife Veronica, they have been here since November 1998. As well as the excellent choice of Cornish real ales on tap, and all the usual beers, lagers and spirits, the inn is highly regarded for the high standard of its cuisine. Prepared by Veronica and Andrew, the lunchtime menu is a tasty mix of freshly cut sandwiches and baguettes and other tempting snacks whilst the evening menu features, among other dishes, the house speciality - curries. There are always several from which to choose and the inn's special curry nights (with even more choice) are always a popular event. Add to this the excellent accommodation at the inn, in a cottage across the square and the adjacent camping site and The North Inn is near perfect.

Opening Hours: Mon-Sat 11.00-23.00; Sun 12.00-22.30

Food: Bar meals and snacks, À la carte, Themed nights

Credit Cards: Visa, Electron, Switch, Solo

Accommodation: 2 double rooms both en suite, Self catering cottage, Camping site

Facilities: Beer garden, Car parking

Entertainment: Longship Singers rehearse here regularly

Local Places of Interest/Activities: Pendeen Lighthouse, Beach 1 mile, Levant Steam Engine 1 mile, Carn Euny Ancient Village 4 miles, Walking, Cycling, Horse riding, Fishing, Sailing, Bird watching

Internet/Website: andrew.coak@btinternet.com

34   The Pendarves Arms

1 Prosper Hill,
Gwithian,
near Hayle,
Cornwall TR27 5BW
Tel: 01736 753223

Directions:

From junction 31 on the M5
take the A30 round Bodmin
towards Penzance. After passing by Camborne turn right
on to a minor road, through
Kehelland and, at the junction with the B3301, turn left.
The Pendarves Arms lies on
this road.

Found in the heart of this picturesque and ancient village of thatched cottages and farm houses, **The Pendarves Arms** is a splendid Victorian inn built of mellow Cornish stone. Standing on the roadside, with its stone walls softened in summer by hanging baskets, the inn is as stylish inside as it is from the road. A cosy and inviting place, from the pitched ceiling beams of this quaint old inn hang a vast collection of decorative mugs that has been continued by owners Steve and Denise Hodgson. Here too can be found excellent, Yorkshire hospitality - a curious find in Cornwall but then Steve and Denise come from the county and only moved here after having fallen in love with the area after coming here on holiday.

As a Yorkshireman, Steve ensures that there is a good range of well kept real ales and bitters here as well as the usual lagers, ciders and spirits. While her husband is looking after customers drinking needs, Denise takes charge of the food and, thanks to her culinary flair and the couple's hard work, The Pendarves Arms is a very popular place to eat, particularly in the summer when it is essential to book a table in the separate non-smoking dining area. The menu varies continuously and, along with daily specials board, there is always a superb choice of interesting, homecooked dishes. Denise's homemade steak and ale pie is a popular local treat and the traditional Sunday roasts, including real Yorkshire pudding, draw people from far and wide. This is an excellent inn, offering the very best hospitality, that is a pleasure to find.

Opening Hours: Mon-Sat 11.00-15.00, 18.30-23.00; Sun 12.00-15.00, 19.00-22.30; Dec-Mar closed Thu 11.00-15.00

Food: Bar meals and snacks, Traditional Sunday lunch

Credit Cards: None

Facilities: Beer garden, Car parking, Children's room

Local Places of Interest/Activities: Beach 1 mile, Tehidy Country Park 4 miles, St Ives 7 miles, Godolphin House 7 miles, Walking, Fishing, Sailing, Swimming, Bird watching, Golf, Surfing

The Queens Arms **35**

Botallack,
St Just,
near Penzance,
Cornwall TR19 7QG
Tel: 01736 788318

Directions:

From junction 31 on the M5 take the A3 round Bodmin to Penzance. From the town take the A3071 to St Just and then the B3306 towards St Ives. The Queens Arms lies down a minor road, on the left, just outside St Just.

Originally built as a private house, **The Queens Arms** first became an inn in 1873 when it was called The New House. Twenty four years later it was known by its present name although there was a short spell in the early 20th century when it was named after Edward VII. A traditional old English inn with a small walled patio garden to the front, this attractive stone building is are characterful inside as its age would suggest. Warm and cosy, with plenty of atmosphere, recent refurbishments have, fortunately, included the restoration of the magnificent painted ceilings above the stairs. Picked out in gentle colours, the plaster relief panels depict various ornate figures.

A delightful, family run inn, landlords Deborah and Philip Badminton are helped by cousin Mark and his wife Marta and together they continue the tradition of offering excellent Cornish hospitality. The real ales served from the bar include those from local brewery, Skinners, which also go by some interesting sounding names - why not try Spriggans or Betty Stoggs, which take their names from characters in Cornish folklore. Delicious typically English bar meals are served at both lunchtime and in the evening throughout the summer and the tasty fare is homecooked by Deborah and Marta. A busy and bustling place that is well frequented by local people, The Queens Arms is particularly popular on Sundays when they serve a marvellous roast lunch.

Opening Hours: Summer - Mon-Sat 11.00-23.00; Sun 12.00-22.30: Winter - Mon-Fri 18.00-23.00; Sat 12.00-15.00, 18.00-23.00; Sun 12.00-15.00, 18.00-22.30

Food: Bar meals and snacks, Traditional Sunday lunch

Credit Cards: None

Facilities: Patio garden, Car parking

Entertainment: Occasional live music

Local Places of Interest/Activities: Coast, Levant Steam Engine 1 mile, Carn Leskys 2 miles, Carn Euny Ancient Village 4 miles, Land's End 6 miles, Walking, Cycling, Horse riding, Fishing, Sailing, Bird watching

36   The Royal Standard Inn

The Square,
Gerrans,
near Truro,
Cornwall
Tel/Fax: 01872 580271

Directions:

From junction 31 on the M5 take the A30 to Bodmin and continue beyond the town and take the A391 to St Austell. Take the A390 then the A3078 towards St Mawes. At Trewithian turn left to Gerrans and The Royal Standard Inn lies in the village centre.

A splendid and imposing cream and red painted building that is hard to miss, **The Royal Standard Inn** is over 250 years old and, so the story goes, that a visiting King Henry VIII gave the pub its name. While the inn is easy to find, its superb lawned garden is hidden well and the sun trap can be found through a small gate leading from the car park. Inside, the old features of this delightful building remain though they are somewhat obscured by the enormous amount of memorabilia that hangs from every available wall and beam. There are hundreds of photographs of the surrounding area, a collection of Toby jugs, copper and brassware, fishing tackle and, finally, paintings by local artists. Certainly cosy and rather eccentric, this colourful interior reflects the personality of popular landlord Alan Sievwright who is a well known and welcoming host. His wife Sheila, who manages the food side of the inn, whilst sharing her husband's enthusiasm for life goes about it more quietly!

Real ales, draught bitters and a good selection of wines are the order of the day from the bar whilst the menu of delicious bar snacks and meals provides everything from open 5" diameter covered baps and local Cornish pasties to authentic Indian curries. Though there is plenty of room here to eat, the inn also has a take away service that is ideal with so much glorious countryside and coast on the door step. Finally, The Royal Standard has a selection of comfortable accommodation that will suit those wishing to linger longer on the Roseland peninsula.

Opening Hours: Mon-Sat 12.00-14.30, 18.30-23.00; Sun 12.00-15.00, 19.00-22.00

Food: Bar meals and snacks

Credit Cards: Visa, Access, Delta, Switch, Solo, Electron, Maestro

Accommodation: 1 double, 1 single room

Facilities: Beer garden, Car parking

Local Places of Interest/Activities: St Mawes Castle 2 miles, Trelissick Gardens 3 miles, Trewithen House 8 miles, Walking, Cycling, Horse riding, Fishing, Bird watching, Sailing

The Sawles Arms **37**

Carthew,
near St Austell,
Cornwall PL26 8XH
Tel: 01726 850317

Directions:

From junction 31 on the M5 take the A30 to Bodmin and continue to the roundabout at the end of the dual carriageway. Turn left on to the A391 towards St Austell. Just beyond Stenalees at the roundabout go straight on along the B3274 and The Sawles Arms lies just down this road.

Found opposite the village green, **The Sawles Arms** is a delightful old inn that lies in a real picture postcard setting. Dating back to the 17th century, this pretty black and white inn is covered with colourful hanging baskets in the summer when, also, its well maintained and secluded rear beer garden is the perfect place to enjoy the sunshine, glorious views and the inn's hospitality. Landlords, Graham, who is locally known as Fred, and Steph Boyling, came here in November 1999 after farming in the area for over 20 years. Although they have been here a relatively short time they have turned around the fortunes of this charming inn and certainly put The Sawles Arms on the map of southern Cornwall.

As the building is old it is not surprising to find that, inside, it has low, beamed ceilings and lovely feature fireplaces. With a very homely and inviting interior that is full of character, this charming inn is just the place to enjoy the excellent range of real ales - from the local St Austell brewery - and other usual drinks that are served from the bar. Whilst Graham is playing host, Steph takes control of the kitchen where the delicious menus of homemade traditional pub food are created. A welcome treat for anyone who appreciates well prepared food at sensible prices it is easy to see why the inn has become so popular in recent times.

Opening Hours: Mon-Sat 11.00-23.00; Sun 12.00-22.30

Food: Bar meals and snacks

Credit Cards: None

Facilities: Beer garden, Car parking

Entertainment: Occasional live music

Local Places of Interest/Activities: Wheal Martyn Museum 1 mile, Eden Project 3 miles, St Austell 3 miles, Beaches 4 miles, Bodmin and moor 8 miles, Walking, Cycling, Horse riding, Fishing, Sailing, Bird watching

38   The Ship Inn

Polmear,
Par,
Cornwall PL24 2AR
Tel: 01726 812540
Fax: 01726 813717

Directions:

From junction 31 on the M5 take the A30 to Bodmin and continue to the roundabout at the end of the dual carriageway. Turn left on to the A391 towards St Austell and continue until the junction with the A390 and turn left. At the next roundabout turn right onto the A3082 and The Ship Inn lies in the village centre.

Dating back to the early 18th century, **The Ship Inn** is a splendid old building that, as well as being found in the main road through the village, also lies close to the sandy beaches of St Austell Bay. Owned and personally run by a local family, David Matthews and his mother and father, Ann and Chris, this large establishment has plenty to offer both locals and visitors alike. The interior of this charming old inn is as full of character as its age would suggest and, along with the original ceiling beams, many other features have withstood the test of time including several interesting over style fireplaces. The restaurant, on the first floor, is a particularly interesting room as, not only is it stylishly furnished and decorated, but the magnificent timbers of the roof can be seen. Outside too there is much for the inn's customers: to side and rear are well maintained gardens where, not only is there a bandstand, but also a play area for children.

From the cosy and inviting bar visitors can enjoy a variety of real ales, including some from local breweries, as well as draught lager, cider and spirits, whilst there is also a tasty range of bar snacks and meals served at both lunchtime and in the evening. For more formal dining, the restaurant (open Tuesday to Saturday and Sunday lunchtime) is perfect. A well known and popular place for a celebration meal, the menus here are sure to excite even the most jaded palate. This is a splendid inn that has a lot to offer its visitors.

Opening Hours: Mon-Sat 11.00-23.00; Sun 12.00-22.30

Food: Bar meals and snacks, À la carte

Credit Cards: Visa, Access, Delta, Switch, Amex, Diners

Accommodation: 2 self catering cottages, 6 static caravans (log cabins to be introduced in 2001)

Facilities: Beer garden, Car parking, Children's play area

Entertainment: Regular live music from the bandstand during the summer

Local Places of Interest/Activities: St Austell Bay and beaches, Eden Project 2 miles, St Austell 3 miles, St Catherine's Castle 3 miles, Restormel Castle 6 miles, Walking, Fishing, Sailing, Bird watching

Internet/Website:
dmattoose@properjob.fsbusiness.co.uk

The Ship Inn

Portloe,
Cornwall TR2 5RA
Tel: 01872 501356

Directions:

From junction 31 take the A30 and then the A391 to St Austell. From the town follow the A390 and then the A3078 towards St Mawes. Approximately 1 mile after Tregony turn left and follow the signposts to Portloe. The Ship Inn lies in the centre of the village.

At the heart of this pretty Cornish fishing village is **The Ship Inn**, a delightful old place that has been painted an attractive blue and white and lies on the narrow road down to the small harbour. A charming and picturesque place, with views out over the village and bay beyond, this inn has a lovely tea garden where, in the summer, cream teas are served along with the usual pub fare. Inside, The Ship Inn is equally delightful, with the open plan bar decorated with a mass of nautical memorabilia and paintings by local artists.

Landlords, Mandy and Keith Johns are locals born and bred and decided to manage this inn as they knew it well as customers. In a warm and friendly, family atmosphere, today's customers can enjoy an excellent choice of real ales, wines and spirits from the bar and also taste some delicious homecooking. Everything is prepared here by Mandy and the house speciality, seafood, is a treat not to be missed. However, there is plenty besides fish to tickle the tastebuds and the inn's traditional Sunday lunches are also a popular occasion here. Add to this the well appointed accommodation and The Ship Inn is a perfect place to stay whilst exploring this wonderful part of the Cornish coast.

Opening Hours: Mon-Sat 11.00-23.00; Sun 12.00-22.30

Food: Bar meals and snacks, Traditional Sunday lunch

Credit Cards: Visa, Access, Delta, Switch, Diners

Accommodation: 1 double room, 1 twin room, both en suite

Facilities: Beer garden, Car parking

Entertainment: Darts

Local Places of Interest/Activities: Coast and coastal walks, Lost Gardens of Heligan 6 miles, Trewithen House 6 miles, St Mawes Castle 7 miles, Truro 9 miles, Walking, Cycling, Horse riding, Fishing, Sailing

Internet/Website:
shipinn@johns.swinternet.co.uk

40   The Tolcarne Inn

Newleyn,
near Penzance,
Cornwall TR18 5AH
Tel: 01736 363074

Directions:

From junction 31 on the M5 take the A30 round Bodmin to Penzance. From the town take the B3315 to Newlyn and The Tolcarne Inn lies on the seafront.

Found overlooking the beach, **The Tolcarne Inn** has been battered by the winds and the sea since it was built in 1717 - or at least that is the date cut into the granite from which the whole building is constructed. Constantly under threat of flooding, one particular gale, the Great Ash Wednesday Storm of 1962, saw the boulders of the town's sea defences thrown around like pebbles and the inn's foundations open to flooding from the extremely high tide of 19 feet and 2 inches! The inn was restored and the sea wall rebuilt though unfortunately now, due to its necessary height, it does obscure the views out to sea from the inn's ground floor windows. The interior of the inn, however, shows no signs of that devastating night and it is a marvellous place of low beamed ceilings that simply oozes olde worlde charm and character.

Landlords Maura and Alan Thompson have been here since December 1999, although Maura has worked here for some time, and fortunately they have not had to contend with any trouble from the sea. They have though, in the short time that they have been here, worked hard and the reputation of the inn is climbing rapidly. With a splendid selection of drinks at the bar to keep both locals and visitors happy, they also serve a delicious menu of tasty and tempting dishes that makes the pub so popular that booking is essential for the Sunday lunches and throughout the summer months. A true local inn, with a warm welcome to visitors, The Tolcarne Inn also shows paintings by local artists on loan from Newlyn Gallery.

Opening Hours: Mon-Fri 11.00-15.00, 18.00-23.00; Sat 11.00-23.00; Sun 12.00-15.00, 19.00-22.30

Food: Bar meals and snacks, À la carte, Tradtional Sunday lunch

Credit Cards: Visa, Access, Delta, Switch

Facilities: Beer garden, Car parking

Entertainment: Quiz nights

Local Places of Interest/Activities: Newlyn harbour, Penzance 1 mile, Carn Euny Ancient Village 4 miles, Land's End 8 miles, Walking, Cycling, Horse riding, Fishing, Sailing, Bird watching

2 East Cornwall

PLACES OF INTEREST:

Altarnun   43
Ashton   43
Bodmin Moor   44
Boscastle   45
Bude   45
Camelford   45
Dobwalls   46
Fowey   46
Launceston   46
Liskeard   47
Looe   47
Lostwithiel   48
Minions   49

Murrayton   50
Polperro   50
Port Isaac   50
Portquin   50
St Cleer   51
St Endellion   51
St Keyne   51
Saltash   51
Tintagel   52
Torpoint   52
Whitsand Bay   52

PUBS AND INNS:

The Carpenters Arms,
   Lower Metherell   53

Church House Inn, Linkhorne   54

Coombe Barton Inn,
   Crackington Haven   55

The Cornish Arms, Pendoggett   56

The Cornish Inn, Gunnislake   57

The Countryman, North Petherwin   58

The Crow's Nest, Port Isaac   59

The Darlington Inn, Camelford   60

The Earl of Chatham, Lostwithiel   61

The Halfway House Inn,
   Twowatersfoot   62

The Harbour Moon, West Looe   63

The Jubilee Inn, Pelynt   64

The London Inn, Kilkhampton   65

The Maltsters Arms, Chapel Amble   66

The Napoleon Inn, Boscastle   67

The Old Inn, St Breward   68

The Smugglers Inn, Cawsand   69

The Snooty Fox, Morval   70

The Tree Inn, Stratton   71

The Hidden Inns of the West Country

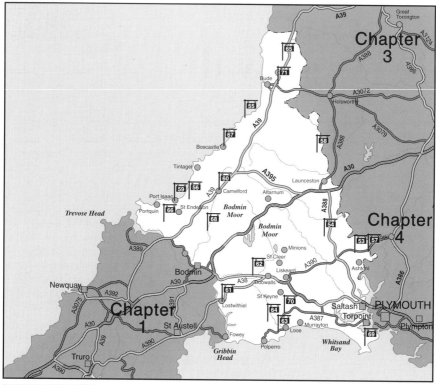

© MAPS IN MINUTES ™ (1998)

53 **The Carpenters Arms**, Lower Metherell

54 **Church House Inn**, Linkhorne

55 **Coombe Barton Inn**, Crackington Haven

56 **The Cornish Arms**, Pendoggett

57 **The Cornish Inn**, Gunnislake

58 **The Countryman**, North Petherwin

59 **The Crow's Nest**, Port Isaac

60 **The Darlington Inn**, Camelford

61 **The Earl of Chatham**, Lostwithiel

62 **The Halfway House Inn**, Twowatersfoot

63 **The Harbour Moon**, West Looe

64 **The Jubilee Inn**, Pelynt

65 **The London Inn**, Kilkhampton

66 **The Maltsters Arms**, Chapel Amble

67 **The Napoleon Inn**, Boscastle

68 **The Old Inn**, St Breward

69 **The Smugglers Inn**, Cawsand

70 **The Snooty Fox**, Morval

71 **The Tree Inn**, Stratton

Please note all cross references refer to page numbers

Cornwall is separated from the rest of mainland Britain by the River Tamar, which rises just northeast of Bude and forms the boundary with Devon down to the river's estuary on the south coast. The natural barrier of the Tamar has, over the centuries, preserved Cornwall's Celtic heritage - still very much in evidence today. Place names beginning with Tre, Pol and Pen are the most common reminders. Others are the many ancient remains of crosses, holy wells and prehistoric sites throughout the countryside.

This area of Cornwall is dominated by the bleak expanse of Bodmin Moor, which covers some 80 square miles. There are also a great many reminders of the presence of Roman and Norman occupation.

Northeastern Cornwall is renowned for its fine dairy products (especially cheeses), and has many connections with the author Thomas Hardy and the poet John Betjeman. And while nowhere in Cornwall is more than 20 miles from the sea, the northeast coast is unique in many respects. Particularly around Boscastle and Tintagel, this is a landscape dominated by high cliffs. Of course the sea has always played an important part in life in the villages of Cornwall - in addition to fishing and trawling, dealing in contraband was once a common way of supplementing income, as the coastline offers many convenient hiding places expansive enough to accommodate even the largest haul of ill-gotten goods.

Where the north is dominated by high cliffs, the south is a series of secluded rocky coves and bays. The inescapable romance of the landscape, which has inspired writers, artists, natives and visitors for centuries, is complemented by gentle Gulf Stream breezes, assuring mild weather throughout spring, summer and autumn. This part of Cornwall is renowned for its characterful resorts, miles of beaches, bustling quaysides and busy market towns.

PLACES OF INTEREST

ALTARNUN

This charming Bodmin Moor village lies in the steep-sided valley of Penpont Water. It features a 15th century packhorse bridge and outstanding, largely 15th century parish church standing in a superb position on a rise above the peat-stained river. Sometimes referred to as the 'Cathedral of the Moors', this surprisingly grand moorstone structure is dedicated to St Nonna, the mother of St David, patron saint of Wales. It has a tall pinnacled tower and an unusually light and spacious interior which contains a carved rood screen, a decorated Norman font and a wonderful series of over 70 Tudor bench ends whose carvings create a charming picture of 16th century village life.

In the churchyard there are several fine examples of the work of Altarnun-born sculptor Nevill Northey Bunard, who carved the bust of John Wesley which stands over the door of the Meeting House by the stream.

ASHTON

A group of interesting hidden places can be found within a few miles of each other, six miles upstream from the spectacular twin bridges over the River Tamar at Saltash. One of the most appealing National Trust properties in England can be found buried in the lanes to the east of the A388 Saltash-to-Callington road. **Cotehele House** is a low granite manor house set around three courtyards, which was largely built in

44

Tudor times by Sir Richard Edgcumbe and his son, Piers.

In the 1550s, the family moved their main residence southwards to Mount Edgcumbe, a more accessible site overlooking Plymouth Sound; since then, Cotehele has been left relatively unaltered, except for the addition of the semi-fortified northwest tower in 1627. Inside, the Tudor great hall contains a remarkable collection of early armour and weaponry, and there are some exceptional tapestries and period furni-

Cotehele House

ture in the other rooms. The house incorporates some charming individual features, including a secret spy-hole to the great hall, a private chapel, and a tower clock with a bell, but no face or hands, which is believed to be the oldest working example of its kind in Britain.

The grounds of Cotehele House are some of the most delightful in the West Country. Above the house, there is an enclosed formal garden with a wide, shallow pond - below it, the ground falls away in a steep-sided combe which contains a spectacular collection of mature rhododendrons, azaleas and other flowering shrubs.

The garden's most enchanting feature - a medieval stone dovecote with a domed roof - stands beside a deep stream-fed pool between the house and the Tamar. At the foot of the combe, a tiny chapel stands on a promontory, 70 feet above the river's edge. This was built in the 15th century by Sir Richard Edgcumbe, a Lancastrian, to show thanks for his escape from the Yorkist forces of Richard III who had been pursuing him through Cotehele woods. Edgcumbe avoided capture by placing a stone in his cap and throwing it into the fast-flowing waters of the Tamar, a ploy which made his pursuers think he had jumped to his death.

Cotehele was once a large working estate with its own flour mill, cider press, smithy and workshops; now restored to working order, these lie in a valley half a mile away from the main house and are open to visitors. Similarly, **Cotehele Quay** was once a significant river port with its own wharves, warehouses and lime kilns. Several of its once-derelict 18th and 19th century buildings have been given new life: one houses a branch of the **National Maritime Museum**, while another is an excellent tearoom.

BODMIN MOOR

The bleak expanse of Bodmin Moor stretches either side of the A30. This 80 square-mile area of granite upland is characterised by saturated moorland and weather-beaten tors. The exposed area to the north of the main road supports the 1,377-foot hill known as **Brown Willy**, the highest point in Cornwall.

Almost as high, and standing on National Trust-owned land a bit to the northwest, is **Rough Tor**, a magnificent viewpoint which is also the site of a memorial to the men of the

Bodmin Moor

Wessex Regiment killed in the Second World War. This dramatic area of the moor is best approached from the northwest along the lane leading up from the A39 at Camelford.

Like Dartmoor, Bodmin Moor is covered in prehistoric remains. Typical of many are the scattered Bronze Age hut circles and field enclosures which can be seen on the side of Rough Tor. Slightly south of this lies the **Fernacre Stone Circle**. Also Bronze Age, it contains more than 30 standing stones and is the largest of this kind of structure on the Moor.

Evidence of even earlier occupation can be found between the A30 and **Hawks Tor**, the site of a Neolithic henge monument known as the **Stripple Stones**.

BOSCASTLE

Lying on a delightful, unspoilt stretch of the north Cornwall coastline, this was a thriving seaport up to the 19th century and is now used by local inshore fishermen and visitors. The National Trust own and protect the harbour area as well as a considerable amount of the land and coastline in north Cornwall. This ancient and picturesque fishing community stands in a combe at the head of a remarkable S-shaped inlet from the Atlantic.

Boscastle harbour's inner jetty was built by the renowned Elizabethan seafarer, Sir Richard Grenville, when the village was prospering as a fishing, grain and slate port. The outer jetty was added 350 years later when Boscastle was being developed as a seaport for the manganese and iron ore mines near Launceston. This latter structure was accidentally blown up by a stray mine during the Second World War, and had to be repaired by the National Trust at considerable expense.

The Trust owns the harbour and much of the coastline around Boscastle. The spectacular slate headlands on either side of the community provide some excellent - if demanding - walking. The village itself is set around a steep broad thoroughfare lined with attractive houses, inns and shops, most of which cater for the holiday-maker. A tourist information centre is lo-

cated in the old forge by the harbour; there is also an interesting **Witchcraft Museum** which contains some

sinister relics of the ancient black arts. The esteemed author Thomas Hardy was a regular visitor to Boscastle when he worked as an architect on the restoration of the church at St Juliot, two miles southeast. The village appears as 'Castle Boterel' in Hardy's early novel, *A Pair of Blue Eyes*. Other attractions in the village include the **Cave Holography & Illusion Exhibition**, and **Lye Rock**, a great place for puffin-spotting.

BUDE

Bude, with its sweeping expanse of sand and Atlantic breakers rolling in from the west, seems to change its character with every change in the weather - a winter gale can make it seem like a remote outpost clinging to the edge of the world, while a warm summer breeze transforms it into a genial holiday town with some excellent facilities for beach-lovers, surfers and coastal walkers. It enjoys its status as a prime north coast resort with find sandy beaches, rock pools, and tidal swimming pool.

The town stood at the northern end of the now-disused **Bude Canal**, an ambitious early 19th century inland waterway which was intended to connect the Atlantic with the English Channel by way of the River Tamar. The only stretch to be completed, that between Bude and Launceston, was largely used for transporting seaweed, sand and other fertilisers to inland farms. Abandoned when the railway arrived in the 1890s, the two mile long section at the northern end has now been restored for use as a recreational amenity. The small fort guarding the northern entrance to the canal was built in the 1840s as an eccentric private residence, and the old forge on the canalside has been converted into an interesting **Museum** exploring Bude's maritime heritage. The Bude-Stratton Historical Folk Exhibition, also on the canal, and the **World of Nature** in the town centre, are two more fascinating places to visit.

CAMELFORD

This small former wool town contains an interesting museum of rural life, the **North Cornwall Museum** and **Art Gallery**, housed in a converted coach house, and the **Museum of Historic Cycling**. Its **Crowdy Reservoir** makes an excellent spot for trout fishing.

Boscastle Cottages

46

DOBWALLS

The popular **Dobwalls Adventure Park** and **Mr Thorburn's Edwardian Countryside** can be found on the northern edge of the village from which it takes its name. The park contains a number of contrasting attractions, including the Forest Railway, a two mile long miniature steam railway whose locomotives and rolling stock are based on the old North American railroad. There is also an indoor railway museum and an extensive adventure playground. The charming Edwardian countryside museum features a permanent exhibition on the life and work of the English wildlife artist, Archibald Thorburn. On site there is also an art gallery and **Cornish Craft Centre**.

The famous **Carnglaze Slate Caverns** lie two miles west in the lovely wooded valley of the River Loveny, a mile to the north on the A38. Slate for use in the building trade was first quarried in these vast man-made caverns in the 14th century. The largest chamber is over 300 foot high and was once used by smugglers as a secret rum store. The lichen on the cavern walls is covered with minute droplets of water which reflect the available light in the most magical way. Visitors can see the remains of the tramway which was built to haul the stone to the surface from the lower levels, and at the deepest level there is a subterranean pool which is filled with the clearest blue-green water.

FOWEY

The lovely old port and historic seafaring town of Fowey (pronounced Foy) guards the western entrance to the river from which it takes its name. The narrow lanes and alleyways of the old town rise abruptly from the water's edge in a pleasant mixture of architectural styles from Elizabethan to Edwardian.

The deep water harbour has been used as an anchorage for seagoing vessels since the time of the ancient Romans, and china clay continues to be exported from the whitened jetties which lie half a mile or so upstream. The town's long history is closely linked with its maritime traditions. During the Hundred Years War, local mariners recruited to fight the French became known as the 'Fowey Gallants'; some refused to disband, and instead formed a notorious gang of pirates who would attack any vessel straying too close to this stretch of coast.

Following a devastating French raid in 1457, a chain was stretched across the estuary mouth at night to deter hostile ships from entering the harbour.

Present-day Fowey is a peaceful community which is connected by vehicle ferry to Bodinnick on the eastern bank, and by passenger ferry to Polruan. The harbour is filled with pleasure craft from all over Britain and continental Europe, and there a number of fine old buildings which are worth closer inspection, for example the **Noah's Ark Museum**, housed in one of the oldest structures in Fowey, the medieval town hall in Trafalgar Square, which is occupied by another interesting local museum, and the Ship Inn, a part-15th century building with a Victorian facade which was once the town house of the Rashleigh family.

The Rashleigh family seat, **Menabilly**, lies to the southeast of the town and was subsequently the home of Daphne du Maurier, who used the setting - rechristened 'Manderley' - in her famous novel, *Rebecca*. Another of Fowey's literary residents was the Cornish novelist Sir Arthur Quiller-Couch, who lived for over 50 years at the Haven on the Esplanade. There are some excellent beaches nearby.

LAUNCESTON

Launceston (the local pronunciation is *Lan-son*) is one of the most pleasant inland towns in Cornwall. For centuries it was an important regional capital which guarded the main overland route into the county. Shortly after the Norman invasion, William the Conqueror's half-brother, Robert of Mortain, built a massive **Castle** here on an elevated site above the River Kensey. From this castle fort, subsequent Earls of Cornwall tried to govern the fiercely inde-

Launceston Castle

pendent Cornish people. A fine example of a motte and bailey castle, the outer bailey is now a public park; there is also a round double keep, the outer walls of which are 12 foot thick in places. Also in its time used as a gaol, where prisoners were kept in appalling conditions in this decaying fortress, its inmates included founder of the Quakers, George Fox.

Launceston boasts a number of fine old buildings and churches. In medieval times a settlement grew up around an Augustinian priory on the northern side of the River Kensey. It is here that the original parish **Church of St Stephen** stands. Nearby there is a Byzantine-style Roman Catholic church, built early in the 20th century. The oldest surviving ecclesiastical building in the town is the 12th century **Church of St Thomas**, near the southern end of the medieval footbridge that crosses the river - surprisingly, within this tiny building stands the largest Norman font in Cornwall.

Some of the most impressive stonework in the area is used in the **Church of St Mary Magdelene**, a 16th century granite structure built by a local landowner after the tragic death of his wife and son. He assembled the finest stonemasons in Cornwall to create, in their memory, a remarkable cornucopia of ornamental carving which covers nearly every surface of the building. Elsewhere in Launceston, the streets around the castle are filled with handsome buildings dating from Georgian times and earlier, including the National Trust-owned **Lawrence House** in Castle Street. Housing an interesting town museum, this was built in 1753 and contains some fine plasterwork ceilings.

Launceston Steam Railway

The art gallery near the medieval **South Gate**, the only remaining vestige of Launceston's town walls, is

also worth a visit. To the west of the town, a **Steam Railway** runs along the Kensey valley. Other nearby attractions include **Tamar Otter Park** and **Trethorne Leisure Farm**.

LISKEARD

Standing on an undulating site between the valleys of the East Looe and Seaton rivers, Liskeard is a pleasant old market town which was one of Cornwall's five medieval Stannary towns (the others being Bodmin, Lostwithiel, Truro and Helston). The name comes from the Latin word for tin, *stannum*, and these five towns were the only ones licensed to weigh and stamp the metal. The town has a long history as a centre for mineral extraction: for centuries, the medieval Cornish tinners brought their smelted tin down from Bodmin Moor for weighing, stamping and taxing, then in the early 19th century, great quantities of copper ore from the nearby **Caradon mines** and granite from the **Cheesewring quarries** were loaded onto barges here and despatched to the coast along the newly-constructed Looe canal. In the 1850's, the canal was replaced by the Looe valley branch of the Great Western Railway, a scenic stretch of line which still operates today although its industrial cargoes have long been replaced by passenger holiday traffic.

Thankfully now bypassed by the busy A38 Plymouth to Bodmin road, Liskeard's narrow streets contain a number of interesting old buildings, including the curious Italianate **Guildhall** and **Stuart House**, a handsome Jacobean residence in which Charles I is believed to have stayed for a week during the English Civil War. Perhaps Liskeard's most unusual feature can be found in Well Lane, where an arched grotto marks the site of **Pipe Well**, a medieval spring which is reputed to have curative powers.

LOOE

At the mouth of the East and West Looe rivers stands the bustling coastal resort and fishing port of Looe. Originally two separate towns facing each other across the estuary, **East** and **West Looe** were first connected by a bridge in the early 15th century, and were officially incorporated in 1883. The present seven-arched

48

bridge dates from the 19th century and is wide enough to carry the A387 Polperro road.

As early as 1800, a bathing machine was constructed at the top of Looe's sandy beach, and when visitors began to arrive in numbers with the coming of the railway in 1859, the town began to develop as a resort. More recently, Looe has established itself as Britain's premier shark-fishing centre, regularly hosting an International Sea Angling Festival.

Over the years, Looe has evolved into a small seaside resort which has managed to retain a good deal of its original character, despite the annual invasion of holiday-makers. The old quarters on either side of the river are mazes of narrow lanes lined with old stone fisherman's cottages and inns, some of which are partially constructed from old ships' timbers. The 16th century **Guildhall** in East Looe is now an impressive local museum. The **Living from the Sea Museum** and **Southeast Cornwall Discovery Centre** also merit a visit.

In summer, pleasure boats depart from the quay for trips along the coast to Polperro and Fowey, and boat trips can also be taken to **St George's Island** half a mile offshore. Now a

Looe

privately-run bird sanctuary, this was once the refuge of the notorious pirate and smuggler, Black Joan, who along with her brother Fyn terrorised the population of this lonely stretch of coast. The **Looe Valley Line** runs from Liskeard to Looe, taking in Coombe, St Keyne and many breathtaking local sights, with walks available from each station.

LOSTWITHIEL

This attractive small market town stands at the head of the Fowey estuary at the historic lowest bridging point on the river. One of Cornwall's medieval Stannary towns, tin and other raw metals were brought here for assaying and onward shipping until upstream mining activity caused the anchorage to silt up, forcing the port to move down-river to the estuary mouth. Present-day Lostwithiel is an atmospheric touring and angling centre whose long history has left it with a legacy of interesting old buildings, many of which are set in characteristic narrow alleyways, or opes. The remains of the 13th century great hall which served as the treasury and stannary offices can be seen in Quay Street, and in Fore Street there is a fine example of an early 18th century arcaded **Guildhall** which now serves as the civic museum. The nearby municipal offices date from later in the century, as does the old grammar school in Queen Street, and elsewhere in the town there are some fine Georgian residences and shop fronts. The **old malt house** is worth finding for its unusual plaque, declaring 'Walter Kendal founded this house and hath a lease for 3,000 years beginning 29 September 1652.'

Lostwithiel's 14th century parish **Church of St Bartholomew** has a rare octagonal spire; one of only six in the county, its style is reminiscent of the church architecture of northern France. Another unusual feature is the row of upper windows in the aisle, or clerestory, which is one of only four in Cornwall. The early 14th century font is unusually large and richly carved. During the Civil War, the Parliamentarians made this the focus for their anti-Royalist feeling when they brought a horse into the church and provocatively christened it Charles 'in contempt of his sacred Majesty'.

The spectacular National Trust-owned property, **Lanhydrock House**, lies midway between the A38 and B3269 north of Lostwithiel. Prior to the Dissolution of the Monasteries, the 400 acre estate belonged to Bodmin's Augustinian priory of St Petroc, then in 1620 it was acquired by the Robartes family, in whose possession it remained until it passed to the National Trust in 1953. The house is set in a superb position in the valley of the River Fowey and is approached along an avenue of sycamore and beech trees, some of which were originally planted over three centuries ago. Visitors pass through an imposing 17th century gatehouse

Lanhydrock House

ways onto the ramparts. The road to the south passes close to the site of a disused mine which was once the largest source of iron ore in Cornwall. Material was transported from here by tramway to Lostwithiel, and then by barge to Fowey for loading onto seagoing vessels. **Bradock Down**, to the east, was the site of a famous Royalist victory.

MINIONS

Here in this exposed former mining community, on the southeastern fringe of Bodmin Moor, stands **Hurlers Stone Circle**, an impressive Bronze Age temple consisting of three stone circles arranged in a line. According to Cornish legend, the circles were formed when teams of local men were turned to stone for hurling (playing the game that is a Celtic form of hockey) on the Sabbath.

Half a mile away to the north stands the spectacular natural granite formation known as **The Cheesewring**. Another local legend has it that this was the haunt of a druid who possessed a golden chalice which never ran dry and provided thirsty passersby with and endless sup-

which, along with the north wing, is one of the few parts of the original structure to have escaped the fire which tore through the building in 1881.

Thankfully, the magnificent first floor gallery in the north wing survived; over 115 feet long, it is illuminated by broad mullioned windows and contains a remarkable plasterwork ceiling showing scenes from the Old Testament which is believed to be the work of the Abbott family, master plasters of North Devon.

Because of the fire, most of Lanhydrock House is a Victorian reconstruction built in the 1880s to the original 17th century design. The updated interior contains a maze of comfortably appointed rooms, over 40 of which are now open to the public. Highlights include the estate offices, servants' quarters, buttery and nursery, which together create a unique picture of life in an opulent Victorian country mansion. The grounds contain an attractive woodland shrubbery, and a much-photographed formal garden and parterre which is overlooked by the small estate church of St Hyderoc.

A mile and a half downstream, the imposing Norman keep of **Restormel Castle** stands on a promontory overlooking the wooded valley of the River Fowey. The fortress was built in the early 12th century by Edmund, Earl of Cornwall, and is remarkably well preserved for its age. The walls of the massive circular shell are 30 feet high in places, and the whole structure is surrounded by a deep dry moat which is lined with flowers in spring. The castle was in use until the 16th century, and was reoccupied for a time by Parliamentarian forces during the English Civil War. Now under the care of English Heritage, visitors can climb a series of walk-

The Cheesewring

ply of water. The story was partially borne out in 1818 when archaeologists excavating a nearby burial chamber discovered a skeleton clutching a golden cup - dubbed the Rillaton Cup, it is now in the British Museum. The lovely **Siblyback Reservoir** is less than two miles west of Minions.

50

MURRAYTON

Here in a sheltered, wooded valley is the home of a famous **Monkey Sanctuary** - the world's first protected colony of Amazonian Woolly monkeys, established in 1964. It was set up to provide a stable setting for Woolly monkeys rescued from lives of isolation in zoos and as pets. The monkeys are allowed to roam freely and visitors are able to view them, along with a variety of other animals and birds, at close quarters. Regular talks and indoor displays explain more about monkey life and their natural habitat, the Amazonian Rainforest.

POLPERRO

This lovely old fishing community is many people's idea of the archetypal Cornish village. It stands at the point where a steep-sided wooded combe converges with a narrow tidal inlet from the sea. Its steep narrow streets and alleyways are piled high with white-painted fishermen's cottages, many of which have now been converted into art galleries and specialist shops.

All routes seem to lead down to Polperro's highly photogenic double harbour, a working fishing port which normally contains an assortment of attractive inshore fishing vessels. The mouth of the inner harbour was fitted with movable timber gates after a southeasterly storm destroyed over 20 boats which were sheltering there in the early 19th century (they have now been replaced by a modern tidal floodgate).

Polperro has had a long association with smuggling: the practice was so rife in the 18th century that many of the village's inhabitants were involved in shipping, storing or transporting contraband goods. To combat the problem,

Polperro Harbour

H M Customs and Excise established the first 'preventive station' in Cornwall here in the early 1800s. The atmosphere and events of those days are brought to life in a fascinating **Smugglers' Museum** which can be found near the inner harbour.

Another attraction is a model village of old Polperro, which is set within pleasant flower-filled gardens. Houses of interest include **Couch's House** (1595), **House on Props**, and the **Old Watch House**. A cliffpath leads to bays and beaches. Modern Polperro has had to succumb to the holiday industry - in summer, cars are banned from the narrow streets.

PORT ISAAC

This lovely old fishing community of stone and slate houses is divided by narrow alleyways, or *drangs* (one goes by the charming name of 'Squeeze-Belly Alley'), and has a lovely small beach.

At one time, huge quantities of herring were landed here. After the arrival of the railway, these were gutted and packed in the village's many fish cellars before being despatched by train to Britain's inland centres of population by train. One of these old cellars is now an inshore lifeboat station, while others are used at boathouses or retail outlets.

PORTQUIN

This picturesque coastal hamlet is overlooked by a Regency faux-Gothic folly on **Doyden's Point**. When Portquin's slate trade was ended by the coming of the railways, it went through such a severe period of decline that at one time outsiders thought that the entire population had been washed away in a great storm. The village remained deserted for decades, but was eventually purchased and restored by the National Trust. Today it is a seasonal community with a very pleasant atmosphere which is arranged around a clutch of National Trust-owned holiday cottages. The offshore rock formations are known as the Cow and Calf.

Just west of Portquin, the small peninsula of land to the north and east of the Camel Estuary is a lovely stretch of country which is entirely free of through traffic. The table-topped **Pentire Head**, to the extreme northwest, offers some excellent walking with magnificent views over the Camel Estuary. The northernmost tip, **The Rump**, is a promontory of hard greenstone which has been eroded into a series of extraordinary pinnacles; this was the site of an Iron Age hill fort, one of three on the headland. The area is known for its wild tamarisk, an elegant flowering shrub more commonly found around the shores of the Mediterranean. Pentire Head was saved from commercial development in the 1930s after local campaigners raised enough funds to purchase the land and donate it to the National Trust.

St Cleer

This sizable village lies in the heart of bleak former mining country on the southern fringe of Bodmin Moor. The settlement is arranged around the parish church, a largely 15th century building with a striking granite tower and a Norman doorway which has survived from an earlier building. To the northeast of the churchyard, another 15th century granite structure marks the site of a holy well whose waters are reputed to have restorative powers. Visitors to such holy wells commonly leave a personal item such as a handkerchief behind them - these can sometimes be seen hanging from nearby branches.

Half a mile east of the village centre stands **Trethevy Quoit**, a massive enclosed Neolithic chamber which originally formed the core of a vast earthwork mound. The largest structure of its type in Cornwall, it is believed to be around 5,000 years old and has much in common with those found in west Penwith. On the opposite (western) side of the village, the **Doniert Stone** is a tall stone cross which was erected as a memorial to King Durngarth, a Cornish king who is thought to have drowned in the nearby River Fowey around 870 AD. Sadly now broken into two pieces, it is carved with a Latin inscription which, translated, reads 'Erected for Doniert for the good of his soul.' A little further west, the River Fowey descends for half a mile through dense broad-leaved woodland in a delightful series of cascades known as **Golitha Falls**, as well as the delightful Siblyback Lake.

St Endellion

This charming village has a church built of Lundy island granite and dedicated to St Endelienta, a Celtic saint who lived solely, so they say, on milk - and who passed away after her trusty cow was killed in a dispute with a farmer. The village also hosts a twice-yearly music festival. Nearby, **Long Cross Victorian Gardens** offer a chance to visit a peaceful and attractive haven resplendent with 19th century plants and plantings.

St Keyne

This small village is home to the fascinating **Paul Corin's Mechanical Music Centre**, a unique museum of mechanical instruments housed in a lovely old mill which stands near the bridge over the East Looe River, half a mile east of the centre of the village. Exhibits include street, cafe and fairground organs, all of which are kept in working order and played on a regular basis.

One of the more unusual episodes in St Keyne's history took place during the reign of the Catholic Mary Tudor, when the local rector and his wife (who had married during the reign of the Protestant Edward VI) were dragged from their bed in the middle of the night and placed on the village stocks.

Another famous holy well, known as **St Keyne Well**, lies a mile south of the village beneath a great tree which is said to bear the leaves of four different species. According to local legend, the first member of a newly-married couple to drink from the spring will be the one who wears the trousers, a notion which captured the imagination of Victorian newlyweds and brought them here in their thousands.

Saltash

Saltash's near-perpendicular streets feature many buildings of interest, including the 17th century **Guildhall** and **Mary Newman's cottage** (home of Mrs Francis Drake). Tamar River cruises depart from here. Brunel's **Iron Railway**

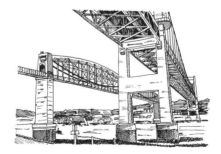

Tamar Bridge and Iron Bridge

Bridge opened in 1859, and the suspension road bridge in 1961. **Saltash Galleries** on the High Street features works by local artists covering a wide range of artistic styles and media.

TINTAGEL

The romantic remains of **Tintagel Castle** stand on top of **Tintagel Head**. Prior to a series of rock falls in the 19th century, this formidable headland was connected to the mainland by a natural stone bridge; now only a narrow isthmus remains. Many like to believe that this was the birthplace of the legendary King Arthur, or even that it was the site of Camelot, the mythi-

Tintagel Castle

cal headquarters of the Knights of the Round Table (other possibilities are Caerleon in Wales and South Cadbury in Somerset). Fragments of a Celtic monastic house dating from the 6th century have been uncovered on the headland; their origins coincide with the activities of the Welsh military leader on which the Arthurian legends are thought to be based; however, the fortification we see today was founded by Reginald Earl of Cornwall, the illegitimate son of Henry I, in the 12th century, over 600 years after Arthur would have died. Whatever the true heritage of Tintagel castle, the scramble down towards the sea and back up to its clifftop site 250 feet above the Atlantic is a breathtaking experience.

Tintagel, of course, owes much of its popularity to the Arthurian connection. One of its most noteworthy attractions is '**King Arthur's Halls**'; these were built in the 1930's by devotees of the legends and include the '**Hall of Chivalry**', a room with over 70 stained-glass windows depicting the coats of arms of the Knights of the Round Table. Elsewhere, Arthurian eating places and souvenir shops abound.

Perhaps the finest building in Tintagel is the **Old Post Office**, a small 14th century slate-built manor house which in the 19th century found new life as a letter-receiving station. Now owned by the National Trust, this charming and strangely organic-looking structure has been carefully restored to its Victorian livery.

A good sandy beach can be found a couple of miles to the south of Tintagel at **Trebarwith Strand**, one of the few breaks in the wild craggy cliffscape.

TORPOINT

For those wishing to cross the Tamar Estuary (here called the *Hamoaze*) by car, a 24-hour vehicle ferry plies back and forth between Devonport and Torpoint. The latter stands on the northern arm of the Rame peninsula and is a small industrial boat-building and dormitory town which faces the naval dockyard across the Estuary.

The atmosphere is very different at **Antony House**, a delightful National Trust-owned property which lies between the A374 and the estuary of the River Lynher, a mile and a half northwest. Considered one of the finest early Georgian country mansions in Cornwall, it was constructed between 1718 and 1729 of pale silver-grey stone brought in by sea from Pentewan, near Mevagissey.

WHITSAND BAY

The most impressive stretch of beach in southeast Cornwall is found along the shore here. More a series of coves than a continuous expanse of sand, the bay runs between Portwrinkle and Rame on the southwestern side of the Rame peninsula. To gain access to the beach, visitors should park in one of the car parks arranged at intervals along this highly scenic stretch of coast road, and then descend by way of a steep footpath. Lifeguards are on duty at busy times.

The Carpenters Arms 53

Lower Metherell,
near Callington,
Cornwall PL17 8BJ
Tel: 01579 350242
Fax: 01579 350242

Directions:

From Plymouth take the A3064 to Saltash and then the A388 towards Launceston. At Callington turn right on to the A390 and then follow the signposts to Lower Metherell and The Carpenters Arms can be found 1 mile from Cotehele House.

Dating back to the 15th century, **The Carpenters Arms** is a charming and picturesque typical old Cornish pub that is built of the local stone. The inn acquired its name from the carpenters who stayed here whilst constructing near by Cotehele House during Tudor times. Though the level of hospitality since those days has greatly improved, many of the inn's original features, which the carpenters would recognise, remain, including the flagstone floors and old oak beams. Surprisingly, as the inn does not lie on the coast, there is a nautical theme here and as well as a mass of pictures and other memorabilia, there is plenty of gleaming brassware on display.

Well known locally for its excellent hospitality, licensees, Linda and Michael Mutter, take great pride in this wonderful English country inn. There is a fine selection of real ales, as well as all the usual drinks, at the bar and the tasty menu of delicious homecooked bar meals and lunches is well worth taking the time to sample. Local fish, meat and vegetables are used and, whilst in the summer the barbecues are popular, the Sunday roast lunches are a treat that can be enjoyed throughout the year. In good weather, when the attractive patio style beer garden comes into its own, or in the cosy warmth of the bar in winter, this is a marvellous inn that is an ideal place for either a short stay or a relaxing break during a journey.

Opening Hours: Mon-Sun 12.00-15.00, 18.00-23.00 (winter 19.00-23.00)

Food: Bar meals and snacks, Sunday lunches, Summer barbecues

Credit Cards: Visa, Access, Switch

Accommodation: 1 double room en suite

Facilities: Patio garden, Car parking

Entertainment: Darts

Local Places of Interest/Activities: Cotehele House 1 mile, Kit Hill 2 miles, Morwellham Quay Museum 3 miles, Bodmin Moor 5 miles, Walking, Bird watching, Fishing

54   Church House Inn

Linkhorne,
near Callington,
Cornwall PL17 7LY
Tel: 01579 363631

Directions:

From junction 31 on the M5 take the A30 to Launceston and then the A388 towards Saltash. Turn right off the A388 to Bray Shop, continue over the crossroads to the T junction and turn left. At the telephone box turn right and Church House Inn lies opposite St Melor's Church.

The history of this delightful country inn is sketchy though it is known that the **Church House Inn** was built, at the latest, in 1906. However, this attractive stone built inn, which is painted a traditional black and white, gives the appearance of having been here for centuries. Inside the story is the same and the timeless atmosphere is helped by the wealth of ceiling beams, horses brasses, open fire and exposed stone walls. A warm and inviting family inn, where locals and visitors are all greeted as friends, landlord Nigel Payne must be proud of the success of his first venture into the licensing trade.

As a country pub in the heart of some excellent walking country, offering good food and drink is essential and the well stocked bar certainly provides all that could be needed in the way of liquid refreshment - as well as the two real ales, usual beers, lagers and spirits there is also an extensive wine list. Food too plays an important part of life here and, whilst bar food is available at lunchtime, the separate restaurant has an impressive evening menu. All the dishes are homecooked and the substantial menu includes a range of specialities such as Steak Mignons, Sherry Chicken and the Church House Curry. Vegetarians too have their own imaginative menu and children too are well looked after. A place well worth seeking out this is a charming village inn that the whole family can enjoy.

Opening Hours: Tue-Thu 19.00-23.00; Fri-Sat 12.00-15.00, 19.00-23.00; Sun 12.00-15.00, 19.00-22.30

Food: Bar meals and snacks, À la carte, Vegetarian and Children's menu

Credit Cards: Visa, Access, Delta, Switch, Amex, Diners

Facilities: Car parking, Functions catered for

Entertainment: Skittles, Darts

Local Places of Interest/Activities: Hurlers Stone Circle 4 miles, King Doniert's Stone 6 miles, Bodmin Moor 6 miles, Launceston 7 miles, Beaches 12 miles, Walking, Horse riding, Fishing, Bird watching

Coombe Barton Inn | 55

Crackington Haven,
near Bude,
Cornwall EX23 0JG
Tel: 01840 230345
Fax: 01840 230788

Directions:

From junction 31 on the M5 take the A30 to Launceston and, after passing the town, turn right on to the A395. At the junction with the A39 turn right towards Bude and, at Collamoor Head, turn left on to the B3263. Turn right at Tresparrett Posts and follow the signs of Crackington Haven and the Coombe Barton Inn lies on the coast.

Situated on the north Cornwall coast, the **Coombe Barton Inn** has to have one of the most stunning positions that it is possible to have. With the rising heathland behind of Bodmin Moor, the inn overlooks the soft sands of Crackington Haven, a quiet bay with abundant rock pools that has been used in numerous films and television programmes. The inn was originally built, around 200 years ago, for a slate quarry owner and, whilst the slate was landed in the bay, those living in the house also had a marvellous view. Today, the inn is owned by John and Nicola Cooper who, along with their son Nick and daughter-in-law Pettina, have been running this delightful place since 1978.

There are large picture windows in most of the rooms which bring the glorious colours of the sea, beach and moorland right inside the room and, so as not to over-shadow this effect, the interior is decorated throughout in gentle muted colours. A very popular place, not just for the scenery, the Coombe Barton Inn has a fine reputation not only for its splendid selection of drinks - including several locally brewed real ales - but also for the excellent food available. In comfortable surroundings, diners can enjoy a delicious and varied menu but the house speciality, fish, is certainly a treat not to be missed. A popular place, where booking is essential at weekends, the traditional Sunday carvery draws families on an outing from miles around. Finally, in this glorious setting, visitors to the area can also make use of the inn's superb bed and breakfast accommodation.

Opening Hours: Mon-Fri 11.00-15.00, 18.00-23.00; Sat 12.00- 5.00, 18.00-23.00 (12.00-23.00 in summer); Sun 12.00-15.00, 18.00-22.30 (12.00-22.30 in summer)

Food: Bar meals and snacks, À la carte, Traditional Sunday lunch

Credit Cards: Visa, Access, Delta, Switch, Amex, Diners

Accommodation: 6 double rooms, 3 en suite

Facilities: Car parking, Children welcome

Local Places of Interest/Activities: Crackington Haven, Bodmin Moor 2 miles, Bude 9 miles, Walking, Cycling, Horse riding, Fishing, Sailing, Bird watching

56   The Cornish Arms

Pendoggett,
near Port Isaac,
Cornwall PL30 3HH
Tel: 01208 880263
Fax: 01208 880335

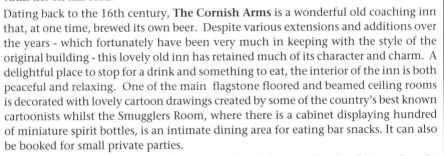

Directions:

From junction 31 on the M5 take the A30 to Launceston. After passing by the town turn right on to the A395 and then left on to the A39. Travel approximately 1 mile along the A39 then turn right on to the B3314. Continue to Pendoggett and The Cornish Arms lies on this road.

Dating back to the 16th century, **The Cornish Arms** is a wonderful old coaching inn that, at one time, brewed its own beer. Despite various extensions and additions over the years - which fortunately have been very much in keeping with the style of the original building - this lovely old inn has retained much of its character and charm. A delightful place to stop for a drink and something to eat, the interior of the inn is both peaceful and relaxing. One of the main flagstone floored and beamed ceiling rooms is decorated with lovely cartoon drawings created by some of the country's best known cartoonists whilst the Smugglers Room, where there is a cabinet displaying hundred of miniature spirit bottles, is an intimate dining area for eating bar snacks. It can also be booked for small private parties.

A free house serving an excellent range of real ales as well as keg bitters, draught lagers, cider and stout, The Cornish Arms has an excellent reputation for the high standard of its cuisine. Served in the cosy and intimate surroundings of the elegant dining room, there is a select and well chosen menu that includes several fish dishes - the house speciality. For less formal dining but with equal quality and imagination, the bar menu is ideal. Here too fish features but there are many other tasty alternative that range from freshly cut sandwiches to the inn's mouthwatering steak and kidney pie. As might be expected, the accommodation here matches the very high standards set by the rest of the hospitality on offer at The Cornish Arms and a stay here is treat to be thoroughly enjoyed.

Opening Hours: Mon-Sat 11.00-23.00; Sun 12.00-22.30

Food: Bar meals and snacks, À la carte

Credit Cards: Visa, Access, Delta, Switch, Amex

Accommodation: 7 double and twin rooms, 6 en suite and 1 with private bathroom, "Coachmans Suite"

Facilities: Beer garden, Car parking, Functions catered for

Local Places of Interest/Activities: Tregeare Rounds 1 mile, Coast 1 mile, Long Cross Victorian Gardens 2 miles, Eden Project 2 miles, Walking, Cycling, Horse riding, Fishing, Sailing, Surfing, Bird watching, Golf

Internet/Website: cornisharms@aol.com

The Cornish Inn 57

The Square, Fore Street,
Gunnislake,
Cornwall PL18 9BW
Tel: 01822 834040 (Bar)
Fax: 01822 834843

Directions:

From junction 31 on the M5 take the A30 to Okehampton, then, approximately 2 miles further on, the A386 to Tavistock. Continue on the A390 towards Liskeard and The Cornish Inn can be found just over the county border.

Found at the heart of this once prosperous though still pleasant old mining town, **The Cornish Inn** is an impressive old black and white building lying on the main road through Gunnislake. Dating back to 1723, when it was built as a mine captain's house, the premises became a pub in 1839 and, finally, The Cornish Inn in the 1950s. Acquired in November 1999 by Maggie Beaton and run by her with the help of son Colin Jeffery and also Ad Chapman, although this is their first venture it is already proving to be a great success. The interior is as charming and full of character as the outside would suggest and, fortunately for today's visitors, many of the inn's original features remain, including the low beamed ceilings and the emphasis on offering visitors superb hospitality.

As well as the excellent range of well kept real ales and local cider served from the bar, The Cornish Inn has a fast growing reputation for the high standard of the delicious meals served here. There is a separate bar and restaurant menu but which ever is chosen customers can rest assured that all the homecooked dishes are prepared from only the best and freshest local ingredients. Add to this the well appointed guest rooms and The Cornish Inn must surely prove to be one of the better inns in the county and also a welcome introduction to Cornish hospitality.

Opening Hours: Mon-Sat 11.00-23.00; Sun 12.00-23.00, supper hours licence.

Food: Bar meals and snacks, À la carte

Credit Cards: Mastercard, Visa, American Express

Accommodation: 11 double rooms, 7 en suite

Facilities: Car parking, Children welcome

Entertainment: Regular live music, Quiz nights, Plasma television with Sky Sports 1,2 & 3

Local Places of Interest/Activities: Morwellham Quay Museum 2 miles, Tavistock 3 miles, Dartmoor National Park 7 miles, Saltash 8 miles, Walking, Cycling, Horse riding, Fishing, Bird watching

Internet/Website:
e-mail:dawcolone@aol.com
website: http://travellerschoice.net

58 The Countryman

Langdon Cross,
North Petherwin,
near Launceston,
Cornwall PL15 8NL
Tel: 01566 785333
Fax: 01566 785333

Directions:

From junction 31 on the M5 take the A30 to Launceston. From the town take the B3254 towards Bude and The Countryman can be found on the roadside approximately 5 miles from Launceston.

A very appealing country inn situated on the main route to Bude, **The Countryman** is a delightful thatched building that is at least 100 years old. A former wheelwright's, this did not become an inn until 1988 and this low, white painted thatched building has made a perfect transition to its new trade. With an interior as charming as the outside would suggest, it would be hard to find a more attractive country inn. Cosy, warm and inviting, both the bar area and the restaurant have low beamed ceilings, comfortable chairs and large fireplaces to add an extra glow in the winter. Meanwhile, during fine weather customers can make good use of the inn's excellent beer garden. Not is this a large, well maintained and pleasant place to sit and enjoy the sun shine but there is also a children's play area and a football pitch for the really energetic.

Very much a family inn, The Countryman is owned and run by Dee and Phil Sargent along with the assistance of their daughters Michelle and Joanne and their son-in-law Steve. Excellent food combined with a fine selection of real ales and locally brewed cider is very much order of the day here. Such is the inn's reputation for the high standard of its cuisine that booking for the restaurant is essential throughout the summer and for their traditional Sunday lunches. Each day the à la carte menu is supplemented by tempting specials and the house speciality - sea food - really is a treat not to be missed. Add to this the equally high quality accommodation and The Countryman is certainly an inn that no discerning visitor should miss.

Opening Hours: Mon-Sat 11.00-23.00; Sun 12.00-22.30

Food: Bar meals and snacks, À la carte, Traditional Sunday lunch

Credit Cards: Visa, Access, Delta, Switch, Amex, Diners

Accommodation: 1 double, 1 family room, 1 twin, 1 single all en suite

Facilities: Beer garden, Car parking, Children's play area

Entertainment: Occasional live music

Local Places of Interest/Activities: Lawrence House 3 miles, Launceston Steam Railway 3 miles, Bodmin Moor 7 miles, Beaches 10 miles, Walking, Golf, Horse riding, Fishing

The Crow's Nest

4 The Terrace,
Port Isaac,
Cornwall PL29 3SG
Tel: 01208 880305

Directions:

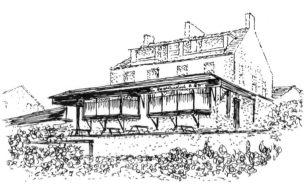

From junction 31 on the M5 take the A30 to Bodmin and then the A389 to Wadebridge. From the town take the B3314 to St Endellion and, about 1 mile further on, turn left on to the B3267. The Crow's Nest is situated on the coast, adjacent to the main car park.

Overlooking Port Isaac Bay, **The Crow's Nest** is very aptly named as it stands on the cliff top and from here there are spectacular views across the bay to Tintagel Head. Originally two private houses that were built in the late 19th century, the premises became first a hotel and then an inn, The Shipwright, in 1985. Today's owners, Mike and Michelle, came here in April 2000 and, having first renamed the inn, they set about a complete refurbishment. The new decor and furnishings in both the bar and restaurant and in the guest rooms, is stylish and very much in keeping with the high standard of hospitality that Mike and Michelle offer their customers.

The large picture windows of the bar and restaurant not only give the interior a light and airy feel but allow visitors to enjoy the views when the weather is not pleasant enough to sit on the front terrace. As well as the excellent range of real ales, stouts, lagers and ciders available from the bar, The Crow's Nest prides itself on the superb menu of homecooked food that is served throughout the day and into the evening. Michelle is the chef and, as well as the quality bar snacks and light meal menu during the day, she prepares a mouthwatering range of dishes for the evening. Freshly cooked to order and with an emphasis on quality, it is not surprising that it is necessary to book a table in advance so as not to be disappointed. A popular inn that offers the very best in hospitality as well as its glorious setting, The Crow's Nest is well worth a visit.

Opening Hours: Mon-Sat 11.00-23.00; Sun 12.00-22.30

Food: Bar snacks and home-cooked meals

Credit Cards: None

Accommodation: 2 double rooms and 2 twin rooms all en suite, Self catering flat for 2001

Facilities: Terrace garden

Entertainment: Occasional live music

Local Places of Interest/Activities: Coast, Long Cross Victorian Gardens 1 mile, Tregeare Rounds 3 miles, Camel Trail 6 miles, Tintagel 8 miles, Walking, Fishing, Sailing, Bird watching

60 The Darlington Inn

Market Place,
Camelford,
Cornwall PL32 9PG
Tel: 01840 213314

Directions:

From junction 31 on the M5 take the A30 to Launceston. Continue for 3 miles and then turn right on to the A395. At the junction with the A39 turn left towards Wadebridge, After approximately 3 miles The Darlington Inn lies in the centre of Camelford.

Found in the heart of this ancient village, **The Darlington Inn** has a history that matches Camelford for its depth and richness. Dating back to the 13th century, the inn became an important posting house and inn in the 16th century as the not only did stage coach travellers rest here in front of roaring fires but so did the King's messengers. This inn, first called The Darlington Arms in the early 18th century when ownership passed to the Earl of Darlington, has also played a part in the political process in the village and, as well as being a place for parties on each side to meet, drink and feast, it is still from the inn's balcony that the election results are announced. Still dispensing excellent hospitality to locals and visitors alike, The Darlington Inn is now in the very capable and experienced hands of landlords Mike and Pauline Meredith.

A truly old building that has as much character and charm as its history would suggest, a visit here is an excellent introduction to the very best Cornish hospitality. The selection of real ales served from the bar always includes at least one local brew although there are also seasonal brews which also feature alongside the draught lagers and ciders. Food too is a key element here and, as well as locally caught fish, the meat comes from a local butcher and as much produce as possible is sourced locally for these interesting homecooked dishes. Add to this the superb accommodation which includes Pauline's hearty traditional English breakfast and The Darlington Inn is an ideal place from which to explore North Cornwall.

Opening Hours: Mon-Sat 11.00-15.00, 18.00-23.00; Sun 12.00-22.30

Food: Bar meals, Cream teas in summer

Credit Cards: Visa, Access, Delta, Switch, Amex, Diners

Accommodation: 3 doubles all en suite

Facilities: Car parking

Entertainment: Regular live music

Local Places of Interest/Activities: Bodmin Moor 3 miles, Beaches 4 miles, Tintagel Head 5 miles, Tregeare Rounds 5 miles, Walking, Cycling, Horse riding, Fishing, Sailing, Bird watching

The Earl of Chatham | **61**

Grenville Road,
Lostwithiel,
Cornwall PL22 0BN
Tel: 01208 872269

Directions:
From junction 31 on the M5 take the A30 towards Bodmin. From the town take the B3268 to Lostwithiel and The Earl of Chatham can be found by following the brown signs.

Dating back to the 17th century, **The Earl of Chatham** is an attractive and quaint old inn that lies down a quiet street in the heart of this old stannery town. Named after William Pitt the Younger, who was also the Earl of Chatham, this delightful and traditional Cornish inn has a great deal of charm that goes hand in hand with excellent hospitality. Landlords, Robert and Dorothy Saunders, have been here since October 1999 and, with the help of resident manager, Tony Poole, they have created the perfect village inn where locals come to meet, enjoy a drink and catch up on the recent news whilst visitors are greeted warmly.

Well known for the fine selection of real ales, most of which are from local breweries, as well as the usual draught lagers, ciders and spirits, The Earl of Chatham also has a fine reputation for the high standard of its cuisine. Served at both lunchtime and in the evening the interesting menu incorporates dishes from England and the Mediterranean with a particular emphasis on Portugal. Finally, the accommodation here is not only comfortable and of the same high quality as the rest of the inn but guests are greeted each morning with a gargantuan homecooked breakfast. Visitors to the town might also be interested to learn that Robert and Dorothy have two other businesses in Lostwithiel. Lawrence House Stores, housed in the former home of Captain Lawrence who served under Captain Bly, is a specialist grocery store offering, in particular, health, organic and Cornish produce. Meanwhile, Langmaids, which lies opposite Lawrence House, is a green grocery and fish mongers that stocks only the freshest local produce.

Opening Hours: Mon-Sat 11.00-23.00; Sun 12.00-22.30; Food 12.00-14.00, 18.00-21.00

Food: Bar meals and snacks, À la carte, Themed evenings

Credit Cards: Visa, Access, Delta, Switch, Amex, Diners

Accommodation: 4 double,1 single room

Facilities: Beer garden, Car parking, Children and dogs welcome

Entertainment: Live music every Saturday evening

Local Places of Interest/Activities: Rostormel Castle 1 mile, Lanhydrock 2 miles, Beach 4 miles, Bodmin 5 miles, Walking, Horse riding, Fishing, Sailing

62 The Halfway House Inn

Twowatersfoot,
near Liskeard,
Cornwall PL14 6HR
Tel: 01208 821242
Fax: 01208 821242

Directions:

From junction 31 on the M5 take the A38 to Liskeard and continue from approximately 7 miles. The Halfway House Inn lies on this road, midway between Liskeard and Bodmin.

Found in the quiet hamlet of Twowatersfoot, which takes its name from the meeting of two rivers, the Fowey and the Neot, **The Halfway House Inn** is literally that as it lies midway between Liskeard and Bodmin. A former coaching house that was built in the 1850s, this inn lies in an outstanding location, on the edge of Bodmin Moor, and is also has, to the rear and side, its own splendid riverside gardens. Although the building was gutted by fire in May 1999, owner Steven Couzens has completely refurbished the inn with no expense spared and the result is a charming and elegant establishment with a traditional and relaxed atmosphere.

Well known for serving excellent real ales and a fine choice of wine, what makes The Halfway House Inn so popular is the marvellous menus served here. Steven is an experienced chef, like his father, and so diners can be assured that they are in very good hands here. There are several menus which themselves are supplemented by a mouthwatering list of daily specials so that the choice here is wide and varied and sure to please everyone. The emphasis is on presenting dishes that use the top quality fresh local produce and fish, naturally, features heavily amongst the tempting dishes. Vegetarians too are very well catered for and, with one smoking and one non smoking restaurant, there is plenty of space for all to dine in comfort. A well known and highly regarded inn locally, it is essential to book a table at the weekends.

Opening Hours: Mon-Sat 11.00-15.00, 18.00-23.00; Sun 12.00-15.00, 19.00-22.30

Food: Bar meals and snacks, À la carte, Vegetarian

Credit Cards: Visa, Access, Delta, Switch, Amex, Diners

Facilities: Beer garden, Car parking, Children welcome, Functions catered for

Local Places of Interest/Activities: Bodmin Moor, Dobwalls Family Adventure Park 2 miles, King Doniert's Stone 4 miles, Coast 9 miles, Walking, Cycling, Horse riding, Fishing, Bird watching

The Harbour Moon | 63

Quay Road,
West Looe,
Cornwall PL13 2BU
Tel: 01503 262873
Fax: 01503 262655

Directions:

From junction 31 on the M5 take the A38 through Saltash and continue to Trerulefoot. Turn left on to the A387 to West Looe. The Harbour Moon can be found on the quayside.

A delightful inn that overlooks West Looe's harbour, **The Harbour Moon** is an attractive place which, during the summer, is bedecked with a mass of hanging baskets and window boxes. Used as a billet for American soldiers stationed nearby during World War II, the older part of the inn and its more recent extension, with massive picture windows, provides much more comfort that the GIs would have received. The bar, in the extension, has a mass of old artefacts and memorabilia hanging from the walls and ceiling. Here customers can expect, and receive, an excellent pint of real ale and there is also a good selection of draught lagers and ciders from which to choose.

Owners, Nigel and Ali have been here since 1989 and, whilst establishing the inn as a well known place for a drink and a tasty selection of bar meals and snacks, have opened a Bistro in the original building with its olde world charm and character. In the relaxed surroundings here diners can enjoy a delicious and tempting menu of dishes that marry together the superb fresh produce of Cornwall with the style and flair of modern cuisine. Naturally fish and seafood feature heavily and the freshness is assured as it all comes from the fishermen working out of West Looe. Add to this the homely and comfortable accommodation here and visitors will find that The Harbour Moon has everything for a stay in this delightful part of Cornwall.

Opening Hours: Mon-Sat 11.00-23.00; Sun 12.00-22.30

Food: Bar meals and snacks, À la carte

Credit Cards: Visa, Access, Delta, Switch, Amex, Diners

Accommodation: 1 double room, 1 twin room and 1 family room

Facilities: Car parking, Children welcome

Entertainment: Regular karaoke

Local Places of Interest/Activities: Beaches and coast, Polperro 3 miles, Fowey 8 miles, Dobwalls Family Adventure Park 8 miles, Bodmin Moor 9 miles, Walking, Cycling, Horse riding, Fishing, Sailing, Bird watching

Internet/Website: harbourmoon@aol.com

64 The Jubilee Inn

Jubilee Hill,
Pelynt,
near Looe,
Cornwall PL13 2JZ
Tel: 01503 220312
Fax: 01503 220920

Directions:

From junction 31 on the M5 take the A38 to Plymouth. At Trerule Foot, beyond Saltash, take the A387 to Looe to the junction with the B3359. Turn right to Pelynt and The Jubilee Inn lies in the village.

Once a medieval farmhouse, **The Jubilee Inn**, one of Cornwall's finest free houses and inns, dates from the 16th century and though originally called The Axe it changed its name to The Jubilee in 1887 to commemorate Queen Victorian's 50th wedding anniversary. First impressions are always important and this splendid inn will certainly impress. Painted a delicate shade of pink, the front façade is topped with ornate crowns and, throughout the summer, there are a mass of colourful flower filled hanging baskets, tubs and window boxes to add an extra vibrancy. Today's owners, Gary and Veronica Rickard, though only here since the beginning of 1999, have plenty of experience in running top class establishments and, as Gary's great, great, great, great grandfather's daughter once ran the inn, they have also family connections - if from long ago.

Stepping inside this delightful building is just like stepping back in time. Many of the building's splendid original features remain and are picked out by the recent re-decoration whilst all the rooms are furnished to the very highest standards with furniture and ornaments that sit well in this historic building. As well as the excellent bar, the restaurant here is marvellous and offers a sumptuous menu that reflects the very best in Cornish cuisine. Less formal dining can be taken from the equally superb bar menu and, during the summer, there are barbecues outside in the peaceful surrounds of the inn's charming garden. Naturally, the accommodation here is also second to none.

Opening Hours: Mon-Fri 11.00-15.00, 18.00-23.00; Sat 11.00-23.00; Sun 12.00-22.30

Food: Bar meals and snacks, À la carte, Traditional Sunday lunch, Barbecues

Credit Cards: Visa, Access, Delta, Switch, Amex, Diners

Accommodation: 11 en suite doubles

Facilities: Large garden, Car parking, Children welcome

Local Places of Interest/Activities: Polperro 2 miles, Beaches 3 miles, Fowey 5 miles, Bodmin Moor 7 miles, Eden Project 10 miles, Walking, Cycling, Horse riding, Fishing, Golf, Sailing, Swimming.

Internet/Website: rickard@JubileeInnfreeserve.co.uk

The London Inn 65

Kilkhampton,
near Bude,
Cornwall EX23 9QR
Tel: 01288 321665
Fax: 01288 321651

Directions:

From junction 31 on the M5 take the A30 to Okehampton and then follow signs to Holsworthy. Continue towards Bude and, at the Red Post roundabout, turn right on to the B3254. At the junction with the A39 turn right and The London Inn lies on this road.

Dating back to the 17th century, **The London Inn** is an eyecatching, cream and brown painted old coaching inn that does not take its name from the stagecoach route on which it lies but from the fishing vessels that were once so common along the north Cornwall and Devon coasts. As pretty as a picture during the summer when the front of the building is bedecked with colourful hanging baskets, this is indeed an excellent time to come to this inn as, to the rear, there is a large and well maintained beer garden that is secluded from the road. A pleasant and traditional English pub inside, the key feature here is the unusual wooden bar surround that is sure to catch people's attention. If the bar does not the splendid array of drinks served here surely will: there are always at least three real ales on tap, including a local brew, and traditional Somerset draught cider.

However, landlords Angela and John Leigh do not end their hospitality there as The London Inn has a good local reputation for the delicious and varied menus of tasty, homecooked food. Taken in either the bar or the separate dining area, there are sandwiches, salads and other tempting dishes for a light meal or, for those who have worked up an appetite, an à la carte menu that concentrates on presenting traditional English cooking at its best. Both children and vegetarians are also well catered for so the whole family will enjoy eating here. Finally, in the inn's grounds are three self catering cottages that can be booked through South West Holiday Cottages (01752 260711).

Opening Hours: Mon-Fri 12.00-15.00, 18.00-23.00; Sat 11.00-23.00; Sun 12.00-15.00, 19.00-22.30

Food: Bar meals and snacks, À la carte, Traditional Sunday lunch, Children's menu

Credit Cards: Visa, Access, Delta, Switch, Amex, Diners

Accommodation: 3 self catering cottages

Facilities: Beer garden, Car parking, Children welcome

Local Places of Interest/Activities: Upper and Lower Tamar Lakes 2 miles, Beach 4 miles, Bude 5 miles, Walking, Cycling, Horse riding, Fishing, Sailing, Swimming, Bird watching

66 The Maltsters Arms

Chapel Amble,
near Wadebridge,
Cornwall PL27 6EU
Tel: 01208 812473

Directions:

From junction 31 on the M5 take the A30 to Launceston. Continue along this road a further 3 miles then turn right on to the A395. At the junction with the A39 turn left. After approximately 12 miles turn right on to the B3314 and follow the signs to Chapel Amble. The Maltsters Arms lies in the village centre.

The Maltsters Inn is a real picture postcard pub - a delightful whitewashed stone building that is over 300 years old with a splendid thatched canopy over the main front door - which overlooks the village green. However, this has not always been such a pleasant place as, many years ago, it had to close when it became a meeting place for bargees on the River Amble and ladies of dubious reputation! The interior of this ancient inn is also full of charm and character with its beamed ceilings throughout, flagstone floors, inglenook fireplace and exposed stone walls. The various different bar areas and restaurant are decorated differently and whilst one has a nautical theme another has hundreds of key-rings - old and new - hanging from its beams.

A true family inn, not only are children welcomed here but owners Marie and David Gray are helped in the running of this excellent free house by their head chefs daughter Libbe and son-in-law (to be in Oct) Daniel, eldest daughter Ann and son-in-law David who is the bar manager. As well as the superb range of real ales, include special Cornish brews, The Maltsters Inn has an enviable reputation for the high standard of cuisine served here. Booking is essential due to the popularity of the restaurant and, once tried, it is easy to see why. The marvellous à la carte menu is in the modern British style and whilst there is plenty of choice, the daily fish menu is certainly a house speciality that is certainly not worth missing.

Opening Hours: Mon-Sat 12.00-15.00, 18.00-23.00; Sun 12.00-15.00, 18.00-22.30

Food: À la carte

Credit Cards: Visa, Access, Delta, Switch, Amex, Diners

Facilities: Car parking

Local Places of Interest/Activities: Long Cross Victorian Gardens 2 miles, Tregeare Rounds 3 miles, Beach 4 miles, Pencarrow House 4 miles, Walking, Horse riding, Fishing, Bird watching

The Napoleon Inn

67

High Street,
Boscastle,
Cornwall PL35 0BD
Tel: 01840 250204

Directions:

From junction 31 on the M5 take the A30 to Launceston. Continue past the town then take the A395 to Davidstow. Just beyond the village turn right, cross over the A39 and continue to the B3266. Turn right to Boscastle (on the coast midway between Bude and Wadebridge) and The Napoleon Inn lies in the heart of the village.

The Napoleon Inn is an attractive 16th century pub at the top of Boscastle in the old part of this picturesque harbour village which many visitors to the area miss. It is the oldest inn in Boscastle with slate floors, old beams, an exposed clome oven and roaring log fires in the winter.

Real ales are served straight from the barrel - from the local St Austell and Bass breweries - and food is served lunchtime and evenings in the bars and evenings in "Boney's Bistro". The two different menus are on chalkboards and constantly change as the food is all homemade using fresh local produce. A choice of traditional roasts is also on the Sunday menus.

The hosts Mike and Jo Mills, who took over in October 1999, have returned to Boscastle after a 24 year absence. Mike, an ex musician, had a country rock band called "Free Spirit" in the 1970's/80's. He now joins local musicians in the traditional Friday night sessions at the Napoleon, with a variety of instruments including guitars, banjo, fiddle etc. - many people join in singing. With good food and drink and a warm welcome step back in time to 1549.

Opening Hours: Mon-Sat 11.00-14.30, 18.00-23.00; Sun 12.00-15.00, 18.00-23.00

Food: Bar meals, Evening Bistro

Credit Cards: Visa, Access, Delta, Switch, Maestro

Facilities: Garden, Sun Terrace, Car parking

Entertainment: Live music every Friday, Traditional pub games including Skittles & Toad-in-the-Hole, Wednesday quiz nights

Local Places of Interest/Activities: Tintagel 3 miles, Bodmin Moor 8 miles, Coast and coastal walks, Horse riding, Bird watching, Historical area

68   The Old Inn

Churchtown,
St Breward,
Bodmin Moor,
Cornwall PL30 4PP
Tel: 01208 850711
Fax: 01208 851671

Directions:

From junction 31 on the M5 take the A30 towards Bodmin. After passing Launceston, continue for a further 16 miles and, just after Temple, turn right and follow the signs to St Breward. The Old Inn lies on the far side of the village.

This village not only boasts, at 700 feet, Cornwall's highest church, but also its highest inn - **The Old Inn**. Dating back to the 11th century, when it was originally built to house those working on the village church, next door, this splendid and ancient building became an inn in the 1500s. A place of atmosphere and character, the inn has, over the years, been the haunt of smugglers who moved their contraband by night over the lonely and treacherous moorland. This ancient land is still a wilderness today and it is also the home of numerous prehistoric temples, holy wells, stone circles and the legendary Beast of Bodmin.

Surrounded by exposed stone walls, with low beamed ceilings above, and warmed by roaring log fires, customers can enjoy a splendid choice of real ales as well as all the usual drinks from the inn's bar. Owners, Darren Wills and Simon Hetherington, who came here in Spring 1999, have also gained an enviable reputation for the cuisine served here along with their bar. Darren, a local man, is chef of the team and it is his flair and imagination that has created the marvellous and extensive menu. The fish served here comes from Port Isaac and the meat is also local so everything is as fresh as possible and, with the addition of at least 15 daily specials, there is also plenty of choice to suit every palate. The bar menu too is equally impressive and it is not surprising that it is necessary to book a table in the beautiful, cottage style restaurant to avoid disappointment.

Opening Hours: Mon-Thu 11.00-15.00, 18.00-23.00; Fri-Sat 11.00-23.00; Sun 12.00-22.30

Food: Bar meals and snacks, À la carte

Credit Cards: Visa, Access, Delta, Switch, Amex, Diners

Facilities: Beer garden, Car parking

Entertainment: Occasional live music and discos

Local Places of Interest/Activities: Pencarrow House 5 miles, Bodmin 7 miles, Tintagel 7 miles, Coast 8 miles, Walking, Cycling, Horse riding, Fishing, Bird watching

Internet/Website: dwtheoldinn@aol.com

The Smugglers Inn **69**

The Square,
Cawsand,
near Torpoint,
Cornwall PL10 1PF
Tel: 01752 822309

Directions:

From Plymouth take the ferry to Torpoint and then the A374 to Antony. From the village take the B3247 towards Millbrook then follow the signs for Cawsand and The Smugglers Inn lies in the heart of the village.

Dominating the village square, **The Smugglers Inn** is an imposing cream coloured building that dates from around 1650 and was certainly the haunt of smugglers who gave the inn its name. A traditional, comfortable and homely inn, licensee Penny Farley, with the aid of her pleasant staff, has created a warm and friendly pub that welcomes not only regulars but visitors to this delightful part of Cornwall. Penny trained as a nurse before entering the licensing trade and her warm personality, along with experience gained in Buckinghamshire, is very much part of the appeal of this inviting inn.

As well as stocking all the usual drinks behind the bar, there is also a good selection of real ales and guest beers served here. Meanwhile, those looking for good, honest homecooking need look no further. Served in the separate restaurant area, the menu is a simple list of dishes that use fresh, locally produced ingredients. The seafood, a speciality here, is all locally caught and the homemade soups are a particular treat. This is excellent English cuisine at its best and Penny also sells free range eggs from a local farm. Very much a village pub, The Smugglers Inn is a charming place in which to spend some time relaxing and enjoying the generous hospitality in this quiet and unspoilt fishing village.

Opening Hours: Winter: Mon, Wed-Fri 12.00-15.30, 19.00-23.00; Tue, Sat-Sun 12.00-23.00; Summer Mon-Sun 12.00-23.00

Food: Bar meals and snacks, Children's menu

Credit Cards: Visa, Access, Switch

Facilities: Car parking nearby, Sells free range eggs

Entertainment: Occasional live music, Traditional pub games, Pool

Local Places of Interest/Activities: Mount Edgcumbe 2 miles, Antony House 5 miles, Plymouth 6 miles, On the coast, Walking, Sailing

Internet/Website:
www.cornwallbusiness.net/smugglers

70

The Snooty Fox

Morval,
near Looe,
Cornwall PL13 1PR
Tel: 01503 240233

Directions:

From junction 31 on the M5 take the A38 through Saltash and continue to Trerule Foot. Turn left on to the A387 towards East Looe. The Snooty Fox lies on this road, 3 miles from East Looe.

Separate from the main road by its large and well established garden, **The Snooty Fox** is an excellent country inn and hotel that was originally a farmhouse. With glorious views in all directions over the rolling countryside of south Cornwall, this well known local inn is an ideal place from which to enjoy both good hospitality and the surrounding country. All the rooms here, the restaurant, bar and guest rooms, have large windows that not only give the interior a light and spacious feel but also provide wonderful backdrops to the rooms. Carefully and stylishly furnished and decorate, owners Steve and June Wright have created a perfect inn for both locals and visitors alike.

Well known for stocking a superb range of real ales, including the locally brewed Doom bar, the selection of draught lagers, ciders and wines here is extensive. The restaurant too is a popular place - booking is essential for the popular Sunday lunch carvery - and the reputation that Steve and June have gained for the high standard of cuisine is enviable. Whether it is the à la carte menu in the restaurant or the less formal bar menu, there is plenty of choice and certainly something to excite even the most jaded palate. Children are also welcomed here and, along with the outstanding accommodation, The Snooty Fox is an ideal place for a family break.

Opening Hours: Mon-Sat 11.00-23.00; Sun 12.00-22.30; Closed Sun February and March

Food: Bar meals and snacks, À la carte

Credit Cards: Visa, Access, Delta, Switch, Amex, Diners

Accommodation: 6 double rooms, 1 family room, 1 single room, 7 en suite

Facilities: Large garden, Car parking, Children welcome, Functions catered for

Local Places of Interest/Activities: Looe 3 miles, Beaches and coast 3 miles, Polperro 6 miles, Liskeard 6 miles, Bodmin Moor 7 miles, Walking, Cycling, Horse riding, Fishing, Sailing, Bird watching

The Tree Inn

71

Fore Street,
Stratton,
Cornwall EX23 9DA
Tel: 01288 352038

Directions:

From junction 31 on the M5 take the A30 to Okehampton and then the A386, A3079 and A3072 to Holsworthy. Continue on the A3072 towards Bude and The Tree Inn lies just before the junction with the A39.

A splendid old building dating back to the 13th century, **The Tree Inn**, with its delightful courtyard garden, is not only a very hospitable place but also one with a history attached. The headquarters of Sir Beville Grenville, the Royalist captain who led his troops to victory at nearby Stamford Hill in May 1643, the inn was also the birthplace of Antony Payne. Born in 1610, Payne, at over 7 feet tall and weighing 38 stones, was the last of the Cornish giants. A servant of the Grenvilles, after Charles II had been restored to the throne, Payne became Yeoman of his Guard but the Cornishman returned to Stratton on his retirement and died here in 1691. The interior of this lovely inn matches the interesting history attached to it and the bar and restaurant, which are situated on either side of the courtyard, are both full of character with the original old beams that were taken from shipwrecks and massive, thick walls.

Owners Lynn Watkins and Michael Coogan have been here since November 1998 and it is their flair and style that have gone into creating this marvellous and elegant inn. As well as serving an excellent range of real ales, there is a good selection of draught lagers, ciders and stouts to refresh visitors. Food is served in the bar, or for more formal dining, in the restaurant but, whichever is chosen, the varied menus are sure to both tempt and excite. As children are made equally welcome here and the inn offers first class accommodation, The Tree Inn is a superb place for a family holiday or a relaxing break.

Opening Hours: Mon-Sat 11.00-23.00; Sun 12.00-22.30

Food: Bar meals and snacks, À la carte, Traditional Sunday lunch

Credit Cards: Visa, Access, Delta, Switch, Amex, Diners

Accommodation: 5 double rooms, 1 en suite

Facilities: Courtyard garden, Car parking

Entertainment: Regular live folk music

Local Places of Interest/Activities: Stamford Hill 1 mile, Bude 2 miles, Beach 3 miles, Dartmoor National Park 22 miles, Walking, Cycling, Horse riding, Fishing, Sailing, Swimming, Bird watching

Internet/Website: www.thetreeinn.co.uk

This page is left intentionally blank

3 North Devon

PLACES OF INTEREST:

Arlington   75
Barnstaple   76
Belstone   77
Bideford   77
Braunton   78
Clovelly   78
Great Torrington   78
Hartland   79
Ilfracombe   79

Lynmouth   79
Muddiford   80
North Tawton   80
Okehampton   80
Stoke   81
Westward Ho!   81
Woolacombe   81

PUBS AND INNS:

The Black Venus Inn, Challacombe   83

The Coach and Horses, Horns Cross   84

Ebrington Arms, Knowle   85

Foxhunters Inn, West Down   86

The Golden Inn, Highampton   87

The Half Moon Inn, Sheepwash   88

The Hunters' Inn, Heddons Valley   89

The Molesworth Arms, Pyworthy   90

The Old Union Inn, Stibbs Cross   91

Royal Oak Country Inn, Dolton   92

The Stag Hunters Hotel, Brendon   93

The Thatched Inn, Abbotsham   94

The Windsor Arms, Bradiford   95

The Wrey Arms, Sticklepath   96

The Hidden Inns of the West Country

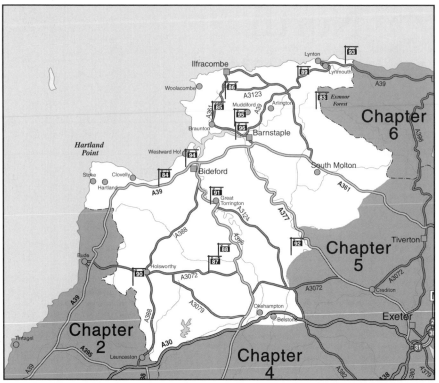

© MAPS IN MINUTES ™ (1998)

83	The Black Venus Inn, Challacombe	90	The Molesworth Arms, Pyworth
84	The Coach and Horses, Horns Cross	91	The Old Union Inn, Stibbs Cross
85	Ebrington Arms, Knowle	92	Royal Oak Country Inn, Dolton
86	Foxhunters Inn, West Down	93	The Stag Hunters Hotel, Brendon
87	The Golden Inn, Highampton	94	The Thatched Inn, Abbotsham
88	The Half Moon Inn, Sheepwash	95	The Windsor Arms, Bradiford
89	The Hunters' Inn, Heddons Valley	96	The Wrey Arms, Sticklepath

Please note all cross references refer to page numbers

NORTH DEVON

To the north and west, the puckered green hills of North Devon roll away to the coast; to the south lie the wildest stretches of Dartmoor with the great peaks of High Willhays and Yes Tor rising to more than 2,000 feet. At this height they are, officially, mountains, but quite puny compared with their original altitude: geologists believe that at one time the surface of Dartmoor stood at 15,000 feet above sea level. Countless centuries of erosion have reduced it to a plateau of whale-backed granite ridges with an average height of around 1,200 feet.

Dartmoor's most characteristic topographical features are its tors, great chunks of fragmented granite which have stood up to 60 million years of ice, rain and wind better than the less-resistant rock which once surrounded them. There are some 200 of these distinctive outcrops on the moor. After so many millions of years of erosion, the moor has become strewn with fragments of surface granite, or moorstone. It was because of this ready-to-use stone that Dartmoor became one of the most populous areas of early Britain, its inhabitants using the easily quarried granite to create their stone rows, circles, and burial chambers. Stone was also used to build their distinctive hut-circles of which there are more than 1,500 scattered across the moor.

In the whole of England there are only three areas which the Council for the Protection of Rural England has officially designated as "tranquil", and one of them is North Devon. This is the heartland of Lorna Doone Country and the homeland of Tarka the Otter, who has given his name to a 180-mile trail of footpath, cycle-way and rail link that winds its way around this wonderfully unspoilt region. The captivating scenery, the picturesque villages and the relaxed lifestyle help to explain why so many visitors fall under its spell.

The North Devon Coast is glorious stretch of coastline that runs from the Somerset border to Barnstaple, offering some of the grandest coastal scenery in the country, and a beach, Woolacombe, which has been named as one of the Top Ten Beaches in the world. This 3 mile expanse of golden sands has also gained both the Blue Flag accolade for safety and cleanliness, and a Premier Resort Award for the quality of its amenities.

The two major settlements in this area are Ilfracombe and Braunton. Most of the other settlements are villages or hamlets linked by a network of country lanes meandering around rolling hills.

PLACES OF INTEREST

ARLINGTON

Arlington Court (National Trust) was home to the Chichester family from 1534 until the last owner, Rosalie Chichester, died childless in 1949. (Sir Francis Chichester, famous as an aviation pioneer and as the first solo round-the-world sailor, was born 2 miles away at Shirwell.) The present house was built in 1822 to an unambitious design by the Barnstaple architect Thomas Lee, and extended some 40 years later by Sir Bruce Chichester, who also added the handsome stable block. When he died in 1881, he left the house and its 2,775 acre park to his daughter Rosalie, along with a staggering mountain of debts. Only 15 years old when she inherited the estate, Rosalie managed to keep it intact and stayed on at Arlington Court until her death at the age of 83.

76

The interior is something of a museum to Rosalie's various interests, with displays of her collections of porcelain, pewter, shells, snuff boxes, and more than a hundred model ships, some made by French soldiers captured during the Napoleonic wars. Intriguingly, Rosalie never saw the most valuable work of art amongst her possessions: after her death, a watercolour by William Blake was discovered on top of a wardrobe where it had lain forgotten for over 100 years. It is now on display in the white drawing room.

Rosalie Chichester also turned the grounds of Arlington Court into something of a nature reserve. An 8 mile long perimeter fence was erected to protect the native wildfowl and heron populations, and the Shetland ponies and Jacob sheep grazing the fields are descendants of those introduced by Rosalie. The stable block now houses a unique collection of horse-drawn carriages, with rides available at most times.

BARNSTAPLE

Barnstaple takes its floral decorations very seriously. The town began its association with the Britain in Bloom movement in 1991 and just five years later crowned its efforts by winning the Gold award for the "Prettiest Floral Town in Europe" in the Entente Florale Competition. Wherever you turn there are magnificent displays - a haycart full of flowers outside the police station and civic centre, a giant postage stamp outside the Post Office, or a stunning model of a train at the entrance to the railway station.

Barnstaple

The town enjoys a superb location at the head of the Taw estuary, at the furthest point downstream where it was possible to ford the river. The first bridge across the Taw was built in the late 1200s, but the present impressive structure, 700 feet long with 16 arches, dates from about 1450 although it has been altered and widened many times.

Barnstaple is the administrative and commercial capital of the region, a pre-eminence it already enjoyed when the Domesday Book recorded it as one of only four boroughs in the county, with its own Mint and regular market. There are still produce markets on Tuesdays and Fridays, but the **Pannier Market** is open every weekday. This huge glass-roofed building covering some 45,000 square feet was built in 1855 and resembles nothing more than a major railway station. Each day of the week has a different emphasis: crafts on Monday and Thursday, for example, antiques on Wednesday. The Market takes it name from the pannier baskets in which country people would carry their produce to the town. Just across from the Pannier Market is Butchers Row, a quaint line of booth-like Victorian shops built mostly of wood and with a brightly painted wooden canopy. Back in 1855, they were occupied exclusively by butchers, but now you'll find a variety of goods on sale, seaweed amongst them. Each week in season 300 pounds of it are sold, most of which apparently ends up as a breakfast dish, served with bacon and an egg on top.

In the High Street stands the rather austere **Guildhall**, built in the Grecian style in 1826 and housing some interesting civic memorabilia: portraits, regalia and silverware. The **Church of St Peter and St Paul** dates back to the early 1300s but, after having its spire twisted by a lightning strike in 1810, it suffered even more badly under the heavy hand of the Victorian restorer, Sir Gilbert Scott. Much more appealing are the charming 17th century **Horwood's Almshouses** nearby, and the 15th century **St Anne's Chapel**, which served for many years as the town's grammar school. It is now a museum with a schoolroom re-created as it might have been in the late 17th century when John Gay, author of *The Beggar's Opera*, was numbered amongst its pupils.

Another interesting museum has the unusual distinction of being housed in a former signal box. The **Lynton and Barnstaple Railway Museum** records the history of the narrow-guage railway that ran between Barnstaple to Lynton from 1898 to 1935.

One of Barnstaple's most enduring industries has been pottery, made here continuously since the 13th century. In Litchdon Street, the **Royal Barum Pottery** welcomes visitors to its workshop, museum and well-stocked shop.

Walkers along the **Tarka Trail** will know Barnstaple well as the crossover point in this figure-of-eight long-distance footpath. Inspired by Henry Williamson's celebrated story of Tarka the Otter, the 180-mile trail wanders through a delightful variety of Devon scenery - tranquil countryside, wooded river valleys, rugged moorland, and a stretch of the North Devon coast, with part of the route taking in the "Tarka Line" railway in order to get the best views of the locations described in the novel. A guide book is available covering the whole trail; and there are pamphlets detailing individual sections.

BELSTONE

Surrounded by the magnificent scenery of the Dartmoor National Park, Belstone is a picturesque village with a triangular village green (complete with stocks), a church dating back to the 13th century, and a splendid pub, The Tors. A path from Belstone village leads up to the ancient standing stone circle known as the **Nine Stones**, although there are actually well over a dozen of them. Local folklore claims that these

Belstone Stocks

stones under Belstone Tor were formed when a group of maidens was discovered dancing on the Sabbath and turned to stone. The problem with this story is that the stone circle was in place long before the arrival of Christianity. It is also claimed that the mysterious stones change position when the clock strikes noon. What is certain is that the view across mid-Devon from this site is quite breathtaking.

BIDEFORD

77

Named the "Little White Town" by Charles Kingsley, this attractive town set beside the River Torridge was once the third busiest port in Britain. The first bridge across the shallow neck of the Torridge estuary was built around 1300 to link Bideford with its aptly-named satellite village, East-the-Water. That bridge must have been very impressive for its time. It was 670 feet long and built of massive oak lintels of varying length which created a series of irregular arches between 12 and 25 feet apart. These erratic dimensions were preserved when the bridge was rebuilt in stone around 1460 (the old bridge was used as scaffolding), and despite widening during the 1920s they persist to this day. Unusually, **Bideford Bridge** is managed by an ancient corporation of trustees, known as *feoffees*, whose income, derived from property in the town, not only pays for the upkeep of the bridge but also supports local charities and good causes. A new high-level bridge a mile or so downstream, opened in 1987, has relieved some of the traffic congestion and also provides panoramic views of the town and the Torridge estuary.

Bideford received its Market Charter from Henry III in 1272 (on May 25th to be precise), and markets still take place every Tuesday and Saturday. Since 1883 they have been held in the splendid Pannier Market building, reckoned to be one of the best surviving examples of a

Lundy Island Lighthouse

78

Victorian covered market.

One excursion from Bideford that should not be missed is the day trip to **Lundy Island** on the supply boat, the *MS Oldenburg*. Lundy is a huge lump of granite rock, 3 miles long and half a mile wide, with sheer cliffs rising 500 feet above the shore. Its name derives from the Norse *lunde ey*, meaning "puffin island", and these attractive birds with their multi-coloured beaks are still in residence, along with many other species. More than 400 different birds have been spotted on Lundy, and you might also spot one of the indigenous black rats for whom the island is their last refuge. The island has a ruined castle, a church, a pub, a shop selling souvenirs and the famous stamps. There's even a hotel, but if you hope to stay overnight you must book well ahead.

BRAUNTON

Braunton claims the rather odd distinction of being the largest village in Devon. It's a sizeable community, spreading along both sides of the River Caen, with some handsome Georgian houses and a substantial church reflecting Braunton's relative importance in medieval times. The church is dedicated to St Brannoc, a Celtic saint who arrived here from Wales in the 6th century. It's said that his bones lie beneath the altar of the present 13th century church, a story which may well be true since the building stands on the site of Saxon predecessor.

There's fascinating evidence of Saxon occupation of this area in **Braunton Great Field**, just to the southwest of the village. This is one of very few remaining examples of the Saxon open-field strip system still being farmed in Britain. Around 350 acres in total, the field was originally divided into around 700 half-acre strips, a furlong (220 yards) long, and 11 yards wide. Each strip was separated by an unploughed "landshare" about 1 foot wide. Throughout the centuries many of the strips have changed hands and been combined, so that now only about 200 remain. A medieval wall divides the southern edge of the Great Field from the now reclaimed Braunton Marsh, formerly an area of common grazing land. To the west, both the field and the marsh are bounded by a wide expanse of high sand dunes known as **Braunton Burrows**, the southern part of which is a designated nature reserve noted for its migrant birds, rare flowers and insects. Beyond the dunes lie the 3 mile long **Saunton Sands**, one of the most impressive sandy beaches in the West Country.

CLOVELLY

Even people who've never been to Devon have probably heard of this unbelievably quaint and picturesque village that tumbles down a steep hillside in terraced levels. Almost every flower-strewn cottage is worthy of its own picture postcard and from the sheltered little harbour there is an enchanting view of this unique place. The only access to the beach is on foot or by donkey, although there is a Land Rover service from the Red Lion Hotel for those who can't face the climb back up the hill. The only other forms of transport are the sledges which are used to deliver weekly supplies. During the summer months, there are regular boat trips around the bay, and the *Jessica Hettie* travels daily to Lundy Island with timings that allow passengers to spend some six hours there, watching the seals and abundant wildlife. The **Clovelly Pottery**, opened in 1992, displays an extensive range of items made by Cornish and Devon potters. In the nearby workshop, for a small fee, visitors can try their hand at throwing a pot.

GREAT TORRINGTON

Castle Hill commands grand views along the valley of the River Torridge. (There's no view of the castle: that was demolished as long ago as 1228. Its site is now a bowling green.) On the opposite bank of the river is the hamlet of Taddiport where the tiny 14th century church by the bridge was originally the chapel of a leper hospital: its inmates were not permitted to cross over into Torrington itself.

Torrington's May Fair is still an important event in the local calendar, and has been since 1554. On the first Thursday in May, a Queen is crowned, there is maypole dancing in the High Street, and a banner proclaims the greeting "Us be plazed to zee 'ee."

The town can also boast one of the West Country's leading tourist attractions, **Dartington Crystal**, where visitors can see skilled craftsmen blowing and shaping the crystal, follow the history of glass-making from the Egyptians to the present day, watch a video presentation, and browse amongst some 10,000 square feet of displays. The enterprise was set up in the 1960s by the Dartington Hall Trust to provide employment in an area of rural depopulation: today, the beautifully designed handmade crystal is exported to more than 50 countries around the world.

HARTLAND

Anyone interested in attractive stoneware will want to visit the **Hartland Pottery** in North Street. Here visitors can watch the various processes of making oven to tableware. Functional oil lamps are a popular item, as are the Chunglazed pieces, a particularly lovely deep blue colour that originated during the Sung Dynasty, 960-1279 AD.

From the village, follow the signs to **Hartland Abbey**. Founded in 1157, the Abbey was closed down in 1539 by Henry VIII, who gave the building and its wide estates to William Abbott, Sergeant of the Royal wine cellars. His descendants still live here. The house was partly rebuilt in the mid-18th century in the style known as Strawberry Hill Gothic, and in the

Hartland Abbey

1850s the architect George Gilbert Scott added a front hall and entrance. The Abbey's owner, Sir George Stucley, had recently visited the Alhambra Palace in Spain which he much admired. He asked Scott to design something in that style and the result is the elegant Alhambra Corridor with a blue vaulted ceiling with white stencilled patterns. The Abbey has a choice collection of pictures, porcelain and furniture acquired over many generations and, in the former Servants' Hall, a unique exhibition of documents dating from 1160. There's also a fascinating Victorian and Edwardian photographic exhibition which includes many early photographs.

ILFRACOMBE

With a population of around 11,000, Ilfracombe is the largest seaside resort on the North Devon coast. Up until 1800, however, it was a small fishing and market town relying entirely on the

sea both for its living and as its principal means of communication.

The boundaries of the old town are marked by a sheltered natural harbour to the north, and a part-Norman parish church half-a-mile away to the south. The entrance to the harbour is guarded by **Lantern Hill**, a steepsided conical rock which is crowned by the restored medieval Chapel of St Nicholas. For centuries, this highly-conspicuous former fishermen's chapel doubled as a lighthouse, the light

Ilfracombe Harbour

being placed in a lantern at the west end of the building. Today, Lantern Hill provides a spectacular view of Ilfracombe's old street plan, busy harbour, and craggy coastline.

Like so many west country resorts, Ilfracombe developed in response to the early 19th century craze for sea bathing. The **Tunnel Baths**, with an extravagant Doric facade, were opened in Bath Place in 1836, by which time a number of elegant residential terraces had been built on the hillside to the south of the old town.

For walkers, the coastal path provides some spectacular scenery, whether going west to **Capstone Point**, or east to **Hillsborough Hill**.

LYNMOUTH

For centuries, the people of Lynmouth subsisted on agriculture and fishing, especially herring fishing and curing. By good fortune, just as the herring shoals were moving away to new waters, the North Devon coast benefited from the two new enthusiasms for "Romantic" scenery and sea bathing.

Lynmouth's setting beside its twin rivers is undeniably beautiful, but it has also proved to be tragically vulnerable. On the night of August 16th, 1952, a cloudburst over Exmoor deposited 9 inches of rain onto an already saturated moor. In the darkness, the normally placid

East and West Lyn rivers became raging cataracts and burst their banks. Sweeping tree trunks and boulders along with it, the torrent smashed its way through the village, destroying dozens of houses and leaving 31 people dead. That night had seen many freak storms across southern England, but none had matched the ferocity of the deluge that engulfed this pretty little village. An earlier exceptional storm, in 1899, involved the Lynmouth lifeboat in a tale of epic endurance. A full-rigged ship, the *Forest Hall*, was in difficulties off Porlock, but the storm was so violent it was impossible to launch the lifeboat at Lynmouth. Instead, the crewmen dragged their 3½ ton boat, the *Louisa*, the 13 miles across the moor. Along the way they had to negotiate Countisbury Hill, with a gradient of 1,000 feet over 2 miles, before dropping down to Porlock Weir where the *Louisa* was successfully launched and every crew member of the stricken ship saved.

Cliff Railway

Lynton is connected to its sister-village Lynmouth by an ingenious **cliff railway** which, when it opened on Easter Monday 1890, was the first of its kind in Britain. A gift from Sir George Newnes, the publisher and newspaper tycoon, the railway is powered by water, or rather by two 700 gallon water tanks, one at each end of the 450 foot track. When the tank at the top is filled, and the one at the bottom emptied, the brakes are released and the two passenger carriages change place.

MUDDIFORD

Less than 2 miles east of Muddiford, **Marwood Hill Gardens** offers visitors some 18 acres of trees and shrubs, many of them rare and unusual. The collection was started more than half a century ago and now includes an enormous number and variety of plants. The three lakes, linked by the largest Bog Garden in the West Country, are busy with ducks and multi-coloured carp. From spring, when camellias and magnolias are in bloom, through to the brilliant hues of Autumn, the gardens provide a continuous spectacle of colour.

NORTH TAWTON

North Tawton was once an important borough governed by a *portreeve*, an official who was elected each year until the end of the 19th century. This scattered rural community prospered in medieval times but the decline of the local textile industry in the late 1700s dealt a blow from which it never really recovered. The little town also suffered badly from the ravages of a fire which destroyed most of the older and more interesting buildings.

However, a few survivors can still be found, most notably **Broad Hall**, dating from the 15th century.

OKEHAMPTON

From Celtic times Okehampton has occupied an important position on the main route to Cornwall. For centuries this strategic location brought considerable prosperity to the town, but with the huge growth in car ownership from the 1970s onwards traffic congestion in its narrow streets became intolerable. Fortunately, the A30 now bypasses the town and it has recovered the character of a quiet, rather old-fashioned town.

Romantically sited atop a wooded hill and dominating the surrounding valley of the River Okement are the remains of **Okehampton Castle** (English Heritage). This is the largest medieval castle in Devon and the ruins are still mightily impressive even though the castle was dismantled on the orders of Henry VIII after its owner, the Earl of Devon, was convicted of treason.

A good place to start a tour of the town is the **Museum of Dartmoor Life**, housed in a former mill with a restored water wheel outside. In the surrounding courtyard, you will also find the Dartmoor National Park Visitor Centre, craft and gift shops, and a tearoom. Amongst the town's interesting buildings are the 15th century **Chapel of Ease** and the **Town Hall**, a striking three-storey building erected in 1685 as a private house and converted to its current use

Museum of Dartmoor Life

in the 1820s. And don't miss the wonderful Victorian arcade within the shopping centre which is reminiscent of London's Burlington Arcade.

STOKE

St Nectan's Church is generally regarded as one of the finest churches in Devon. Its tower soars 128 foot high, and inside there's a Norman font, a fine screen and carved bench-ends. A mile further west is **Hartland Quay**. Exposed to all the wrath of Atlantic storms, it seems an inhospitable place for ships, but it was a busy landing-place from its building in 1566 until the sea finally overwhelmed it in 1893. Several of the old buildings have been converted into a comfortable hotel; another is now a museum recording the many wrecks that have littered this jagged coastline.

About three miles to the north of the Quay, reached by winding country lanes, is **Hartland Point**. On Ptolemy's map of Britain in Roman times, he names it the "Promontory of Hercules", a fitting name for this fearsome stretch of upended rocks rising at right angles to the sea. There are breathtaking sea and coast views and a lighthouse built in 1874.

WESTWARD HO!

Is there any other place in the world that has been named after a novel? Following the huge success in 1855 of Charles Kingsley's tale of Elizabethan derring-do, a company was formed to develop this spectacular site with its rocky cliffs and 2 miles of sandy beach. The early years were troubled. A powerful storm washed away the newly-built pier and most of the houses. When Rudyard Kipling came here in 1874 as a pupil at the United Services College, he described "Twelve bleak houses by the shore".

Today Westward Ho! is a busy holiday resort well worth visiting for its beach and the nearby **Northam Burrows Country Park**, 670 acres of grazed burrows rich in flora, fauna and migratory birds, and offering tremendous views across Bideford Bay.

An unusual event at Westward Ho! is the Pot Walloping Festival, which takes place in late spring. Local people and visitors join together to throw pebbles which have been dislodged by winter storms back onto the famous ridge, after which exercise pots of a different kind also get a walloping.

WOOLACOMBE

The glorious stretch of golden sands at Woolacombe is justifiably regarded as the finest beach in North Devon, and this favoured resort lies between two dramatic headlands, both now protected by the National Trust. The sands and rock pools are a delight for children, and surfers revel in the monster waves rolling in from the Atlantic.

Back in the early 1800s, Woolacombe was little more than a hamlet. With the craze for sea bathing, the two families who owned most of the land here, the Fortescues and the Chichesters, began building villas and hotels in the Regency style and these now give the old part of Woolacombe a very special charm and character.

This page is left intentionally blank

The Black Venus Inn   83

Challacombe,
near Barnstaple,
Devon EX31 4TT
Tel: 01598 763251

Directions:

From junction 27 on the M5 take the A361 towards Barnstaple and then the A399 towards Combe Martin. 9 miles further on, take a right turn on to the B3358. The Black Venus Inn can be found just off this road, to the right, close to the county border with Somerset.

At least 400 years old, the interestingly named **Black Venus Inn** is a splendid old stone built inn that has a wonderful situation in the Exmoor National Park. A picturesque and attractive inn, with japonica growing up its walls, there is a large car park opposite and a well maintained beer garden to the side that is an ideal place to take in this glorious setting as well as sample the fare on offer. Inside, this historic building is full of Devon character and charm: the low ceilings still have the original beams intact, the stone fireplace in the restaurant has a hand carved wooden surround and on the walls are items of bygone agricultural times.

The Black Venus Inn is landlords Jennifer and Adrian Lidbury's first pub and they have taken to its extremely well. Perhaps, Jennifer's background in farming and herbalism or Adrian's previous experience in engineering is a help but it is probably their open and friendly personalities that have made this a popular place with both visitors and locals. Concentrating on local ales and cider, the bar is a cosy place to enjoy a drink, some good conversation and a snack. There is also a comprehensive menu available in the restaurant which is supplemented by a daily changing specials board - the list of homemade dishes is sure to satisfy even the biggest of appetites. Jennifer's butcher and greengrocer guarantee local produce. In the heart of walking and riding countryside, this is a charming inn that makes a super stopping point at either midday or in the evening.

Opening Hours: Mon-Sat 11.00-23.00; Sun 12.00-22.30

Food: Restaurant, bar meals and snacks, morning coffee, afternoon tea, take away.

Credit Cards: Visa, Access, Delta, Switch, Amex

Facilities: Beer garden, Car parking

Entertainment: Pool, Darts

Local Places of Interest/Activities: Exmoor National Park 1 mile, Arlington Court 5 miles, Combe Martin Wildlife and Dinosaur Park 6 miles, Lynton and Lynmouth Cliff Railway 7 miles, Coast 6 miles, Walking, Bird watching, Horse riding

Internet/Website:
e-mail:jlidbury@aol.com
website: Blackvenusexmoor.co.uk

84   The Coach and Horses

Horns Cross,
near Bideford,
Devon EX39 5DH
Tel: 01237 451214

Directions:

From junction 27 on the M5 take the A361 to Barnstaple and then the A39 around Bideford towards Bude. The Coach and Horses can be found on the main road, 5 miles from Bideford.

Originally built in the 1600s as a coaching inn on the busy Bideford to Bude stagecoach route, the aptly named **Coach and Horses** is still offering excellent refreshment and accommodation to weary travellers. A delightful and charming inn, the interior of which still evokes the style of days gone by, it is managed by Di Staddon and Martyn Wonnacott who, though this is their first venture, have really put the Coach and Horses on the map. As well as many of the building's original features still being present, the splendid bar is particularly distinctive as it is made from American Ash and, during the winter, the relaxed ambience of the cosy interior is warmed by an old wood burning stove.

However, wonderful surroundings do little to satisfy customers' thirst and hunger and, again, The Coach and Horses excels. From the magnificent bar there are several superb real ales and bitters from which to choose. The menu here is equally impressive and, wherever possible, the produce used is both local and fresh. As Martyn was previously a farmer, the high quality of the ingredients is assured and, though the menu is simple, the dishes represent the best in English country cooking. Finally, the accommodation here can be found in a separate building to the rear of the main inn and, whilst the comfortable and stylish rooms are on the first floor, the ground floor is taken up with the well fitted out children's play room.

Opening Hours: Mon-Sat 11.00-23.00; Sun 12.00-22.30

Food: Bar meals and snacks

Credit Cards: None

Accommodation: 2 double rooms, 1 twin room, all en suite

Facilities: Children's play room, Car park

Entertainment: Card game Euchre, Darts

Local Places of Interest/Activities: Big Sheep Adventure Park 3 miles, Milky Way Adventure Park 2 miles, Clovelly 4 miles, Westward Ho! 6 miles, Tarka Cycle Path 5 miles, Walking, Cycling, Horse riding, Fishing

Ebrington Arms | 85

Winsham Road,
Knowle,
near Braunton,
Devon EX33 2LW
Tel: 01271 812166

Directions:

From junction 27 on the M5 take the A361 to Barnstaple and continue on this road towards Ilfracombe. The Ebrington Arms can be found by turning right in the village of Knowle, into Winsham Road, 2 miles after passing through Braunton.

Although the **Ebrington Arms** has been tastefully and sympathically extended over the years to increase the available accommodation the original 18th century stone building can still be identified. Inside, there are no such divisions between the old and the less old as this delightful establishment has a true English country inn atmosphere that is timeless. The cosy snug bar is very well frequented by the regular, local clientele whilst there is also a comfortable lounge bar and a separate restaurant. The cellar at the Ebrington Arms is well stocked and, apart from the three real ales on tap and the usual beers and lagers, there is a choice of 15 malt whiskies and an extensive wine list on offer here.

Food too plays an important part in the life of the inn and whilst the bar menu offers a tasty range of superb, homecooked hot and cold dishes, the evening à la carte menu is a magnificent. The house speciality is fish and the mouthwatering fish and seafood dishes are supplemented by an ever changing list of daily specials that are imaginatively prepared by the inn's chef. However, meat eaters and vegetarians are most definitely not forgotten and the same imaginative and flair is put into creating each splendid offering. Becoming increasingly well known for their fabulous menus, Roger and Dena Sells, the landlords, have certainly put their years of experience in the hotel trade to excellent use. A charming place to find that will definitely satisfy the whole family the Ebrington Arms is well worth taking the time to seek out.

Opening Hours: Mon-Sat 12.00-15.00, 18.00-23.00; Sun 12.00-15.00, 19.00-23.00

Food: Bar meals and snacks, À la carte

Credit Cards: Visa, Mastercard, Delta, Switch

Facilities: Children's play area, Car parking, Functions catered for

Entertainment: Traditional pub games, Skittles

Local Places of Interest/Activities: Marwood Hill 3 miles, Braunton Burrows Nature Reserve 4 miles, Ilfracombe 6 miles, Beach 4 miles, Barnstaple 7 miles, Walking, Fishing, Bird watching

86 Foxhunters Inn

West Down, nr Ilfracombe,
Devon EX34 8NU
Tel: 01271 863757
Fax: 01271 879313

Directions:
From junction 27 on the M5 take the A361 to Barnstaple and continue on the road in the direction of Ilfracombe. Just over 3 miles after Braunton the Foxhunters Inn can be found on the main road.

An attractive stone built old coaching inn, the **Foxhunters Inn** dates back over 300 years and, in that time, this delightful country pub has been offering superb hospitality to travellers and local people alike. Full of atmosphere and charm, this lovely old building has roaring log fires in winter, low ceilings with a mass of aged oak beams and gleaming brassware inside, with, for the summer, a well maintained beer terrace which overlooks the rolling north Devon countryside.

Local businessman, Graham Toms and his partner Sue, took over this historic old inn in December 1999 and, whilst they have undertaken an extensive refurbishment programme since then, the character of the Foxhunters Inn has remained. Other improvements and developments are planned that will enhance further the facilities here. As well as concentrating on serving traditional, local real ales from the bar, Graham and Sue have extended the range of meals offered here and now the Foxhunters Inn is a well respected place to eat with an enviable reputation for the high standard of the cuisine. The menu provides a range of superbly cooked dishes whilst on Sunday there is a marvellous carvery that draws people from far and wide. Add to this the comfortable country inn accommodation and the Foxhunters Inn is the perfect place to stay with the family whilst exploring this picturesque area of north Devon.

Opening Hours: Mon-Sun 11.00-24.00

Food: Restaurant, Bar meals, Sunday carvery

Credit Cards: Visa, Access, Delta, Switch, Amex, Diners

Accommodation: 9 double rooms all en suite

Facilities: Beer terrace, Car parking

Entertainment: Occasional live entertainment

Local Places of Interest/Activities: Chambercombe Manor 3 miles, Marwood Hill 4 miles, Barnstaple 8 miles, Brauton Burrows 7 miles, Saunton Sands Beach 6 miles, Walking, Bird watching, Surfing, Sailing, Horse riding

The Golden Inn 87

Highampton,
near Beaworthy,
Devon EX21 5LT
Tel: 01409 231200

Directions:

From Okehampton take the A386 north to Hatherleigh and then the A3072 west. The Golden Inn lies 4 miles down the road.

Dating back to the 16th century, **The Golden Inn** is a charming, long, typical Devonshire cob building that has managed to retain its thatched roof. As can be expected with an inn of this age, The Golden Inn has all the character and atmosphere of days gone by - there are open inglenook fireplaces, adding warmth and cheer on winter's nights, exposed beams and an interesting assortment of memorabilia on the walls. Purchased by Karen and Tony Knight in 1996, this attractive and popular inn is well frequented by local people who enjoy the warm welcome they receive and the relaxed atmosphere of the place.

Both Karen and Tony enjoy going out to inns and pubs - when they have the time - and, therefore, they understand exactly what makes a place popular with both locals and visitors. Customers at The Golden Inn can therefore expect and receive the very best in hospitality. As a freehouse, the bar here serves an excellent range of real ales, which changes from time to time, as well as all the usual beers, lagers and spirits. There is, too, a superb selection of world wide wines that not only adds a finishing touch to a meal here but which can also be drunk by the glass. The menu, a list of traditional pub meals - many with an extra twist - is all prepared by Karen who not only uses the finest and freshest local ingredients but also prides herself on the imaginative presentation. Well known and highly regarded in the area, it is particularly advisable to book a table in the cosy dining room for The Golden Inn's Sunday lunch.

Opening Hours: Mon-Sat 11.30-15.00, 18.30-23.00; Sun 12.00-16.00, 19.00-22.30

Food: Meals available at both lunchtime and evening, Traditional Sunday lunch

Credit Cards: none

Facilities: Large beer garden with glorious views, Large car park

Entertainment: Pool, Darts, Skittles, Quiz nights

Local Places of Interest/Activities: Fishing, Golf, Walking, Dartmoor National Park 11 miles

88 The Half Moon Inn

Sheepwash,
near Hatherleigh
Devon EX21 5NE
Tel: 01409 231376
Fax: 01409 231673

Directions:

From Exeter take the A30 west to Okehampton then the A386 north to Hatherleigh. Turn left onto the A3072 to Highampton then right to Sheepwash and The Half Moon Inn lies 1 mile down the road.

Records show that **The Half Moon Inn** was already well established in 1795 when, despite the small size of Sheepwash (even today there are less than 250 inhabitants), there were three rival inns in the village. However, by 1900, they had all disappeared whilst The Half Moon had expanded - taking in the former Dame school and a milliner's shop. Remarkably, in almost a century the inn has only had five landlords. The current owners, the Inniss family, arrived in 1958, and during their time here they have assured the inn's outstanding reputation for hospitality, unique homely atmosphere and its excellent facilities for fishermen. The family owns its own private fishing on 10 miles of the River Torridge, and, for those new to fishing, tackle is available for hire and Charles Inniss will give tuition.

Meanwhile, back at the inn, brother Benjie Inniss has given his name to Benjie's Bar - just the place to settle down in the evening and listen (or tell) some fishing yarns. A welcoming bar with a magnificent log fire as its focal point, guests will find fine beers and a wide range of malt and blended whiskies served from the bar while there is also a splendid cellar of over 200 fine wines which Benjie is happy to show to guests. Bar snacks are available here at lunchtime and, in the evening, The Half Moon's stylish restaurant is open to both residents and nonresidents alike.

Opening Hours: Mon-Sat 11.00-14.30, 18.00-23.00; Sun 12.00-14.30, 19.00-22.30

Food: Bar snacks lunchtime, à la carte restaurant in the evening

Credit Cards: Visa, Access, Mastercard, Switch

Accommodation: 14 double rooms all ensuite

Facilities: Children and dogs welcome, Private river and stillwater fishing, Rod room, Games room

Local Places of Interest/Activities: Dartmoor National Park 12 miles, North Devon coast 15 miles, Tarka Trail 3 miles, Golf, Walking, Horse riding

Internet/Website: http://www.halfmoon.demon.co.uk

The Hunters' Inn

Heddons Valley,
near Parracombe,
Devon EX31 4PY
Tel: 01598 763230
Fax: 01598 763636

Directions:

From junction 27 on the M5 take the A361 towards Barnstaple. After passing South Molton take the A399 towards Combe Martin. The Hunters' Inn can be found just off this road by following the signposts after passing through Blackmoor Gate.

The Hunters' Inn is a delightful country inn offering traditional, friendly hospitality that must have one of the most splendid situations of any English inn - in the gentle folds of Heddon Valley which, during the 19th century, became known as the Switzerland of England. There has been an inn here for many years and it started life in the kitchen of a thatched farmhouse which the farmer's wife dispensing beer from a barrel to local farmers who came here to enjoy a gossip over their mugs of ale. In 1868, the farm was taken over by the Berry family and, whilst they continued farming the land, they also expanded the ale house by adding buildings and it soon became a favourite haunt of visitors on walking tours. Now an inn in the proper sense, the buildings burnt to the ground in 1895 and the present inn was constructed, in this Swiss chalet style, a year later.

Today, The Hunters' Inn is still family run and Clifford Johnson, the owner, has a wealth of experience in the hotel business gained in Park Lane, London. This is an inn of charm and character that very much lives up the expectation created by the marvellous external appearance. As well as serving a good range of well kept real ales, beers and lagers, there is a fine wine list that complements perfectly the à la carte menu served in the restaurant. More casual dining can be taken from the bar menu but, whether formal or informal, the high standard of the dishes is maintained. With a choice of accommodation and traditional cream teas served in the summer, The Hunters' Inn is a delightful hidden away place that is well worth seeking out.

Opening Hours: Mon-Sat 11.00-23.00; Sun 11.00-22.30

Food: Bar meals and snacks, À la carte

Credit Cards: Visa, Access, Delta, Switch, Amex

Accommodation: 7 double rooms en suite, 2 double rooms shared bathroom

Facilities: Gardens, Children's play area, Car parking, Functions room

Local Places of Interest/Activities: Combe Martin Wildlife and Dinosaur Park 4 miles, Arlington Court 5 miles, Lynton and Lynmouth Cliff Railway 4 miles, Exmoor National Park 5 miles, Coast 1 mile, Walking, Bird watching, Horse riding

90 The Molesworth Arms

Pyworthy,
Holsworthy,
Devon EX22 6SU
Tel: 01409 254669

Directions:

From Okehampton take the A3079 then the A3072 to Holsworthy. Follow the A3072 through the town towards Bude then, at Holsworthy Golf Course, turn left signposted The Molesworth Arms.

Dating back to 1905, **The Molesworth Arms** is a splendid stone built pub that, despite its modest exterior, is surprisingly spacious inside. Though not quite 100 years old, this is a place of atmosphere and charm - there are exposed oak beams, flag stone floors and roaring log fires in winter. A true village inn, owners Chris and Lisa Gilbert, have created the perfect place for a quiet drink and good conversation where no one is a stranger for long.

Whether sitting in the bar with company or playing any one of the traditional pub games, there is an excellent range of well kept real ales, lagers and beers, as well as a good selection of world wide wines, to help quench customers' thirst. The Molesworth Arms is also fast gaining a reputation for the delicious menu of grills, traditional pub meals and sandwiches which are served either in the bar or in the cosy restaurant. Chris is the chef of the partnership and, as well as producing a mouthwatering menu of homemade snacks and light meals there are several house specialities that certainly should not be overlooked. Ensuring that customers not only receive quality but also quantity, the inn is very popular and it is advisable to book for their renowned Sunday lunch.

Opening Hours: Mon-Sat 11.00-15.00, 18.30-23.00; Sun 12.00-15.00, 19.00-22.30. Closed Monday lunchtimes except Bank Holidays

Food: Food available 12.00-2.00 and 6.30-9.30, Traditional Sunday lunches

Credit Cards: Visa, Mastercard, Switch, Amex, Delta

Facilities: Beer garden, Families welcome, Functions catered for

Entertainment: Darts, Skittles, Pool

Local Places of Interest/Activities: Golf, Horse riding, Walking, North Devon and North Cornwall coast 9 miles.

The Old Union Inn 91

Stibbs Cross,
Torrington,
Devon EX38 8LH
Tel: 01805 601253
Fax: 01805 601253

Directions:
From Bideford take the A386 then the A388 towards Holsworthy. The Old Union Inn lies on the A388 at the crossroads with the B3227.

An attractive and typical north Devonshire pub, **The Old Union Inn** is a large and imposing white 16th century building that is hard to miss. Full of character and charm, the inn has lost none of its age old feel over the years and today's customers can enjoy the warmth from the old inglenook fireplace just as people have over the last few centuries. Cosy and comfortable whatever the time of year, the pub walls are decorated with all manner of interesting and unusual memorabilia which is sure to be the subject of one or two conversations.

Today, The Old Union Inn is owned and personally run by Carol and John McKay who came here after returning from 16 years in South Africa. Whilst John was busy working in computers, Carol managed a large social club and the skills she learnt there, as well as the couple's natural flair for making people feel instantly at ease, have only benefited the customers of the inn. As well as the excellent selection of real ales, key beers, stouts, lagers and spirits served from the bar, The Old Union also offers customers a delicious menu of homemade bar snacks and meals. All cooked to order - and perfection - Carol's homemade pies are a house speciality well worth taking the time to seek out. Traditional nursery puddings are also a mouthwatering addition to the menu. A place for good conversation, as well as good food, drink and hospitality, those looking for a traditional inn need look no further.

Opening Hours: Summer - Mon-Sun 12.00-23.00; Winter - Mon-Sun 12.00-15.00, 17.00-23.00

Food: Bar meals and snacks all day

Credit Cards: None

Accommodation: 1 double room ensuite; 2 double rooms with shared bathroom

Facilities: Beer garden, Children's playarea, Dogs welcome

Entertainment: Darts, Bar billiards, Quiz nights, Large screen satellite TV

Local Places of Interest/Activities: Fishing, Shooting, Walking, North Devon coast 8 miles

92 Royal Oak Country Inn

The Square,
Dolton,
Devon EX19 8QF
Tel: 01805 804288
Fax: 01805 804288

Directions:

From junction 31 on the M5 take the A30 and then the A377 towards Barnstaple. After passing through Copplestone take the B3220 towards Great Torrington and, after 12 miles, turn left on to the B3217. The Royal Oak Country Inn can be found approximately 2 miles down this road, beside the village church.

Situated in the heart of this attractive village, **The Royal Oak Country Inn** was described, by travel writer SH Burton more than a quarter of a century ago, as 'a mouthwatering and thirst quenching establishment of great charm, enhanced by its thatched neighbours'. Though Burton was delighted by his visit here many years before the present landlords, Jayne and Matt Sevier arrived from the New Forest, the compliments are just as much in order now as they were then. Dating back to the 16th century, although some parts are thought to be older, this grand old building features old beamed ceilings, open log fires and a wealth of colourful hanging baskets of flowers.

A popular place for a sociable game of skittles or to enjoy good conversation, many come here to also sample the inn's huge choice of beverages, including real ales from small, local independent breweries, which is thought to be the most extensive in Devon. The comprehensive menu of delicious homecooked bar snacks and meals is also worthy of a second or third glance whilst those looking for more formal dining can enjoy the delights of the à la carte menu in the attractive restaurant. Certainly a place for all the family, whilst the adults are taking advantage of the inn's superb drinks the children have their own, safe play area in the well maintained and pleasant beer garden.

Opening Hours: Mon-Fri 11.30-14.30, 18.30-23.00; Sat 11.30-14.30, 18.00-23.00; Sun 12.00-14.30, 19.00-22.30

Food: Bar meals and snacks, À la carte

Credit Cards: Visa, Access, Delta, Switch, Amex, Diners

Accommodation: 3 twin rooms all en suite, 1 twin room with separate bathroom

Facilities: Beer garden, Children's play area, Car parking, Functions catered for

Entertainment: Regular live music, Darts, Skittles, Pool

Local Places of Interest/Activities: Tarka Trail passes in front of inn, Great Torrington 6 miles, Okehampton 11 miles, Beach 12 miles, Walking, Cycling, Horse riding, Fishing

The Stag Hunters Hotel | 93

Brendon,
near Lynton,
Devon EX35 6PS
Tel: 01598 741222
Fax: 01598 741352

Directions:
From junction 25 on the M5 take the A358 to Williton and then the A39 to Minehead and on towards Lynton. One mile before Countisbury turn left and The Stag Hunters lies a short distance away.

Found in the gloriously unspoilt valley of the River Lyn **The Stag Hunters Hotel** is a splendid family run hotel which offers superb old fashioned hospitality in a part of English were old traditions and values remain. Surrounded by its own five acres of paddocks and a delightful garden, the nearby river can be fished for salmon and trout and this ancient stone built hotel is well placed for many of north Devon's historic attractions.

The welcoming bar serves a wide choice of beers, ales, wines and spirits and it is also the place to try the highly regarded local Exmoor real ale. The food here too is very much influenced by the hotel's location and the splendid à la carte menu, served in the atmospheric restaurant, offers seasonal Devon fare along with locally caught seafood. The less formal, bar menu is equally tempting and, again is a wonderful choice of homecooked dishes that feature of the very best that Devon has to offer. Not only can guests also enjoy a very pleasant and relaxing nights sleep in one of the comfortable and well appointed guest rooms but their is stabling here for eight horses - so the hack can come too. Well behaved dogs need not be left behind as they can be accommodated in their owners' rooms. A magnificent Devon country hotel that has is a welcome and inviting place to stay, the charm of The Stag Hunters Hotel begins, rather than ends, with its splendid setting. A place well worth seeking out this is a hidden inn that has a special appeal to those looking for old fashioned, high quality hospitality.

Opening Hours: Mon-Sun 12.00-23.00

Food: Bar meals and snacks, À la carte

Credit Cards: Visa, Mastercard, Switch, Eurocard, Solo

Accommodation: 14 double rooms all en suite

Facilities: Beer garden, Car parking, Stabling, Paddocks, Dogs welcome

Entertainment: Regular sing songs

Local Places of Interest/Activities: Watersmeed Ho 1 mile, Foreland Point 2 miles, Lynton and Lynmouth Cliff Railway 3 miles, Exmoor National Park 2 miles, Coast 1 mile, Walking, Fishing, Horse riding, Bird watching

Internet/Website: staghunters@netscapeonline.co.uk

94 The Thatched Inn

Abbotsham,
near Bideford,
Devon EX39 5BA
Tel: 01237 471321
Fax: 01237 471321

Directions:

From junction 27 on the M5 take the A361 through Tiverton to Barnstaple and then the A39 around Bideford towards Bude. The Thatched Inn lies just off the main road, approximately 2 miles from Bideford, behind the Big Sheep.

As its name would suggest, **The Thatched Inn** does indeed have a thatched roof and, before becoming converted into an inn, it was three stone built 15th century cottages. A picturesque and very charming country inn, there is a delightful beer garden where adults can sit and enjoy the glorious north Devon countryside whilst children can play on the swings. The interior of this ancient inn is equally charming and also full of character as many of the building's original features remain along with a large wood burning stove that adds an extra warmth in the winter. Gleaming brassware hangs from walls and ceiling beams and, not surprisingly for such an old place, there is also a resident ghost though his or her story is unknown.

Before buying the inn in 1993, Leslie Robert Heard was a local farmer and he has certainly taken to the licensing trade like a duck to water. This splendid inn has a fine reputation locally for its excellent selection of real ales and there is also a wide range of wines from which to choose. The menu of freshly prepared traditional pub fare, including the house speciality homemade pies, is supplemented by an everchanging boards of daily specials which are sure to tempted even the most jaded palate. Taken in either the bar area or in the non smoking dining room, a meal in this convivial company is well worth taking the time to enjoy. Finally, visitors to this area of north Devon can take further advantage of The Thatched Inn's hospitality by staying in the inn's self catering holiday cottage.

Opening Hours: Mon-Sat 11.00-23.00; Sun 12.00-22.30

Food: Bar meals and snacks, Traditional Sunday lunch

Credit Cards: Visa, Access, Delta, Switch, Amex, Diners

Accommodation: Self catering holiday cottage, sleeps 6

Facilities: Large beer garden, Car parking

Local Places of Interest/Activities: Big Sheep Adventure Park, Bideford 2 miles, Westward Ho! 2 miles, Appledore and North Devon Maritime Museum 4 miles, Northiam Burrows Nature Reserve 4 miles, Walking, Fishing, Bird watching

The Windsor Arms   95

Bradiford,
near Barnstaple,
Devon EX31 4AD
Tel: 01271 343583

Directions:

From junction 27 on the M5 take the A361 to Tiverton and then on to Barnstaple. The Windsor Arms can be found just north of the town.

Dating back to 1837, **The Windsor Arms** was originally constructed as a bakehouse and, just a short while later, in 1857, it was converted into the Windsor Hotel. An attractive stone building, the interior of The Windsor Arms is a real rabbit warren and, as well as the two bar areas, there is a small and intimate dining room. The building's original features, including the open fireplaces, and the decorative brassware hanging from the walls and ceiling beams all add together to give the inn a cosy and inviting atmosphere - one of the several reasons why the inn is so popular. Meanwhile, around the back of the inn is a large, enclosed heated patio area that was once the hotel's courtyard and it is a marvellous place to sit out even when the evening is chilly. Here too, in a self contained building, is the games room which not only has all the usual pub games but also table skittles and a splendid 1950s one armed bandit.

Superb hospitality is the key at The Windsor Arms and landlords Keith and Angie Higginson have certainly established a fine reputation for their inn. As well as providing a pleasant and enjoyable ambience, the couple also serve wonderful food and drink. The menu, an uncomplicated list of traditional favourites, with some more exotic dishes thrown in, this is the ideal place for good homecooking. Children too are catered for and, as well as having their own menu, there are also special areas set aside in the pub for them.

Opening Hours: Mon-Sat 12.00-15.00, 18.00-23.00; Sun 12.00-15.00, 18.00-22.30

Food: Bar meals and snacks, Traditional Sunday lunch, Children's menu

Credit Cards: Visa, Access, Delta, Switch, Amex, Diners

Facilities: Patio garden, Children's areas

Entertainment: Traditional pub games

Local Places of Interest/Activities: St Anne's Chapel Museum in Barnstaple, Marwood Gardens 3 miles, Tapeley Park 6 miles, North Devon Maritime Museum in Appledore 7 miles, Beaches 7 miles, Walking, Horse riding, Sailing

96 The Wrey Arms

Bickington Road,
Sticklepath,
Barnstaple,
Devon EX31 2BX
Tel: 01271 376000
Fax: 01271 376000

Directions:

From junction 27 on the M5 take the A361 to Barnstaple. From the town centre take the A3125 towards Bideford and The Wrey Arms can be found on the outskirts of Barnstaple.

Situated on the outskirts of this old market town, which is also the oldest regional borough in England, **The Wrey Arms** is a large inn that sits back from the main Barnstaple to Bideford road. Built in 1936, this pub has a typical 1930s exterior that is half brick and half mock Tudor. The spacious interior is equally full of between the wars character and one bar has been refurbished to add to the warmth of the already comfortable surroundings. A popular and inviting inn, The Wrey Arms is a family run establishment with Mark Rogers and his wife Gina as landlords ably assisted by Gina's mother, Brenda, who manages the kitchen.

The three real ales served from the bar rotate every two or three weeks and, along with all the usual drinks, they can be enjoyed in either one of the inn's two comfortable bars areas or outside in the secluded beer garden and patio. Food too is an important aspect of life at The Wrey Arms and the menus comprise of traditional English pub dishes created from fresh local produce. Whilst customers food and drinks needs are being so capably catered for, entertainment is also provided with both music and a wealth of pub games being played enthusiastically by both locals and visitors alike.

Opening Hours: Mon-Sat 11.00-23.00; Sun 12.00-22.30

Food: Bar meals and snacks, Traditional pub food

Credit Cards: Visa, Access, Delta, Switch, Amex, Diners

Accommodation: 1 family room, 5 twin rooms, 1 single room all en suite

Facilities: Beer garden, Car parking, Functions catered for

Entertainment: Regular live music, Discos, Karaoke, Pool, Skittles, Darts, Shove H'penny

Local Places of Interest/Activities: St Anne's Chapel Museum in Barnstaple, Marwood Gardens 3 miles, Tapeley Park 6 miles, North Devon Maritime Museum 7 miles, Beaches 7 miles, Walking, Horse riding, Fishing, Sailing

4 South Devon

PLACES OF INTEREST:

Ashburton   100
Bovey Tracey   100
Brixham   100
Buckfastleigh   101
Castle Drogo   101
Dartmouth   101
Dawlish   102
Dawlish Warren   102
Kingsbridge   102
Loddiswell   103
Moretonhampstead   103
Newton Abbot   103
North Bovey   103

Paignton   103
Plymouth   104
Postbridge   105
Salcombe   106
Tavistock   106
Teignmouth   106
Torquay   107
Totnes   107
Wembury   108

PUBS AND INNS:

The Anchor Inn, Ugborough   109
The Bell Inn, Bovey Tracey   110
The Blacksmiths Arms, Lamerton   111
Bridford Inn, Bridford   112
Bullers Arms, Chagford   113
The Castle Inn, Lydford   114
The Chip Shop Inn, Chipshop   115
The Church House Inn, Churchstow   116
The Church House Inn, Rattery   117
The Church House Inn,
   Stokeinteignhead   118
The Crabshell Inn, Kingsbridge   119
The Dolphin Inn, Kenton   120
The George Inn, Buckfastleigh   121
The Globe Inn, Frogmore   122

The Journey's End Inn, Ringmore   123
The Ley Arms, Kenn   124
The Live and Let Live Inn,
   Landscove   125
The London Inn, Horrabridge   126
London Inn, South Brent   127
The Plough Inn, Ipplepen   128
Port Light Inn, Bolberry Down   129
The Post Inn, Whiddon Down   130
The Ring O' Bells, West Alvington   131
The Rose and Crown, Yealmpton   132
The Toby Jug Inn, Bickington   133
Two Mile Oak, Abbotskerswell   134
White Thorn Inn, Shaugh Prior   135

The Hidden Inns of the West Country

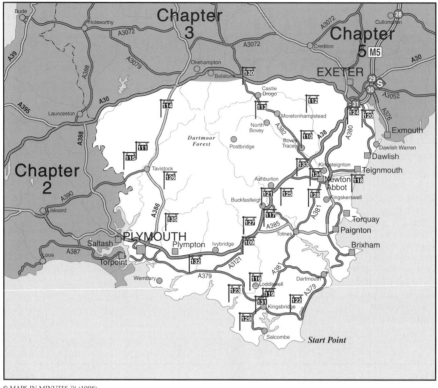

© MAPS IN MINUTES ™ (1998)

109 The Anchor Inn, Ugborough

110 The Bell Inn, Bovey Tracey

111 The Blacksmiths Arms, Lamerton

112 Bridford Inn, Bridford

113 Bullers Arms, Chagford

114 The Castle Inn, Lydford

115 The Chip Shop Inn, Chipshop

116 The Church House Inn, Churchstow

117 The Church House Inn, Rattery

118 The Church House Inn, Stokeinteignhead

119 The Crabshell Inn, Kingsbridge

120 The Dolphin Inn, Kenton

121 The George Inn, Buckfastleigh

122 The Globe Inn, Frogmore

123 The Journey's End Inn, Ringmore

124 The Ley Arms, Kenn

125 The Live and Let Live Inn, Landscove

126 The London Inn, Horrabridge

127 London Inn, South Brent

128 The Plough Inn, Ipplepen

129 Port Light Inn, Bolberry Down

130 The Post Inn, Whiddon Down

131 The Ring O' Bells, West Alvington

132 The Rose and Crown, Yealmpton

133 The Toby Jug Inn, Bickington

134 Two Mile Oak, Abbotskerswell

135 White Thorn Inn, Shaugh Prior

Please note all cross references refer to page numbers

If you think the title "The English Riviera" might be a little presumptuous, just take a look at all the palm trees in this part of Devon. You see them everywhere here: not just in public parks and expensively maintained hotel gardens, but also giving a Mediterranean character to town house gardens, and even growing wild. They have become a symbol of the area's identity, blazoned on leaflets, brochures, T-shirts, shop fronts, key-rings and hats.

The first specimen palm trees arrived in Britain in the 1820s, and it was soon discovered that this subtropical species took kindly to the genial climate of South Devon. Today there are literally thousands of them raising their spiky tufted heads above the more familiar foliage of English gardens. To the uninitiated, one palm tree may look much like another, but experts will point out that although the most common variety growing here is *Cordyline australis* (imported from New Zealand), there are also Mediterranean Fan Palms, *Trachycarpus fortunei* from the Chusan Islands in the East China Sea, and Date Palms from the Canary Islands. The oldest palm tree on record in the area is now over 80 years old and more than 40 feet high.

The Mediterranean similarities don't end there. Torquay, like Rome, is set on seven hills and the red-tiled roofs of its Italianate villas, set amongst dark green trees, would look equally at home in some Adriatic resort. The resemblance is so close that in one film in the Roger Moore television series, *The Saint*, a budget-conscious producer made Torquay double for Monte Carlo.

The South Hams have been dubbed "The frutefullest part of all Devonshire' by one writer describing this favoured tract of land lying south of Dartmoor, bounded by the River Dart to the east and the River Erme to the west. The climate is exceptionally mild, the soil fertile and the pastures well watered. But the rivers that run off Dartmoor to the sea, slicing north-south through the area, created burdensome barriers to communications until fairly recent times. This comparative isolation kept the region unspoilt, but also kept it poor. For the most part, the South Hams is a charmed landscape of drowsy villages linked by narrow country lanes running between high banks on which wildflowers flourish: thanks to an enlightened County Council in the 1950s and 1960s, the verges were never assaulted with massive quantities of herbicides as in other areas. The South Hams coastline presents enormous variety with some of the most spectacular cliff scenery in Devon running from the Erme to Start Point; and in contrast a long, low-lying stretch of beach extending north towards Dartmouth. No fewer than ten South Hams beaches won awards in 1997, with Blackpool Sands near Dartmouth achieving "Resort" status for its excellent facilities. The eastern boundary of the South Hams is the enchanting River Dart, surely one of the loveliest of English rivers. Rising in the great blanket bog of the moor, the Dart flows for 46 miles and together with its tributaries drains the greater part of Dartmoor.

South Dartmoor boasts just one minor road crossing the moor from east to west. In the remainder of this huge area of dome-shaped granite the most frequently seen living creatures are the famous Dartmoor ponies which have been here since at least the 10th century. The moor is notorious for its abundant rainfall, - an annual average of 60 inches, twice as much as falls on Torbay, a few miles to the east. In some of the

100

more exposed westerly fringes, an annual rainfall of 100 inches is common. In prehistoric times the climate was much drier and warmer. The moor then was dotted with settlements and this Bronze Age population left behind them a rich legacy of stone circles, menhirs, burial chambers, and single, double or even triple rows of stones. The row of 150 stones on Stall Moor above Burrator Reservoir is believed to be the longest prehistoric stone row in the world. Wild and untamed as it looks now, the moor has seen a considerable amount of commercial activity. Tin has been mined here since at least the 12th century as the many streamers, gullies and adits bear witness. Lead, copper, iron, and even arsenic have all been mined at some time. This activity has left the moor pitted with the scars of disused mine workings, ruined pump and smelting houses, although most of them are now softened by a cloak of bracken and heather.

PLACES OF INTEREST

ASHBURTON

This appealing little town lies just inside the boundary of the Dartmoor National Park, surrounded b y lovely hills and with the River Ashburn splashing through the town centre. Municipal history goes back a long way here, to 821AD in fact, when the town elected its first Portreeve, the Saxon equivalent of a Mayor. The traditional office continues to the present day, although its functions are now purely ceremonial. But each year, on the fourth Tuesday in November, officials gather to appoint not just their Portreeve but also the Ale Tasters, Bread Weighers, Pig Drovers and even a Viewer of Watercourses.

BOVEY TRACEY

This ancient market town takes its name from the River Bovey and the de Tracy family, who received the manor from William the Conqueror. The best-known member of the family is Sir William Tracy, one of the four knights who murdered Thomas à Becket in Canterbury Cathedral. To expiate his crime Sir William endowed a church here, dedicated to St Thomas. That building was destroyed by fire and the present church is 15th century with a 14th century tower. Its most glorious possession is a beautifully carved screen of 1427, a gift to the church from Lady Margaret Beaufort, the new owner of the manor and the mother of King Henry VII.

Walkers will enjoy the footpath that follows the trackbed of the former railway from Moretonhampstead to Newton Abbot, skirting the River Bovey for part of its length. Another interesting place to visit in the town is River-side Mill, run by the Devon Guild of Craftsmen. The Guild presents changing craft exhibitions and demonstrations and the mill also contains a Museum of Craftsmanship, a study centre and a shop.

Just to the north of Bovey Tracey is **Parke**, formerly the estate of the Tracy family but now owned by the National Trust and leased to the Dartmoor National Park as its headquarters. The Centre can also provide details of the many nature trails, woodland and riverside walks in the area, including one to the famous **Becky Falls** where the Becka Brook makes a sudden 70 foot drop.

BRIXHAM

In the 18th century Brixham was the most profitable fishing port in Britain, and fishing is still the most important activity in this engaging little town, although the trawlers now have to pick their way between flotillas of yachts and tour boats. On the quay there are stalls selling freshly caught seafood and around the harbour a maze of narrow streets where you'll find a host of small shops, tea rooms and galleries.

Brixham's lighthouse has been called "the highest and lowest lighthouse in Britain". There's only one of them, in fact, and it's only 15 feet high, but beneath it is a 200 foot high cliff rising at the most easterly point of Berry Head. The lighthouse stands within **Berry Head Country Park** which is noted for its incredible views (on a good day as far as Portland Bill, 46 miles away), its rare plants (like the white rock-rose) and its colonies of sea birds such as fulmars and kittiwakes nesting in the cliffs.

BUCKFASTLEIGH

Dominating the small market town of Buckfastleigh is **Buckfast Abbey**, a Benedictine monastery built in the Norman and Gothic styles between 1907 and 1938. If you've ever wondered how many people it takes to construct an Abbey, the astonishing answer at Buckfast is just six. Only one of the monks, Brother Peter, had any knowledge of construction, so he had to check every stone that went

Buckfast Abbey

into the fabric. A photographic exhibition at the Abbey records the painstaking progress that stretched over 30 years. Another monk, Brother Adam, became celebrated as the bee-keeper whose busy charges produced the renowned Buckfast Abbey honey. The Abbey gift shop also offers the famous Buckfast Tonic Wine, recordings of the Abbey choristers and a wide range of religious items, pottery, cards and gifts.

CASTLE DROGO

Castle Drogo (National Trust) was the last "castle" to be built in England. It was the brain child of Julius Drewe, a founder of the Home and Colonial Stores who retired at the age of 33 with a colossal fortune. He was inordinately proud of his Norman ancestor, Drogo, from whom the nearby village of Drewsteignton takes its name. So he commissioned Sir Edwin Lutyens to "build a medieval fortress to match the grandeur of the site" - 900 feet above the River Teign and with superb views across Dartmoor. Built of granite, the castle took almost 20 years to

complete, from 1911 until 1930, and architectural opinion about its merits is divided, to say the least. One writer thought Castle Drogo "about as romantic as one of Julius's grocery stores"; another

Castle Drogo

compared its straight lines and sharp angles to the brutalist buildings on London's South Bank. But the views are fabulous.

DARTMOUTH

Queen Victoria called the Dart the "English Rhine", perhaps thinking of the twin castles of Dartmouth and Kingswear that guard its estuary. It was her ancestor, Alfred the Great, who developed Dartmouth as a strategic base, and the town's long connection with the senior service is reflected in the presence here of the Royal Naval College. The spectacular harbour is still busy with naval vessels, pleasure boats and ferries, and particularly colourful during the June Carnival and the Dartmouth Regatta in late August. For centuries, this entrancing little town clinging to the sides of a precipitous hill was one of England's principal ports. During the 1100s, Crusaders on both the Second and Third Crusades mustered here, and from here they set sail. In its sheltered harbour, Elizabeth's men o'war lay in wait to pick off the stragglers from the Spanish Armada. Millions of casks of French and Spanish wine have been offloaded onto its narrow quays. And in 1620, the *Mayflower* put in here for a few days for repairs before hoisting sail on August 20th for Plymouth and then on to the New World where they arrived three months later. The quay from which they embarked later became the major location for the BBC-TV series, *The Onedin Line*, and was also seen in the feature film *Sense and Sensibility* star-

102

ring Emma Thompson and Hugh Grant.

Geoffrey Chaucer visited the town in 1373 in his capacity as Inspector of Customs and is believed to have modelled the Shipman in his *Canterbury Tales* on the character of the then Mayor of Dartmouth, John Hawley. Hawley was an enterprising merchant and seafarer who was also responsible for building **Dartmouth Castle** (English Heritage). Dramatically sited, it guards the entrance to the Dart estuary and was one of the first castles specifically designed to make effective use of artillery. In case the Castle should prove to be an inadequate deterrent, in times of danger a heavy chain was strung across the harbour to **Kingswear Castle** on the opposite bank. (Kingswear Castle is privately owned and not open to the public).

Also worth seeking out are **The Butterwalk**, a delightful timber-framed arcade dating from 1640 in which the Dartmouth Museum occupies the ground floor.

Two other buildings in Dartmouth should be mentioned. One is the **railway station**, possibly the only one in the world which has never seen a train. It was built by the Great Western Railway as the terminus of their line from Torbay and passengers were ferried across to Kingswear where the railway actually ended. The station is now a restaurant. The other building, which is inescapable, is the **Britannia Royal Naval College** (not open to the public). This sprawling red and white building, built between 1899 and 1905, dominates the northern part of the town as you leave by the A379 towards Kingsbridge.

DAWLISH

This pretty seaside resort, with one of the safest beaches in England, has the unusual feature of a main railway line separating the town from its seafront. The result is, in fact, much more appealing than it sounds. For one thing, the railway keeps motor traffic away from the beachside, and for another, the low granite viaduct which carries the track has weathered attractively in the century and a half since it was built. The arches under which beach-goers pass create a kind of formal entrance to the beach and the Victorian station has become a visitor attraction in its own right.

By the time Brunel's railway arrived here in 1846, Dawlish was already well-known as a fashionable resort with scores of new villas springing up along the Strand. Earlier improvers had already "beautified" the River Daw, which flows right through the town, by landscaping the stream into a series of shallow waterfalls and surrounding it with attractive gardens like **The Lawn**. Until Regency times, The Lawn had been a swamp populated by herons, kingfishers and otters. Then in 1808, the developer John Manning filled in the marshy land with earth removed during the construction of Queen Street. Today, both The Lawn and Queen Street still retain the elegance of those early-19th century days.

Dawlish has attracted many admiring visitors, amongst them Jane Austen (one of whose characters cannot understand how one could live anywhere else in Devon but here), and Charles Dickens, who, in his novel *Nicholas Nickleby*, has his hero born at a farm nearby. Both of these great literary figures arrived not long after the first houses were built along the Strand. That was in 1803. Up until then, Dawlish was just a small settlement beside the River Daw, located about a mile inland in order to be safe from raiders. This is where the 700-year old church stands, surrounded by a small group of thatched cottages.

DAWLISH WARREN

Dawlish Warren is a mile-long sand spit which almost blocks the mouth of the River Exe. There's a golf course here and also a 55 acre **Nature Reserve**, home to more than 450 species of flowering plants. For one of them, the Jersey lily, this is its only habitat in mainland England. Guided tours of the Reserve, led by the Warden, are available during the season.

KINGSBRIDGE

The Kingsbridge Estuary is not, strictly speaking, an estuary at all (no river runs into it), but a *ria*, or drowned valley. Whatever you call it, this broad expanse of water provides an attractive setting for this busy little town, an agreeable spot in which to spend an hour or two strolling along the quayside or through the narrow alleys off Fore Street bearing such graphic names as Squeezebelly Passage.

In the centre is **The Shambles**, an Elizabethan market arcade whose late-18th century upper floor is supported on six sturdy granite pillars. Above the church, the former Kingsbridge Grammar School, founded in 1670, now houses the **Cookworthy Museum of Rural Life**, named after William Cookworthy, who was born at Kingsbridge in 1705. Working as an apothecary at Plymouth, William encountered traders from the Far East who had brought back porcelain from China. English pottery makers despaired of ever producing such delicate cups and plates, but Cookworthy identified the basic ingredient of porcelain as kaolin, huge deposits of which lay in the hills just north of Plymouth. Ever since then, the more common name for kaolin has been China clay.

LODDISWELL

After the Norman Conquest, Loddiswell formed part of the 40,000 acre estate of Judhel of Totnes, a man with an apparently insatiable appetite for salmon. Instead of rent, he stipulated that his tenants should provide him with a certain number of the noble fish: Loddiswell's contribution was 30 salmon a year.

The benign climate of South Devon has encouraged several viticulturalists to plant vineyards in the area. The first vines at **Loddiswell Vineyard** were planted in 1977 and since then its wines have been laden with awards from fellow wine-makers and consumer bodies. The Vineyard welcomes visitors for guided tours or walkabouts on weekday afternoons from Easter to October, and also Sunday afternoons in July and August.

MORETONHAMPSTEAD

Moreton, as this little town is known to local people, has long claimed the title of "gateway to east Dartmoor", a role in which it was greatly helped by the branch railway from Newton Abbot which operated between 1866 and 1964. This is the gentler part of Dartmoor, with many woods and plantations, and steep-sided river valleys. Within easy reach are picture-postcard villages such as Widecombe-in-the-Moor, striking natural features like Haytor, and the remarkable Bronze Age stone hut-circle at Grimspound.

One of the most interesting buildings in Moreton is the row of **Almshouses** in Cross Street. Built in 1637, it is thatched and has a striking arcade supported by sturdy granite columns. The almshouses are now owned by the National Trust but are not open to the public. Just across the road from the almshouses is **Mearsdon Manor Galleries**, the oldest house in Moreton, dating back to the 14th century.

The ground floor of the manor is now a very pleasant traditional English tea room. In total contrast, the remaining rooms contain an astonishing array of colourful, exotic artefacts collected by the owner, Elizabeth Prince, on her trips to the Far East. There are Dartmoor-pony-sized wooden horses, Turkish rugs, Chinese lacquered furniture, finely-carved jade - a veritable treasury of Oriental craftsmanship.

NEWTON ABBOT

Newton Abbot is an ancient market town which took on a quite different character in the 1850s when the Great Western Railway made it the centre of its locomotive and carriage repair works. Neat terraces of artisans' houses were built on the steep hillsides to the south; the more well-to-do lived a little further to the north in Italianate villas around Devon Square and Courtenay Park.

NORTH BOVEY

In any discussion about which is the "loveliest village in Devon", North Bovey will be one of the leading contenders. Set beside the River Bovey, it is quite unspoiled, with thatched cottages grouped around the green and the 15th century church.

PAIGNTON

Today, Torquay merges imperceptibly into Paignton, but in early Victorian times Paignton was just a small farming village, about half a mile inland, noted for its cider and its "very large and sweet flatpole cabbages". The town's two superb sandy beaches, ideal for families with young children, were to change all that. A pier and promenade add to the town's appeal, and throughout the summer season there's a packed programme of specials events, including a Children's Festival in August, funfairs and various firework displays.

The most interesting building in Paignton is undoubtedly **Oldway Mansion**, built in 1874 for Isaac Singer, the millionaire sewing-machine manufacturer. Isaac died the following year and it was his son, Paris, who gave the great mansion its present exuberant form. Paris added a south side mimicking a music pavilion in the grounds of Versailles, a hallway modelled on the Versailles Hall of Mirrors, and a sumptuous

104

ballroom where his mistress Isadora Duncan would display the new, fluid kind of dance she had created based on classical mythology. Paris Singer sold the mansion to Paignton Borough Council in 1946 and it is now used as a Civic Centre, but many of the splendid rooms (and the extensive gardens) are open to the public free of charge, and guided tours are available.

An experience not to be missed in Paignton is a trip on the **Paignton and Dartmouth Steam Railway**, a seven mile journey along the lovely Torbay coast and through the wooded

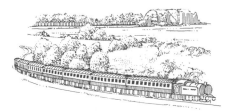

Paignton and Dartmouth Steam Railway

slopes bordering the Dart estuary to Kingswear where travellers board a ferry for the ten-minute crossing to Dartmouth. The locomotives and rolling stock all bear the proud chocolate and gold livery of the Great Western Railway, and on certain services you can wine and dine in Pullman style luxury in the "Riviera Belle Dining Train". During the peak season, trains leave every 45 minutes or so.

The town's other major attraction is **Paignton Zoo**, set in 75 acres of attractive botanical gardens, home to some 300 species of world animals. A registered charity dedicated to protecting the global wildlife heritage, the Zoo is particularly concerned with endangered species such as the Asiatic lions and Sumatran tigers which are now provided with their own forest habitat area, and orang utans and gorillas who roam freely on large outdoor islands, free from cages.

PLYMOUTH

Although Plymouth is one of the most celebrated names in British maritime history, it was surprisingly late in the day before its po-

tential as one of the finest deep-water harbours in Europe was recognised. Only towards the end of the 13th century were the first quays erected and it wasn't until Elizabethan times that it became the main base for the English fleet guarding the western Channel against an attack from Spain.

Perhaps the best way of getting to know this historic city is to approach Plymouth Hoe on foot from the main shopping area, along the now-pedestrianised Armada Way. It was on the Hoe on Friday, July 19th, 1588, that one of the most iconic moments in English history took place. Commander of the Fleet, and erstwhile pirate, Sir Francis Drake was playing bowls here when he was informed of the approach of the Spanish Armada. With true British phlegm, Sir Francis completed his game before boarding *The Golden Hind* and sailing off to harass the Spanish fleet. A statue of Sir Francis, striking a splendidly belligerent pose and looking proudly to the horizon, stands on the Hoe which is still an open space, combining the functions of promenade, public park and parade ground.

Just offshore, the striking shape of **Drake's Island** rises like Alcatraz from the deep swirling waters at the mouth of the River Tamar. In its time, this stark fortified islet has been used as a gunpowder repository (it is said to be riddled with underground tunnels where the powder was stored), a prison, and a youth adventure centre.

Two miles from the Hoe, Plymouth's remarkable **Breakwater** protects the Sound from the destructive effects of the prevailing south-westerly winds. Built between 1812 and 1840, this massive mile-long construction required around 4 million tons of limestone. The surface was finished with enormous dove-tailed blocks of stone, and the structure rounded off with a lighthouse at one end.

On a clear day, it's possible to see the famous **Eddystone Lighthouse**, 12 miles out in the Channel. The present lighthouse is the fourth to be built here. The first, made of timber, was swept away in a huge storm in 1703 taking with it the man who had built the lighthouse, the shipowner Winstanley. In 1759, a much more substantial structure of dovetailed granite blacks was built by John Smeaton. It stood for 120 years and even then it was not the lighthouse but the rocks on which it stood which began to collapse. The lighthouse was dismantled and re-erected on the Hoe where, as **Smeaton's**

Tower, it is one of the city's most popular tourist attractions. From the top, there are good views of Millbay Docks, Plymouth's busy commercial port which was once busy with transatlantic passenger liners. Today, the docks handle a variety of merchant shipping, including the continental ferry services to Brittany and northern Spain. To the east, the view is dominated by **The Citadel**, a massive fortification built by Charles II, ostensibly as a defence against seaborne attack. Perhaps bearing in mind that Plymouth had resisted a 4-year siege by his father's troops during the Civil War, Charles' Citadel has a number of gun ports bearing directly on the city. The Citadel is still a military base, but there are guided tours available.

Near the Citadel is Plymouth's oldest quarter, the **Barbican**. Now a lively entertainment area filled with restaurants, pubs, and an innovative small theatre, it was once the main trading area for merchants exporting wool and importing wine. Close by are the **Mayflower Steps** where the Pilgrim Fathers boarded ship for their historic voyage to Massachusetts. The names of the Mayflower's company are listed on a board on nearby Island House, now the tourist information office. Many other emigrants were to follow in the Pilgrim Fathers' wake, with the result that there are now more than forty communities named Plymouth scattered across the English-speaking world.

A number of interesting old buildings around the Barbican have survived the ravages of time and the terrible pasting the city received during the Second World War. **Prysten House**, behind St Andrew's Church, is a 15th century priest's house; the **Elizabethan House** in New Street has a rich display of Elizabethan furniture and furnishings, and the **Merchant's House** in St Andrew's Street is generally regarded as Devon's finest Jacobean building. A fascinating exhibit in the Merchant's House is the **Park Pharmacy**, a genuine Victorian pharmacy complete with its 1864 fittings and stocked with such preparations as Ipecacuanha Wine (one to 2 tablespoonfuls as an emetic) and Tincture of Myrrh and Borax, "for the teeth and gums".

Locally, the Tamar estuary is known as the Hamoaze, (pronounced ham-oys), and it's well worth taking one of the boat trips that leave from the Mayflower Steps. This is certainly the best way to see Devonport Dockyard, while the ferry to Cremyll on the Cornish bank of the Tamar drops off passengers close to Mount Edgcumbe Country Park and the old smuggling village of Cawsand.

The blackest date in Plymouth's history is undoubtedly March 21st, 1941. On that night, the entire centre of the city was razed to the ground by the combined effects of high-explosive and incendiary bombs. More than 1,000 people were killed; another 5,000 injured. After the war, the renowned town planner Sir Patrick Abercrombie was commissioned to design a completely new town centre. Much of the rebuilding was carried out in the 1950s, which was not British architecture's Golden Age, but almost half a century later the scheme has acquired something of a period charm.

The new city has some excellent facilities, including a first-rate **Museum and Art Gallery**, near Drake Circus, the Theatre Royal with its two auditoria in Royal Parade, the Arts Centre in Looe Street, and the Pavilions complex of concert hall, leisure pool and skating rink at the foot of Western Approach.

On the southern edge of the city stands one of Devon's grandest mansions, **Saltram House** (National Trust). Built during the reign of George II for the Parker family, this sumptuous house occupies a splendid site overlooking the Plym estuary. In the 1760s Robert Adam was called in, at enormous expense, to decorate the dining room and "double cube" saloon, which he accomplished with his usual panache. There are portraits of the Parkers by the locally born artist Sir Joshua Reynolds, and amongst the fine furniture, a magnificent four-poster bed by Thomas Chippendale. Other attractions include the great kitchen with its fascinating assortment of period kitchenware, an orangery in the gardens, and the former chapel, now a gallery displaying the work of West Country artists.

POSTBRIDGE

Postbridge's its famous **Clapper Bridge** probably dates back to the 14th century. Spanning the East Dart River, the bridge is a model of medieval minimalist construction with just three huge slabs of granite laid across solid stone piers. Not wide enough for wheeled traffic, the bridge would originally have been used by pack horses following the post road from Exeter into Cornwall.

106

SALCOMBE

Standing at the mouth of the Kingsbridge "Estuary", Salcombe enjoys one of the most beautiful natural settings in the country. Sheltered from the prevailing west winds by steep hills, it also basks in one of the mildest micro-climates in England. It's not unusual to see mimosa, palms, and even orange trees in the terraced gardens rising from the water's edge. The peaceful gardens at **Overbecks** (National Trust), overlooking Salcombe Bar, have an almost Mediterranean character.

Like other small South Devon ports, Salcombe developed its own special area of trading. Whilst Dartmouth specialised in French and Spanish wine, at Salcombe high-sailed clippers arrived carrying the first fruits of the pineapple harvest from the West Indies, and oranges from the Azores. That traffic has ceased, but pleasure craft throng the harbour and a small fishing fleet still operates from Batson Creek, a picturesque location where the fish quay is piled high with lobster creels. The town's sea-faring history is interestingly evoked in the **Salcombe Maritime & Local History Museum** in the old Customs House on the quay.

The coastline to the south and west of Salcombe, some of the most magnificent in Britain, is now largely owned by the National Trust. Great slanting slabs of gneiss and schist tower above the sea, making the clifftop walk here both literally and metaphorically breathtaking. At Bolt Head, the rock forms a jagged promontory protruding onto the western approaches to the Kingsbridge estuary, and further west, the spectacular cliffs between Bolt Head and Bolt Tail are interrupted by a steep descent at Soar Mill Cove. After rounding Bolt Tail, the footpath drops down to the sheltered sandy beach of Hope Cove.

TAVISTOCK

Tavistock was one of Devon's four Stannary Towns. The name comes from the Latin word for tin, *stannum*, and these four towns (the others are Ashburton, Chagford and Plympton) were the only ones licensed to weigh and stamp the metal.

For most of its recorded history, Tavistock has had only two owners. From 974 until 1539 the town was the property of Tavistock Abbey. Then Henry VIII closed the Abbey and sold the

building, along with its vast estates to John Russell whose family, as Earls and Dukes of Bedford, owned most of the town until 1911. The present town centre is essentially the creation of the Russell family, who after virtually obliterating the once-glorious Abbey, created a completely new town plan. Later, in the 1840s, Francis the 7th Duke diverted some of the profits from his copper mines to build the imposing Guildhall and several other civic buildings. He also remodelled the Bedford Hotel, and constructed a model estate of artisans' cottages on the western side of the town.

One of the legacies of the Abbey is the annual three-day fair, granted in 1105, which has now evolved into Goose Fair, a wonderful traditional street fair held on the second Wednesday in October. Tavistock was also permitted to hold a weekly market which, almost 900 years later, takes place every Friday in the Pannier Market, so named because country folk used to arrive carrying their produce in pannier bags. There's also an antiques and crafts market on Tuesdays, and a Victorian market on Wednesdays when many of the stallholders appear in period costume.

TEIGNMOUTH

Teignmouth has something of a double personality. On the coastal side is the popular holiday resort with its 2 miles of sandy beaches, a splendid promenade almost as long, and a pier. There's also a 25 foot high lighthouse which serves no apparent purpose apart from looking rather fetching. The residential area contains much fine Regency and Georgian building. Particularly noteworthy are the Church of St James with its striking octagonal tower of 1820, and the former Assembly Rooms, a dignified colonnaded building which now houses the Riviera Cinema. Teignmouth's Georgian past is recalled on Wednesdays during the season when local people dress up in 18th century costume.

On the river side of the town is the working port, approached by the narrowest of channels. The currents here are so fast and powerful that no ship enters the harbour without a Trinity House pilot on board. **The Quay** was built in 1821 when there was great demand for granite from the quarries on Haytor Down. Amongst the many buildings constructed in this durable stone were London Bridge (the one now in the USA) and the British Museum. The main export today is potter's clay from pits beside the River Teign, but boat building continues on a small scale.

The seafront naturally is a major attraction with its wide promenade, sandy beach, safe bathing, and Grand Pier offering all the traditional entertainments as well as newer ones such as King Neptune's Seabed Band.

TORQUAY

In Victorian times, Torquay liked to be known as "The English Naples", a genteel resort of shimmering white villas set amongst dark green trees and spread, like Rome, across seven hills. It was indisputably the west of England's premier resort, with imposing hotels like the Imperial and the Grand catering for "people of condition" from across Europe. At one time the town could boast more royal visitors to the square mile than any other resort in the world. Edward VII came here on the royal yacht Britannia and anchored in the bay. Each evening he would be discreetly ferried across to a bay beneath the Imperial Hotel and then conducted to the first floor suite where his mistress, Lily Langtry, was waiting.

The town's oldest building is **Torre Abbey**, founded in 1195 but largely remodelled as a Georgian mansion by the Cary family between 1700 and 1750. The Abbey was sold to Torbay Council in 1930 and, together with its extensive gardens, has been open to the public ever since. **Torquay Museum** has an interesting exhibition of photographs recording her life, as well as a pictorial record of Torquay over the last 150 years, and displays chronicling the social and natural history of the area. Amongst the Museum's other treasures are many items discovered at **Kents Cavern**, an astonishing complex of caves regarded as "one of the most important archaeological sites in Britain".

Excavations in the 1820s revealed an remarkable collection of animal bones - the remains of mammoths, sabre-toothed tigers, grizzly bears, bison, and cave lions. These bones proved to be the dining-room debris of cave dwellers who lived here some 30,000 years ago, the oldest known residents of Europe. The caves are open daily, all year, offering guided tours, a sound and light show, a gift shop and refreshment room.

Just a mile or so from the town centre is **Cockington Village**, a phenomenally picturesque rural oasis of thatched cottages, a working forge, and the Drum Inn designed by Sir Edward Lutyens and completed in 1930. From the village there's a pleasant walk through the park to **Cockington Court**, now a Craft Centre and Gallery. Partly Tudor, this stately old manor was for almost three centuries the home of the Mallock family. In the 1930s they formed a trust to preserve "entire and unchanged the ancient

Cockington Village

amenities and character of the place, and in developing its surroundings to do nothing which may not rather enhance than diminish its attractiveness". The Trust has been spectacularly successful in carrying out their wishes.

TOTNES

Totnes proudly claims to be the second oldest borough in England. This captivating little town claims to have been founded by an Ancient Trojan named Brutus in the 1200BC. The grandfather of Aeneas, the hero of Virgil's epic poem The Aeneid, Brutus sailed up the River Dart, gazed at the fair prospect around him and decided to found the first town in this new country which would take its name, Britain, from his own. **The Brutus Stone**, set in the pavement of the main shopping street, Fore Street, commemorates this stirring incident when both the town and a nation were born. Well, it could be true. The town sent its first Member of Parliament to London in 1295, and elected the first of its 630-odd Mayors in 1359.

The first recorded evidence of this town, set on a hill above the highest navigable point on the River Dart, doesn't appear until the mid-10th century when King Edgar established a mint here. The Saxons already had a castle of

108

sorts here, but the impressive remains of **Totnes Castle** are Norman, built between the 1100s and early 1300s. Towering over the town, it is generally reckoned to be the best-preserved motte and bailey castle in Devon.

A substantial section of Totnes' medieval town wall has also survived. The superb **East Gate**, which straddles the steep main street, is part of that wall, and although grievously damaged by fire in 1990 has been meticulously restored. Just a little way down the hill from East Gate is the charming **Guildhall** of 1553, a remarkable little building with a granite colonnade. It houses both the Council Chamber (which is still in use) and the underground Town Gaol (which is not).

The town's Elizabethan heritage really comes alive if you are visiting on a Tuesday in summer. You will find yourself stepping into a pageant of Elizabethan colour, for this is when the people of Totnes array themselves in crisp, white ruffs and velvet gowns for a charity market which has raised thousands of pounds for good causes.

At 70 Fore Street is the **Totnes Museum**, housed in an attractive half-timbered Elizabethan building whose upper floors overhang the street. One of the fascinating exhibits here honours a distinguished son of Totnes, Charles Babbage (1791-1871) whose "Analytical Machine" is universally acknowledged as the forerunner of the electronic computer. The Museum display records his doomed struggle to perfect such a calculator using only mechanical parts. A little further up the hill, in High Street, the Butterwalk and Poultry-walk are two ancient covered shopping arcades whose upper storeys

Totnes Museum

rest on pillars of granite, timber or cast iron.

For centuries Totnes was a busy river port, and down by Totnes Bridge, an elegant stone structure of 1828, the quay was lined with warehouses, some of which have survived and been converted into highly desirable flats. Nearby, on the Plains, stands a granite obelisk to the famous explorer William Wills, a native of the town who perished from starvation when attempting to re-cross the Australian desert with Robert Burke in 1861.

One excursion from Totnes not to be missed is the breathtakingly beautiful river trip to Dartmouth, 7 miles downstream. This stretch of the river has been called the "English Rhine", and the comparison is no exaggeration. During the summer there are frequent departures from the quay by the bridge. Another memorable journey is by steam train along the 7 mile stretch of the **Primrose Line** which runs through the glorious scenery of the Dart Valley to Buckfastleigh.

Even this list of attractions isn't exhaustive. Anyone interested in photography will want to visit **Bowden House Photographic Museum** with its vast collection of photographs, photographic bygones, vintage and classic cameras, all housed in a grand Tudor and Queen Anne mansion. Bowden House also claims to be seriously haunted. Visitors frequently authenticate sightings of monks, of gentlefolk in 18th century costume, and of a pathetic figure known as "Little Alice". Needless to say, the Halloween Night candlelit tours of the house are extremely popular.

WEMBURY

Wembury church makes a dramatic landmark as it stands isolated on the edge of the cliff, and the coastal path offers spectacular views of the Yealm estuary to the east, and Plymouth Sound to the west. The path is occasionally closed to walkers when the firing range is in use, so look out for the red warning flags. The **Great Mew Stone** stands a mile off-shore in Wembury Bay. This lonely islet was inhabited until the 1830s when its final residents, the part-time smuggler Sam Wakeham and his family, gave up the unequal struggle to make a living here. The Mew Stone is now the home of seabirds who surely can't take kindly to its use from time to time by the HMS Cambridge gunnery school on Wembury Point.

The Anchor Inn 109

Lulterburn Street,
Ugborough,
Devon PL21 0NG
Tel: 01752 892283
Fax: 01752 690722

Directions:

From Plymouth take the A38 east to Ivybridge. From Ivybridge turn off the main road on to the B3213 and follow the signs to Ugborough and The Anchor Inn lies 3 miles from the town.

This hillside village, which looks north, over the main road, to Ugborough Beacon and the southern reaches of Dartmoor, is home to **The Anchor Inn**. A particularly pretty village inn, with bench seating out at the front, this was originally built as three cottages in the 14th century. Inside, the inn is just as attractive and, with many of the cottages' features still in place, such as the leaded windows, oak beams and open fireplaces, there is a cosy and friendly atmosphere. As well as the lounge area, with its thatched bar, there is a charming, intimate restaurant, where the ceiling beams have been covered with a collection of bells.

Managed by Sheelagh Jeffreys, on behalf of her daughter Samantha, The Anchor Inn is well known locally for the excellent quality and range of the dishes served here. The à la carte menu, served in either the bar or the restaurant, is supplemented by an everchanging specials board and the choice on offer is, certainly, extensive. Taking their influence from around the world, the selection ranges from local Devon beef to ostrich, wild boar, alligator and bison. Vegetarians are also well catered for and the wine list too provides an interesting selection from around the globe. However, the high standard of hospitality on offer here does not end with food and drink as, to the rear of the inn, there are seven self contained cabins that provide the perfect opportunity for a quiet, undisturbed break.

Opening Hours: Mon-Sun 10.30-15.00, 17.00-23.30

Food: À la carte served in bar and restaurant

Accommodation: 7 double cabins all ensuite and self contained

Facilities: Bench seating to the front, Large car park

Entertainment: Occasional live music

Local Places of Interest/Activities: Dartmoor National Park 1 mile, Dartmoor Wildlife Park 6 miles, Beaches 7 miles, Walking, Riding, Sailing

110

The Bell Inn

Town Hall Place,
Bovey Tracey,
Devon TQ13 9AA
Tel: 01626 833495

Directions:

From junction 31 on the M5 take the A38 towards Plymouth. Just after Chudleigh, turn right on to the B3344 to Bovey Tracey. Continue through the town to the market square and The Bell Inn.

Found in the heart of this ancient market town, which takes its name from the River Bovey and the Norman de Tracey family, **The Bell Inn** is a splendid old inn that was originally built as three cottages. A place that is hard to miss, if the light and dark green painted exterior does not catch the eye the comical murals will certainly grab the attention of passers-by. Though landlords, Keith and Sandra Cowie, only moved here from the Midlands a short while ago, they have settled into life at The Bell and in Bovey Tracey with great ease - their pub is popular with locals who find the relaxed surroundings ideal for meeting up with friends. However, visitors to the inn will find this a friendly place where no one remains a strange for long.

Although this was once three buildings, the interior has been sympathetically altered to create one large bar area without losing any of the original character. So among the ceiling beams, gleaming brassware and mass of curios displayed on the walls customers can enjoy a drink from the splendid selection from the bar. Well kept real ales and scrumpy cider are popular but there are also all the usual spirits and a range of wines from which to make a choice. This is chiefly a drinking pub but there is a small menu of tasty bar snacks for those who are hungry and, in an elevated section of the bar, customers can amuse themselves by playing traditional pub games. Visitors will be glad to hear that The Bell Inn also offers bed and breakfast accommodation in a choice of four comfortable guest rooms.

Opening Hours: Mon-Fri 12.00-15.00, 17.00-23.00; Sat 12.00-15.30, 18.00-23.00; Sun 12.00-15.30, 19.00-22.30

Food: Bar snacks

Credit Cards: None

Accommodation: 4 double rooms all en suite

Facilities: Limited car parking on street

Entertainment: Pool, Darts

Local Places of Interest/Activities: House of Marbles and Rare breeds Farm in Bovey Tracey, Dartmoor National Park 1 mile, Ugbrooke 3 miles, Beaches 9 miles, Walking, Horse riding, Fishing, Bird watching

The Blacksmiths Arms   111

Lamerton,
near Tavistock,
Devon PL19 8QR
Tel: 01822 612962

Directions:

From Plymouth take the A386 to Tavistock and then the B3362 towards Launceston. After about 2 miles take the right turn to Lamerton and The Blacksmiths Arms can be found in the village.

A farming community, on the edge of Dartmoor, Lamerton is home to **The Blacksmiths Arms**, a 17th century inn that has been owned and personally run by Janie and Robert White since October 1999. Having both been in farming locally all their lives they have taken to pub life quickly and with ease - it could be in the blood as Robert's great grandfather ran this pub in the 1920s. A splendid, well maintained building from the outside, once inside the inn is warm and inviting - with an atmosphere that reflects the building's age. Real fires add a warm glow in winter and the spacious interior has been divided into a comfortable open bar area and a separate, more intimate dining room.

As well as serving a superb selection of well kept real ales, wines and ciders, plus all the usual drinks, The Blacksmiths Arms offers a delicious menu of homecooked food that is also supplemented by the ever changing specials board. All the ingredients - meat, fish and vegetables - are produced locally and, with Robert and Janie's farming experience visitors can expect only the very best. Well known locally, this is a particularly popular place for Sunday lunch so booking is advisable.

Opening Hours: Mon-Sat 11.30-14.30, 18.30-23.00; Sun 12.00-15.00, 19.00-22.30

Food: Bar meals and snacks for lunch and dinner, Traditional Sunday lunches

Credit Cards: Visa, Mastercard, Delta, Switch

Facilities: Beer garden, Children's play area, Disabled and baby changing facilities

Entertainment: Darts, Pool

Local Places of Interest/Activities: Dartmoor National Park to the east, Fishing, Walking, Golf

112 Bridford Inn

Bridford,
near Exeter,
Devon EX6 7HZ
Tel: 01647 252436
Fax: 01647 252436

Directions:

From Exeter take the A30 towards Okehampton then, at Pocombe Bridge, turn left on to the B3212. After 4 miles turn on to the B3193 and, over the bridge, take the left turn then the first right turn and Bridford Inn lies in the village.

Once three cottages in this old lead mining village surrounded by wooden valleys on the edge of Dartmoor, **Bridford Inn** dates back to the 17th century and has not only views over the countryside but also overlooks the parish church. A place of charm and character, owners Guy and Rena came here in summer 1999 and they have maintained the olde worlde atmosphere of the place. With a large inglenook fireplace, exposed beams and local memorabilia hanging from the stone walls, the feeling here is very much of a place that has changed little over the centuries.

However, visitors of yesteryear will certainly notice a difference in the standard of the hospitality offered to today's patrons. As well as the comprehensive selection of drinks, including real ales and wine by the bottle or glass, Bridford Inn is famous for its menu. Winners of many prestigious awards for their cuisine, including having been an Egon Ronay entrant, the secret of the inn's success is not only in the fine preparation but also in the careful selection of fresh local ingredients. Taken either in the bar or in the separate dining room, this is an excellent place for a quiet pub lunch or a celebratory evening meal. Add to this the large beer garden, where petanque is played in the summer, and the geniality of the regular customers, including the inn sponsored cricket team, and no one need look further for the ideal village inn.

Opening Hours: Mon-Sat 12.00-14.30, 18.00-23.00; Sun 12.00-15.00, 19.00-22.30

Food: Extensive menu for lunch and dinner, Traditional Sunday lunches

Credit Cards: Visa, Mastercard, Switch, Delta

Facilities: Beer garden, Private dining room

Entertainment: Live music, Theme weeks, Darts, Quizzes

Local Places of Interest/Activities: Canonteigh Falls 3 miles, Kennick Reservoir 1 mile, Walking, Horse riding, Sailing

Internet/Website: bridfordinn@virgin.net

Bullers Arms

7 Mill Street,Chagford,
near Newton Abbot,
Devon TQ13 8AW
Tel: 01647 432348
Fax: 01647 432810

Directions:

From junction 31 on the M5 take the A38 and then the A382 towards Moretonhampstead. Passing through the town and continue for 3 miles before turning left on to the B3192. Go into the village of Chagford, turn right at the T junction and the Bullers Arms lies on the right.

Situated in the centre of this typical Devon rural village, the **Bullers Arms** is an attractive old cream and dark green painted inn that dates back, in parts, to the 16th century. Despite its roadside location, behind the inn, there is, unexpectedly, a large beer garden that remains a pleasant secluded oasis of peace and tranquillity. Though the interior has been modernised over the years, the work has been carried out in a tasteful and sympathetic manner and many of the buildings original features remain including the ceiling beams and large stone fireplace.

Very much a place for regular customers to meet and catch up on the local news, landlords Stephen and Sheila Luxton warmly welcome visitors to the area and, as well as being an inviting place, the hospitality here is well worth seeking out. There is always a choice of local real ale from the bar, along with all the usual drinks, and the wine list here is extensive. Food too is an important part of life at the Bullers Arms and the menus are impressive. The tasty bar meals and snacks menu is accompanied by a splendid list of dishes that include not only old favourites such as steaks and fresh fish but also a range of curries and vegetarian options. Children too have their own menu and, so that all the family can enjoy the delights of the Bullers Arms, pets are also welcome.

Opening Hours: Mon-Fri 11.00-14.30, 18.00-23.00; Sat 11.00-23.00; Sun 12.00-22.30

Food: Bar meals and snacks, À la carte

Credit Cards: Visa, Access, Delta, Switch, Amex, Diners

Accommodation: 1 double room, 2 twin rooms, all en suite

Facilities: Beer garden, Car parking, Children and pets welcome

Entertainment: Darts, Chess

Local Places of Interest/Activities: Dartmoor National Park, Castle Drago 3 miles, Finch Foundry 6 miles, Hound Tor Medieval Village 6 miles, Walking, Cycling, Horse riding, Fishing, Bird watching

114

The Castle Inn

Lydford,
near Okehampton,
Devon EX20 4BH
Tel: 01822 820241/820242
Fax: 01822 820454

Directions:

From junction 31 on the M5 take the A30 towards Launceston. After passing Okehampton turn left on to the A386 towards Plymouth and, at Downton, turn right into Lydford. The Castle Inn lies on the main road through the village.

Dating back to the 13th century, when it was built to house the stone masons working on the construction of the village church, **The Castle Inn** is a wonderful, traditional country inn that is a pleasure to visit. The pink façade, with its verandah, is not only eyecatching but also somewhat misleading as, inside, this inn has a much older character. The low beamed ceilings of the ground floor rooms have bowed over the years and, in every nook and crannies, there is a wealth of memorabilia on display - from old pictures to commemorative plates. Ancient fireplaces glow with log fires and the rooms are furnished with splendid antique pieces that add to both the comfort and character of the inn.

Managed by Michael and Lyn Hazelton this is a marvellous inn that provides customers with top class country hospitality. Bar meals and snacks are served throughout the inn and, weather permitting, in the glorious, secluded garden whilst, in the evenings visitors can opt for a delicious meal in the inn's highly acclaimed restaurant. An atmospheric room that provides an intimate environment for diners, both the table d'hote and à la carte menus change regularly and offer a tantalising choice of imaginative and exciting dishes that are prepared with flair and served with style. Finally, the inn's top class accommodation offers guests the opportunity to relax in delightful surroundings of individually styled rooms.

Opening Hours: Mon-Fri 11.30-15.00, 18.00-23.00; Sat 11.30-23.00; Sun 12.00-22.30

Food: Bar meals and snacks, Table d'hote, À la carte

Credit Cards: Visa, Access, Delta, Switch

Accommodation: 8 double rooms and 1 single room all en suite

Facilities: Large beer garden, Car parking, Functions catered for

Entertainment: Quiz nights, Occasional music, Occasional country entertainment

Local Places of Interest/Activities:

Lydford Castle, Lydford Gorge 1 mile, Dartmoor National Park, Walking, Horse riding, Fishing, Bird watching

Internet/Website: castleinnlyd@aol.com

The Chip Shop Inn 115

Chipshop,
Tavistock,
Devon PL19 8NT
Tel: 01822 832322

Directions:

From Tavistock take the A390 towards Gunnislake. After approximately 2 miles turn right at Gulworthy Cross and opposite the school Chipshop is signposted.

Found at the heart of this old hamlet, that was built on the profits of first the local tin mining and then copper mining industries, **The Chip Shop Inn** dates back to the early 18th century. Its name, however, has nothing to do with fried potatoes but comes from the 1800s, in the heyday of the copper mining, when the miners were paid for their labour in tokens, or 'chips', which could be exchanged for goods at the local shop - also owned by the mine owner. Today, the inn's owners, Steve and Debbie Kirkham, only accept sterling in exchange for food and drink!

A large black and white building, with colourful, flower filled baskets hanging from every conceivable point during the summer, The Chip Shop Inn is a place well worth taking a detour to find. With exposed beams, traditional flag stone floors and interesting memorabilia on the walls, this is an inn with character, atmosphere and charm. A meeting place for locals, where visitors are assured a warm welcome, the real ales served from the bar are considered 'the best in Devon' whilst there is also an excellent selection of wine and all the usual other drinks. In the short time that they have been here, since autumn 1999, Steve and Debbie have also made a name for themselves by serving an extensive menu of tasty snacks and meals that range from old favourites like sausage and chips to sizzling Cantonese seafood. With regular live entertainment, a children's play area in the beer garden and dogs welcome, this is the perfect inn for all the family.

Opening Hours: Mon-Fri 12.00-14.30, 17.00-23.00; Sat and Sun all day (Sun until 22.30)

Food: Bar meals and snacks for lunch and dinner

Credit Cards: None

Facilities: Skittle alley used as function room, Beer garden, Children's play area,

Dogs welcome

Entertainment: Live entertainment regularly, Skittles, Darts, Assorted other bar games, Conker tournament

Local Places of Interest/Activities: Morwellham Quay Museum 3 miles, Dartmoor National Park to the east, Walking, Riding, Birdwatching

116 | The Church House Inn

Churchstow,
Kingsbridge,
Devon TA7 3QN
Tel: 01548 852237

Directions:

From Exeter take the A38 and then the A384 to Totnes. From here take the A381 to Kingsbridge and, at the roundabout before entering Kingsbridge, take the A379 towards Plymouth and The Church House Inn lies 1 mile along the road.

First built as a rest house for Benedictine monks in the 13th century, **The Church House Inn** is a wonderful stone built pub that is still offering the very best in hospitality to any one entering its doors. Many of the building's original features remain, including the great beams, thick stone walls, great stone fireplace complete with bread oven and even a 30 foot well, which all add to the unique olde worlde atmosphere of excellent free house. Owned and personally run by Elizabeth and Robert Robinson since early 1998, this is a warm and friendly family run inn that welcomes visitors as well as acting as a central meeting place for the people of Churchstow - the local theatrical group, of which Liz and Robbie are members, met here regularly.

Known for keeping an excellent pint or two of real ale, The Church House Inn is justly acclaimed for the superb menu that it offers. An extensive list of old favourites, the extra hungry should make straight for the house mixed grill - a banquet on a single plate. All homemade the dishes range from soups and sandwiches to steaks and pies and the menu is supplemented by an everchanging specials board. From Wednesday to Saturday evenings and Sunday lunchtime, The Church House Inn serves a carvery that is making its way into local legend and so booking is essential to avoid disappointment. Finally, with ample space for functions and an attractive selfcatering cottage at the rear of the main building, The Church House Inn has a lot to offer those looking for a somewhere different to stay.

Opening Hours: Mon-Sat 11.00-15.00, 18.00-23.00; Sun 12.00-15.00, 19.00-22.30

Food: Bar meals and snacks, Carvery Wed-Sat evenings and Sun lunch

Credit Cards: Visa, Access, Delta, Switch

Accommodation: 3 bedroom selfcatering cottage

Facilities: Function rooms, Courtyard beer garden, Children and dogs welcome

Local Places of Interest/Activities: Golf, Walking, Riding, Beach 3 miles

Internet/Website:
Robbie@churchill.freeserve.co.uk

The Church House Inn 117

Rattery,
near Totnes,
Devon TQ10 9LD
Tel: 01364 642220

Directions:
From Exeter take the A38 south towards Plymouth. One mile after Dean Prior take the minor road to the left, signposted Rattery, and The Church House Inn can be found approximately 1 mile away.

The Church House Inn, a listed building, dates back to 1028 and it is reputedly the oldest building in England. A home to monks whilst the parish church was being constructed, it remained in the hands of the Church until 1946 when it finally became the aptly named Church House Inn. Today, it is owned by Jill and Brian Evans, who, along with their dedicated team, welcome both visitors and locals to their splendid free house.

As befits a building of this age, there are open log fires and sturdy oak beams but the marvellous relaxed atmosphere comes from the warm welcome that everyone receives here. Those interested in history will enjoy reading the list of local vicars on display, which also confirms the building's age, whilst all will be taken with the excellent hospitality here. Opening for morning coffee, the inn stocks a wide range of real ales, beers and lagers, as well as having a good cellar of wines from around the world, and there is also a superb menu of traditional English fare served throughout the day. Taken in either the cosy bar area or the separate dining room the choice is sure to suit everyone's tastes.

Opening Hours: Mon-Sun 11.00-14.30, 18.00-23.00

Food: Bar meals and snacks throughout the day

Credit Cards: None

Facilities: Outside terrace with seating,

Dining room used for functions, Children and dogs welcome

Local Places of Interest/Activities:
Dartington Crystal and Cider Press Centre 3 miles, South Devon Railway 3 miles, Totnes 4 miles, Walking, Birdwatching, Sailing

118 The Church House Inn

Stokeinteignhead,
near Newton Abbot,
Devon TQ12 4QA
Tel: 01626 872475
Fax: 01626 872475

Directions:

From junction 31on the M5 take the A38 and then the A380 to Newton Abbot. At the roundabout at the end of the dual carriageway turn left to Combeinteignhead and, from the village, right to Stokeinteignhead. The Church House Inn lies in the centre of the village.

An attractive and picturesque place, **The Church House Inn** dates back to the 12th century when it was built as a home for stone masons working on the construction of the village church. Its license to served beer and ale was first granted, by the Church, in the 13th century and, though it has been extended over the years, this grand old building remains relatively unchanged. However, in 1993 the inn's thatch caught fire and, though the fire burned for some 17 hours, restoration of the devastated first floor and roof were completed by the end of that year and the inn reopened. Landlords Jim and Corinna Wilson, who were here at the time of the fire, have also fortunately stayed on and they continue to offer the generous hospitality that has been a hall mark of this ancient inn for centuries.

The interior of this friendly and inviting inn is full of character and charm and many of the building's original features can still be seen: the oak panelling, beamed ceilings and large stone fireplaces. The addition of a magnificent display of copper utensils provides a truly cosy and homely feel. An excellent place for a drink, either in the comfortable bar or outside in the well maintained beer garden, The Church House Inn also has a fine reputation for the high standard of its cuisine. Corinna runs the kitchen from which the delicious array of homecooked dishes are produced and the interesting menus provide a tantalising choice that are sure to satisfy even the most jaded diner.

Opening Hours: Mon-Sat 11.00-15.00; 17.30-23.00; Sun 12.00-15.00, 18.00-22.30

Food: Bar meals and snacks, À la carte, Traditional Sunday lunch

Credit Cards: Visa, Access, Delta, Switch

Facilities: Beer garden, Car parking, Functions catered for

Entertainment: Quiz nights, Darts

Local Places of Interest/Activities: Coast 1 mile, Babbacombe Model Village 2 miles, Torquay 3 miles, Newton Abbot 4 miles, Bradley Manor House 5 miles, Walking, Horse riding, Fishing, Sailing, Bird watching

The Crabshell Inn · 119

Embankment Road,
Kingsbridge,
Devon TQ7 1JZ
Tel: 01548 852345
Fax: 01548 852262

Directions:

From Exeter take the A38 then the A381 to Kingsbridge. Once in the town take the A379 and The Crabshell Inn lies on the right hand side of the road.

Found in this attractive little town, the **Crabshell Inn** is a charming 200 year old inn that lies right on the quay side. The interior, with its central open fireplace, exposed stone walls and beamed ceilings, is very much in character with the age of the building. Owners, Keith and Sue Rooker came here from Birmingham in 1988 and, along with the considerable help of their grown up daughters, Jane and Samantha, assistant manager Flora and assistant chef "Fudge" - not to mention their five grandchildren - have made this a very family orientated place with a welcoming atmosphere.

Downstairs, in the large open bar, the separate Parrot Room, which is named after the bird that died in 1981 and the Buttery Restaurant, visitors can enjoy a glass of real ale, local cider, wine or lager as well as delicious homecooked bar snacks or meals. The menu is extensive and covers all possible occasions from sandwiches and cream teas to full gourmet experiences. Fish is a house speciality and so features heavily and, with Salcombe and Plymouth being so close, the fish is always very fresh. For more formal dining there is the first floor Water's Edge Restaurant whilst take away meals are also available. With a large beer garden overlooking Kingsbridge's estuary with free moorings, and a special children's room, this is the perfect place to come to when a drink and excellent food is the order of the day.

Opening Hours: Mon-Sat 11.00-23.00; Sun 12.00-22.30

Food: Bar meals, snacks and à la carte in either bar, restaurant or on the quay

Credit Cards: Visa, Access, Delta, Switch

Facilities: Large beer garden, Children's room, Function room, Moorings for boats

Entertainment: Occasional music evenings, Themed nights

Local Places of Interest/Activities: Sailing, Fishing, Walking, Beaches, Bird watching, New swimming pool and Leisure Centre

120   The Dolphin Inn

Fore Street,
Kenton,
Devon EX6 8LD
Tel: 01626 891371
Fax: 01626 891371

Directions:
From junction 31 on the M5 take the A379 towards Dawlish. The Dolphin Inn can be found in the centre of Kenton, 3 miles from Exminster.

Found in the heart of picturesque village which is close to the Exe estuary, **The Dolphin Inn** is an attractive 17th century building that has an enclosed courtyard garden. The eyecatching cream and black exterior of this grand old inn makes it hard to miss and The Dolphin is one place that certainly should appear on everyone's itinerary of south Devon. Much larger inside than the road frontage would initially suggest, this splendid building is a wealth of beams and gleaming brassware. The key feature of the comfortable lounge bar is the magnificent cast iron open fire range, complete with bread oven, that adds a warm glow and a homely touch to this pleasant place during the winter. Here, visitors and locals alike can enjoy not only the relaxed atmosphere but also an excellent pint or two of real ale from the bar.

However, whilst ensuring that all the drinks here reach her customers in tip top condition, landlady, Helen Savory has gained an enviable reputation for the inn's restaurant. Along with head chef, Keith Ratcliffe, who is well known locally, the menus served here are a particular treat. As the inn is so close to the sea, fish and seafood is a speciality although the menu also includes an interesting and imaginative selection of both meat and vegetarian dishes. Everything is cooked to order and the selection of homemade sweets is too tempting to miss. For less formal dining there is the equally tempting bar snacks menu and also a carvery area for those who enjoy roast dinners throughout the week, not just on Sundays.

Opening Hours: Mon-Sat 11.00-23.00; Sun 12.00-22.30 (closed afternoons in winter)

Food: Bar meals and snacks, À la carte, Carvery, Traditional Sunday lunch

Credit Cards: Visa, Access, Delta, Switch

Facilities: Beer garden, Car parking nearby

Entertainment: Darts

Local Places of Interest/Activities: Powderham Castle, Beach 3 miles, Devon and Exeter Racecourse 4 miles, Ugbrooke 6 miles, Exeter 6 miles, Walking, Sailing, Horse riding, Fishing, Bird watching

The George Inn | 121

*50-51 Old Plymouth
Road,
Buckfastleigh,
Devon TQ11 0DH
Tel: 01364 643727
Fax: 01364 643727*

Directions:
Take the A38 from Exeter
towards Plymouth.
Three miles after passing
through Ashburton, turn
on to the B3380 and The
George Inn lies a mile
down this road.

At the heart of this old market town, which is dominated by Buckfast Abbey which is still the home of Benedictine monks, lies **The George Inn**. A typical coaching inn, situated by the side of the old main road between Exeter and Plymouth, which is now mercifully quiet, The George has been offering excellent hospitality to weary travellers for several centuries. Today, this charming family run inn continues the tradition whilst also acting as a meeting place for the townsfolk of Buckfastleigh.

The interior very much reflects the age of this 18th century building, there are open fires and the original ceiling beams, and the atmosphere created is relaxed and cosy. As well as the usual range of drinks served in the open plan bar area, visitors can also enjoy morning coffee and afternoon tea whilst, for lunchtime and in the evening, there is a splendid bar menu. Offering a choice of dishes, from light snacks to full meals, the tasty list is supplemented by a blackboard of mouthwatering daily specials and tempting puddings. Eaten either in the bar, or the separate dining room, which is dominated by a large grand piano, there is sure to be something here for everyone. Finally, in the true tradition of an old inn, The George Inn offers excellent accommodation in delightful, individually decorated and furnished guest rooms.

Opening Hours: Mon-Sun 11.30-15.00, 18.00-23.30; All day in summer

Food: Bar meals and snacks, morning coffee, afternoon tea

Credit Cards: Visa, Access, Switch

Accommodation: 7 double rooms all en suite

Facilities: Skittle alley used also as function room, Outside seating, Children and dogs (by prior arrangement) welcome

Entertainment: Wine and themed evenings, Quiz nights

Local Places of Interest/Activities: Buckfast Abbey, Buckfast Butterfly and Dartmoor Otter Sanctuary, Dartmoor National Park, Walking, Riding, Bird watching

122

The Globe Inn

Frogmore,
near Kingsbridge,
Devon TQ7 2NR
Tel: 01548 531351
Fax: 01548 531351

Directions:

From junction 31 on the M5 take the A38 towards Plymouth and continue to the Loddiswell and Shirehorse Centre exit. Follow the signs on A3121 and then the B3196 to Loddiswell and then Kingsbridge. From the town take the A379 towards Dartmouth for 3 miles and The Globe Inn lies in the centre of Frogmore.

The pretty village of Frogmore is not only well placed for magnificent scenery, uncrowded beaches and historic towns and villages but it is also the home of **The Globe Inn**. Overlooking Frogmore Creek, this picturesque 18th century Devonshire coastal inn provides wonderful, traditional English hospitality that is tailored to the needs of the 21st century family. Perhaps, this seems a little strange when visitors first meet landlords, John and Lynda Horsley, who come from Australia but they have certainly not only embraced English inn keeping with style and enthusiasm but they are also a welcoming and personable couple who greet everyone as friends.

There are two bars - the sportsmans with its flagstone floor, pool table and darts, and the lounge bar with its open fire and nautical memorabilia - and both are well stocked with a good range of real ales and farmhouse ciders. Food too is important here and, as well as the extensive menu of bar snacks and meals, there is an everchanging menu served in the inn's candlelit restaurant. From traditional pub fare to the more exotic there is something to suit every taste and pocket. Locally caught seafood appears on the list of house specialities as does a variety of other delicious dishes including Barbary duck and Chicken Stilton. Whilst providing excellent food and drink in relaxed and comfortable surroundings, The Globe Inn also offers visitors a choice of accommodation that is ideal for families and those wishing to explore the south Devon coast.

Opening Hours: Mon-Sat 11.30-15.00, 17.30-23.00; Sun 12.00-15.00, 18.30-22.30

Food: Bar meals and snacks, À la carte

Credit Cards: Visa, Access, Delta, Switch, Amex

Accommodation: 6 doubles, 3 en suite

Facilities: Beer garden, Children's play area, Car parking, Functions catered for

Entertainment: Theme nights, Darts, Pool

Local Places of Interest/Activities: Coast 3 miles, Kingsbridge 3 miles, Woodlands Leisure Park 7 miles, Walking, Cycling, Horse riding, Fishing, Bird watching, Golf

Internet/Website:
horsley@theglobeinn.co.uk

The Journey's End Inn 123

Ringmore,
near Kingsbridge,
Devon TQ7 4HL
Tel: 01548 810205

Directions:

From Exeter take the A38 towards Plymouth then turn off on to the A3121 to Modbury. From here follow the signs for Ringmore and The Journey's End Inn is found off the B3392 near the coast.

The pretty coastal village, just back from the sea, is home to the splendid 13th century **Journey's End Inn**, that was originally built to house the stone masons working on the village church. In the late 16th century, it became one of a chain of 'new inns' that were established throughout the country by Elizabeth I to encourage travellers and merchants. A charming and attractive building the pub's unusual name is taken from the play, Journey's End, by RC Sherrif who wrote the last chapters whilst staying here.

Today a freehouse owned and personally run by Debbie and Grahame Gillam, the couple, who have only been here since summer 1999, have gained an enviable reputation for the friendly atmosphere and excellent food that they offer. Certainly a place for real ale connoisseurs - there are six at any one time served from the cask - those who enjoy a tipple have plenty of choice including many bottled lagers, real cider, 15 different malt whiskies and an extensive wine list. Whilst Debbie is playing hostess, catching up with regular visitors and welcoming new, Grahame, the chef of the partnership, is busy putting together the delicious range of homecooked dishes that make up the well chosen menu. Specialising in fresh local produce, the standard menu offers a superb range of dishes and, throughout the year, there are a series of themed menu evenings which prove very popular.

Opening Hours: Winter - Tue-Sat 12.00-15.00, 18.00-23.00; Sun all day; Summer - Mon-Sun all day

Food: Bar meals and snacks, à la carte

Credit Cards: Visa, Access, Delta, Switch

Accommodation: 1 double room ensuite, 1 family room ensuite

Facilities: Beer garden, Conservatory dining room, Children and dogs welcome

Entertainment: Music evenings, Themed evenings, Quizzes, Twice yearly beer festival

Local Places of Interest/Activities: Beach 1 mile, Walking, Riding, Golf

Internet/Website: JourneyEnd@aol.com

124 The Ley Arms

Kenn,
near Exeter,
Devon EX6 7UW
Tel: 01392 832341
Fax: 01392 832873
Directions:
From junction 31 on the M5 take the A38 towards Plymouth. After approximately 2 miles turn left into Kenn and The Ley Arms can be found in the village centre.

Dating back to 1290, **The Ley Arms** is a marvellous old thatched inn, the long frontage of which curves along the side of the road. Originally built as a home for stone masons working on the local church this splendid building makes an idyllic country pub in a particularly picturesque setting and with the River Kenn running along the bottom of the car park. Naturally, with a building as old as this there is a wealth of ceiling beams which, fortunately, have withstood the test of time and renovators whims. Add to this the curios on the walls, the wood burning stove and the old slate flooring and The Ley Arms is a delightful inn full of olde worlde charm and character.

Landlords Robert Underhill and his wife have only been here since November 1999 but they have certainly made their mark. Not only is this a well known pub for the high quality and range of real ales, beers, spirits and wines served here but Robert's wife, who is a Roux brothers trained chef, has taken charge of the food served here. The menus are indeed very tempting and, whilst there are many old pub favourites, the imaginative and interesting dishes reflect the great attention to detail and flair which is a hall mark of this inn. The menus change with the seasons to ensure that customers can enjoy the very best of local produce and dining here is a treat to be savoured.

Opening Hours: Mon-Sat 11.00-15.00, 17.30-23.00; Sun 12.00-22.30

Food: Bar meals and snacks, À la carte, Sunday carvery

Credit Cards: Visa, Access, Delta, Switch, Amex, Diners

Facilities: Car park, Functions catered for

Entertainment: Darts, Skittles

Local Places of Interest/Activities: Devon and Exeter Racecourse 2 miles, Powderham Castle 3 miles, Exeter 4 miles, Dartmoor National Park 5 miles, Beaches 6 miles, Walking, Horse riding, Fishing, Sailing

The Live and Let Live Inn 125

Landscove,
near Ashburton,
Devon TQ13 7LZ
Tel/Fax: 01803 762663

Directions:

From junction 31 on the M5 take the A38 towards Plymouth. At the Ashburton roundabout turn left and follow the signs for Landscove. Continue for 3 miles and The Live and Let Live Inn can be found in the village on the left.

Found in the heart of this quiet village, **The Live and Let Live Inn** is an attractive and picturesque inn that has a small walled beer garden to the front. Built in the early 1800s as a house, it did not become an inn until 1840 and, today, it still has the appeal of a private home, with the two bay windows on either side of the front door. Inside, the inn is very quaint and cosy and, as well as a mass of beams and brassware, the small bar has wood panelled walls which all add to the cosy atmosphere. A warm and inviting inn, particularly in winter when the woodburning stove is lit, this is a pleasant and friendly inn that offers charming hospitality to all the family.

From the bar customers can enjoy an excellent range of drinks, including two real ales and local scrumpy cider, and, for wine lovers, there is an extensive list featuring country wines and wine from around the world. The separate restaurant is also a small and intimate room and here customers are treated to a fine menu of tasty homecooked dishes. The wholesome list of traditional pub food ranges from light meals through to succulent steaks, fresh fish and several vegetarian options. The high standard of service and cuisine here has ensured that landlords, Bob and Wendy Langdon and their son Mark, have firmly established The Live and Let Live Inn as one of the best places to eat and drink in the area.

Opening Hours: Mon-Sat 11.30-15.00, 18.30-23.00; Sun 12.00-15.00, 19.00-22.30

Food: Bar meals and snacks, À la carte

Credit Cards: Visa, Access, Delta, Switch, Amex, Solo

Facilities: Beer garden, Car parking, Functions catered for

Entertainment: Theme nights, Darts

Local Places of Interest/Activities: Buckfast Butterfly and Otter Sanctuary 2 miles, South Devon Railway 2 miles, Buckfast Abbey 3 miles, Dartmoor National Park 3 miles, Totnes 4 miles, Beaches 8 miles, Walking, Cycling, Horse riding, Fishing

126

The London Inn

23 Station Road,
Horrabridge,
Yelverton,
Devon PL20 7ST
Tel: 01822 853567
Fax: 01822 853567

Directions:
From Plymouth take the A386 towards Tavistock. The London Inn can be found just off the road, in Horrabridge, 1 mile further on from Yelverton.

In the heart of this old village, which boasts a medieval bridge with arched recesses for pedestrians across the River Walkham, lies **The London Inn**, an early 18th century building that has been a centre of village life for all of its 200 years. Stepping into The London Inn is like taking a walk back in time - many of the buildings original features have been preserved including the exposed beams, open fires and stone walls - and the atmosphere created is one of warmth and friendliness. Very much a family pub, Alison and Philip Grimes, the hosts, have been here since 1997 and they are ably assisted, during college holidays, by their two children, Simon and Emma.

With a comfortable main bar, a delightful restaurant and a cosy village public bar, there is a corner here to suit every occasion whether dropping in for a quick drink and a chat or for a celebratory meal. As well as keeping a fine selection of real ales, keg beers, lagers, ciders and wines, the inn has an enviable reputation for the high standard of the food served here. All homecooked and prepared from the freshly local produce, the menus range from tasty bar snacks to full à la carte and, as well as the giant London Inn mixed grill, the house speciality is fish - both sea and freshwater. A place well worth finding, visitors are sure to receive a warm welcome from everyone including Alison and Philip's three lovely boxer dogs.

Opening Hours: Mon-Sat 11.00-23.00; Sun 12.00-22.30

Food: À la carte and bar snack menu served all day

Credit Cards: Visa, Access, Delta, Switch

Facilities: Beer garden, Large car park, Function room

Entertainment: Quiz nights, Pool, Darts, Euchre (a card game)

Local Places of Interest/Activities: Buckland Abbey 3 miles, Garden House 1 mile, Dartmoor National Park, Fishing, Walking, Golf

London Inn 127

Exeter Road,
South Brent,
Devon TQ10 9DF
Tel: 01364 73223

Directions:

From junction 31 on the M5 take the A38 towards Plymouth. Approximately 2 miles after Dean Prior turn right on to the B3213 and follow the signs for South Brent. The London Inn lies on the main road through the village.

Found in the heart of this village, which lies just within Dartmoor National Park, the **London Inn** is a large and imposing black and white building that is hard to miss. Dating back, at least, to the 18th century, this old coaching inn stands on the once busy London to Plymouth route and would, a couple of hundred years ago, be a busy and bustling place. Today, things are a little quieter in this pleasant backwater but the London Inn continues to offer superb hospitality to both locals and visitors alike.

Recently refurbished to a high standard, this excellent inn has two bar areas, a separate restaurant and, outside, a large beer garden with children's play area complete with rabbits and budgies. The old wood panelling has survived the redecoration programme which has added a nautical theme to this country inn and, amongst all the seafaring memorabilia, there is also a large aquarium. As well as offering a fine selection of real ales, lagers and ciders from the bar, the menus served in both the bars and the restaurant range from mouthwatering sandwiches and juicy steaks to superb fresh fish and tempting desserts. There are also some delicious house specialities such as Chicken Forrestier and Glastonbury Lamb. However, this is not all that landlords Graham and Ann Marie Bloomfield have to offer as there is also comfortable accommodation here that matches the same high standards as the rest of the inn.

Opening Hours: Mon-Sat 11.00-23.00; Sun 12.00-22.30

Food: Bar meals and snacks, À la carte

Credit Cards: Visa, Access, Delta, Switch, Amex, Diners

Accommodation: 5 double rooms all en suite

Facilities: Large beer garden, Car parking, Functions catered for

Entertainment: Regular live music and discos, Darts, Pool

Local Places of Interest/Activities:
Dartmoor National Park, Buckfast Butterfly and Dartmoor Otter Sancturay 5 miles, South Devon Railway 5 miles, Totnes 7 miles, Beaches 12 miles, Walking, Cycling, Horse riding, Fishing, Bird watching

128 The Plough Inn

Fore Street,
Ipplepen,
Devon TQ12 5RP
Tel: 01803 812118
Fax: 01803 812118

Directions:

From junction 31 on the M5 take the A38 and then the A380 to Newton Abbot. From the town take the A381 towards Totnes and, after approximately 4 miles, turn right following the signs for Ipplepen. Continue through the village and The Plough Inn can be found on the left.

Dating back to the 18th century, **The Plough Inn** is an attractive old inn that stands back from the road and has an attractive courtyard style front garden. Inside, the inn is equally pleasing and, despite having been renovated over the years, the character of the building remains very much in tact. There is a wealth of ancient beams holding up the low ceilings and, as well as the abundance of brassware, farm implements are on display in every available place. There is even an old bicycle hanging from one of the beams. Cosy and intimate, this is a charming place to visit at any time of year though in the winter the interior is warmed by the heat from the open fire and, in the summer, customers can enjoy the delightful secluded rear beer garden.

However, whilst ambience is an important aspect of any inn so is the food and drink on offer. The Plough Inn, under the management of landlord Eric Hales, is certainly one place where customers will not be disappointed. As well as the excellent range of real ales, beers, lagers, ciders, spirits and wines, the menu here is a tempting list of tasty dishes that range of fresh fish to steaks and mixed grills with both children and vegetarians amply catered for. This is also a village inn and a popular meeting place for those living in the area which gives The Plough a friendly and relaxed atmosphere that all can enjoy.

Opening Hours: Mon-Sat 11.30-23.00; Sun 12.00-22.30

Food: Bar meals and snacks, Traditional Sunday lunch

Credit Cards: None

Facilities: Beer garden, Car parking, Family room, Functions catered for

Entertainment: Occasional live entertainment, Regular quiz nights, Darts, Pool

Local Places of Interest/Activities: Compton Castle 2 miles, Bradley Manor 3 miles, Newton Abbot 4 miles, Totnes 5 miles, Torquay 5 miles, Paignton 6 miles, Walking, Cycling, Horse riding, Fishing, Sailing

Internet/Website: ipplepen.com

Port Light Inn

Bolberry Down,
near Salcombe,
Devon TQ7 3DY
Tel: 01548 561384
* or 07970 859992*
Fax: 01548 561668

Directions:

From Exeter take the A38 then the A381 to Kingsbridge. Follow the A381 towards Salcombe and, at Marlborough, take the right turn to Bolberry and The Port Light Hotel lies near the coast.

Situated on a particularly scenic stretch of Devon's southwest coast, **Port Light Hotel, Restaurant and Inn** is well placed for enjoying the area's best known feature - the sun setting over the sea. A former golf club house that also saw service during World War II as a radar station, Port Light has an enviable position, a unique cliff top position, nearly 450 feet above sea level, and it is surrounded by acres of National Trust coastal countryside.

An independent inn that is owned and personally run by Sean and Sonya Hassall, Port Light has gained an excellent reputation, including recognition in many leading guides, for the very high standard of their cuisine. Fresh local fish is the house speciality but the extensive menus also include a range of other interesting dishes that combine the traditional flavours with a Mediterranean twist. Served in either the welcoming bar area, the conservatory, or the attractive dining room, a meal here is a treat worth savouring and there is also the view from the window to remember. Finally, Port Light has one other welcome feature for dog lovers as a well behaved family pet can easily be accommodated here and Sean and Sonya even offer Doggie Breaks throughout the year.

Opening Hours: Mon-Sat 11.00-14.30, 18.30-23.00; Sun 11.00-14.30, 18.30-22.30

Food: Bar meals, À la carte in restaurant, conservatory and bar

Credit Cards: Visa, Access, Delta, Switch

Accommodation: 5 double rooms ensuite

Facilities: Children and pets welcome,

Disabled facilities, Large car park

Local Places of Interest/Activities:
Overbeck's Museum 2 miles, Walking, Sailing, Riding, Windsurfing, Golf

Internet/Website: www.portlight-salcombe.co.uk

130   The Post Inn

Exeter Road,
Whiddon Down,
Okehampton,
Devon EX20 2QT
Tel: 01647 231242

Directions:

From Exeter take the A30 towards Okehampton. At the Merrymeet roundabout turn left on to the A382 and The Post Inn lies 200 yards from the junction.

Built in the 16th century, **The Post Inn** is a charming old place with an interesting history. Originally one of a chain of roadside inns that supplied fresh horses to the King's couriers as they rode around the country taking his messages, the inns later became the obvious choice as posting stations when the Royal Post service began in 1635. Though the job of postmaster has long since been taken away from inn keepers, it was only in 1964 that this inn shortened its name from The Post Office Inn. Today, owners Graham and Miriam Short very much carry on the old traditions of an inn and, whilst no longer playing a part in the postal service, visitors can certainly expect excellent hospitality.

Cosy, comfortable and still with many of the building's original features, both the bar and dining area are charming places for a quiet drink, delicious meal and good conversation. As a freehouse, there is an ever changing selection of real ales, including those from local breweries, from the bar as well as all the usual beers, lagers and spirits. Wine drinkers also have plenty of choice and local wine too features on the list. The Post Inn has an equally fine reputation for its homecooked food and the steaks and game pies - the house specialities - are certainly well worth travelling to discover. Sunday lunch too is popular and, as this is Devon, cream teas also feature here.

Opening Hours: Mon-Sat 11.00-23.00; Sun 12.00-22.30

Food: Bar meals and snacks, Traditional Sunday lunches, Cream Teas

Credit Cards: Visa, Mastercard, Switch, Delta

Facilities: Beer Garden, Children's play area, Dogs welcome in bar

Entertainment: Theme nights, Quizzes

Local Places of Interest/Activities: On the edge of Dartmoor National Park, Finch Foundry 3 miles, Castle Drago 2 miles, Grimspound 7 miles, Walking, Birdwatching, Riding

The Ring O' Bells

131

West Alvington,
near Kingsbridge,
Devon TQ7 3PG
Tel: 01548 852437

Directions:
From Exeter take the A38 then the A381 to Salcombe. Follow the road through the town and The Ring O' Bells can be found 3/4 mile out of the town, up a hill.

Found high above the Kingsbridge estuary, **The Ring O' Bells** is an attractive Victorian inn with a large veranda from which there are glorious views over the interesting coastline. A warm and welcoming village local, with open fires and pictures and artefacts of historic local interest adorning the walls, the atmosphere of the inn ensures that everyone has a relaxing time whilst enjoying the exceptional hospitality. As well as the comfortable bar area, the ideal place for a pint or two of well kept real ale and a friendly conversation, The Ring O' Bells has an spacious restaurant.

Owner, George Holdsworth, who is very ably assisted by his wife Rosemary, is a chef and, since coming here in summer 1999, he has put The Ring O' Bells on the culinary map of south Devon. The delicious menus are displayed around in the inn on blackboards and they include a range of dishes, from fish to venison, but there is one overriding theme - all are homemade and all are prepared from the freshest local ingredients. The pudding menu, again all homemade, is a splendid list that includes many, many favourites. Prepared by George's mother, her pudding making skills are becoming a local legend. Finally, there is also a superb choice of accommodation, either at The Ring O' Bells itself or, just under a mile away, at George and Rosemary's country house.

Opening Hours: Mon-Sat 11.00-15.00, 18.00-23.00; Sun 12.00-22.30

Food: À la carte throughout

Credit Cards: Visa, Access, Delta, Switch

Accommodation: 4 double rooms all ensuite; further 4 double rooms all ensuite at proprietor's country residence

Facilities: Functions catered for, baby sitting service, packed lunches available

Local Places of Interest/Activities: Golf, Sailing, Watersports, Walking

Internet/Website:
brandonthedude@netscapeonline.co.uk

132 | The Rose and Crown

Market Street,
Yealmpton,
near Plymouth,
Devon PL8 2EB
Tel: 01752 880223

Directions:

From junction 31 on the M5 take the A38 towards Plymouth. At the Ugborough roundabout turn left on to the A3121 and then continue on the A379 towards Plymouth. The Rose and Crown lies in the heart of Yealmpton.

Dating back as far as the 15th century, **The Rose and Crown** is a splendid coaching inn with a fine Georgian front façade that stands in the heart of this pretty south Devon village. Added to and modernised over the years, the interior of the inn harks back to the days of horse travel and, as well as the oak panelling remaining, there are numerous old pictures of the area hanging from the walls. Well known locally for its excellent range of real ales - there is always a local brew on tap - there is also a good selections of wines available at the bar as well as all the usual drinks. A very popular place, where customers can also take advantage of the delightful beer garden, complete with purpose built children's play area, in the summer, landlords Carolyn and Ian McLellan have certainly made a success of their first venture into the licensing trade.

However, this is not all that The Rose and Crown has to offer customers as Carolyn and Ian have also worked hard to offer visitors a fine choice of food. The extensive exciting menus, for both lunchtime and in the evening, cover a wide variety of dishes including many old pub favourites as well as exotic Far Eastern curries, fresh fish and tantalising desserts. Taken in the bar or in the separate dining area, though the inn is large the fame of The Rose and Crown's cuisine has spread and booking a table is necessary to avoid disappointment.

Opening Hours: Mon-Thu 11.00-14.30, 17.30-23.00; Fri-Sat 11.00-23.00; Sun 12.00-22.30

Food: Bar meals and snacks, Table d'hote, À la carte

Credit Cards: Visa, Access, Delta, Switch

Accommodation: 1 family room, 1 double, 1 twin, 1 single

Facilities: Beer garden, Children's play area, Car parking, Functions catered for

Entertainment: Pool, Darts, Dominoes, Cards

Local Places of Interest/Activities: National Shire Horse Centre, Flete House 3 miles, Beach 3 miles, Plymouth 5 miles, Walking, Cycling, Horse riding, Fishing, Sailing

The Toby Jug Inn   133

Bickington,
near Newton Abbot,
Devon TQ12 6JZ
Tel: 01626 821278

Directions:

From Exeter take the A38 towards Plymouth and, at the Drum Bridges roundabout, turn on to the old A38 following the signs to Bickington. The Toby Jug Inn lies approximately 3 miles down the road.

Dating back to the 17th century **The Toby Jug Inn** is a large and imposing building that lies on the main road through the village. Looking very much like an old coaching inn, The Toby Jug is delightful and traditional old pub where welcoming hospitality is certainly order of the day. Full of character and charm, the interior, which is divided into the main bar, Stable bar and dining room, has stone floors, exposed stone walls and a mass of fascinating local memorabilia hanging from the walls and ceiling beams. There are, too, wonderful old fireplaces with beautiful rustic seating beside for those who wish to warm themselves after a day out in the glorious surrounding countryside.

Since coming here in 1997, host, Mike Barron, who believes in the tradition of English pubs and inns, has achieved his aims of creating the same. A place much loved by the locals, visitors here can enjoy the very best in both food and drink. The menu of freshly prepared homecooked food - there are two chefs slaving away in the kitchen - offers everything from a tasty sandwich to a three course gourmet meal and fresh local fish is the house speciality. With both children and dogs also welcome here, there is also a large beer garden for everyone to enjoy in the summer, The Toby Jug Inn is ideal for families and those looking for a real English country pub.

Opening Hours: Mon-Fri 11.00-15.00, 17.00-23.00; Sat and Sun all day (Sun until 22.30)

Food: Bar meals, snacks and à la carte in bar or dining room

Credit Cards: Visa, Access, Delta, Switch

Facilities: Beer garden, Small animal enclosure, Children and dogs welcome

Entertainment: Music evenings occasionally, Darts, Cards

Local Places of Interest/Activities: Dartmoor National Park 3 miles, Gorse Blossom Miniature Railway and Woodland Park 1½ miles, Walking, Golf, Fishing

134

Two Mile Oak

Totnes Road,
Abbotskerswell,
near Newton Abbot,
Devon TQ12 6DF
Tel: 01803 812411
Fax: 01803 812411

Directions:

From junction 31 on the M5 take the A38 and then the A380 to Newton Abbot. From the town take the A381 towards Totnes and the Two Mile Oak inn can be found just 2 miles from Newton Abbot.

Found in the heart of this picturesque village, the **Two Mile Oak** inn is a charming, long narrow white washed building that dates back to the 14th century. Formerly a coaching inn, it is still adjacent to the main Newton Abbot to Totnes road, this lovely establishment is surrounded by well kept gardens, with a patio area, and there are glorious views over the local farmland. Inside, this inn is equally delightful and many of the building's original features, such as the low beamed ceilings, open fires and wood floors, remain. Part of the cosy lounge bar has been converted from what was the coaching inn's horse barn and here too can be seen the old holding cell where prisoners on their journey to Dartmoor were kept whilst their guards rested.

Landlords Karen and Mark have been here since 1999 and, though a young and enthusiastic couple, their experience in the hotel trade has ensured that they manage the Two Mile Oak with comfortable ease. Well known locally for its excellent choice of cask conditioned ales, a board in the bar also shows details of the inn's wine list. Likewise, the daily specials to the pub's splendid menu are displayed on a chalkboard. The varied menu includes a wide range of choice, including several imaginative vegetarian choices, and such exotic delights as ostrich steaks also feature. A lively and friendly inn and a great favourite with local people, Karen and Mark arrange various events during the summer such as live music and outdoor barbecues.

Opening Hours: Mon-Sat 11.00-23.00; Sun 12.00-22.30

Food: Bar meals and snacks, À la carte, Traditional Sunday lunch, Barbecues in summer

Credit Cards: Visa, Access, Delta, Switch

Facilities: Beer garden, Car parking,

Children welcome

Entertainment: Occasional live music

Local Places of Interest/Activities: Bradley Manor 2 miles, Compton Castle 2 miles, Babbacombe Model Village 5 miles, Beach 5 miles, Torquay 5 miles, Walking, Cycling, Horse riding, Fishing, Swimming, Golf

White Thorn Inn 135

Shaugh Prior,
near Plymouth,
Devon PL7 5HA
Tel: 01752 839245

Directions:

From junction 31 on the M5 take the A38 towards Plymouth. At Plympton turn right on to the B3416 and then right again on to the B3147. Continue to Lee Moor and then turn left following the signs to Shaugh Prior and the White Thorn Inn lies in the centre of the village.

Situated on high ground and with panoramic views from its garden across the rolling moorland of Dartmoor, the **White Thorn Inn** is a large country pub that is hard to miss in this quiet Dartmoor village. Purpose built in 1932, the inn looks much more established than its years and the cottages next door were the original village pub. Despite its relatively new construction, the interior of the White Thorn Inn is surprisingly traditional and there are a wealth of beams that are typical of the mock Tudor style of the 1930s. To add further to the old fashioned and established air of the pub, gleaming brasses hang from the walls, along with a numerous pictures, and there is a log burning fire which provides not only a focal point but also a warm glow in winter.

Serving a good range of drinks from the bar, including several real ales, landlords Geoff and Anna Beddard also provide their customers with a delicious menu of homecooked dishes. Ranging from the usual bar snacks and sandwiches through to the sumptuous grills and fresh fish, the White Thorn specialities, which include curry, steak and Guiness pie and chilli, both the choice and the quality of the meals ensures that the inn remains a popular place for both locals and visitors. The traditional Sunday lunch is a particularly well attended feast and booking is usually essential. With good food and drink and the delightful garden, which includes plenty of safe climbing frames, swings and a Wendy house for the children, this must be the ideal family inn.

Opening Hours: Mon-Fri 11.30-15.00, 19.00-23.00; Sat 11.00-23.00; Sun 12.00-22.30

Food: Bar meals and snacks, Traditional Sunday lunch

Credit Cards: None

Facilities: Large beer garden, Car parking, Children's play area, Functions catered for

Entertainment: Darts

Local Places of Interest/Activities: Dartmoor National Park, Dartmoor Wildlife Park 4 miles, Plymouth 5 miles, Beaches 10 miles, Walking, Cycling, Horse riding, Fishing, Climbing, Bird watching

This page is left intentionally blank

5 East Devon

PLACES OF INTEREST:

Axminster 139
Budleigh Salterton 139
Colyton 140
Dalwood 140
Exeter 140
Exmouth 142
Honiton 142
Otterton 143

Ottery St Mary 143
Seaton 143
Shute 144
Sidmouth 144

PUBS AND INNS:

The Artful Dodger, St Davids 145
The Awliscombe Inn, Awliscombe 146
The Blacksmiths Arms, Plymtree 147
The Bowd Inn, Bowd Cross 148
The Butterleigh Inn, Cullompton 149
The Crown and Sceptre, Newton St Cyres 150
Dartmoor Railway Inn, Crediton 151
Fishponds House, Luppitt 152
The Lamb Inn, Silverton 153
New Fountain Inn, Whimple 154
The Old Court House, Chulmleigh 155

The Old Inn, Kilmington 156
The Passage House Inn, Topsham 157
The Prospect Inn, Exeter 158
The Royal Oak, Chawleigh 159
The Seven Stars, Winkleigh 160
The Sir Walter Raleigh, East Budleigh 161
The Three Tuns Inn, Silverton 162
The White Hart Inn, Woodbury 163
The White Lion Inn, Bradninch 164
The Wyndham Arms, Kentisbeare 165

The Hidden Inns of the West Country

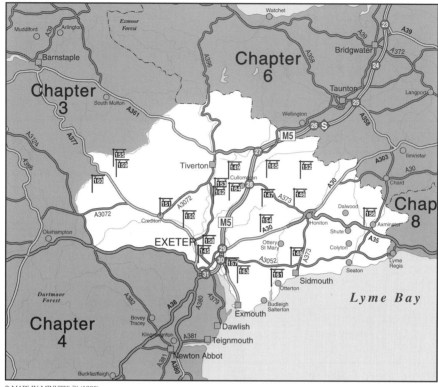

© MAPS IN MINUTES ™ (1998)

145	The Artful Dodger, St Davids		156	The Old Inn, Kilmington
146	The Awliscombe Inn, Awliscombe		157	The Passage House Inn, Topsham
147	The Blacksmiths Arms, Plymtree		158	The Prospect Inn, Exeter
148	The Bowd Inn, Bowd Cross		159	The Royal Oak, Chawleigh
149	The Butterleigh Inn, Cullompton		160	The Seven Stars, Winkleigh
150	The Crown and Sceptre, Newton St Cyres		161	The Sir Walter Raleigh, East Budleigh
151	Dartmoor Railway Inn, Crediton		162	The Three Tuns Inn, Silverton
152	Fishponds House, Luppitt		163	The White Hart Inn, Woodbury
153	The Lamb Inn, Silverton		164	The White Lion Inn, Bradninch
154	New Fountain Inn, Whimple		165	The Wyndham Arms, Kentisbeare
155	The Old Court House, Chulmleigh			

Please note all cross references refer to page numbers

No less a traveller than Daniel Defoe thought the landscape of East Devon the finest in the world. Acres of rich farmland are watered by the rivers Axe, Otter and Madford, and narrow, winding lanes lead to villages that are as picturesque and interesting as any in England. Steep-sided hills rise towards the coastline where a string of elegant Regency resorts remind the visitor that this part of the coast was one of the earliest to be developed to satisfy the early 19th century craze for sea bathing. Three river valleys, those of the Axe, the Sid and the Otter, cut through the hills of east Devon to meet the sea at Lyme Bay. They provide the only openings in the magnificent 20 mile long stretch of rugged cliffs and rocky beaches. Even today, the only way to explore most of this part of the coast is on foot along the magnificent South West Coast Path.

In the early 1800s, the Prince Regent's fad for sea bathing brought an influx of comparatively affluent visitors in search of healthy relaxation. Their numbers were augmented by others whose European travels had been rendered impossible by Napoleon's domination of the Continent. Between them, they transformed modest little coastal towns into fashionable resorts, imbuing them with an indefinable "gentility" which still lives on in the elegant villas, peaceful gardens and wide promenades.

PLACES OF INTEREST

AXMINSTER

This little town grew up around the junction of two important Roman roads, the Fosse and the Icknield, and was important in medieval times for its Minster beside the River Axe. Its name has entered the language as the synonym for a very superior kind of floor-covering which first appeared in the early 1750s. Wandering around London's Cheapside market, an Axminster weaver named Thomas Whitty was astonished to see a huge Turkish carpet, 12 yards long and 8 yards wide. Returning to the sleepy little market town where he was born, Thomas spent months puzzling over the mechanics of producing such a seamless piece of work. By 1755 he had solved the problem, and on Midsummer's Day that year the first of these luxurious carpets was revealed to the world. The time and labour involved was so prodigious that the completion of each carpet was celebrated by a procession to St Mary's Church and a ringing peal of bells. Ironically, one distinguished purchaser of an Axminster carpet was the Sultan of Turkey who in 1800 paid the colossal sum of £1,000 for a particularly fine specimen. But the inordinately high labour costs involved in producing such exquisite hand-tufted carpets crippled Whitty's company. In 1835, their looms were sold to a factory at Wilton. That was the end of Axminster's pre-eminence in the market for top-quality carpets, but echoes of those glorious years still reverberate. **St Mary's Church** must be the only house of worship in Christendom whose floor is covered with a richly-woven carpet, and a new factory in Woodmead Road is now busy making 20th century Axminster carpets. Visitors are welcome.

Running off Axminster's market square is Silver Street where Whitty's carpet factory stood until it was destroyed by fire in 1827. His house, which stands close by, survived and is now the Law Chamber.

BUDLEIGH SALTERTON

With its trim Victorian villas, broad promenade and a spotlessly clean beach flanked by 500 foot high red sandstone cliffs, Budleigh Salterton retains its 19th century atmosphere of a genteel resort. Victorian tourists "of the better sort" noted with approval that the 2 mile long beach was of pink shingle rather than sand. (Sand attracted the rowdier kind of holiday-maker). The steeply-shelving beach was another deterrent, and the sea here is still a place for paddling rather than swimming.

One famous Victorian visitor was the celebrated artist Sir John Everett Millais, who stayed during the summer of 1870 in the curiously-shaped house called **The Octagon**. It was beside the beach here that he painted his most famous picture, *The Boyhood of Raleigh*, using his two sons and a local ferryman as the models.

The name Budleigh Salterton derives from the salt pans at the mouth of the River Otter which brought great prosperity to the town during the Middle Ages. The little port was then busy with ships loading salt and wool, but by 1450 the estuary had silted up and the salt pans flooded.

COLYTON

This is a very appealing small town of narrow winding streets and interesting stone houses. Throughout its long history, Colyton has been an important agricultural and commercial centre with its own corn mill, tannery, sawmill and iron foundry.

Many of the older buildings are grouped around the part-Norman **Church of St Andrew**, a striking building with an unusual 15th century lantern tower, and a Saxon cross brilliantly reconstructed after its broken fragments were

Church of St Andrew, Colyton

retrieved from the tower where they had been used as building material. Nearby is the **Vicarage** of 1529, and the **Old Church House**, a part-medieval building enlarged in 1612 and used

as a grammar school until 1928.

Look out also for the **Great House** which was built on the road to Colyford by a wealthy Elizabethan merchant. Half a mile to the north of Colyton, **Colcombe Castle** contains some exceptional 16th and 17th century remains, including an impressive kitchen hearth.

DALWOOD

Dalwood's **Loughwood Meeting House** is one of the earliest surviving Baptist chapels in the country. When it was built in the 1650s the site was hidden by dense woodland, for the Baptists were a persecuted sect who could only congregate in out of the way locations. Under its quaint thatched roof, this charming little building contains a simple whitewashed interior with early 18th century pulpits and pews. The chapel was in use until 1833, then languished for many years until it was acquired by the National Trust in 1969. It is now open all year round with admission by voluntary donation.

EXETER

The city stands on a rise above the River Exe at what was once its lowest fording point. Protected by valleys to the north and south and by the Haldon Hills to the west, a settlement has existed on this important strategic site since the days of the Celts. The ancient Romans made Isca their southwestern stronghold, capturing it in around AD 56 and constructing a military fort which they expanded into a city over the next century. Around this new regional capital, they built a massive defensive wall in the shape of an irregular rectangle within which the city remained right up until the 18th century.

During the Dark Ages that followed the departure of the Roman legions in the 5th century, Exeter was twice occupied by the Vikings. William I then captured the city in 1086 following a siege that lasted 18 days. To defend their new conquest, the Normans built **Rougemont Castle**, the gatehouse and tower of which can still be seen in Rougemont Gardens to the north of the city centre.

The finest Norman legacy in Exeter, however, is undoubtedly **St Peter's Cathedral**, which stands within its own attractive close to the west of Southernhay Gardens. The original structure was built in the 11th and 12th centuries; however, with the exception of the two sturdy tow-

Exeter Cathedral

Shearmen. Inside there is some exceptional carved panelling, a collection of rare silver, and a remarkable pair of fulling shears weighing over 25 pounds and measuring over 4 feet.

Exeter's importance as a centre of the wool trade developed throughout the Tudor and Elizabethan periods, with raw fleeces, spun yard and finished cloth being traded in the market in considerable quantities. Woollen products of all kinds were exported to the major cities of Europe.

Following a long period of decline which began in the mid-19th century, Exeter Quay underwent a dramatic revival in the 1980s when many of its old warehouses and maritime buildings were renovated and reopened as restaurants, shops and commercial units. The Custom House, one of the most handsome 17th century buildings in Exeter (and one of the first to be constructed of brick), can be found here.

ers, the body of the cathedral was demolished in 1260 and rebuilt over the next 90 years. A remarkable astronomical clock can be found on the north wall of the transept. Dating from around 1400, its twin blue and gold faces indicate the phases of the moon as well as the time of day; its inscription, translated from the Latin, reads "The hours perish and are reckoned to our account."

In addition to the cathedral, the centre of Exeter once contained over 30 churches, seven monasteries and several other ecclesiastical institutions. St Nicholas' Priory, an exceptional example of a small Norman priory, is now an interesting museum where visitors can view the original prior's cell, the 15th century kitchen and the imposing central hall with its vaulted ceiling and solid Norman pillars. One of Exeter's most rewarding attractions is its unique labyrinth of **Underground Passages**, which were built by the cathedral clergy in medieval times to regulate the water supply and provide safe passage between the city's many ecclesiastical houses. Guided tours around this fascinating subterranean world are available all year round and are strongly recommended.

Exeter's most impressive non-ecclesiastical medieval building can be found in the partly pedestrianised High Street. The **Guildhall** was built by the powerful craftsmen's guilds in the late 15th century, its splendid portico having been added a century later. On occasion, the main chamber is still used for formal meetings of the city burghers, making this one of the oldest municipal buildings in Britain still in use. One a smaller scale, the **Tucker's Hall** was built in 1471 for one of the city's most powerful wool guilds - the Company of Weavers, Fullers and

The Customs House, Exeter Quay

By the time it was completed in 1681, large quantities of sugar, rice, tea and other commodities were being landed at the quay, requiring an official presence of some consequence. The Custom House was therefore constructed to an impressive standard, with fine plasterwork ceilings and balustraded staircases which are worth seeing. Visitors are admitted by arrangement with HM Customs and Excise, though casual visitors are generally welcomed. Exeter Quay is also the location of the internationally renowned **Maritime Museum**, the world's largest collection of boats. Exhibits include an Arab dhow, a reed boat from Lake Titicaca in South America, and the *Cygnet*, an eccentric rowing dinghy which was used to ferry guests to wild parties on her even more eccentric sister vessel, the *Swan*.

142

The character of modern Exeter was much altered by the effects of Second World War bombing, carried out, it was claimed, in revenge for Allied attacks on the historic city of Lubeck. The devastating raids of May 1942 destroyed much of the medieval and Georgian city. Large areas of the city had to be rebuilt in the 1950s, often in the form of modern shopping centres, though it is amazing that so many buildings did survive the raids.

EXMOUTH

Exmouth, with its 2 miles of seafront and its sandy beaches, has attracted visitors since the early 18th century. The oldest seaside resort in Devon, even before the arrival of the railway

Exmouth Harbour

in 1861 the wealthy and fashionable were coming here in large numbers to reap the benefits of the sea air and saltwater bathing.

Originally a small fishing port formed from the parishes of Littleham and Withycombe Regis, the population of Exmouth rose dramatically between 1800 and 1900. Much of this development was inspired by the Rolle family, owners of Littleham Manor, who were responsible for constructing some of the town's most elegant late Georgian terraces. One of the finest seafront promenades on the south coast runs along the great sea wall, which was built in stages between 1840 and 1915.

HONITON

Honiton is the ''capital'' of east Devon, a delightful little town in the valley of the River Otter and the ''gateway to the far southwest''. It was once a major stopping place on the Fosse Way, the great Roman road that struck diagonally across England from Lincoln to Exeter. Honiton's position on the main traffic artery

to Devon and Cornwall brought it considerable prosperity, and its broad, ribbon-like High Street, almost two miles long, testifies to the town's busy past. By the 1960s, this busyness had deteriorated into appalling traffic congestion during the holiday season. Fortunately, the construction of a by-pass in the 1970s allowed Honiton to resume its true character as an attractive market town.

Although Honiton was the first town in Devon to manufacture serge cloth, the town is much better known for a more delicate material, Honiton lace. Lace-making was introduced to east Devon by Flemish immigrants who arrived here during the reign of Elizabeth I. By the end of the 17th century, some 5,000 people were engaged in the industry, most of them working from their own homes making fine "bone" lace by hand. Children as young as five were sent to "lace schools" where they received a rudimentary education in the three Rs, and a far more intensive instruction in the intricacies of lace-making.

Almost wiped out by the arrival of machine-made lace in the late 1700s, the industry was given a new lease of life when Queen Victoria insisted upon Honiton lace for her wedding dress and created a new fashion for lace that persisted throughout the century. The traditional material is still made on a small scale in the town and can be found on sale in local shops, and on display in **Allhallows Museum**. This part-15th century building served as a school for some 300 years but is now an interesting local museum housing a unique collection of traditional lace and also, during the season, giving daily demonstrations of lacemaking.

Allhallows Schoolroom was one of the few old buildings to survive a series of devastating fires in the mid-1700s. However, that wholesale destruction had the fortunate result that the new buildings were gracious Georgian residences and Honiton still retains the pleasant, unhurried atmosphere of a prosperous 18th century coaching town.

Another building which escaped the flames unscathed was **Marwood House** in the High Street. It was built in 1619 by the second son of Thomas Marwood, one of Queen Elizabeth's many physicians. Thomas achieved great celebrity when he managed to cure the Earl of Essex after all others had failed. (He received his Devonshire estate as a reward.) Thomas was equally successful in preserving his own health, living to the extraordinary age of 105.

Some buildings on the outskirts of the town are worth a mention. **St Margaret's Hospital**, to the west, was founded in the middle ages as a refuge for lepers who were denied entry to the town itself. Later, in the 16th century, this attractive thatched building was reconstructed as an almshouse. To the east, an early-19th century toll house known as **Copper Castle** can be seen. The castellated building still retains its original iron toll gates. And just a little further east, on Honiton Hill, stands the massive folly of the **Bishop's Tower**, erected in 1842 and once part of Bishop Edward Copplestone's house.

OTTERY ST MARY

The glory of Ottery St Mary is its magnificent 14th century **Church of St Mary**. From the outside, St Mary's looks part mini-Cathedral, part Oxford college. Both impressions are justified since, when Bishop Grandisson commissioned the building in 1337, he stipulated that

Church of St Mary

it should be modelled on his own cathedral at Exeter. He also wanted it to be "a sanctuary for piety and learning", so accommodation for 40 scholars was provided. The interior is just as striking. The church's medieval treasures include a brilliantly-coloured altar screen, canopied tombs, and a 14th century astronomical clock showing the moon and the planets which still functions with its original machinery.

Ottery's vicar during the mid-18th century was the Rev John Coleridge, whose 13th child grew up to become the celebrated poet, Samuel Taylor Coleridge. The family home near the church has since been demolished, but in one of his poems Samuel recalls:

"my sweet birth-place, and the old church-tower Whose bells, the poor man's only music, rang

From morn to evening, all the hot Fair-day."

A bronze plaque in the churchyard wall honours Ottery's most famous son. It shows his profile, menaced by the albatross that features in his best-known poem, *The Rime of the Ancient Mariner.*

It's a delight to wander around the narrow, twisting lanes that lead up from the River Otter, admiring the fine Georgian buildings amongst which is an old wool manufactory by the riverside, a dignified example of early industrial architecture. An especially interesting time to visit Ottery is on the Saturday closest to November 5th. The little town's Guy Fawkes celebrations include a time-honoured, and rather alarming, tradition of rolling barrels of flaming tar through the narrow streets.

OTTERTON

Opposite Otterton, on the western bank of the River Otter, is **Bicton Park**. The park is best known for its landscaped gardens which were laid out in the 1730s by Henry Rolle to a plan by André Le Nôtre, the designer of Versailles. There is also a formal Italian garden, a remarkable palm house known as The Dome, a world-renowned collection of pine trees, and a lake complete with an extraordinary summer house, "The Hermitage". Its outside walls are covered with thousands of tiny wooden shingles, each one individually pinned on so they look like the scales of an enormous fish. Inside, the floors are made from deer's knucklebones. The Hermitage was built by Lady Louise Rolle in 1839 as an exotic summer-house; any occupation during the winter would have been highly inadvisable since the chimney was made of oak.

SEATON

This small seaside town, before it developed as a resort, lay half a mile inland. Attractively framed by some impressive coastal scenery, much of the architecture is Victorian and Edwardian, though the parish church of St Gregory dates from the 14th century. Perhaps the most noteworthy feature of the town is the **Seaton Tramway**, a 3 mile stretch of track running along the western bank of the River Axe to Colyton. Operated by an enthusiastic team of devotees, many of them volunteers, the open tramcars are popular with holiday makers in summer and birdwatchers in winter; the latter

144

benefit from being able to glide along the estuary, seemingly without causing

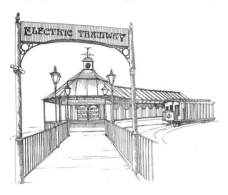

Seaton Tramway

disturbance to the local feathered population.

SHUTE

Shute Barton (National Trust) is an exceptional example of a medieval manor house. Dating from the 1380s, only two wings of the original building have survived, but they include some remarkably impressive features such as the Great Hall with its massive beamed ceiling, and the ancient kitchen with a huge range capable of roasting an ox whole. Entry is by way of a Tudor gatehouse. Shute Barton was owned by the Pole family, a local dynasty which is commemorated by some grand monuments in St Michael's Church, amongst them an overbearing memorial to Sir William Pole which depicts the Master of the Household to Queen Anne standing on a pedestal and dressed in full regalia. More appealing is the 19th century sculptured panel, seven feet high and framed in alabaster, which shows Margaret Pole greeting her three little daughters at the gates of heaven.

SIDMOUTH

Sidmouth's success, like that of many other English resorts, had much to do with Napoleon Bonaparte. Barred from their favoured Continental resorts by the Emperor's conquest of Europe, the leisured classes were forced to find diversion and entertainment within their own island fortress. At the same time, sea bathing had suddenly become fashionable so these years

were a boom time for the south coast, even as far west as Sidmouth which until then had been a poverty-stricken village dependent on fishing.

Sidmouth's spectacular position at the mouth of the River Sid, flanked by dramatic red cliffs soaring to over 500 feet and with a broad pebbly beach, assured the village's popularity with the newcomers. A grand Esplanade was constructed, lined with handsome Georgian houses, and between 1800 and 1820 Sidmouth's population doubled as the aristocratic and well-to-do built substantial "cottages" in and around the town. Many have since been converted into impressive hotels such as the **Beach House**, painted strawberry pink and white, and the **Royal Glen** which had been the residence of the Duke of Kent. The Duke came here in 1819 in an attempt to escape his numerous creditors, and it was here that his infant daughter, Victoria, had her first view of the sea. Later, as Queen, she presented a stained-glass window to the parish church in memory of her father.

A stroll around the town reveals a wealth of attractive Georgian and early Victorian buildings; in all, Sidmouth can boast nearly 500 listed buildings. Curiously, the Victorians seemed incapable of creating architecturally interesting churches and Sidmouth's two 19th century churches are no exception. But it's worth seeking out the curious structure known as the **Old Chancel**, a glorious hotch-potch of styles using bits and pieces salvaged from the old parish church and elsewhere, amongst them a priceless window of medieval stained glass.

Also well worth a visit is **Sidmouth Museum**, near the seafront, which provides a vivid presentation of the Victorian resort, along with such curiosities as an albatross's swollen foot once used as a tobacco pouch. There's an interesting collection of local prints, a costume gallery and a display of fine lace. One of the most striking exhibits in the museum is the "Long Picture" by Hubert Cornish which is some 8 feet long and depicts the whole of Sidmouth seafront as it was around 1814.

Demure though it remains, Sidmouth undergoes a transformation in the first week of August each year when it plays host to the International Folklore, Dance and Song Festival, a cosmopolitan event which attracts a remarkable variety of Morris Dancers, Folk Singers and even Clog Dancers from around the world.

The Artful Dodger | 145

Red Cow Village,
St Davids,
Exeter
Devon EX4 4AX
Tel: 01392 274754

Directions:

From junction 29 on the M5 follow the signs for St Davids Station and then take the A377 towards Crediton. The Artful Dodger lies on the outskirts of the city.

Situated on a corner, along the main road out of Exeter towards Crediton, **The Artful Dodger** is a handsome old building that, with its long white painted frontage, is hard to miss. Built in the mid 18th century, or possibly earlier, this attractive town inn, unusually, has a large rear beer garden that makes it a place well worth making for particularly during the summer. Very much a family run inn, today's landlords, Troy and Jon have been here since 1997 and they bought the property from Troy's mother who was here from 1988.

Although Jon is originally from Australia, the beers served here are truly English and, as well as the selection of rotating real ales, there is also draught cider and a fine wine list. The menu of interesting and tasty dishes, that are served throughout the day, not only includes traditional pub favourites but also create your own pizzas and juicy burgers and then there is always the specials board. An attractive, warm and welcoming atmosphere makes this a delightful town inn that is well worth seeking out and, whilst the open plan design of the interior is modern, many of the building's original features and the tradition of offering excellent hospitality, remain.

Opening Hours: Mon-Sat 11.00-23.00; Sun 12.00-22.30

Food: Bar meals and snacks

Credit Cards: None

Facilities: Beer garden, Limited car parking

Entertainment: Occasional live music, Darts, Pool

Local Places of Interest/Activities:
Historic sights of Exeter, Devon and Exeter Racecourse 5 miles, Dartmoor National Park 5 miles, South Devon coast 10 miles, Walking, Cycling, Horse riding, Fishing, Bird watching

146   The Awliscombe Inn

Awliscombe,
Honiton,
Devon EX14 3PJ
Tel: 01404 42554

Directions:
From junction 28 on
the M5 take the A373
towards Honiton and
The Awliscombe Inn
lies 8 miles down this
road.

In the heart of the lovely village of Awliscombe is **The Awliscombe Inn**, a marvellous old place, full of history and character, that has graced the village for over 200 years. Clad in ivy and with a large beer garden and a secluded patio courtyard, this is the perfect country inn. Bought, in March 1999, by Angela Read, a charming lady with over 20 years experience at the top level of management, the visitors' book that she keeps confirms that this is an establishment of excellence.

The large main bar, with its warm glow from logs burning in the inglenook fireplace, is a cosy and comfortable place for a drink. And there is indeed a fine selection including cask ale, keg beer, spirits and a worldwide range of wine by the glass or bottle. Like the bar, the two dining rooms - one nonsmoking the other smoking - are also decorated and furnished in a manner in keeping with the age and style of this rustic inn. Here, visitors can treat themselves to a wonderful meal of good country pub fare all homecooked, from fresh produce, by Angela and her chef, Robert Avery. A delightful mix of traditional with a hint of modern cuisine, the menu changes regularly depending on the seasons and what was found at the local fish market. Finally, the inn's equally superb accommodation is very much in the same style as the rest of The Awliscombe Inn - professional, friendly and relaxed. It is also private from the pub and so will suit those with children.

Opening Hours: Mon-Sat 11.00-14.30, 18.00-23.00; Sun 12.00-15.00, 19.00-22.30

Food: Lunches and dinners

Credit Cards: Visa, Mastercard, Switch, Delta

Accommodation: 1 double room ensuite, 1 twin room ensuite

Facilities: Beer garden, Patio courtyard, Skittle alley used for private functions

Entertainment: Pool

Local Places of Interest/Activities: Walking, Birdwatching, Honiton 1½ miles

The Blacksmiths Arms 147

Plymtree,
near Cullompton,
Devon EX15 2JU
Tel: 01884 277474

Directions:

Take junction 28 off the M5 on to the A373 Honiton road, turn right just after Dulford and The Blacksmiths Arms can be found in the centre of Plymtree.

Renowned for being one of the longest villages in the country Plymtree is an attractive old settlement, with a Saxon church, that is also home to **The Blacksmiths Arms.** Originally built in the 16th century though much added to later, this splendid inn's imposing Georgian façade is hard to miss. Still very much a centre for village life, the pub's large open bar, complete with its original fireplace, has photographs of Plymtree's cricket and skittles teams up on the wall. When not involved in a game, the teams congregate here to enjoy a pint or two of the pub's excellent selection of real ales, keg beers and lagers as well as celebrate their wins and commiserate their losses.

However, hosts Liz and John also offer a warm welcome to visitors who are sure to enjoy the friendly, relaxed atmosphere of this traditional village inn. As well as the excellent reputation the couple have gained for their marvellous hospitality since arriving here in May 1999, Liz is justly proud of the pub's food for which it is becoming increasingly well respected. Freshly prepared from local produce the menu of traditional English dishes is all homecooked and, particularly at Sunday lunch time, it is advisable to book. As a place to meet, drink and eat, The Blacksmiths Arms is second to none and, along with the regular music and quiz nights, there is always something to look forward to.

Opening Hours: Mon 18.00-23.00; Tue-Sat 12.00-23.00; Sun 12.00-22.30

Food: Meals available all day, Traditional Sunday lunches

Credit Cards: None

Facilities: Beer garden, Function and meeting room

Entertainment: Skittles alley, Boules piste, Quizzes, Live music

Local Places of Interest/Activities: Honiton 8 miles, Walking, Cycling, Horse riding

148 The Bowd Inn

Bowd Cross,
Sidmouth,
Devon EX10 0ND
Tel: 01395 513328
Fax: 01395 516362

Directions:

From Exeter take the A3052 towards Sidmouth and The Bowd Inn lies at the crossroads with the B3176 Sidmouth road in the village of Bowd Cross.

Situated on the main road between London and Penzance, **The Bowd Inn**, which is named after this small hamlet and is derived from the Old English meaning 'under the hill', has been offering travellers excellent hospitality for many years. Built in 1651, originally as a series of farm buildings, today this splendid Grade II listed inn is as attractive a place as anyone could wish to find. Hard to miss with its traditional thatched roof, The Bowd Inn has developed in recent years into a charming old hostelry that is not only a popular meeting place for the locals but also a delightful place much loved by holidaymakers new to the area.

As charming and full of character inside as the impressive exterior would suggest, hosts Richard and Shirley, who have been here since 1995, have gained an enviable reputation for the warm and friendly atmosphere here. The superb decor, low ceilings, log fires, cosy snugs and traditional flag stone floors all add to the informal air of this wonderful old inn. With an extensive cellar where there is not only a fine choice of real ales, lagers, beers and ciders but also an extensive range of wines, many, even champagne, served by the glass, this is certainly a place for a quiet drink and a chat. However, what draws many to this lovely place is the imaginative homecooked menu of old favourites and modern delights that are conjured up in the kitchen at both lunchtime and in the evening and served in the attractive and comfortable Library styled dining area.

Opening Hours: Summer - Mon-Sat 11.00-23.00; Sun 12.00-22.30. Winter hours flexible

Food: Bar meals and snacks served all day

Credit Cards: Visa, Mastercard, Amex, Diners, Switch, Delta

Facilities: Beer garden, Terrace, Children's play area

Entertainment: Live music every two weeks, Darts, Dominoes, Shove Ha'penny, Board games

Local Places of Interest/Activities: Sidmouth and the coast 2 miles, Donkey Sanctuary 4 miles, Sidbury Castle Iron Age hill fort 4 miles, Walking, Riding

The Butterleigh Inn 149

Butterleigh,
Cullompton,
Devon EX15 1PN
Tel: 01884 855407
Fax: 01884 855600

Directions:

Take junction 28 from M5 into Cullompton, turn right at the Manor Hotel crossroads, follow the signs to Butterleigh and The Butterleigh Inn lies in the village centre.

Found in the charming countryside setting, set back off the main road through the village, **The Butterleigh Inn** is a splendid 400 year old traditional Devonshire cob building that has been a delightful country inn for many years. Purchased by Jenny Hill in 1998 and managed by her with the help of her brother Andy and his partner Deirdre, this is very much a friendly family inn where both locals and visitors are sure to enjoy the relaxed and homely atmosphere. Full of character, the inn has several cosy, small bar areas, each of which offers the perfect place for customers to settle down and enjoy some fine hospitality and good conversation. The feeling of time having stood still is enhanced by the flag stone floors, ancient fireplaces and the interesting array of local memorabilia decorating the walls. Whilst customers can expect a good selection of real ales - Cotleigh Brewery is always available - kegs beers, lagers and ciders, there is also a fine range of worldwide wines from which to choose. Well known for their food, The Butterleigh Inn has a frequently changing menu of homemade dishes that range from potato skins filled with chilli beef and vast Ploughman's lunches to steaks and interesting vegetarian dishes. Add to this the daily specials board and the mouthwatering pudding menu and everyone is sure to find the perfect dishes for a tasty and satisfying lunch or dinner. Finally, for glorious summer days, the inn has an attractive and secluded beer garden surrounded by the hills of Devon.

Opening Hours: Mon-Sat 12.00-14.30, 18.00-23.00 (Fri 17.00-23.00); Sun 12.00-15.00, 19.00-22.30

Food: Bar meals and snacks 12.00-14.00, 19.00-21.45 (Sun until 21.30)

Credit Cards: Visa, Mastercard, Switch, Solo

Facilities: Beer garden, Children under 14 lunchtimes only, Dogs welcome

Entertainment: Darts, Cribbage, Cards, Shove ha'penny, Chess, Dominoes

Local Places of Interest/Activities: Bickleigh Castle and Bickleigh Mill Visitor Centre 3 miles, Tiverton 3 miles, Fursdon 4 miles

150 The Crown and Sceptre

Newton St Cyres,
Exeter,
Devon EX5 5DA
Tel: 01392 851278

Directions:
From Exeter take the A396 then the A377 towards Crediton. The Crown and Sceptre lies 3 miles along the A377.

Lying in the pretty village of Newton St Cyres, which was mentioned in the Domesday Book, **The Crown and Sceptre** is a lovely old coaching inn dating back to the early 19th century. Although the inn has seen many changes over the years, this is still a place where both locals and visitors receive the very best of hospitality from Ann Franklin, Kay Rigg and their staff. Partners in this new venture, Ann, a nurse, and Kay, a trained chef, came here in July 1999 and from the start they have ensured the success of this warm and friendly inn. Comfortable and cosy inside, with real fires in the winter, there is a charming beer garden for the summer, with a patio, feature bridge over a stream and a children's play area.

The restaurant, which is as atmospheric as the rest of the inn, provides the perfect setting in which to enjoy the delicious dishes that are all prepared under Kay's watchful eye. And, with the world famous Quickes Farm, producers of Quickes Traditional Mature Cheddar, in the village, the ploughman's lunch is a must. The bar not only stocks a good selection of wines with which to complement a meal but there are also several real ales, keg beers, lagers and all the usual spirits from which to choose. Finally, another popular addition to life at the pub made by Ann and Kay are the live music evenings on most Fridays - featuring many different styles, from jazz to steel bands, which certainly fill the bar.

Opening Hours: Mon-Fri 11.00-15.00, 17.00-23.00; Sat 11.00-23.00; Sun 12.00 - 22.30

Food: Bar meals and snacks all day, Traditional Sunday lunches

Credit Cards: Visa, Mastercard, Switch

Facilities: Beer garden, Children's play area

Entertainment: Live music, Quizzes

Local Places of Interest/Activities: Exeter 4 miles, Walking, Riding, Beach 11 miles

Dartmoor Railway Inn | 151

Station Road,
Crediton,
Devon EX17 3BX
Tel: 01363 772489

Directions:

From Exeter take the A377 to Crediton and The Dartmoor Railway Inn lies on the edge of the town.

As well as being the birthplace of one of the very few Britons to become fully fledged saints - St Boniface was born here in AD 680 and the town is twinned with Dokkum in Friesland, on the outskirts of which Boniface was murdered, and Fulda in Germany, where he is buried - Crediton is also the home of **The Dartmoor Railway Inn**. Built in 19th century, at the same time as the London and South Western Railway reached the town, this is a typical railway hotel of its day. Solid and imposing from the outside, once inside visitors will find cosy log fireplaces, an attractive decor and a comfortable and relaxing atmosphere in which to enjoy the delights of this inn. Hosts, Jim and Carol came here in March 1999 but this is actually Jim's second spell at The Dartmoor Railway as he was its landlord for six years in the 1970s.

A friendly and welcoming couple, with 30 years experience in the trade, Jim and Carol are the driving force behind the success of the inn. With a well stocked cellar and a splendid range of real ales, keg beers and ciders on tap customers are sure to be able to enjoy their favourite tipple whilst engaging in conversation - the key entertainment at The Dartmoor Railway Inn. Jim's excellent homecooked menu of fresh fish dishes, soups made from secret recipes, succulent steaks and the ever changing specials board has also put the inn on the culinary map of Devon. Very much a popular choice with those in the area, the Sunday carvery lunch of roast beef grown locally (Jim knows the farmer) is a treat not to be missed.

Opening Hours: Mon-Sat 12.00-15.00, 18.00-23.00; Sun 12.00-15.00, 19.00-22.30

Food: Bar meals available all day , Traditional Sunday lunches, à la carte, evening meals

Credit Cards: Visa, Mastercard, Switch, Delta

Accommodation: 2 double rooms, 1 twin room, all with shared bathroom

Facilities: Patio garden, Skittles alley used for functions

Local Places of Interest/Activities: The Tarka Line lies opposite the inn, Local church with memorial to St Boniface and Sir Henry Redvers Buller (hero of the Relief of Ladysmith)

152 Fishponds House

Luppitt,
Honiton,
Devon EX14 0SH
Tel: 01404 891287/891358
Fax: 01404 891109

Directions:

Leave the M5 at junc 25 and from Taunton, take the B3170 signposted Corfe and Trull. Take the right turn signed Smeatharpe. Through the village, take the right turn signposted Fishponds House, which is 500 yards on the right.

Built in 1201 for the Lake Keeper who provided fish to the monks at Dunkeswell Abbey, **Fishponds House** is one of the area's best kept secrets. Hidden away in some 45 acres of grounds this ancient house, which has been added to over the years, is now an attractive and delightful inn offering the very best in the hospitality. The large open bar, with its stone walls, exposed beams and inglenook fireplace, has been stylishly decorated to show off the original character of this old building. Likewise, the separate restaurant provides the perfect setting for an intimate dinner. Here, guests can enjoy a delicious menu of both traditional and modern English food accompanied by wine from the comprehensive worldwide list. Alternatively, less formal, but equally well prepared and presented, there is a menu of tasty snacks and lighter meals served in the bar which is also popular for its good range of local real ales.

Accommodation too is high on the list of priorities at Fishponds House and to ensure that guests make the most of their stay here manager, Anne-Marie Spalding ensures a friendly, welcoming atmosphere in which to relax.

Opening Hours: All day during the summer; Winter - Mon-Sat 11.00-15.00, 17.30-23.00; Sun 12.00-15.00, 19.00-22.30

Food: Restaurant for lunch and dinner

Credit Cards: Visa, Mastercard, Switch

Accommodation: 3 double rooms, 9 twin rooms, 2single rooms

Facilities: Fishing, Tennis court, Pets welcome by prior arrangement, Functions catered for

Local Places of Interest/Activities: Dunkeswell Abbey ruins in the village, Blackdown Hills, Walking, Riding, Fishing

The Lamb Inn
153

47 Fore Street,
Silverton,
Devon EX5 4HZ
Tel: 01392 860272

Directions:

Take junction 28 off the M5 into Cullompton then take the B3181 following signs to Killerton House. Through Bradninch follow the signs to Silverton and The Lamb Inn lies 3 miles along the road.

Found in this pleasant village, that is so well placed for many of east Devon's attractions and glorious countryside, lies the 300 year old **Lamb Inn**. Purchased, in February 1999 by Alan and Jane Isaac, they couple completely refurbished the interior of this old inn before opening their doors. However, non of this delightful building's original character and charm has been lost - a superb inglenook fireplace adds warmth of a cold night, there are slate floors throughout the main bar and dining room and photographs of the local bowling team hang from the walls. Very much a family run village pub, not only is there a good selection of real ales, including local brewery ale direct from the cask, an extensive wine list and all the usual lagers and spirits but, for the hungry, there is a mouthwatering menu of tasty dishes, including imaginative vegetarian options.

However, what gives The Lamb Inn is special atmosphere is the friendly and welcoming manner of hosts, Alan and Jane. Before opening the inn they had farmed locally for over 20 years and, while they still have an interest in farm they still own, they also have a son at agricultural college whilst their two daughters help out in the inn. This is also a place for locals to meet and, as well as the bell ringers coming here to quench their thirst after bell ringing practice, the bowling club are regular visits and there are darts and quiz league teams representing the pub. Those looking for good food, drink and company should look no further.

Opening Hours: Mon-Fri 11.00-14.30, 17.30-23.00; Sat 11.00-23.00; Sun 12.00-22.30

Food: Bar meals and snacks available lunchtime and evening, Traditional Sunday lunches

Credit Cards: Visa, Mastercard, Switch, Delta

Facilities: Car park, Non smoking dining room

Entertainment: Darts, Quizzes

Local Places of Interest/Activities: Killerton House 2 miles, Bickleigh Castle 3 miles, Tiverton 6 miles, Walking, Golf, Fishing

154 New Fountain Inn

Church Road,
Whimple,
Exeter,
Devon EX5 2TA
Tel: 01404 822350

Directions:
From Exeter take the A30 towards Honiton. After 5 miles follow signs to Whimple and the New Fountain Inn lies in the village.

Found at the heart of this delightful old village, with its ancient central square and cider apple orchards, the **New Fountain Inn** is a lovely old village pub. Built originally as two cottages which were converted into an inn over 200 years ago, many of the buildings' old features can still be seen. Both the bars and the dining area have been tastefully decorated - memorabilia and old local photographs adorn the walls - and the open fireplaces add a warm glow in the winter months. However, during the summer, visitors can make use of the large, well maintained beer garden whilst children can play safely in their own special area or watch the goats and chickens in the animal enclosure.

The attractive surroundings, the pleasant atmosphere and the excellent hospitality offered at the New Fountain Inn are all down to owners, Paul and Gill Mallett. Paul, who was born and brought up in Whimple, purchased the inn in 1990 and the couple have become very much involved in village life. Recommended by CAMRA, the real ales served here are well worth tasting and the New Fountain Inn also has a fine reputation for the delicious homecooked meals and snacks on offer. All prepared on the premises from fresh local produce, the menu is complemented by a daily specials' board. A real family run pub, Paul and Gill's daughter Michelle and son Christopher also help out, this is a charming place in which to spend some time. Finally, planning permission has been granted to convert the inn's barn into a local village heritage museum - something more to look forward to here.

Opening Hours: Mon-Sat 12.00-14.30, 18.30-23.00; Sun 12.00-15.00, 19.00-22.30

Food: Bar meals and snacks

Credit Cards: Visa, Mastercard, Switch

Facilities: Heritage museum, Beer garden, Large car park

Entertainment: Theme nights, Darts, Quizzes

Local Places of Interest/Activities: Killerton Gardens 5 miles, Cadhay 3 miles, Fernwood Gardens 2 miles, Golf, Walking, Beach 8 miles

The Old Court House · 155

South Molton Street,
Chulmleigh,
Devon EX18 7BW
Tel: 01769 580045
Fax: 01769 581146

Directions:
From junction 27 on the M5 take the A361 towards Barnstaple. After 15 miles turn off at the Rose Ash services but follow the signposts for Chulmleigh. On entering the village, turn right at The Red Lion and The Old Court House lies 200 yards up this road.

A splendid old stone coaching inn **The Old Court House** is not only a superb example of 17th century architecture but it also retains its thatched roof. A valuable resting place to merchants and travellers of those days, in 1644, some 10 years after it was built, the inn is reputed to have been visited by Charles I whilst he was on his tour of the West Country in the first wheeled carriage. A reminder of those days can be found in one of the guest bedrooms where a magnificent Royal House of Stuart Coat of Arms is moulded on the wall. Another function of the inn, in days gone by, was as a Court House and the cut away sections in the low oak beams in the main bar were made to allow the helmeted guards to stand upright during court sessions.

This wonderful and ancient inn not only offers visitors a true taste of history but, at the hands of landlords Sam and Mrs Paddy Moyse, excellent drink, food and hospitality can be found here. Serving a fine range of real ales and West Country cider in the bar, there is also a comprehensive menu of delicious and traditional pub food that includes a mouthwatering selection of savoury suet puddings. Whilst the interior of this friendly family run inn is both comfortable and inviting, there is a charming cobbled courtyard style beer garden for summer's days. Finally, the accommodation provided, which matches the same high standards as the rest of The Old Court House, comes as either bed and breakfast or self catering.

Opening Hours: Mon-Sat 12.00-23.00; Sun 12.00-22.30

Food: Bar meals and snacks, Home-made specials

Credit Cards: Visa, Access, Delta, Switch, Amex, Diners

Accommodation: 1 en suite Family room, 1 Four-poster room, 1 self contained flat

Facilities: Beer garden, Children and pets welcome, Functions catered for

Entertainment: Traditional pub games incl. Karem (Burmese snooker) and K'nobble

Local Places of Interest/Activities: Tarka Trail 2 miles, Dartmoor National Park 12 miles, Exmoor National Park 15 miles, Walking, Cycling, Horse riding, Fishing, Golf

156 The Old Inn

Kilmington,
Axminster,
Devon EX13 7RB
Tel: 01297 32096
Fax: 01297 35533

Directions:

From Honiton take the A35 towards Bridport and The Old Inn can be found on the right some 7 miles along the road.

Found in the heart of the Kilmington and on the edge of the Blackdown Hills area of outstanding beauty, **The Old Inn** is indeed just that - ancient. Though there have been additions made over the years, the original building is believed to date from 1440 and, with its thatched roof, this Grade II listed building is hard to miss. Though the landlord and lady, Owen and Lynne Davies have not been here for long, they came to the inn in July 1999, they have certainly made their mark. Not only have they made a great impact with the locals - this is the place for meeting and conversation in the village, but they have created a traditional inn of character and charm where good conversation, a relaxed style and fine hospitality go hand in hand.

The delightful lounge bar, housed in the original 15th century part of the inn, and the 18th century public bar both provide a cosy and traditional setting for meeting friends and enjoying a drink from the fine selection behind the bar. Food too is an important part of life at The Old Inn and an excellent menu of both meals and bar snacks has been created by the inn's chef, Eric, a Frenchman who has worked in many prestigious establishments throughout the world. However, busy though Owen and Lynne have obviously been, they still find time to ride and keep two horses in the stables at the rear of the inn. Anyone venturing around the back, and there is a secluded beer garden here too, will also find the village cricket pitch. Naturally, the home team retire to the inn for a hard earned drink after their game.

Opening Hours: All day during the summer; Winter - Mon-Sat 11.30-14.30, 17.30-23.00; Sun 12.00-14.30, 19.00-22.30

Food: Lunches and dinners

Credit Cards: Visa, Mastercard, Amex, Switch, Delta

Facilities: Beer garden, Skittle alley

Local Places of Interest/Activities: Axminster 1 mile, Seaton Tramway 3 miles, Loughwood Meeting House 2 miles

Website/Internet: theoldinn@netlineuk.net

The Passage House Inn 157

Ferry Road,
Topsham,
near Exeter,
Devon EX3 0JN
Tel: 01392 873653
Fax: 01392 879065

Directions:

From junction 30 on the M5 take the minor road signposted Topsham. At the roundabout in the village take the 3rd exit down Ferry Road and The Passage House Inn lies approximately 100 yards down the road on the left.

Situated on the waterfront of this old town, that has been declared a conservation area due to the large number of splendid 17th and 18th century merchants' houses, **The Passage House Inn** fits in very well with its neighbours. Built during the port's great period of prosperity and with marvellous views over the Exe estuary, this imposing old inn has much to offer both its regular customers and those visiting the area. As carefully and meticulously maintained inside and it is outside, the interior of this superb inn is full of old beams and brass lanterns that all add to the ageless atmosphere here.

The excellent range of real ales, beers and lagers served at the bar are complemented by the extensive wine list that offers a carefully selected choice of non vintage and vintage wines from around the world. The menus here have also been carefully chosen and, while the list of tempting dishes ranges from succulent sandwiches to juicy steaks, fish is the house speciality. Landed at nearby fishing villages daily, the fish is brought directly to the inn each day and the blackboard displays the varieties available. Served either plain, or with one of the inn's freshly made sauces, this is certainly a treat not to be missed and a must for anyone who enjoys fish at its best. With fine hospitality, a comfortable setting and the glorious views from the beer garden, The Passage House Inn has to be one of the most perfect places to enjoy a relaxing drink and good food.

Opening Hours: Mon-Sat 11.00-23.00; Sun 12.00-22.30

Food: Bar meals and snacks, À la carte

Credit Cards: Visa, Access, Delta, Switch, Amex

Facilities: Beer garden, Car parking

Local Places of Interest/Activities: Exeter 4 miles, Exmouth 5miles, Powderham Castle 5 miles, Beach 7 miles, Walking, Horse riding, Fishing, Bird watching

158 The Prospect Inn

The Quay,
Exeter,
Devon EX2 4EB
Tel: 01392 273152
Fax: 01392 273152

Directions:

From junction 29 on the M5 follow the signs to the centre of Exeter and then to The Quay. The Prospect Inn can be found along the quayside.

Situated on Exeter's historic quay, **The Prospect Inn** is a splendid 17th century pub that will be familiar to viewers of the 1970s television series *The Onedin Line* as it was filmed here. This marvellous location, in the heart of the city's old port, is must for visitors where, amid the old warehouse that now house craft shops and museums, they can also enjoy the delights of this equally historic old inn. There is seating to the front of the inn, with views over what is still a bustling place, whilst, inside this popular inn, there is one large bar area separated into three levels. The theme here is, naturally, nautical and the numerous pictures on the walls celebrate the many aspects of the seafaring life. There is even a massive ship's wheel hanging from the ceiling which leaves no one in any doubt that they are in a once important old port town.

However, it is not just its interesting location and its resident ghost that brings people to The Prospect Inn but also the excellent hospitality that can be found here. Landlord Ady Taylor, who has been here since 1992, ensures that there is a good choice of beers, ales and lagers on tap, including four real ales, to quench the thirst of his customers. Meanwhile, those also looking for a tasty meal will not be disappointed. The menus vary from lunchtime to evening but the superb quality, service and choice remains constant and, whether it is a light lunch or a three course dinner, the list of imaginative dishes from around the world is sure to please everyone.

Opening Hours: Mon-Sat 11.00-23.00; Sun 12.00-22.30

Food: Bar meals and snacks, À la carte

Credit Cards: Visa, Access, Delta, Switch

Facilities: Car parking close by

Entertainment: Regular live music, Darts

Local Places of Interest/Activities: Historic quayside, Exeter Cathedral, Devon and Exeter Racecourse 4 miles, Powderham Castle 6 miles, Beach 9 miles, Walking, Cycling, Horse riding, Fishing, Sailing

The Royal Oak 159

Chawleigh,
near Chulmleigh,
Devon EX18 7HG
Tel: 01769 580427

Directions:

Leave M5 at junction 27 and take the A361 to Tiverton. Then take the B3137 through Nomansland and the B3042 to Chawleigh and The Royal Oak is in the centre of the village.

Dating back to the 14th century, **The Royal Oak** is a wonderful old cob building, complete with a slate roof, that can be found in the heart of this equally charming Devonshire village. Full of atmosphere and character, there are two comfortable bar areas, one with a magnificent inglenook fireplace where log blaze in the hearth of cold winter's nights and the other with a piano, pool table and juke box. However, what really draws people to the inn, apart from the delightful company and excellent beer, is the delicious and unusual food on offer.

The Royal Oak has been owned and personally run by Juerg and Linda Mehlin since 1997 and, though Linda comes from London both she and her Swiss husband have been living in Switzerland for the past 30 years. Though they both take charge in the kitchen, it is the interesting menu of Swiss dishes, prepared by Juerg, that most people come here to try. Not just cheese fondue, there is cheese raclette, Rösti potatoes, liver Swiss style, diced pork Zurich and a whole host of other dishes along with the more traditional English pub favourites - Linda's speciality. Eaten in either of the two bar areas or in the intimate dining room, the food here is well worth seeking out and, for the Sunday lunches, booking a table is essential.

Opening Hours: Mon 19.00-23.00; Tue-Sat 12.00-15.00, 19.00-23.00; Sun 12.00-22.30

Food: Meals available all day, Sunday lunches, Swiss cuisine a speciality

Credit Cards: Visa, Mastercard, Delta

Accommodation: 3 double rooms, 2 single rooms

Facilities: Beer garden, parking

Entertainment: Pool, Skittles, Darts, Pianist twice a month, Quizzes

Local Places of Interest/Activities: Fishing, Walking, Horse riding, Golf

160 The Seven Stars

High Street,
Winkleigh,
Devon EX19 8HX
Tel: 01837 83344
Fax: 01837 83344

Directions:

From junction 31 on the M5 take the A30 and then the A377 towards Barnstaple. After passing through Copplestone take the B3220 towards Great Torrington and The Seven Stars can be found just off this road, in the heart of Winkleigh.

A splendid old building that is at least 300 years old, **The Seven Stars** is a striking black and white inn that stands on the main road through the village. Up until the beginning of the 20th century, this grand old inn was graced by a thatched roof but, following a fire, it was replaced with slate tiles. However, inside, much of the building's original features remain which all adds to the pleasant atmosphere of this traditional Devon village inn. The wealth of beams and oak panelling maintain the old fashioned air here whilst the slate floor is a particularly interesting and unusual feature - it is circular in design and originally came from Canary Wharf, London.

Since coming here in May 1999, landlords David and Sheila Babb have worked hard, and obviously succeeded, in creating a warm and friendly environment for both locals and visitors alike. There are always two real ales on tap at the bar, as well as local cider and all the usual drinks, whilst the menu of tasty, traditional homecooked bar meals and snacks is sure to satisfy even the most fussy of eaters. Very much a place for the people of Winkleigh and the surrounding area to meet up and enjoy excellent hospitality, new customers are made very welcome and never remain strangers for long.

Opening Hours: Mon-Fri 11.30-23.00; Sat 11.00-23.00; Sun 12.00-22.30

Food: Bar meals and snacks, Traditional Sunday lunches

Credit Cards: Visa, Access, Delta, Switch, Amex, Diners

Facilities: Beer garden, Car parking

Entertainment: Regular live music, Darts, Skittles, Pool

Local Places of Interest/Activities: Local cider factory, Okehampton 9 miles, Finch Foundry 9 miles, Dartmoor National Park 10 miles, Walking, Cycling, Horse riding, Fishing, Bird watching

Internet/Website:
babb@7stars.fsnet.co.uk

The Sir Walter Raleigh | 161

High Street,
East Budleigh,
Devon EX9 7ED
Tel: 01395 442510

Directions:
From Exeter take the A376 to Exmouth and then the B3178 towards Budleigh Salterton. Just after bypassing Budleigh take the left turn into East Budleigh and The Sir Walter Raleigh lies on the main street.

Thought to have been built in the 15th century, **The Sir Walter Raleigh** named after the illustrious Elizabethan adventurer and courtier who was born at nearby Hayes Barton 100 years later. It was around the time that Raleigh was setting sail on his voyages of discovery that the village also lost its position as a port when the river began to silt up leaving the ships without water. Today, this is a charming unspoilt village of attractive cottages and non more so than the picturesque exterior of this thatched inn. A place of atmosphere and antiquity, the inn has many of its original features, including the beam work, and is a comfortable inn offering the very best in hospitality.

Owned and personally run by Edward and Shirley Truman, the couple have not only earned The Sir Walter Raleigh an enviable reputation for the excellent real ales, wines and other usual drinks from the bar but also they are famous locally for their food. All homemade the dishes, on both the menu and the specials board, reflect the variety of fresh produce in the area - with fish and locally grown meat a speciality. A warm welcome awaits any visitors who find themselves entering this delightful village inn and, with a beer garden opening in summer 2000, there is even more reason to seek out The Sir Walter Raleigh.

Opening Hours: Mon-Sat 11.30-15.00, 18.00-23.00, Sun 12.00-15.00, 19.00-22.30

Food: Bar meals and snacks available all day

Credit Cards: Visa, Mastercard, Delta, Switch, Solo, JCB

Facilities: Beer garden (Summer 2000), Large car park

Local Places of Interest/Activities: Sir Walter Raleigh's birthplace 1 mile, Bicton Gardens 1 mile, Budleigh Salterton 1 mile, Coast, Walking, Golf

162   The Three Tuns Inn

Exeter Road,
Silverton,
Exeter,
Devon EX5 4HX
Tel: 01392 860352
Fax: 01392 860636

Directions:
Take junction 28 off the M5 into Cullompton then take the B3181 following signs to Killerton House. Continue by following the signs to Silverton and The Three Tuns Inn lies 3 miles along the road.

Built in the 1490s, **The Three Tuns Inn**, nestling in the heart of the village, is certainly one of the oldest inns in Devon. It is probably one of the prettiest as well - a traditional cob building still with its thatched roof, the inn has a colourful display of flower filled hanging baskets and window boxes in the summer months. Purchased by Peter and Diane Collingwood in January 1999, this charming couple offer their customers the very best in hospitality. As attractive inside as the exterior suggests, the warm and friendly atmosphere of The Three Tuns Inn is aided by the exposed original ceiling beams, the roaring open fires and the carefully chosen memorabilia adorning the walls.

Very much a village pub, as it has been for the past 500 years, customers can expect an excellent range of well kept real ales, beers, lagers and spirits served at the bar. Those looking for food will find that they have certainly come to the right place. Served in either the intimate non smoking restaurant or in one of the bars, there is a menu of tempting homecooked dishes that are supplemented by the ever changing specials board. There is also an extensive wine list to add that finishing touch to a meal. Finally the superb accommodation and the charming secluded courtyard beer garden all add up to making The Three Tuns a perfect country inn.

Opening Hours: Mon-Fri 11.30-15.00, 17.50-23.00; Sat 11.30-23.00; Sun 12-22.30

Food: Bar meals and snacks available (12.00-14.00, 17.00-21.30), Traditional Sunday lunches

Credit Cards: Visa, Mastercard, Switch, Delta

Accommodation: 2 double rooms, 2 twin rooms, 1 triple room all ensuite; 1 room suitable for disabled

Facilities: Beer garden, Car park, Non smoking restaurant

Entertainment: Music in garden in summer, Quizzes

Local Places of Interest/Activities: Killerton House 2 miles, Bickleigh Castle 3 miles, Tiverton 6 miles, Walking, Golf, Fishing

Internet/Website: www.eclipse.co.uk/

The White Hart Inn 163

Church Style Lane,
Woodbury,
Devon EX5 1HN
Tel: 01395 232221

Directions:

From junction 30 on the
M5 take the A376 towards
Exmouth. At the Clyst St
George roundabout turn
left onto the B3179 to-
wards Budleigh Salterton
and The White Hart Inn
can be found turning left
in the centre of the village.

Found at the heart of this pretty village, **The White Hart Inn** is a charming old place that dates back to the 14th century. Reputedly built for stone masons working on Exeter Cathedral, this traditional village inn lies down a quiet lane and its rear beer garden opens out on to the village green that also has a children's play area. Sheila Rayson has been the landlady here since 1988 and, over the years, not only has she created the perfect haven for villagers wishing to enjoy the relaxed atmosphere of her delightful inn but she has also welcomed a host of visitors to this quiet place just off the Devon Riviera.

Tastefully decorated and with a mass of heavy oak beams and gleaming horse brasses, this pleasant inn is just the place for good food and drink. Serving real ales from the bar as well as all the usual beers, lagers and spirits, wine lovers will find that they too are catered for with a good selection of wines appearing on the wine list. The menu here also reflects the traditional nature of this old inn and whilst there are some elaborate dishes such as Tournedos Rossini there are many old favourites like fresh fish and chips, fillet steak and juicy freshly cut sandwiches. A well established and popular local inn, The White Hart is a welcoming and inviting place to make for whilst exploring the south Devon coast.

Opening Hours: Mon-Fri 11.00-15.00, 18.00-23.00; Sat 11.00-23.00; Sun 12.00-15.00, 19.00-22.30

Food: Bar snacks and meals, À la carte

Credit Cards: Visa, Access, Delta, Switch, Amex, Diners

Facilities: Beer garden, Car parking, Functions catered for

Entertainment: Regular live music, Darts, Skittles, Pool

Local Places of Interest/Activities: James Countryside Collection 4 miles, Bicton Park 4 miles, Fairlynch Museum 5 miles, Coast 5 miles, Exeter 6 miles, Walking, Sailing, Horse riding, Fishing, Bird watching

164   The White Lion Inn

26 High Street,
Bradninch, Exeter,
Devon EX5 4QL
Tel: 01392 881263

Directions:

From junction 28 of the M5 take the B3181 to Cullompton then follow the signs to Bradninch. The White Lion Inn lies 1 mile down the road, in the village.

Once an important town, larger than Exeter, built on the wealth of the woollen trade and lace industry, Bradninch is also a popular place with American visitors as Daniel Boon was christened here. Now a quiet place, well situated in the heart of the glorious Devon countryside yet close to the motorway and numerous places of interest, Bradninch is also the home of **The White Lion Inn**. Built in 1640, this attractive centrally placed pub has a long frontage that makes it hard to miss whilst, inside, it is as cosy and friendly as every country pub should be. Owned by Chris and Maggie Stobbart-Rowlands, the couple have not only created a warm and pleasant atmosphere since they arrived here in October 1999 but they are also fast gaining an excellent reputation for the good food that is offered here.

In the delightful surroundings of the pub's large open bar, complete with a splendid inglenook fireplace and a display of pictures and paintings by local artists, visitors can enjoy a quiet drink from the wide ranging selection of real ales, beers, lagers, spirits and wines. The delicious homecooked food - prepared by Maggie - includes game dishes when in season and the chalkboard menu changes often. Fresh local produce is an essential ingredient here though there are many different styles of cuisine on offer - from old fashioned steak pie to Thai curry. With equally excellent accommodation available and a charming terraced beer garden this is a superb place to find.

Opening Hours: Winter - Mon-Sat 11.00-14.00; 18.00-23.00 (closed Tuesday am); Sun 12.00-15.00, 19.00-22.30. Summer - all day at the weekend

Food: Meals and bar snacks, Sunday lunch

Credit Cards: Visa, Mastercard, Switch

Accommodation: 3 double rooms, 1 twin room all with shared bathroom

Facilities: Beer garden, Children's play area

Entertainment: Folk music nights, Quizzes, Darts, Theme nights

Local Places of Interest/Activities: Tiverton 6 miles, Bickleigh Castle 5 miles, Killerton 3 miles, Walking, Cycling

Internet/Website:
http://www.yeoldewhitelion.co.uk
e-mail: maggie@yeoldewhitelion.co.uk

The Wyndham Arms 165

Kentisbeare,
near Cullompton,
Devon EX15 2AA
Tel: 01884 266327

Directions:

From junction 28 on the M5 take the A373 towards Honiton. After 1 mile take the road left to Kentisbeare. The pub stands prominently in the village centre.

Found at the heart of this picturesque old village **The Wyndham Arms** is one of Kentisbeare's several medieval buildings. Believed to have been built in the 14th century, the inn has retained much of its charm as well as a sense of history and, in the main bar, the large inglenook fireplace has a back plate dating from 1662 which depicts a lion and a unicorn - indicating the joining of the thrones of England and Scotland in 1603 following the death of Elizabeth I. With a cosy snug bar and a comfortable restaurant, the inn has plenty of space though the friendly, welcoming atmosphere ensures that no one finds themselves lost.

Since coming here in September 1999, licensee Gavin Scott, who has many years experience in the trade, has not only made The Wyndham Arms the centre of attention in the village but also gained an enviable reputation for the high quality of his meals. The comprehensive menu changes on a regular basis but the steaks, very much the house speciality, are always available. Most dishes are homecooked and, as far as possible, only local produce, including cheese and vegetables, is used. Anyone here on a Monday evening will also have the added pleasure of tasting the popular curry. With an excellent cellar, a fine selection of real ales and local scrumpy on tap behind the bar there is everyone's favourite tipple to enjoy - along with music nights, quiz evenings, skittles and much more.

Opening Hours: Mon-Sat 11.00-15.00, 18.00-23.00; Sun 12.00-15.00, 19.00-22.30

Food: Bar meals, snacks and children's menu for lunch and dinner

Credit Cards: Visa, Access, Delta, Switch

Facilities: Skittle alley used also as function room, Beer garden, Children's play area

Entertainment: Pianist once a week, Live music once a fortnight, Quiz nights

Local Places of Interest/Activities: Walking, Cycling, Horse riding, Fishing

Internet/Website: the.wyndham.arms@virgin.net

This page is left intentionally blank

6 South and West Somerset

PLACES OF INTEREST:

Allerford 169
Barrington 169
Bishops Lydeard 170
Bridgwater 170
Burrow Bridge 171
Cadbury Castle 171
Chard 172
Cheddon Fitzpaine 172
Clapton 172
Crewkerne 172
Dunster 173
East Lambrook 174
Exmoor 174
Glastonbury 174
Ilminster 177
Kingsdon 177
Langport 177
Martock 178

Minehead 178
Monksilver 179
Montacute 179
Muchelney 180
Porlock 180
Selworthy 180
Somerton 181
Stoke-sub-Hamdon 181
Taunton 181
Thorne St Margaret 182
Tintinhull 182
Tolland 183
Treborough 183
Washford 183
Watchet 183
Williton 184
Wincanton 184
Yeovil 184

PUBS AND INNS:

The Ashcott Inn, Ashcott 185
The Bell Inn, Evercreech 186
The Candlelight Inn, Bishopswood 187
The Globe Inn, Milverton 188
The Globe, Somerton 189
The Greyhound Inn, Stogursey 190
The Hunters Lodge Inn, Leigh Common 191
The Pilgrims' Rest Inn, Lovington 192

The Ship Inn, Wellington 193
The Swan at Kingston, Kingston St Mary 194
The Three Horseshoes, Batcombe 195
The Travellers Rest, East Pennard 196

The Hidden Inns of the West Country

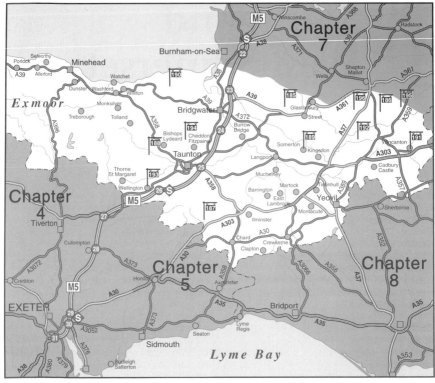

185 The Ashcott Inn, Ashcott

186 The Bell Inn, Evercreech

187 The Candlelight Inn, Bishopswood

188 The Globe Inn, Milverton

189 The Globe, Somerton

190 The Greyhound Inn, Stogursey

191 The Hunters Lodge Inn,
Leigh Common

192 The Pilgrims' Rest Inn, Lovington

193 The Ship Inn, Wellington

194 The Swan at Kingston,
Kingston St Mary

195 The Three Horseshoes, Batcombe

196 The Travellers Rest, East Pennard

The county's plain stretches from Wells and Glastonbury in the north down to Taunton near the boundary with Devon. The western coastline boasts lively and popular seaside resorts such as Watchet and Minehead.

In the far west corner of the county, straddling the border with Devon, can be found the smallest national park in the country - Exmoor. With dramatic coastal cliffs, rolling heather moorland and secluded wooded valleys, Exmoor, though often overlooked in favour of its larger neighbour, Dartmoor, has a character and charm all its own. This was once wild hunting country, and its abundance of prehistoric sites, ancient packhorse bridges and wild deer and ponies easily makes it one of the more romantic and mysterious parts of the country. Not surprisingly, this countryside inspired the writer R. D. Blackmoor; fans of his novel *Lorna Doone* are drawn to the area to visit the places he describes.

A good place to begin exploring this part of the county is from the **Wellington Monument**, the conspicuous 170 foot obelisk which stands on a spur of the Blackdown Hills overlooking the Vale of Taunton Deane, just off the M5. This striking landmark was constructed in honour of the Duke of Wellington on the estate bought for him by the nation following his victory at the Battle of Waterloo. The monument's foundation stone was laid in 1817 following a wave of enthusiastic public support. However, the necessary funds to complete the project did not materialise and a number of radical economies had to be introduced. These included the redesigning of the structure to give it three sides instead of four and the cancelling of an ostentatious cast iron statue of the Duke which had been proposed for the top. As it was, the modified triangular pinnacle remained unfinished until 1854, two years after Wellington's death. Visitors can still make the formidable 235-step climb to the top where they are rewarded with spectacular views across lowland Somerset to Exmoor and the Mendips.

PLACES OF INTEREST

ALLERFORD

Allerford is a lovely old village which has some fine stone cottages and an elegant twin-arched

Packhorse Bridge, Allerford

Packhorse Bridge. Located in Allerford's old school, the **Allerford Museum** (The West Somerset Rural Life Museum) is an imaginatively presented trove of rural life whose exhibits include a Victorian kitchen, laundry and dairy, and an old schoolroom complete with desks, books and children's toys. From Allerford, it is possible to climb back up the hill for the return walk to Minehead, a round trip of about 12 miles. For those preferring a walk on the high moor, a spectacular circular nature walk starts and finishes at the Webber's Post car park at the foot of Dunkery Hill.

BARRINGTON

The beautiful National Trust-owned **Barrington Court** was built in the 1570s from local Ham stone and displays the characteristics of the

170 architectural transformation from Tudor Gothic, with its buttresses and mullioned and transomed windows, to Renaissance, with its twisted finials and chimney stacks. The garden was laid out in the 1920s in a series of themed rooms, including the iris garden, lily garden, white garden and fragrant rose garden. The celebrated landscape architect, Gertrude Jekyll, was brought in to advise on the initial planting and layout, and the garden remains the finest example of her work in the Trust's care. There is also an exceptionally attractive one-acre kitchen garden with apple, pear and plum trees trained along the walls which in season produces fruit and vegetables for use in the restaurant. The nearby estate village of Barrington contains some fine old Hamstone cottages.

BISHOPS LYDEARD

The sizable village of Bishops Lydeard is the southern terminus of the **West Somerset Railway**, a privately-operated steam railway which runs for almost twenty miles to Minehead on the Bristol Channel coast. The longest line of its kind in the country, it was formed when British Rail's 100-year-old branch between Taunton and Minehead was closed in 1971. After a five-year restoration programme, the new company began operating a limited summer service which has steadily grown in popularity. Special attractions include the first class Pullman dining car and the "Flockton Flyer", a steam locomotive which may be recognised for its many appearances on film and television. Services between the line's ten stations run throughout the day between mid-March and end-October.

BRIDGWATER

The ancient inland port and industrial town of Bridgwater stands at the lowest medieval bridging point on the River Parrett. Despite having been fortified since before the Norman invasion, the settlement remained little more than a village until an international trade in wool, wheat and other agricultural produce began to develop in the late Middle Ages. During this period, Bridgwater grew to become the most important town on the coast between Bristol and Barnstaple, and the fifth-busiest port in Britain. The largely 14th century parish **Church of St Mary**, with its disproportionately large

spire, is the only building to survive from this medieval era of prosperity, the castle having been dismantled after the English Civil War, and the 13th-century Franciscan friary and St John's hospital having long since disappeared. The oldest and most interesting part of the town lies between King Street and the West Quay, an area whose layout is medieval, but whose buildings are amongst the finest examples of Georgian domestic architecture in Somerset.

Prior to the construction of a canal dock a short distance downstream early in the 19th century, ships used to tie up on both riverbanks below Bridgwater's medieval three-arched bridge. The last remnant of the castle, **The Water Gate**, can still be seen here on the West Quay, along with a number of fine Georgian residences, the most notable of which, the Lions, was built in 1725.

After a long period of decline brought about by a long-running war with the nation's continental trading partners, Bridgwater underwent something of an industrial renaissance during the first half of the 19th century. The manufacture of Bridgwater glass, which had begun the previous century, continued to expand, and a canal terminus, complete with docks, warehouses, brickworks and retractable railway bridge, was built between 1837 and 1841 a few hundred yards north of the old centre. Finally closed in 1970, the site has been restored and is now a fascinating piece of industrial archeology which is well worth seeing. Bridgwater's manufacturers have long since relocated to the outskirts of town. The most evident of these, a cellophane factory, makes its presence known to residents and visitors alike by its distinctive airborne aroma.

The interior of the parish church is worth seeing for its painting of the *Descent from the Cross* by an unknown Italian artist, and for the fine Jacobean screen which extends across a side chapel. It was from the church tower that the Duke of Monmouth is reputed to have spotted the approaching army of James II the day before the Battle of Sedgemoor. This supposed advantage gave him the inspiration to launch the surprise attack which eventually led to his disastrous defeat in July 1685.

A bronze statue of Bridgwater's most famous son, Robert Blake, can be seen at the top of Fore Street. This celebrated military leader was born in 1598 in the house which now accommodates **Bridgwater's Town Museum**. When in his forties, Blake became an important officer in Cromwell's army and twice defended Taunton against overwhelming Royalist odds, then at the age of fifty, he was given command of the British navy and went on to win a number of important battles against the Dutch and Spanish, so restoring the nation's naval supremacy in Europe. The museum contains a three-dimensional model of the Battle of Santa Cruz, one of his most famous victories, along with a collection of his personal effects.

There is also a similar diorama of the Battle of Sedgemoor and a large collection of locally-discovered artefacts dating from the Neolithic period to the Second World War. Also well worth seeing is Bridgwater's spectacular annual carnival which is held in the town on the first Thursday in November.

BURROW BRIDGE

An interesting pumping station can be seen beside the River Parrett at Burrow Bridge. It contains a fine collection of Victorian pump engines and is open to the public on certain days each year. Burrow Bridge is also the location of the **Somerset Levels Basket and Craft Centre**, a workshop and showroom stocked with handmade basketware. The conspicuous conical hill which can be seen nearby is known as **Burrow Mump**. This isolated knoll is reputed to be the site of an ancient fort belonging to King Alfred, the 9th century King of Wessex, who is thought to have retreated to this lonely spot to escape a Viking incursion. It was during his time here that he is rumoured to have sought shelter in a hut in the nearby village of

Burrow Mump Fort

Athelney and was scolded by the family for burning their cakes. In many ways reminiscent of Glastonbury Tor, Burrow Mump is crowned by the picturesque remains of a medieval church which can be seen from miles around.

171

Burrow Mump is situated in the heart of the low-lying area known as the **King's Sedge Moor**, an attractive part of the Somerset Levels which is drained by the rivers Cary (here renamed the King's Sedgemoor **Drain) and** Parrett. This rich area of wetland is known for its characteristic pollarded willows whose straight shoots, or withies, have been cultivated on a substantial scale ever since the taste for wicker developed during the Victorian era. The traditional craft of basket-making, one of Somerset's oldest commercial activities, once employed thousands of people. Though now very much scaled down, the industry is still alive and well and is even enjoying something of a revival.

CADBURY CASTLE

Cadbury Castle is a massive Iron Age hill fort which is also reckoned by some to be the location of King Arthur's legendary Camelot. This ancient hilltop site was occupied for some 5,000 years from the middle to the Neolithic period right up to the 13th century. Heavily fortified throughout the Iron Age, the Romans are reputed to have carried out a massacre here around 70 AD to put down a revolt by the ancient Britons. A major archeological excavation in the 1960s uncovered a wealth of Roman and pre-Roman remains on the site. It also confirmed the existence of a substantial fortification dating from around 500 AD, the time when King Arthur would have been spearheading the Celtic-British resistance against the advancing Saxons. If Cadbury Castle had indeed been Arthur's Camelot, it is likely that it would have been a timber fortification and not the turreted stone structure mythologised by the storybooks.

The easily-defended hilltop site was again refortified during the reign of Ethelred the Unready, this time against the Danes. The poorly-advised king also established a mint here around 1000 AD, most of the coinage from which was used to buy off the Norse invaders in an act of appeasement which led to the term Danegeld. As a consequence, most of the sur-

172

viving coins from the Cadbury mint are now to be found in the museums of Scandinavia.

The mile-long stroll around Cadbury Castle's massive earthwork ramparts demonstrates the site's effectiveness as a defensive position. Thanks to the magnificent view from the top, troop movements to the north and west would have been easily spotted, and the important route into the Heart of England, the Fosse Way, would have been clearly visible five miles away to the northwest.

Another exceptional view of south Somerset can be had from the summit of **Corton Hill**, two miles to the south. The site of an ancient beacon, it can be reached by following Halter Path Lane from the village of Corton Denham.

CHARD

On the northern approaches to Chard, the A358 Ilminster to Axminster road passes close to two contrasting places of interest. To the west, **Hornsbury Mill** is a 200 year old corn mill which has an impressive working water wheel, and to the east, **Chard Reservoir Nature Reserve** is a conservation area which offers a varied two-mile circular walk through rustling reed beds, broad-leaved woodland and open hay meadows. An important habitat for wildlife, the lake is home to a number of rare bird species, including the kingfisher and great crested grebe.

Despite its rapid postwar development, the centre retains a pleasant village-like atmosphere which is particularly apparent around the broad sloping main street. A good way to find out more about the town's eventful past is to visit the award-winning **Chard Museum** in Godworthy House. This impressive local mu-

Chard Museum

seum is housed in an attractive thatched building at the west end of the High Street.

CHEDDON FITZPAINE

The beautiful **Hestercombe Gardens** lie on the south-facing foothills of the Quantocks just north of the village of Cheddon Fitzpaine. This carefully-restored Edwardian garden is an outstanding example of the professional collaboration between the architect, Sir Edwin Lutyens, and the landscape designer, Gertrude Jekyll. Originally laid out in 1904, Hestercombe was restored in the 1980s by Somerset County Council using Jekyll's original planting scheme as a guide.

CLAPTON

The 10-acre **Clapton Court Gardens** are some of the most varied and interesting in Somerset. Among the many beautiful features are the formal terraces, rose garden, rockery and water garden. The grounds incorporate a large wooded area containing a massive ash tree which, at over 230 years old and 28 foot in girth, is believed to be the oldest and largest in mainland Britain. There is also a fine metasequoia which is already over 80 foot tall, having been planted in 1950 from seed brought back from China.

CREWKERNE

The ancient former market town of Crewkerne developed as a thriving agricultural and market centre during Saxon times and even had its own mint in the decades leading up to the Norman invasion. The magnificent parish **church of St Bartholomew** was built on the wealth generated by the late-medieval boom in the wool industry. A structure of minster-like proportions, it is one of the grandest of the many fine Perpendicular churches to be found in south Somerset.

Unlike most other towns in Wessex whose textile industries suffered an almost total decline, Crewkerne was rejuvenated in the 18th century when the availability of locally-grown flax led to an expansion in the manufacture of sailcloth and canvas webbing. Among the many thousands of sails to be made here were those for HMS *Victory*, Nelson's flagship at the Battle of Trafalgar. The town's resurgence was further boosted by the development of the London-Exeter coaching route at this time, a factor which led to the rebuilding of old Crewkerne in elegant Georgian style. Many fine town houses and inns from this period can still be seen in the centre, most notably in Church and Abbey streets, now an Area of Outstanding Architectural Interest. Less appealing are the northern and southern outskirts of the town which been given up to large-scale light industrial development.

The A30 to the west of Crewkerne climbs onto the aptly-named **Windwhistle Hill**, a high chalk-topped ridge which enjoys dramatic views southwards to Lyme Bay and northwards across the Somerset Levels to the mountains of South Wales. This is also the location of the impressive Windwhistle golf and country club.

The River Parrett Trail passes over the lovely **Haslebury Bridge**, a medieval packhorse bridge, on its way between Bridgwater and Crewkerne. Approximately 50 miles long, the Trail passes through one of Britain's most ecologically sensitive and fragile areas, the Somerset Levels and Moors. Old mills, splendid churches, attractive and interesting villages and towns - and historical sights including Europe's largest Iron Age fort, at Ham Hill in Stoke-sub-Hamdon, up through Langport and beyond. Walkers will also find orchards, peaceful pastureland and traditional industries such as cider making and basket-weaving.

DUNSTER

The ancient fortified settlement of Dunster has an almost fairy-tale appearance when approached along the A39 from the southeast. With its huge turreted castle rising above the trees and distinctive ruined folly on nearby Conygar hill, it is a place well-worth visiting, particularly out of season. **Dunster Castle** was founded by William de Mohun on a natural promontory above the River Avill a few years before the Domesday Book was compiled in 1086. In 1404, it passed to the Luttrells for the then colossal sum of 5000 marks, about £3300, in whose family it remained until Lt. Col. G W F Luttrell presented the property to the National Trust in 1975.

During the English Civil War, Dunster Castle was one of the last Royalist strongholds in the West Country to fall, the garrison finally surrendering after a siege lasting 160 days. The castle underwent some major alterations during the latter part of the 17th century and some of its finest internal features date from this pe-

riod, including the superb plasterwork ceiling in the dining room, and the magnificent balustraded main staircase with its delicately-carved flora and fauna. The banqueting hall contains a unique collection of 16th-century leather hangings, and there are also many fine examples of period furniture throughout the interior.

Further changes to the building by Anthony Salvin in the 19th century completed the transformation from castle to country mansion. Work on the steeply-terraced garden with its striking collection of rare shrubs and subtropical plants was also carried out at this time. Dunster Castle is surrounded by an attractive 28-acre park containing an 18th-century flour mill which was built on the site of a Norman predecessor. Restored to working order in 1979, **Dunster Working Water Mill** continues to produce flour and other cereals for wholesale and retail sale.

The old feudal settlement of Dunster has a wide main street which is dominated by the castle. At the northern end stands the former **Yarn Market**, a small octagonal building erected by the Luttrells around 1600 when the village was a centre of the cloth trade. Indeed, such was its importance that at one time, Dunster gave its name to a type of woollen cloth which was renowned for its quality and strength. The nearby **Luttrell Arms** is over a century older; a private residence which was converted to an inn around 1650, it has a fine

Dunster Yarn Market

174

15th-century porch and a room lined with carved oak panelling. It once belonged to Cleeve Abbey, as did the 14th-century nunnery in Church Street. Dunster's principal medieval monastic house, **Dunster Priory**, was an outpost of Bath Abbey. Now largely demolished, the only parts to survive are its splendid priory church and unusual 12th-century dovecote. This can be seen in a nearby garden and still contains the revolving ladder which was used to reach the roosting birds.

Dunster's former priory church is now one of the finest parish churches in Somerset. Rebuilt of rose pink sandstone by the monks after 1100, its 100 foot tower was added in the 15th century at a cost of 13s 4d per foot, with an extra 20s for the pinnacles. The building's most outstanding internal feature is its fan vaulted rood screen which extends across the nave and aisles, one of the widest and most impressive of its kind in the country. There are also some fine 15th and 16th century fittings, an unusual painting of the Brazen Serpent thought to be by Thornhill, and several monuments to members of the Luttrell family. On the southern edge of the village, the River Avill is spanned by the ancient **Gallox Bridge**, a medieval packhorse bridge which is now under the care of English Heritage.

Dunster's Memorial Hall is home to the lovely **Dolls Museum**, with over 700 dolls from different periods and countries, dressed in delightful outfits and national costumes.

EAST LAMBROOK

The charming hamlet of East Lambrook is home of the beautiful **East Lambrook Manor Garden**. The garden was laid out by the writer and horticulturalist, Margery Fish, who lived at the medieval Ham-stone manor from 1937 until her death in 1969. Her exuberant planting and deliberate lack of formality created an atmosphere of romantic tranquillity which is maintained to this day. Now Grade I listed, the story of the genesis of the project is told in her first book, *We Made A Garden*. The National Collection of cranesbill species geraniums is also kept here.

The low-lying land to the north of East Lambrook is crisscrossed by a network of drainage ditches, or rhines (pronounced reens), which eventually flow into the rivers Parrett,

Isle and Yeo. Originally cut in the early 1800s, the ditches are often lined with double rows of pollarded willows which have come to characterise this part of Somerset. Despite having to be cleared every few years, the rhines provide a valuable natural habitat for a wide variety of bird, animal and plantlife.

EXMOOR

The characteristic heartland of the **Exmoor National Park**, 70 per cent of which lies within Somerset, is a high treeless plateau of hard-wearing Devonian shale which has been carved into a series of steep-sided valleys by the prolonged action of the moor's many fast-flowing streams. Whereas the upland vegetation is mostly heather, gorse and bracken, the more sheltered valleys are carpeted with grassy meadows and pockets of woodland. The deep wooded combes also provide shelter for herds of shy red deer which roam at will, but are seldom seen. Easier to spot are the hardy Exmoor ponies, now almost all cross-breeds, which often congregate at roadside parking areas where there can be rich pickings from holidaymakers.

Exmoor is criss-crossed by a network of paths and bridleways which provide some superb opportunities for walking and pony-trekking. Many follow the routes of the ancient ridgeways across the high moor and pass close to the numerous hut circles, standing stones, barrows and other Bronze and Iron Age remains which litter the landscape. Among the finest examples are the stone circle on Porlock Hill, **Alderman's Barrow** north of Exford, and the delightfully-named **Cow Castle** near Simonsbath. The remarkable medieval packhorse bridge known as **Tarr Steps** lies to the north of the village of Hawkridge, near Dulverton. A superb example of a West Country clapper bridge, it is composed of massive flat stones placed across solidly-built dry stone uprights. The Roman relic known as the **Caractacus Stone** can be seen a couple of miles to the east of here near Spire Cross.

GLASTONBURY

The ancient ecclesiastical centre of Glastonbury, a small town with an immense history, is a mecca for those encompassing such diverse beliefs as paganism, Christianity, Arthurian legend and the existence of UFOs. Before the surrounding Somerset Levels were drained in the 18th century, the dramatic form of **Glaston-**

Glastonbury Tor

Along with mystical energy, the tor offers a magnificent panorama across

175

Somerset to Wells, the Mendips, the Quantocks and the Bristol Channel. The view from the top is most breathtaking on a misty day when the Tor is surrounded by a sea of silver cloud. The striking tower at the summit is all that remains of the 15th century **Church of St Michael**, an offshoot of Glastonbury Abbey which fell into disrepair following the Dissolution of the Monasteries in 1539. In that turbulent year, the tor became a place of execution when the last abbot of Glastonbury, Richard Whiting, and two of his monks were hanged near the summit for opposing the will of Henry VIII.

bury Tor stood out above a great expanse of mist-covered marshland. Known throughout the region as the Isle of Avalon, one of the first outsiders to sail up the River Brue and land at this distinctive conical hill was the early Christian trader, Joseph of Arimathea, who arrived from the Holy Land around 60 AD. According to local legend, Joseph was walking one day on nearby Wearyall Hill when he plunged his staff into the ground. Miraculously, the stick took root and burst into leaf, and this he took as a sign he should found a church. A wattle and daub structure was duly erected at the spot which later became the site of the great **Glastonbury Abbey**.

Joseph's staff is reputed to have grown into the celebrated Christmas-flowering Glastonbury hawthorn, and although the original is believed to have been felled during Cromwellian times by an overzealous Puritan (he was blinded by a flying shard of wood in the process, no doubt as a gesture of retribution), one of its windswept ancestors can still be seen on the crest of Wearyall Hill. In an extended version of the legend, Joseph was accompanied on one of his visits to Glastonbury by his nephew, the young Jesus Christ, an occurrence which is reputed to have provided William Blake with the inspiration for his hymn, Jerusalem.

Glastonbury Tor remains a landmark which can be seen from miles around, although curiously, it is often less conspicuous when viewed from close by. The 520 foot hill has been inhabited since prehistoric times, and excavations on the site have uncovered evidence of Celtic, Roman and pre-Saxon occupation. Because of its unusually regular shape, it has long been associated with myth and legend. For example, in its time it has been identified as the Land of the Dead, the Celtic Otherworld, a Druid's temple, magic mountain, Arthurian hillfort, ley line intersection, and rendezvous point for passing UFOs.

The wooded rise standing between Glastonbury Tor and the town centre is known as **Chalice Hill**. During one of his visits in the 1st century AD, Joseph of Arimathea is supposed to have buried the Holy Grail (the cup used by Christ at the Last Supper) beneath a spring which emerges from the foot of the hill's southern slope. The spring forms a natural well which was partially enclosed within a masonry structure during medieval times. This is now situated in an attractive garden maintained by the **Chalice Well Trust**. The spring water has a high iron content which leaves a curious rust-coloured (some say blood-coloured) residue in its wake. It is also reputed to have curative powers and flows at a constant rate of 25,000 gallons per day into a pool known as the Pilgrim's Bath.

The dramatic remains of **Glastonbury Abbey** can be found to the northwest of Chalice

Glastonbury Abbey

176 Hill in the heart of old Glastonbury. If the legend of Joseph of Arimathea is to be believed, this is the site of the earliest Christian foundation in the British Isles. The abbey is thought to have been founded by King Ine around 700 AD, and under St Dunstan, the 10th century abbot who went on to become the Archbishop of Canterbury, it grew in influence so that by the time of the Norman invasion, it owned estates covering an eighth of the county of Somerset. The abbey continued to grow under the guidance of the Benedictines until a disastrous fire destroyed most of the abbey buildings in 1184.

When the foundations of the replacement great church were being excavated seven years later, a wooden sarcophagus was discovered 16 feet down between the shafts of two ancient crosses. Inside were found the bones of a large man and a slender woman, and one story tells of how the woman's long golden hair seemed in a perfect state of preservation until a monk touched it, transforming it to dust. A lead cross found nearby convinced the abbot that he had discovered the remains of King Arthur and Queen Guinevere, although it was known at the time that this was the burial place of at least three kings from the later, Saxon period.

The abbot's discovery could well be described as timely, given his pressing need for funds to pay for the abbey's reconstruction. Notwithstanding, Glastonbury soon became an important place of pilgrimage, and when the main part of the abbey had been completed in 1278, King Edward himself arrived to witness the final re-interring of Arthur's bones in a magnificent new tomb in the choir. The regenerated great church was a massive 560 feet in length, with a splendid central bell-tower, twin west towers, a unique clock, and a series of shrines to the great and the good.

The abbey continued to wield considerable power until Henry VIII's Dissolution of the Monasteries of 1539 forced it to close. The building was abandoned and soon fell into disrepair: its walls were plundered for building stone and Arthur's tomb was destroyed. A number of impressive remains have nevertheless survived, the best-preserved being **St Mary's Chapel**, the shell of the great church, and the 14th century **Abbot's Kitchen**. The last named is a charming structure with a vaulted roof and a fireplace in each corner which has survived almost intact. The old abbey gatehouse now houses an interesting small museum whose exhibits include a selection of historic artefacts from the site and a model of the abbey as it was at the time of the Dissolution.

The abbey's principal **Tithe Barn** stands on its own to the southeast of the main monastic buildings. Although it is relatively small for such a great estate, it incorporates some fine sculptured detail, notably the carved heads on the corner buttresses and emblems of the four Evangelists on the gables.

During the Middle Ages, Glastonbury Abbey was an internationally renowned centre of learning which attracted scholars and pilgrims from all over Christendom. Such were the eventual numbers that a guesthouse had to be built outside the abbey walls. Originally constructed around 1475, the much ornamented **George and Pilgrims Hotel** can still be seen in the High Street near the Market Cross. The old timber beams of this striking building are adorned with carved angels and the fireplace in the bar is surrounded by Delft tiles which are over two centuries old. The interior is guarded by a series of curious monks' death masks, and at one time, the building was even rumoured to have a subterranean passage leading from the cellar into the abbey grounds.

A couple of doors away, **The Tribunal** is a handsome early 15th-century courthouse which now houses the tourist information office. The two square panels above the doorway each contain the royal emblem of the Tudors, an indication that the king's justice was meted out inside. Among the many fine churches to be found in Glastonbury are **St John's Baptist church** in the High Street, which has an imposing 134ft tower, and St Mary's Roman Catholic church in Magdalene Street, which dates from the outbreak of the Second World War.

A National Trust footpath to the east of Glastonbury leads to **Gog and Magog**, the ancient oaks of Avalon. This famous pair of living antiquities are all that remain of an avenue of oaks which, sadly, was cut down in the 1900s to make way for a farm. One of the felled trees was eleven feet in diameter and was recorded as having over 2000 season rings.

Another historic place of interest can be found to the northwest of Glastonbury town centre in a field beside the road to Godney. This was the site of a prehistoric **Lake Village** which was discovered in 1892 when it was noticed that a section of an otherwise level site was studded with irregular mounds. Thought to date from around 150 BC, the dwellings were built on a series of tall platforms which raised them above the surrounding marshland. An interesting collection of artefacts recovered from the site can be seen in the town museum.

In its time, Glastonbury has been called the Ancient Avalon, the New Jerusalem, and the "Holyest Erthe" in England. It is a place of natural enchantment which attracts an ever-growing number of pilgrims of the new age who are drawn by its unique landscape, atmosphere and quality of light.

One of the greatest mysteries of the locality, indeed one which may possess something of a credibility gap, is difficult to observe except from the air. Much loved and eagerly propounded by those with an interest in astrology, the **Glastonbury Zodiac** was brought to light in 1935 by Katherine Maltwood when she was researching a book on the Holy Grail. According to Maltwood, the 12 signs of the zodiac appear in their correct order as recognisable features of the landscape, their outlines being delineated by streams, tracks, ridges and ancient boundaries. The entire formation lies within a circle with a seven mile radius whose centre lies three miles to the south of Glastonbury near the village of Butleigh. Its origins remain a subject of speculation.

ILMINSTER

The old ecclesiastical and agricultural centre of Ilminster lies near the junction of the A358 and A303. Meaning "minster on the River Isle", the settlement takes its name from church which was founded here by the Saxon King Ine in the 8th century. The borough was recorded in the Domesday Book as having a market and three mills, and during the medieval era it grew to become a thriving wool and lace-making town. This period of prosperity is reflected in the town's unusually large parish church, a magnificent 15th century minster whose massive multi-pinnacled tower is modelled on Wells cathedral. Thanks to a Georgian restoration the interior is surprisingly plain; however, it does contain a number of interesting tombs and monumental brasses. A stroll around the old part of Ilminster reveals a number of lovely old buildings, many of which are constructed of golden Ham stone. These include the chantry

house, the old grammar school and the colonnaded market house.

177

Dillington House, on the outskirts of Ilminster, is a handsome part-Tudor mansion which is the former home of the Speke family. In the time of James II, John Speke was an officer in the Duke of Monmouth's ill-fated rebel army which landed at Lyme Regis in 1685. However, following its disastrous defeat at Sedgemoor, he was forced to flee abroad, leaving his brother, George, who had done no more than shake the Duke's hand, to face the wrath of Judge Jeffreys. The infamous Hanging Judge sentenced poor George to death, justifying his decision with the words, "His family owes a life and he shall die for his brother." Dillington House is currently leased to Somerset County Council and functions as an adult education centre.

KINGSDON

A mile east of Kingsdon lies the delightful National Trust-owned country house and garden of **Lytes Cary**. This late-medieval manor house was built by succeeding generations of the Lyte family, the best-known member of which is Henry Lyte, the Elizabethan horticulturalist who translated Dodoen's Cruydeboeck from the Dutch to create the celebrated work of reference known as Lyte's Herbal. Dedicated to the Queen, it went on to be reprinted several times as an interest in physic gardening began to develop. The present garden is an enchanting combination of formality and eccentricity: there is an open lawn lined with magnificent yew topiary, an orchard filled with quince, pear and apple trees, and a network of enclosed paths which every now and then reveal a view of the house, a lily-pond or a classical statue. The house was built over a long period and incorporates a 14th-century chapel, a 15th-century hall and a 16th-century great chamber.

LANGPORT

The **Langport and River Parrett Visitor Centre** provides visitors with an opportunity to learn about life on the Somerset Levels and Moors, with a hands-on "discovery room", cycle hire and more.

Defended by an earthwork rampart during Saxon times, by 930 Langport was an important commercial centre which minted its own coins. The town's surviving east gate incorporates a curious "hanging" chapel which sits above the arch on an upper level. The tower at Huish Episcopi can be seen through its barrel-vaulted gateway. Langport's own parish church is worth a look for its beautiful stained-glass windows and finely-carved 12th-century lintel over the south doorway.

During the 18th and 19th centuries, Langport flourished as a banking centre, and the local independent bank, Stuckey's, became known for their impressive branches, many of which can still be seen in the surrounding towns and villages trading under the banner of NatWest. At the time of its amalgamation in 1909, Stuckey's had more notes in circulation than any other in the country except the Bank of England.

Throughout history, the Langport Gap has been the site of a number of important military encounters. Two of the most significant occurred over 1000 years apart: the first involved Geraint, King of the Dumnonii in the 6th century, and the second, the Battle of Langport of July 1645, gave Parliament almost total control of the South West during the English Civil War.

MARTOCK

Surrounded by fertile arable land, Martock's long-established affluence is reflected in its impressive part 13th century parish church. A former abbey church which once belonged to the monks of Mont St Michel in Normandy, it boasts one of the finest tie-beams roofs in Somerset, almost every part of which is covered in beautiful carvings.

The old part of Martock contains an unusual number of fine buildings. The National Trust-owned **Treasurer's House** is situated opposite the church. Recently refurbished, this handsome part 13th-century residence incorporates a medieval great hall and cross wing, and a kitchen annexe which was added around 1500. The nearby **Old Court House** is a former parish building which served the locality for 200 years as a grammar school, and to the west, Martock's 17th-century Manor House is the former home of Edward Parker, the man who exposed the Gunpowder Plot after Guy Fawkes had warned him against attending Parliament on the fateful night.

The Somerset Guild of Craftsmen Gallery at Yandles of Martock contains a fascinating range of work made by the county's craftspeople. Items on display include musical instruments, spinning wheels, turned wood, furniture, ceramics, textiles, silver and metalwork.

MINEHEAD

The West Somerset Railway terminates at Minehead, a popular seaside town lying at the foot of the wooded promontory known as North Hill. Despite sounding like a product of the industrial age, this is one of the oldest settlements in the county, having been a busy Bristol Channel port since the time of the Celts. The old harbour lies in the lee of North Hill, making it one of the safest landing places in the West Country. At one time, ships would arrive here with their cargoes of wool and livestock from Ireland, crops from the plantations of Virginia, coal from the valleys of South Wales, and day trippers from Cardiff and Bristol. Today, however, the merchantmen and paddle steamers have gone and the harbour is the peaceful haunt of sailing dinghies and pleasure craft.

A good view of the old port can be had from the **North Hill Nature Trail**, a 3 mile walk which starts near the lifeboat station on the harbourside. Minehead's parish church of St Michael stands in a prominent position below North Hill. A substantial part 14th century building, in past centuries a light was kept burning in the tower to help guide ships into the harbour. The interior contains a number of unusual features, including a rare medieval prayer book, or missal, which once belonged to the Richard Fitzjames, a local vicar who went on to become Bishop of London in 1506.

Minehead's 19th century decline as a port was offset by its gradual expansion as a seaside resort. The local powers that be went to great pains to attract a suitably respectable clientele, and indeed a local bylaw was in force until 1890 which forbad anyone over ten years of age from swimming in the sea "except from a bathing machine, tent, or other effective screen." The arrival of the railway in 1874 failed to trigger the brutal expansion experienced by some other seaside resorts, and during the First World War, Minehead was able to provide an escape from the ravages of war at timeless establishments like the Strand Hotel, where guests were entertained by such stars as Anna Pavlova and Gladys Cooper.

Improvements to Minehead have been gradual. In the 1920s, an impressive municipal park known as **Blenheim Gardens** was built near the seafront which incorporates "Little England", a model country town with its own miniature railway and floodlights. The most momentous change, however, came in 1962 when Billy Butlin opened a holiday camp at the eastern end of the esplanade. Now updated and renamed **Somerwest World**, this popular attraction has done much to transform present-day Minehead into an all-round family resort.

MONKSILVER

A handsome manor house lies the southern edge of Monksilver. Built in the middle of Elizabeth I's reign on the site of a monastic settlement, **Combe Sydenham Hall** was the home of Elizabeth Sydenham, second wife of Sir Francis Drake. According to local legend, after Elizabeth had consented to the marriage, she grew so weary of waiting for Sir Francis to return from his voyages around the world that she resolved to wed another. While on her way to the church, however, a meteorite flew out of the sky and smashed into the ground in front of her, a sign, she thought, that she ought to wait on. The original meteorite, now known as "Drake's Cannonball", is on display in the great hall and is said to bring luck to those who touch it. The 500-acre grounds have been designated a country park and contain a working corn mill complete with water wheel, an Elizabethan-style garden, woodland walks, children's play area and deer park.

The estate also incorporates a modern trout farm which stands on the site of a fully restored Tudor trout hatchery dating from the end of the 16th century. Here, visitors can purchase fresh rainbow trout, smoked trout and a number of other specialist food products made here under the "Monksmill" label. **Nettlecombe Court**, one mile to the west, is an ancient manor which once belonged to the Raleigh family, ancestors of Sir Walter. Later, it passed by marriage to the Cornish Trevelyans, and it is now a field studies centre which is open to visitors on Thursdays only by appointment.

MONTACUTE

The superb National Trust-owned **Montacute House** was built in the 1580s by Edward Phelips,

Queen Elizabeth's Master of the Rolls, and is considered a masterpiece of Renaissance architecture. Constructed of golden Ham stone to an H-shaped design, it is adorned with characteristic open parapets, fluted columns, twisted pinnacles, oriel windows and carved statues. The long gallery, one the grandest of its kind in Britain, houses a fine collection of Tudor and Jacobean portraits which are on permanent loan from London's National Portrait Gallery. Other noteworthy features include the stone and stained-glass screen in the great hall, and Lord Curzon's bath, an Edwardian addition which is concealed in a bedroom cupboard. An established story tells of how Curzon, a senior Tory politician, waited at Montacute in 1923 for news that he was to be called to form a new government. The call never came.

Montacute House stands within a magnificent landscaped park which incorporates a walled formal garden, a fig walk, an orangery, and a cedar lawn formerly known as "Pig's Wheaties's Orchard".

Five hundred years before the present Elizabethan house was built, a controversial castle was constructed on the nearby hill by William the Conqueror's half-brother, Robert, Count of Mortain. The Saxons were angered by his choice of site, for they believed it to be a holy place where King Alfred had buried a fragment of Christ's cross. In 1068, they rose up and attacked the castle in one of the many unsuccessful piecemeal revolts against the Norman occupation. Ironically, a subsequent Count of Mortain was found guilty of treason and forced into founding, and then donating all his lands to, a Cluniac priory on the site now occupied by Montacute village. The castle has long since disappeared, as has the monastery, with the exception of its part 12th century priory church which contains some striking monuments to members of the Phelips family.

Montacute is also home to the **TV & Radio Memorabilia Museum**, hosting a fine collection of vintage radios and radiograms, wireless receivers and early television sets, as well as a variety of books, magazines, annuals and other memorabilia of the great (and sometimes kitsch) world of early TV and radio. The museum also has information on some pleasant local walks in the area.

MUCHELNEY

Muchelney is the location of an impressive part-ruined Benedictine monastery which was founded in Saxon times around 950. During the medieval period, **Muchelney Abbey** grew to emulate its great rival at Glastonbury; however, after the Dissolution of the Monasteries in 1539, the building gradually fell into disrepair and much of its stone was removed to provide building material for the surrounding village. In spite of this, a substantial part of the original structure remains, including the south cloister and abbot's lodge. Now under the custodianship of English Heritage, an exhibition of pottery by John Leach and furniture by Stuart Interiors can be seen in the abbey grounds.

Muchelney's parish church is worth seeing for its remarkable early 17th-century illuminations on the ceiling of the nave. Opposite stands the **Priest's House**, a late-medieval hall house with large Gothic windows which was originally a residence for priests serving at the church across the road. This has been refurbished by the National Trust.

PORLOCK

Porlock is an ancient settlement once frequented by Saxon kings which in recent decades has become a popular riding and holiday centre. The village is filled with lovely old buildings, most notably the 15th-century **Dovery Manor** with its striking traceried hall window, and the largely 13th-century red sandstone parish church with its curious truncated shingle spire, the top section of which was lost in a 17th-century thunderstorm. The church also contains an exceptional font, an unusual Easter sepulchre, and a remarkable double tomb consisting of almost life-size alabaster effigies of Sir John Harrington, who was knighted by Henry V during the Agincourt campaign, and his wife, who lived on for over half a century after Sir John's death in 1418.

Porlock has long had the feel of a community at the end of the world thanks to its position at the foot of **Porlock Hill**, the notorious incline which carries the A39 onto Exmoor. The road rises 1,350 feet in under three miles and in places has a gradient of 1 in 4. A less challenging toll road winds its way through the Lovelace estate from **Porlock Weir**, a hamlet lying on the coast a mile and a half to the northwest of Porlock. Now a small tide-affected har-

bour populated by pleasure craft, this was once an important seaport. The Danes sacked it on a number of occasions in the 10th century, and in 1052, Harold, the future king of England, landed here from Ireland to begin a career which ended at the Battle of Hastings. Now peaceful and picturesque, Porlock Weir offers a number of interesting attractions, including a working blacksmith's forge, a picture gallery, and a glass studio which provides visitors with the opportunity to see lead crystal being made in the traditional manner. A submerged forest, a relic of the last Ice Age, lies a short distance offshore and can be glimpsed at low tide.

SELWORTHY

Selworthy Beacon is part of the 12,400-acre Holnicote Estate. The estate covers four and a half miles of coastline between Minehead and Porlock Bay and is now owned by the National Trust. At Hurlstone Point, the South West Coast Path curves inland to avoid the possibility of landslips in the soft Foreland Sandstone before dropping down to Bossington; however, there is an alternative, more arduous clifftop path which should be attempted by experienced walkers only.

The Holnicote Estate extends over 5 miles inland to the 1,700-foot **Dunkery Beacon**, the highest point on Exmoor. It also incorporates 15 farms, many of them on the high moor, and

Selworthy

a number of small settlements, including Selworthy, a superb model village of whitewashed cob and thatch cottages which was built by Sir Thomas Dyke-Acland to house his estate workers.

SOMERTON

Somerton is a fine old town which was the capital of Somerset for a time under the West Saxons. The settlement grew up around an important crossroads to the northwest of the church. However, an expansion towards the end of the 13th century altered the original layout and created the present open market place with its distinctive **Market Cross** and town hall, both later additions. Between 1278 and 1371, Somerton became the location of the county

Somerton Market Cross

gaol and meeting place of the shire courts. It also continued to develop as a market town, a role which is reflected in such delightfully down-to-earth street names as Cow Square and Pig Street (now Broad Street).

Present-day Somerton is filled with handsome old shops, inns and houses, the majority of which are constructed of local bluish lias limestone. The general atmosphere of mature prosperity is enhanced by the presence of a number of striking early buildings. These include the 17th-century **Hext Almshouses** and the part 13th-century church with its magnificent 15th-century tie-beam roof and unusual transeptal south tower.

STOKE-SUB-HAMDON

Stoke-sub-Hamdon is an attractive village whose eastern part contains a fine part Norman church and whose western part contains the remains of a late medieval priory. The latter was built in the 14th and 15th centuries for the

priests of the now-demolished chantry chapel of St Nicholas. The remains, which include an impressive great hall, are now under the ownership of the National Trust.

To the south of the village lies the 400 foot **Ham Hill** (or Hamdon Hill), the source of the beautiful honey-coloured building stone of which so many of the surrounding villages are constructed. This solitary limestone outcrop rises abruptly from the Somerset plain providing breathtaking views of the surrounding countryside. A substantial hill fort was sited here during the Iron Age which was subsequently overrun by the ancient Romans. The new occupants built their own fortification here to guard the Fosse Way and its important intersection with the road between Dorchester and the Bristol Channel at nearby Ilchester.

A war memorial to 44 local men who died in the First World War stands at the summit of the hill which has now been designated a country park. The combination of the view, the old earthwork ramparts, and maze of overgrown quarry workings make this an outstanding picnic and recreation area.

TAUNTON

Taunton, the county town of Somerset, has only been its sole centre of administration since 1936, previous county towns having been Ilchester and Somerton. The settlement was founded as a military camp by the Saxon King Ine in the 8th century, and by Norman times it had grown to have its own Augustinian monastery, minster and castle. An extensive structure whose purpose has always been more administrative than military, the castle was nevertheless the focus of two important sieges during the English Civil War. A few years later, over 150 followers of the Duke of Monmouth were sentenced to death here by the infamous Judge Jeffreys during the Bloody Autumn Assizes which followed the Pitchfork Rebellion of 1685. Even now, the judge's ghost is said to haunt the castle grounds on September nights.

Taunton's historic Castle is home to the **Somerset County Museum**, a highly informative and impressive museum containing a large and important collection of exhibits on the archaeology, natural and human history of the county. There is a wealth of exceptional material evidence in the archaeology galleries, illuminating prehistoric and Roman Somerset. Notable items include wooden trackways from the Somerset Levels, the Low Ham Roman mosaic and a Bronze Age shield, recently found at South Cadbury. The museum also boasts a special display chronicling the colourful history of the Somerset Light Infantry, as part of the Somerset Military Museum within the castle. Visitors can also explore the medieval almshouse in the castle courtyard.

Somerset's famous County Cricket Ground occupies part of the old priory grounds which once stretched down to the river. A section of

Somerset County Cricket Museum

the old monastic gatehouse known as the Priory Barn can still be seen beside the cricket ground. Now restored, this medieval stone building now houses the fascinating **Somerset County Cricket Museum**.

In common with many other towns and villages in the West Country, Taunton was a thriving wool, cloth-making, and later silk, centre during the late Middle Ages. The profits earned by the medieval clothiers went to build not one, but two huge churches: St James' and St Mary's. Both have soaring Perpendicular towers, which have since been rebuilt, and imposing interiors; the former contains a striking carved stone font and the latter an elegant painted roof adorned with angels. The town centre is scattered with other fine buildings, most notably the timber-framed Tudor House in Fore Street and the 17th-century almshouses. Other visitor attractions include **Vivary Park**, with its ponds, gardens and jogging trail, and the impressive **Brewhouse Theatre and Arts Centre**.

A pleasant walk follows the towpath of the **Bridgwater and Taunton Canal**, a 14-mile inland waterway which was constructed in the 1820s and fully reopened in the summer of

1994 following decades of neglect and a 20 year programme of restoration. A relative latecomer when it first opened in 1827, the canal was constructed as part of an ambitious scheme to create a freight route between Exeter and Bristol which avoided the treacherous journey around the Cornish peninsula.

THORNE ST MARGARET

The Vale of Taunton Deane, the broad valley between the southern Quantocks and the Devon border, contains some of the most fertile farmland in the county. Thanks to its prolonged agricultural prosperity, the area is dotted with fine country houses. Three that are worthy of note can be found to the west of Wellington in the lanes around the village of Thorne St Margaret. **Cothay Manor**, described by Pevsner as "one of the most perfect smaller English manor houses of the late 15th century", stands beside the River Tone a mile to the west of the village; the gardens in particular are worth seeing. The slightly older **Greenham Barton**, which retains its early 15th-century two-storey porch and open hall, is situated a mile to the south; and **Wellisford Manor**, which was built of brick around 1700 in a style reflecting the contemporary architecture of nearby Devon, lies half a mile to the north.

TINTINHULL

Tintinhull House Garden was laid out in the early 20th century. The garden is divided by walls and hedges into a series of distinctive areas, each with its own planting theme. These include a pool garden with a delightful lily- and iris-filled pond, a kitchen garden, and a sunken garden which is cleverly designed to give the impression it has many different levels.

The garden is set in the grounds of **Tintinhull House**, an early 17th-century manor farm to which a spectacular west front was added around 1700. Sadly not open to the public, the house overlooks an attractive triangular green which forms the nucleus of the sprawling village of Tintinhull. A number of other interesting buildings can be seen here, including Tintinhull Court, a part-medieval rectory which was remodelled in the 17th and 18th centuries, the Dower House, which was built by the Napper family in 1687, and St Margaret's parish church, a rare example in Somerset of a rectangular single-cell church.

TOLLAND

The lovely **Gaulden Manor** dates from the 12th century, although the present house is largely 17th century. It once belonged to the Turberville family, a name borrowed by Thomas Hardy for use in his novel, *Tess of the D'Urbervilles*.

Still in use as a family home, the house contains an exceptional collection of period furniture and fine china. The great hall has a su-

Gaulden Manor

perb plaster ceiling and fireplace, and the room known as the chapel boasts a particularly fine oak screen. Set in a beautiful wooded combe, Gaulden Manor is surrounded by a series of small ornamental enclosures known as the "Little Gardens of Gaulden". These include a scent garden, butterfly garden, rose garden, bog garden and Old Monk's fish pond.

TREBOROUGH

Towards Treborough, the land rises into the **Brendon Hills**, the upland area within the Exmoor National Park lying to the east and north of the River Exe. During the mid 19th century, iron ore was mined in significant quantities above the village of Treborough, then carried down a steep mineral railway to the coast for shipment to the furnaces of South Wales. At one time almost 1000 people were employed by the Ebbw Vale Company, strict Nonconformists who imposed a rigorous teetotal regime on their workers. (Those wanting a drink had to walk across the moor all the way to Raleigh's Cross.)

The company also founded a miners' settlement with a temperance hotel and three chapels, which became renowned for the achievements of its choir and fife and drum band. Sections of the old mineral railway can still be made out today, such as the one near the junction of the A39 and the B3190 to the east of

Washford, and the two-mile stretch leading down to the coast at Watchet is now a pleasant footpath. The Brendon Hills also offer some fine walking through attractive woodland and open moorland, and further south, the surprisingly well-assimilated **Wimbleball and Clatworthy Reservoirs** offer some good facilities for picnickers, anglers and watersports enthusiasts.

WASHFORD

At Washford, a lane to the south of the A39 leads to the remains of **Cleeve Abbey**, the only monastery in Somerset to have belonged to the austere Cistercian order. The abbey was founded in 1198 by the Earl of Lincoln in the beautiful valley of the River Washford, or *Vallis Florida*. Many of the great monastic houses were allowed to fall into disrepair following Henry VIII's Dissolution of the Monasteries in 1539. However, the cloister buildings at Cleeve were soon put to domestic use and are now among the most complete in the country.

Somewhat less venerable, but still enjoyable, attractions in Washford include **Tropiquaria** - as its name suggests, this wildlife park features tropical animals; there's also an aquarium, aviary and the chance for visitors to stroke snakes, handle tarantulas and in many other ways get in touch with their wilder side - and the **Torre Cider Farm** - admission free.

WATCHET

Watchet has been a port since Saxon times. In the 6th century, St Decuman is reputed to have landed here from Wales, bringing with him a cow to provide sustenance, and in the 9th and 10th centuries, the settlement was important enough to have been sacked by the Vikings on at least three occasions. By the 17th century, Watchet had become an important paper manufacturing centre, and by the mid 19th, around 30,000 tons of iron ore from the Brendon hills were being exported each year through its docks. Coleridge's imaginary crew set sail from here in "The Rime Of The Ancient Mariner", the epic poem which was written when the author was residing at nearby Nether Stowey.

Unlike many similar-sized ports which fell into disuse following the arrival of the railways, Watchet docks has somehow managed to survive. Despite the total decline in the iron ore trade, sizable cargo vessels continue to tie up here to be loaded with goods bound for the Iberian peninsula and elsewhere.

In recent years, Watchet has also developed as something of a coastal resort whose attractions include an interesting small museum dedicated to local maritime history.

WILLITON

Williton, a former Saxon royal estate, is now a sizable village on the busy holiday route to Minehead and the west Somerset coast. The manor was the home of Sir Reginald Fitzurse, one of Thomas Becket's murderers, who was forced to sell part of it to pay for his journey of repentance to Rome and the Holy Land. The Knights Hospitaller founded an institution here which continued to be known as **Williton Hospital** until the 17th century.

Present-day Williton contains the diesel locomotive workshops of the **West Somerset Railway**, the excellent **Williton Pottery** and, just off the A39 at **Orchard Mill**, a restored water wheel and **The Bakelite Museum** - a must for any fan of this truly amazing man-made wonder, the "pioneer of plastics". A delightful small country manor house, Orchard Wyndham, is situated a mile to the southwest of the village. Built in the 14th century and much-altered since, it has been used as a family home by the Wyndhams for the past four and a half centuries.

WINCANTON

The old cloth-making centre of Wincanton is an attractive former coaching town lying almost exactly half way between London and the long-established naval base at Plymouth. In the heyday of the horse-drawn carriage, up to twenty coaches a day would stop here. At that time the inns could provide lodging for scores of travellers and stabling for over 250 horses. The old sector stands on a draughty hillside above the River Cale. It still contains a surprising number of fine Georgian buildings, some of which were constructed to replace earlier ones destroyed in a town fire in 1747. Apart from the medieval carving of St Eligius in the north porch, the parish church is a Victorian rebuild which only merits a brief look.

Modern Wincanton is a peaceful light industrial town whose best-known attraction is probably its **National Hunt Racecourse**. Horse rac-

ing began in the locality in the 18th century and moved to its present site to the north of the town centre in 1927. Regular meetings are held here between October and May, or for golfing enthusiasts, the racecourse incorporates a challenging nine hole pay and play course which is open throughout the year. Also worth visiting is the beautiful **Hadspen House Garden**, situated beside the A371 Shepton Mallet road, 4 miles northwest of Wincanton.

YEOVIL

With its 28,000 inhabitants and strategic position at the junction of several main routes, Yeovil is the largest centre of population in south Somerset. Despite its up-to-date character, Yeovil's origins go back to the time of the ancient Romans. During the Middle Ages, a lively livestock and produce market was established in the town which continues to be held here every Friday.

Yeovil's parish **Church of St John the Baptist** is the only significant medieval structure to survive, most of its other early buildings having been destroyed in a series of town fires in the 17th century. Perhaps its finest internal feature is the plain brass lectern which is believed to date from around 1450. One of only five still in existence, it is the only one to be found in a parish church.

During the 18th century, Yeovil developed into a flourishing coaching and industrial centre whose output included gloves, leather, sailcloth and cheese. This rapid expansion was enhanced by the arrival of the railway in the mid 19th century, then in the 1890s, James Petter, a local ironmonger and pioneer of the internal combustion engine, founded a business which went on to become one of the largest manufacturers of diesel engines in Britain. Although production was eventually transferred to the Midlands, a subsidiary set up to produce aircraft during the First World War has since evolved into the present-day helicopter plant.

A fascinating museum documenting the social and industrial history of the area from prehistoric and Roman times through to the agricultural and industrial revolutions can be found near the Octagon Theatre in the centre of Yeovil. Situated in Wyndham House in Hendford, the recently-refurbished **Museum of South Somerset** uses a series of imaginative settings to recapture the atmosphere of the times.

The Ashcott Inn

185

50 Bath Road,
Ashcott,
near Street,
Somerset TA7 9QQ
Tel: 01458 210282
Fax: 01458 210282

Directions:
From junction 23 on the M5 take the A39 towards Glastonbury. Ashcott lies 10 miles along this road and The Ashcott Inn can be found on the right.

Dating back to the 16th century, when it was a coaching inn, **The Ashcott Inn** is a splendid old pub and restaurant that continues to offer hospitality to travellers and locals alike. Very much a family inn, the lovely relaxed atmosphere found here is down to the manager's hard work and their warm and friendly personalities. At the back of the inn is a large and well maintained beer garden along with a safe, purpose built play area for children whilst, inside, the inn still retains the character and charm from those long ago coaching days. The ancient ceiling beams have escaped the renovators hands as too has the feature fireplace with woodburning stove and a mass of gleaming horse brasses hang around both the bar and restaurant.

Though The Ashcott Inn has a superb range of drinks, including real ales, served from its bar, the inn has gained an enviable reputation for the high standard of cuisine served in the charming restaurant. The evening menu changes daily and is a mouthwatering array of imaginative dishes that are far removed from the usual pub fare. Carefully put together to cater to all tastes, the delicious homecooked dishes make excellent use of local and seasonal produce. Meanwhile, diners can accompany their meal with a wine taken from the extensive list or try one of the featured wines of the month. Although the lunchtime menu is different it is no less exciting and, once visited, it is easy to see why The Ashcott Inn is so popular.

Opening Hours: Mon-Fri 11.00-15.00, 19.00-23.00; Sat 11.00-23.00; Sun 12.00-22.30

Food: Bar meals and snacks, À la carte

Credit Cards: Visa, Access, Delta, Switch, Amex, Diners

Facilities: Large beer garden, Car parking, Children's play area, Functions catered for

Entertainment: Skittles

Local Places of Interest/Activities: The Shoe Museum at Street 3 miles, Glastonbury 4 miles, Wells 9 miles, Cheddar Gorge 11 miles, Walking, Cycling, Horse riding, Fishing

186   The Bell Inn

Bruton Road,
Evercreech,
Somerset BA4 6HY
Tel: 01749 830287
Fax: 01749 831296

Directions:

From junction 23 on the M5 take the A39 to Glastonbury and then the A361 towards Shepton Mallet. Just south of the town turn right on to the A371 towards Castle Cary and then left on to the B3081. The Bell Inn lies through the village, opposite the church.

The Bell Inn, found in the heart of this pretty Somerset village, lies opposite the village church and close to the delightful main square at Evercreech where the village cross still stands. Built in around the 1700s, this splendid stone building has been added to over the years but the various extensions are now very much incorporated into the whole and the long front façade makes a particularly pleasing picture. Inside, the inn is open plan with the large space being warmed by the woodburning stove that stands in one of the building's two original stone fireplaces. Numerous pictures add a homely touch to the walls and there is a separate cosy and intimate restaurant area that is as relaxed and comfortable as the rest of the inn.

An excellent place to come to for a taste of real Somerset rough cider, there are also four real ales, many other beers, lagers and spirits, and a good selection of wines served from the bar. The extensive menu, which is supplemented by a list of daily specials, is a mouthwatering list of freshly cut sandwiches and pasta dishes through to old favourites like shepherd's pie and peppered duck breast. There really is something here to suit every taste and occasion. However, good food and drink in pleasant surroundings are not all The Bell Inn has to offer customers as there is also superb accommodation here that is not only ideal for families but also for those wishing to explore the many delights of the surrounding area.

Opening Hours: Mon-Sat 11.30-23.00; Sun 12.00-22.30

Food: Bar snacks and meals, À la carte

Credit Cards: Visa, Mastercard, Delta

Accommodation: 1 double room, 2 twin rooms, all en suite

Facilities: Beer garden, Car parking, Functions catered for

Entertainment: Regular live music or Karaoke, Darts, Pool, Skittles

Local Places of Interest/Activities: Royal Bath and Wells Showground 1 mile, East Somerset Railway 3 miles, Hadspen House 5 miles, Wells 8 miles, Glastonbury 9 miles, Walking, Cycling, Horse riding,

The Candlelight Inn   187

Bishopswood,
near Chard,
Somerset TA20 3RS
Tel: 01460 234476

Directions:

From junction 25 on the M5 take the A38 into Taunton and then the B3170 towards Honiton. Approximately 1 mile after passing through Fyfett turn left on to a minor road and The Candlelight Inn lies in the heart of the village.

A traditional and attractive stone building, dating from the 17th century, **The Candlelight Inn** is a perfect country inn with a large and secluded rear garden at the bottom of which runs the River Yarty. Though very rural, this delightfully situated inn is also well placed for Taunton and Yeovil as well as the Devon and Dorset coast. Inside, the story is the same, with many of the building's original features remaining in this inviting inn. Open plan and with a wealth of beams, a centrally placed fire adds a touch of warmth in winter as well as being a focal point to the bar. Comfortable and cosy, this is a friendly pub with a relaxed ambience where both locals and visitors can meet and enjoy the hospitality.

As well as the bar area, there is a games room and also an equally attractive dining room. Well known for its beers, ales and spirits, the landlords, Graham and Karen Robotham have also gained an enviable reputation for the high standard of their cuisine. Karen is a trained chef and the excellent menus, which include light lunches, sandwiches and full à la carte are a tasty mix of traditional pub food and more exotic treats such as chilli con carne and curry. A friendly place, with attentive service, whatever the season, The Candlelight Inn is sure to provide excellent hospitality.

Opening Hours: Mon-Sat 12.00-14.30, 19.00-23.00; Sun 12.00-14.30, 19.00-22.30

Food: Bar meals and snacks, À la carte, Traditional Sunday lunch

Credit Cards: Visa, Access, Delta, Switch

Facilities: Large garden, Car parking, Children welcome, Functions catered for

Entertainment: Skittles, Darts

Local Places of Interest/Activities: Poundisford Park 6 miles, Taunton 8 miles, Wellington Monument 8 miles, South coast 15 miles, Walking, Cycling, Horse riding, Fishing, Golf

188

The Globe Inn

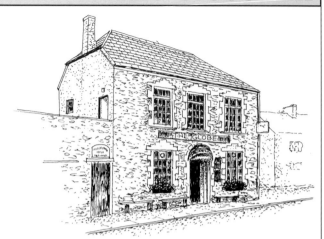

Fore Street,
Milverton,
Somerset TA4 1JX
Tel: 01823 400534
Fax: 01823 401201

Directions:

From junction 26 on the M5 turn north-wards and take the B3187 to Milverton. Continue through the village and The Globe Inn lies on the right.

At the centre of this once thriving weaving village lies **The Globe Inn**, an imposing sandstone building that was built, originally, as a Quakers' meeting house some 400 years ago. Situated right on Milverton's main road, there is, at the back, a three tiered garden (for adults only) which provides a secluded haven from the bustle of everyday village life. Inside, the inn has a Tudor style, complete with beamed ceilings, and the open fire makes not only a fine feature but adds a warm glow in winter. Very much a village inn, where local musicians appear on a regular basis, landlords Stewart and Linda Mudge, also ensure that regulars, and visitors, can enjoy their favourite tipple from the bar which could include one of the local real ales.

Though this is very much a place for people to meet up, have a drink and catch up on the local news, The Globe Inn also has a fine reputation for the high standard of its cuisine. Linda is a classically trained chef so customers can be assured that the tempt-ing dishes on the menus here are certainly different from the local pub fare and are well worth trying. As well as the cosy and intimate restaurant, the inn has a less formal bistro, reach via a tunnel under the building, which is ideal for a more casual meal. To accompany the meal, there is also an extensive wine list. This is a charming inn, that provides good food, drink and comfortable accommodation which lies in the beautiful Vale of Taunton.

Opening Hours: Mon 12.00-23.00; Tue-Thu 12.00-15.00, 17.30-23.00; Fri-Sat 12.00-23.00; Sun 12.00-22.30

Food: Bar meals and snacks, À la carte

Credit Cards: None

Accommodation: 1 double room en suite

Facilities: Beer garden, Limited car parking

Entertainment: Regular live music, Darts, Pool, Skittles

Local Places of Interest/Activities:
Gaulden Manor 3 miles, Taunton 6 miles, West Somerset Railway 7 miles, Beaches 12 miles, Walking, Cycling, Horse riding, Fishing

The Globe

189

Market Place,
Somerton,
Somerset TA11 7LX
Tel: 01458 272474
Fax: 01458 274789

Directions:

From junction 23 on the M5 take the A39 to Street and then the B3151 to Somerton. The Globe lies in the centre of the town.

The ancient capital of Wessex, Somerton is a handsome old market town that has a wealth of old shops, inns and houses and **The Globe**. Situated on the edge of the 13th century market square, this splendid 17th century coaching inn once stood on the main London to the West Country route and so was a bustling place. Although today travellers come by car, this is still very much a popular place where both locals and visitors are treated to the delights of a true English country inn. Outside, at the rear of the inn, there is an attractive walled beer garden, a skittles alley that is well used by the locals and a children's play area. Entering this soft limestone building is like taking a step back in time. The large inglenook fireplace is kept alight throughout the winter and, along with the ancient ceiling beams and mass of curios hanging from the walls, there is a true olde worlde feel.

A well established inn with a strong local following, landlords Chris and Jenny Nightingale have been serving their needs since 1991. As well as the excellent range of drinks, including real ales, served from the bar, The Globe has a well earned reputation for the high standard of its cuisine. Specialising in fish, which is delivered from Cornwall three or four times a week, the menu varies depending on the catch. However, what is never in doubt is the superb menu that is freshly prepared with both style and flair and served in the spacious surroundings of the inn's conservatory restaurant.

Opening Hours: Mon-Sat 11.00-14.30, 17.30-23.00; Sun 12.00-15.00, 19.00-22.30

Food: Bar meals and snacks, À la carte

Credit Cards: Visa, Mastercard, Access, Delta, Switch

Facilities: Beer garden, Car parking, Children's play area, Functions catered for

Entertainment: Skittles, Pool, Darts

Local Places of Interest/Activities: Lytes Cary Manor 3 miles, Priest's House at Muchelney 4 miles, The Shoe Museum at Street 5 miles, Glastonbury 7 miles, Walking, Cycling, Horse riding, Fishing. Golf

190

The Greyhound Inn

1 Lime Street,
Stogursey,
near Bridgwater,
Somerset TA5 1QR
Tel: 01278 732490

Directions:

From junction 23 on the M5 take the A38 to Bridgwater and then the A39 towards Minehead. Approximately 5 miles from Bridgwater turn right on to a minor road signposted Stogursey. Enter the village and turn right into Lime Street just beyond the village church. The Greyhound Inn lies on the left.

Found tucked away in this historic village, **The Greyhound Inn** is a typical village inn that is run by landlords Glenn and Sue. Although Glenn is new to the licensing trade, his partner, Sue, has been in the industry throughout her life and her expertise and the couples amiable nature has certainly helped to make this a popular place with both locals and visitors alike. Very much an inn for all the family: outside there is a large, well maintained beer garden with children's play area whilst, inside, one of the two bars is used as a family room. An attractive and cosy inn, warmed in the winter by the wood burning stove sitting in the fireplace, this is a comfortable place to enjoy the cask conditioned ale and rough cider that is served from the bar along with all the usual drinks.

Food too features here and the menu provides a mouthwatering selection of traditional English pub food. Whilst Friday evening is fish and chip night, the house speciality, homemade pies are always on the menu and children too are catered for with their own special selection of dishes. But, what makes The Greyhound Inn particularly different is the unusual table skittles - there are only two in existence - which is like a miniature skittles alley. The inn also has a normal size alley as well as the more usual pub games that are played here by enthusiastic locals and visitors alike.

Opening Hours: Mon-Fri 12.00-15.00, 17.30-23.00; Sat 12.00-23.00; Sun 12.00-15.00, 19.00-22.30

Food: Bar snacks and meals, Children's menu

Credit Cards: None

Facilities: Beer garden, Children's play area, Car parking, Functions catered for

Entertainment: Occasional live music, Table and normal skittles, Darts, Pool

Local Places of Interest/Activities: Coleridge Cottage 2 miles, Beaches 3 miles, Quantock Hills 5 miles, Bridgwater 7 miles, Walking, Cycling, Horse riding, Fishing, Bird watching

The Hunters Lodge Inn   191

Leigh Common,
near Wincanton,
Somerset BA9 8LD
Tel: 01747 840439
Fax: 01747 840439

Directions:

From junction 18 on the M4 take the A36 and then the A361 to Frome. From the town take the A361, A359 and then the A371 to Wincanton. Leave the town on the A303 towards Andover and take the first exit at Tinklers Hill, signposted Wincanton Racecourse. The Hunters Lodge Inn can be found on the left.

Built in the 18th century as a coaching inn on what was then the main London to Cornwall route, **The Hunters Lodge Inn** is an attractive old building of mellow stone that stands back from the road. The interior of this delightful old inn is as pleasing as the outside would suggest and the cosy feel of the inn is enhanced by the woodburning stove found in one of the building's three fireplaces. The inn's connection with horses - from the coaching days and its closeness to the racecourse - are highlighted by the mass of horse tack that hangs from the walls. As well as the bar area, the inn has a small and intimate restaurant which opens out into the beer garden. Here, not only can adults enjoy their food and drink in the sunshine but there is an aviary in the corner and a large children's play area complete with climbing frames and swings.

Landlord, Ian Bent, grew up in the licensing trade and, though this is first full time venture in the trade, he has a lifetime of experience. This certainly shows as the hospitality and high standard of service found here is both excellent and friendly. There is a choice of three locally brewed real ales from the bar, as well as all the usual drinks, and the inn also has an extensive wine list. The food served here is traditional English pub fayre at its very best and everything is homecooked. In addition to the menu there are daily specials and the fish snacks are also popular, as is the inn's carvery Sunday lunch.

Opening Hours: Mon-Sat 11.00-23.00; Sun 12.00-23.00

Food: Bar meals and snacks, Traditional Sunday lunch

Credit Cards: Visa, Access, Delta, Switch, Diners

Facilities: Beer garden, Car parking,

Children's play area, Functions catered for

Entertainment: Skittles

Local Places of Interest/Activities: Wincanton Racecourse 1 mile, Stourhead Gardens 4 miles, Hadspen House 5 miles, Walking, Cycling, Horse riding

Internet/Website: ynlo@talk21.com

192   The Pilgrims' Rest Inn

Lovington,
near Castle Cary
Somerset BA7 7PT
Tel: 01963 240597

Directions:

From junction 23 on the M5 take the A39 to Street and then the B3151 to Somerton. From here take the B3153 towards Castle Cary and The Pilgrims' Rest Inn can be found at Lovington, midway between Somerton and Castle Cary.

Dating back to, probably, the 17th century, **The Pilgrims' Rest Inn** is a wonderful old stone building that stands by the traffic lights in the centre of the village. The ancient appeal of the whitewashed exterior is continued inside where the inn has retained its low beamed ceilings, exposed stone walls, flagstone floors and inglenook fireplace. Subdivided into cosy, intimate areas, this splendid inn has been owned and personally run by Julian and Sally Mitchison since 1997.

A place that is well worth seeking out, as well as serving three real ales that are brewed in the village, the bar stocks real Somerset cider as well as all the usual drinks and there is also an extensive and well chosen wine list. However, what makes The Pilgrims' Rest Inn different is the food. Described by Julian and Sally as "quietly modern British", the menus here really are special. Everything is homecooked and prepared in the kitchen by Julian and his team and many of the foodstuffs come from the local area: the bacon from Bridport, the butcher is local and the ice creams come from 300 yards away. Whether it is the restaurant's à la carte menu or the less formal bistro bar menu, the range of dishes is wide and the combination of tastes exciting. The attitude to food is as relaxing and refreshing as their dishes and dining here is a delight.

Opening Hours: Tue 19.00-23.00; Wed-Sat 12.00-15.00, 19.00-23.00; Sun 12.00-15.00, 19.00-22.30

Food: Bar meals and snacks, À la carte and fixed price menus

Credit Cards: Visa, Access, Delta, Switch, Amex

Facilities: Beer garden, Car parking, Functions catered for

Local Places of Interest/Activities: Lytes Cary Manor 5 miles, Wincanton Racecourse 7 miles, Glastonbury 8 miles, Walking, Cycling, Horse riding, Bird watching

Internet/Website:
mitchison@pilgrimrest.freeserve.co.uk,
www.pilgrimrest.freeserve.co.uk

The Ship Inn

39 Mantle Street,
Wellington,
Somerset
TA21 8AX
Tel: 01823 662106
Fax: 01823 662106

Directions:
From junction 26 on
the M5 take the A38
into Wellington and
The Ship Inn lies on the
edge of the town, oppo-
site the cinema.

Built in the 1700s, **The Ship Inn** is a traditional old coaching inn that, today, has blended well with the demands of a 21st century town inn. The large open plan bar area, where the pub's piano sits, gives the inn a spacious and airy feel whilst, the modern gas fire adds warmth in winter as well as being a focal point. Though The Ship Inn is not situated on the coast, there is a maritime theme and many of the pictures hanging on the walls are of seafaring scenes.

This popular and attractive inn is managed by Tammie Lynne Lewis, a charming and intelligent young lady who has travelled the world and is now setting about growing the business with the background support of her parents. Things are going well as not only is the inn an excellent place to come to for a pint (or two) of real ale, but the pub food on offer has certainly found a following locally. From sandwiches to steaks, the homecooked dishes are a tasty and filling snack as well as being great value for money. During the season, cream teas are served in the garden which is found in the old courtyard part of the old coaching inn and where, too, there is a skittles alley. A superb place to come to for refreshment, the inn also has comfortable and homely accommodation available which, due to its location, makes The Ship Inn an ideal holiday base.

Opening Hours: Mon-Fri 12.00-14.30, 18.00-23.00; Sat 12.00-23.00; Sun 12.00-15.00, 19.00-22.30

Food: Bar meals and snacks, Cream teas

Credit Cards: None

Accommodation: 1 double room, 1 single room, both with shared bathroom

Facilities: Skittle alley used also as function room, Beer garden, Children's play area, Car parking

Entertainment: Live music on occasional weekends, Skittles, Darts, Pool

Local Places of Interest/Activities: Taunton 6 miles, Wellington Monument 2 miles, West Somerset Railway 5 miles, Beach 15 miles, Walking, Bird watching, Fishing, Horse riding

194   The Swan at Kingston

Kingston St Mary,
near Taunton,
Somerset TA2 8HW
Tel: 01823 451383

Directions:

From junction 25 on the M5 take the A38 into Taunton and then follow the A358 towards Williton. Once through Taunton, follow the signs to Kingston from the main road and The Swan at Kingston can be found to the north of the town.

A delightful 17th century country inn in a picturesque village at the base of the Quantock Hills, **The Swan at Kingston** has lost none of its charm and character over the years. Though it is now open plan inside, the low ceilings, exposed beams and open log fire give this warm and friendly inn a traditional country inn appearance. It is also a comfortable and relaxing place, with well upholstered furniture and tucked away corners for more intimate conversations.

The ideal place for anyone interested in sampling good, well kept real ales, The Swan at Kingston does not allow children. As well as making a name for the pub in the drinks area, landlord Colin Loader, who has been here since 1994, offers customers a mouthwatering menu of homemade dishes. Supplemented by an ever changing daily specials board, the traditional pub fare is highlighted by some tasty house specials that include pork cooked in cider and apple sauce - a real taste of Somerset. On Sunday's the inn is a particularly popular place as the fame of the traditional Sunday roasts has spread far and wide. Booking is therefore essential to avoid disappointment. A popular local pub for the people of the village, visitors here will soon feel at home in this friendly and inviting atmosphere.

Opening Hours: Mon-Sat 11.30-14.30, 18.30-23.00 (Food 12.00-13.45, 19.00-20.45); Sun 12.00-15.00, 19.00-22.30 (Food 12.00-13.45)

Food: Bar meals and snacks, Traditional Sunday lunches

Credit Cards: None

Facilities: Car parking

Local Places of Interest/Activities: Hestercombe 1 mile, Fyne Court 2 miles, Taunton 3 miles, Durleigh Reservoir 5 miles, Walking, Horse riding, Fishing

The Three Horseshoes | **195**

Batcombe,
near Shepton Mallet,
Somerset BA4 6HE
Tel: 01749 850359
Fax: 01749 850615

Directions:

From junction 18 on the M4 take the A46 to Bath and then the A367 and A37 to Shepton Mallet. By pass Shepton Mallet and take the A371 for 1 mile before turning on to the B3081. Take the first left and follow the road through Westcombe and for a further mile to The Three Horseshoes.

Batcombe is an ancient village situated in an Area of Outstanding Natural Beauty and, next the village church, which has one of the finest church towers in Somerset, lies **The Three Horseshoes**. This was once an important centre of the wool industry and, when the inn was built, in the 17th century, Batcombe was a lively and thriving place. Today, things are a little quieter, but the inn maintains the age old tradition of providing excellent hospitality to travellers (and also locals). Through the centuries, The Three Horseshoes has retained many of its original features, there is a huge open fire, a mass of ceiling beams and many quiet alcoves. The assortment of old pictures and prints, and Toby and beer jugs hanging from the walls and beams all add to the olde worlde atmosphere.

From the large open plan bar area, where an excellent range of real ales are served, there is, through an old stone archway, a separate restaurant in what was probably the inn's original coach house. Sitting at elegantly laid tables, customers can enjoy a delicious meal that extends from vegetarian dishes through to game, fowl and fish. Though the surroundings might be old English the menu certainly is not and, prepared with skill and style, a meal here is very much a treat to saviour.

Opening Hours: Mon-Sun 12.00-15.00, 18.30-23.00

Food: À la carte restaurant

Credit Cards: Visa, Access, Delta, Switch

Facilities: Car parking, Function room

Local Places of Interest/Activities: Royal Bath and Wells Showground 4 miles, Longleat 8 miles, Walking, Riding, Horse racing

196   The Travellers Rest

Stone,
East Pennard,
near Shepton Mallet,
Somerset BA4 6RY
Tel: 01749 860069

Directions:

From junction 23 on the M5 take the A39 through Street and Glastonbury until you arrive at the junction with the A37. Take the A37 towards Yeovil. The Travellers Rest lies on the A37 between Pylle and Lydford.

Found amidst the glorious rolling countryside of Somerset, **The Travellers Rest** is just that - an excellent place for passers-by to stop and enjoy some excellent hospitality at a delightful countryside inn. Over 200 years old, this charming roadside inn is full of character with open fireplaces, beamed ceilings and a mass of pictures hanging from the walls. Jeremy and Sue Davies, the landlords, have only been here since summer 1999 but, with over 20 years experience in the licensing trade, customers here are sure to benefit from the couples expertise and amiable manner.

A pint of real ale, there are two served from the bar and both come from local breweries, or a glass of wine from the excellent selection in hand customers can either relax with their drinks in the comfortable bar to take them outside to the delightful beer garden and watch the children playing in their own purpose built area. Food too is important here and the choice of traditional pub favourites is supplemented by a list of daily specials. Everything here is homecooked and represents the very best in traditional English cuisine. For more formal dining their is the separate restaurant though, of course, in fine weather, the glorious views from the garden make eating outside a special treat.

Opening Hours: Mon-Sat 12.00-15.00, 18.30-23.00; Sun 12.00-15.00, 19.00-22.30

Food: Bar snacks and meals

Credit Cards: None

Facilities: Beer garden, Car parking, Children's play area, Functions catered for

Entertainment: Regular live music, Pool

Local Places of Interest/Activities: Royal Bath and Wells Showground 3 miles, Glastonbury 6 miles, Wells 6 miles, The Shoe Museum at Street 7 miles, Walking, Cycling, Horse riding, Fishing

7 North and East Somerset

Places of Interest:

Bath   199
Bristol   202
Burnham-on-Sea   205
Cameley   205
Cheddar   206
Claverton   206
Clevedon   207
Ebbor Gorge   207
Frome   208

Mells   208
Shepton Mallet   209
Stanton Drew   209
Wells   210
Weston-super-Mare   211
Westwood   212
Wookey Hole   212

Pubs and Inns:

Butchers Arms, Bishop Sutton   213

Drum and Monkey Inn, Kenn   214

The Eagle Inn, Highbury   215

The Easton Inn, Easton   216

The Full Moon, Wells   217

The Full Quart, Hewish   218

The Masons Arms, Frome   219

The Old Down Inn, Emborough   220

The Old Mendip Inn, Gurney Slade   221

The Panborough Inn, Panborough   222

The Plume of Feathers, Rickford   223

The Prince of Wales, Dunkerton Hill   224

The Red Lion Inn, Draycott   225

The Ship at Oldford, Oldford   226

The Slab House Inn,
West Horrington   227

The White Hart, Trudoxhill   228

The Woodborough Inn, Winscombe   229

The Hidden Inns of the West Country

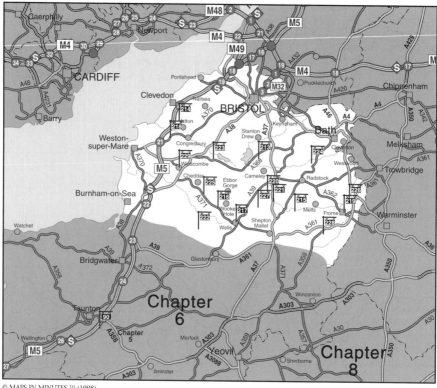

© MAPS IN MINUTES ™ (1998)

213 **Butchers Arms**, Bishop Sutton

214 **Drum and Monkey Inn**, Kenn

215 **The Eagle Inn**, Highbury

216 **The Easton Inn**, Easton

217 **The Full Moon**, Wells

218 **The Full Quart**, Hewish

219 **The Masons Arms**, Frome

220 **The Old Down Inn**, Emborough

221 **The Old Mendip Inn**, Gurney Slade

222 **The Panborough Inn**, Panborough

223 **The Plume of Feathers**, Rickford

224 **The Prince of Wales**, Dunkerton Hill

225 **The Red Lion Inn**, Draycott

226 **The Ship at Oldford**, Oldford

227 **The Slab House Inn**, West Horrington

228 **The White Hart**, Trudoxhill

229 **The Woodborough Inn**, Winscombe

Please note all cross references refer to page numbers

On the northernmost boundary of the county lies Bristol, the largest town of south-west England and a busy industrial and commercial centre. Just a few miles to the southeast lies Bath, a peaceful place of elegant Georgian architecture, whose history as a spa town goes back to Roman times. Separating these two centres from much of the rest of the county are the Mendip Hills. As they are limestone, the hills are full of holes, with caves and potholes and streams that disappear underground.

The Mendips are also home to the well known caves at Wookey Hole and the spectacular Cheddar Gorge, which carves a path through them as well as lending its name to the world-famous cheese. The city of Wells, below the hills, is a charming old town; from here the county's plain stretches out to Glastonbury. Northeastern Somerset's coastline boasts many popular seaside resorts such as Weston-super-Mare.

PLACES OF INTEREST

BATH

Bath is of course one of the most remarkable cities in Britain. It is a glorious concoction of architectural set pieces which have been constructed around the only hot thermal springs in the country since the time of the ancient Romans. Best explored on foot, magnificent examples of the city's Roman, medieval or Georgian heritage lie around almost every corner.

Since time immemorial, over half a million gallons of water a day at a constant tempera-

Roman Baths, Bath

ture of 46°C have bubbled to the surface at this point. The ancient Celts believed the mysterious steaming spring was the domain of the goddess Sulis, and it is likely they were aware of its healing properties long before the arrival of the Roman legions in 43AD. However, the Romans were the first to enclose the spring, and within a few short years of their arrival, they had created the spectacular health resort known as *Aquae Sulis*, a name coined as a gesture to the Celtic population they now controlled. Indeed, they even dedicated the temple adjoining the baths to the joint goddess, Sulis-Minerva, to embody both the Celtic and Roman ideologies.

By the 3rd century, Bath had become so renowned that high-ranking soldiers and officials were coming here from all over the Roman world. Public buildings, such as a temple and forum, were added, and the whole city enclosed behind a stone wall. However, by the year 410, the Empire was crumbling and the last remaining legions were forced to return home. Aquae Sulis was abandoned, and within a few decades the drainage systems failed and the marsh returned.

With the possible exception of Hadrian's Wall, the Roman remains at Bath are the most outstanding to survive in Britain. The main reason for their exceptional state of preservation is that for over a thousand years, they remained buried under several feet of dense alluvial mud. Ironically, the ancient baths remained hidden throughout the entire period

The Hidden Inns of the West Country

200

of Bath's 18th-century renaissance as a spa town and were only rediscovered in the late 19th century; indeed, they were not fully excavated until the 1920s. The restored remains which can be seen today are centred around the **Great Bath**, a rectangular lead-lined pool which is surrounded by steps and the truncated remains of a colonnaded quadrangle. Five separate phases were constructed over a 200 year period which began in the middle of the 1st century. The result is a superb complex of buildings incorporating swimming pools, mineral baths and a series of chambers heated by underfloor air ducts which would have functioned as saunas and Turkish baths. A visit to the Roman Baths includes admission to a fascinating museum of Roman coins, artefacts, jewellery and perhaps the finest exhibit of all, a bronze head of the goddess Sulis Minerva.

The population of Bath fell away during the Dark Ages, and it wasn't until the 8th century that the Saxons founded a nunnery here which put the settlement back on the map. This was later elevated to monastic status when King Edgar of Wessex chose to be crowned "King of all England" here in 973. The present great church was begun in 1499 after its Norman predecessor had been destroyed by fire; however in 1539, Henry VIII's Dissolution of the Monasteries brought work to a halt. The church then had to remain without a roof for three quarters of a century, and indeed, the structure wasn't fully completed until 1901.

With its soaring buttresses, spiky ramparts and vast windows of clear glass, **Bath Abbey** is now considered the ultimate example of English Perpendicular church architecture. Its delicate stone fan-vaulting hangs 70 feet above the nave, and its curious castellated tower is rectangular rather than square because it was built using the pillar-foundations of the earlier building. Inside, there is an unusual 18th century portable oak font and a surprising number of monuments and tablets, more than in any church outside Westminster abbey. Some were erected in memory of the many wealthy invalids who flocked here in the 18th and early 19th centuries and were never well enough to return home.

One tablet in the abbey stands as a memorial to Richard "Beau" Nash, a legendary Bath figure who was one of the three people generally considered responsible for turning Bath

into a fashionable Georgian spa town. He became Bath's Master of Ceremonies, an unpaid yet highly influential position to which he ascended when the previous MC was killed in a duel. He pressurised the corporation into paving, cleaning and lighting the streets, outlawed duelling and the wearing of swords, and set about creating a relaxed social atmosphere in which the gentry (the landed middle-class) could mix on equal terms with their social superiors, the aristocracy. Under his guidance, Bath became elegant and fashionable, and soon began to attract significant numbers of the "right people", not only patrons, but also the architects and entrepreneurs who shared Nash's grand vision for the city. Among these was the architect John Wood who, along with his son (also called John), designed most of the city's finest neoclassical squares and terraces. These included North and South Parades, Queen Square, The Circus, and most notably, **Royal Crescent**, John Wood the Younger's Palladian masterpiece which was the first terrace in Britain to be built to an elliptical design. Bath's third 18th-century founding father was Ralph Allen, an entrepreneur who made his first fortune developing an efficient postal system for the provinces, and who went on to make a second as the owner of the local quarries which supplied most of the honey-coloured Bath-stone to the city's Georgian building sites.

A good place to begin a walk around central Bath is at the **Roman Baths**, whose adjoining **Pump Room** looks much as it did when it was completed in 1796. Now an elegant tearoom, a restorative cup of tea, coffee or spa water can be enjoyed here, often to the accompaniment of live chamber music. Items on show include two sedan chairs, one of which was used as a public taxi by the idle or infirm.

A short distance away from the Pump Room, the magnificent **Pulteney Bridge** spans the River Avon. The only example of the work of Robert Adam in Bath, it was inspired by Florence's Ponte Vecchio and is the only bridge in Britain to incorporate a terrace of buildings. The nearby weir, with its graceful curving steps, is a superb example of Georgian refinement.

Set in beautiful gardens at the end of Great Pulteney Street only 10 minutes' walk from Pulteney Bridge and the centre of the city, the **Holburne Museum** is a jewel in Bath City's crown and one of the finest examples of its elegant Georgian architecture. Originally a spa hotel, the building was adapted for the purposes

Holburne Museum

importance of the city to her life and work. The Centre shop has an unrivalled selection of Jane Austen related books, cards and specially designed gifts.

Gay Street leads through Queen Square to The Circus, a striking example of neoclassical unity of design which is divided into three evenly-proportioned blocks of 11 houses. The street to the northeast leads to the National Trust-owned **Assembly Rooms**, one of the places polite 18th-century society used to congregate to dance, play cards or just be seen. The building was severely damaged during the Second World War and wasn't reopened until 1963. It is now leased to the Bath and North Somerset Council and incorporates an interesting **Museum of Costume**.

The street leading west from the Circus leads to **Royal Crescent**, a superb architectural set piece which is popularly regarded as the climax of Palladian achievement in this most classical of English cities. Built between 1767 and 1774 on a site which then overlooked unspoilt countryside, its huge sweep comprises 30 houses, each of which is divided by a giant Ionic

Royal Crescent, Bath

of a museum by Sir Reginald Blomfield early in the 20th century to house the nucleus of the decorative and fine art collections of Sir William Holburne (1793-1874). On show can be seen superb examples of English and continental silver and porcelain, Italian maiolica and bronzes, together with glass, furniture, miniatures and paintings by such leading English and continental old masters as Gainsborough, Turner, Ramsay, Raeburn and Zoffany. The museum's collection has been added to over the years, with the emphasis remaining on work from the 17th and 18th centuries.

The **Crafts Study Centre** was founded at the Holburne Museum in 1977. This unique establishment incorporates an historic archive of reference books, working notes, documents and photographs relating to leading 20th century artist-craftspeople, along with a permanent exhibition of their work. Items on display include woven and printed textiles, furniture, exquisite calligraphy and ceramics.

Moving to the north of the area once enclosed by Bath's Roman walls, 40 Gay Street is a place all Jane Austen enthusiasts will not want to miss. Here they will find the **Jane Austen Centre**, opened in 1999. Bath was Austen's home during two long visits here at the end of the 18th century, and she made Bath her home from 1801 until 1806. Her novels *Northanger Abbey* and *Persuasion* are largely set in Bath. The Centre offers visitors a chance to find out more about the Bath of Jane Austen's time and the

half column. No. 1 Royal Crescent has been meticulously restored to its original Georgian splendour by the Bath Preservation Trust.

Just along Upper Church Street leading off the Royal Crescent and on to Julian Road, The **Bath Industrial Heritage Centre** offers visitors an insight into the life and times of Mr Jonathan Burdett Bowler, who started his business in Bath in 1872 and described his trade as engineer, brass founder, gasfitter, locksmith and bell-hanger. The business closed in 1969, but remarkably had survived up until this time with its original machinery, Victorian gaslight and everything just as it was nearly 100 years before.

202

The old streets and buildings of Bath are said to be inhabited by an unusual number of ghosts. Two of the most infamous are the Grey Lady, whose characteristic jasmine scent has been detected around the **Theatre Royal** and nearby Garrick's Head inn, and the Black-hatted Man, who is said to appear in and around the Assembly Rooms. Details of a guided Ghost Walk can be obtained from the Tourist Information Centre.

Bath contains an exceptional number of fine art galleries and specialist museums. The **Victoria Art Gallery** near Pulteney Bridge is the city's principal venue for major touring exhibitions. It also has a permanent collection of classical paintings and a smaller gallery displaying work from the area. The **British Folk Art Collection** (formerly the Museum of English Naive Art) in the Paragon is an absorbing anthology of 18th and 19th-century paintings which are characterised by their "direct simplicity". On the same site is the Building of **Bath Museum**, a fascinating collection of models, drawings and illustrations which chronicle the city's unique architectural evolution. **The Museum of East Asian Art** on Bennett Street has a superb collection of Chinese, Japanese, Korean and Southeast Asian artefacts, ranging in date from 5000 BC to the 20th century, all housed in a restored Georgian building. The **William Herschel Museum** pays tribute to the distinguished 18th century astronomer, who discovered the planet Uranus in 1781, here in what was his home, a delightful period house, with displays of his many achievements - and those of his sister Caroline - and their impact on modern science.

The first recorded mailing of a Penny Black postage stamp was made in 1840 at No. 8 Broad Street, now the site of the **Bath Postal Museum**; exhibits include a reconstruction of a Victorian sorting office and a children's activity room. **Sally Lunn's House** in North Parade Passage is thought to be the oldest house in Bath. Its cellar museum contains the kitchen used by the celebrated 17th-century cook who is attributed with inventing the Bath bun. The Bath Industrial Heritage Centre in Julian Road is a re-creation of an aerated water manufactory which provides an insight into one of the city's traditional industries.

Close to Weston on the northern edge of Bath, the ground rises onto Lansdown, a spur of downland which is the site of one the most

remarkable follies in Britain. **Beckford's Tower** was built in the 1820s by the wealthy and eccentric scholar, William Beckford, to house his extensive art collection. Visitors climbing the 156 steps to the belvedere are rewarded with a magnificent view stretching from Wiltshire Downs in one direction to the Black Mountains of Wales in the other. There is also a small museum charting Beckford's extraordinary life in pictures, prints and models.

Another of Bath's follies, **Sham Castle**, was constructed on a hill to the east of the city by the quarry-owner Ralph Allen. Built to be seen from his town house, as its name suggests it is merely a romantic facade which is made even more picturesque by night-time illumination. Later in his career, Allen moved out to **Prior Park**, an ostentatious country mansion on the southeastern edge of Bath which now houses a co-educational school. Designed in classic Palladian style by John Wood the Elder, the house stands within impressive landscaped grounds whose ornamental lakes and superb neoclassical bridge were created under the guidance of Capability Brown and the poet Alexander Pope. The garden enjoys magnificent views.

The National Trust owns 560 acres of countryside and woodland which together form the magnificent **Bath Skyline Walk**. Described in a leaflet obtainable from the National Trust shop in the Abbey Churchyard, the eight-mile footpath offers some spectacular views of Bath's Georgian outline. The route starts above Bathwick to the east of the city and also takes in an Iron Age field system.

BRISTOL

With a population of over 400,000 and a history dating back to the time of the Saxons, Bristol is a diverse regional capital which takes time to get to know. A good place for the visitor to begin is **Brandon Hill**, an area of open ground near the city centre which can be found to the west of the Park Street shopping area. Here, visitors can climb to the top of the **Cabot Tower**, a 100 foot monument standing near the site of a chapel dedicated to St Brendan the Navigator which was erected in memory of another maritime pioneer, John Cabot. The first non-Scandinavian European to set foot on Newfoundland, Cabot's expedition of 1497 was financed by local Bristol merchants.

For centuries, Bristol was a major commercial seaport, and the magnificent view from the top of the tower reveals a complex series of docks and wharves along a curving stretch of water known as the **Floating Harbour**. This semi-artificial waterway was created when the course of the River Avon was diverted to the south early in the 19th century. A massive feat of civil engineering, the work took over five

Bristol Harbour

years to complete and was largely carried out by Napoleonic prisoners using only picks and shovels. Today, the main docks have moved downstream to Avonmouth and the Floating Harbour has become home to a wide assortment of recreational and smaller working craft.

Bristol was founded during Saxon times at the point where the curving River Frome joined the River Avon. This strategically important bridging point at the head of the Avon gorge soon became a major port and market centre, and by the early 11th century the town had its own mint and was trading with other ports throughout western England, Wales and Ireland. In 1067, the Normans began to build a massive stone keep on a site between the present day Floating Harbour and Newgate, a place which is still known as **Castle Park** despite the almost total demolition of the structure at the end of the English Civil War. The heart of the old city lies west of here, around the point where Corn, Broad, Wine and High Streets converge.

Half a mile further west, **Bristol Cathedral** stands at the foot of Park Street on College Green. Founded in about 1140 by Robert Fitzhardinge as the great church of an Augustinian abbey, several original Norman features remain, including the southeast transept walls, chapter house, gatehouse and east side of the abbey cloisters. Elsewhere there is some good 14th century stained glass and a series of striking roof bosses in the north transept. Following the Dissolution of the Monasteries in 1539,

Henry VIII took the unusual step of elevating the church to the status of cathedral, and soon after, the richly-carved choir stalls were added. This was followed over a century later by Grinling **Gibbons'** superbly carved organ case.

The structure wasn't fully **completed** until the 19th century when a new nave was built in sympathetic style to the existing choir. **This** now contains some exceptional monuments and tombs, along with a pair of unusual candlesticks which were donated in 1712 by the rescuers of Alexander Selkirk, the actual castaway on whom Daniel Defoe's character, Robinson Crusoe, was modelled.

During the Middle Ages, Bristol expanded enormously as a trading centre and at one time it was second only to London as a seaport. This medieval trade was built on the export of raw wool and woollen cloth from the Mendip and Cotswold Hills and the import of wines from Spain and southwest France. The city's first major wharf development was carried out at this time - the diverting of the River Frome from its original course into the wide artificial channel now known as **St Augustine's Reach**. A remarkable achievement for its day, the excavation created over 500 yards of new berthing and was crucial for Bristol's developing economy.

The city's increasingly wealthy merchants founded one of the most impressive parish churches in the west of England during this period. Originally set in a suburb to the east of the main channel, the church of St Mary Redcliffe is a wonderful arrangement of pinnacles, flying buttresses and sweeping stained glass windows. Queen Elizabeth I called it "the fairest, goodliest and most famous Parish Church in England". Its soaring 290 foot spire is a 19th century addition to the original 13th century tower, and its ornately decorated north porch was built to an unusual hexagonal design which is reputed to have been influenced by the architecture of China. John Cabot is commemorated in the church, and in the south transept Admiral Sir William Penn, whose son William founded the state of Pennsylvania in the US, is buried. An unusual roof boss in the shape of a circular maze can be seen in the north aisle. A giant replica of this, complete with water channels and raised walkways, can be seen in **Victoria Park**, half a mile away to the south. The sandstone beneath St Mary Redcliffe is riddled

The Hidden Inns of the West Country

with underground passages known as the **Redcliffe Caves**. Interesting guided tours around these unusual natural caverns are conducted from time to time by the City Engineer's Department.

A stroll around Bristol city centre reveals an unusual number of interesting historic buildings. Queen Square, to the northwest of Redcliffe Bridge, is lined with handsome early 18th century buildings, although two sides had to be rebuilt following their destruction in a riot in 1831. The **Theatre Royal** in King Street is the home of the acclaimed Bristol Old Vic theatre company. One of the oldest theatres in the country still in regular use, it was built in the 1760s with a semicircular auditorium, a rare feature for the time. Also in King Street, a striking timber framed merchant's house of 1669 known as **Llandoger Trow** can be seen at its eastern end.

Continuing northwards into the area once contained within the city walls, **The Exchange** in Corn Street was built in the 1740s by the neoclassical architect, John Wood the Elder, whose work is much in evidence at Bath. The interior contains some fine detailing, including three heads symbolically depicting Asia, Africa and America which look down from above the doorways leading off the entrance hall. The four low flat-topped pillars which can be seen outside the Exchange are known as "nails". These are made of bronze and were used by local merchants to transact their business, giving rise to the saying, "to pay on the nail".

The Red Lodge in Park Row contains the only remaining Tudor domestic interior in Bristol. Together with a similar residence called the White Lodge, it was built for Sir John Younge in the 16th century. The building retains a remarkable number of original features, including one of the finest Tudor oak-panelled rooms in Wessex, and is now under the custodianship of the Bristol Museum and Art Gallery.

The elegant **Georgian House** in Great George Street was originally built in 1791 as a merchant's town house. Furnished in the style of the period, its contents have been selected from the permanent collection of the City Museum and Art Gallery, and include purchases made specifically for the house. The main **City Museum and Art Gallery** in Queen's Road occu-

pies an imposing building at the top Park Street. Among its many fine exhibits is an exceptional collection of Chinese glass. Also worth seeing are **John Cabot's House** in Deanery Road and the **Trinity Almshouses** in Old Market Street to the east of the city centre.

Also to the east of town, near the Temple Meads railway station, can be found the oldest Methodist Chapel in the world, built in 1739 and known as **John Wesley's Chapel**, built by this renowned man. At the **British Empire and Commonwealth Museum** in Clock Tower Yard, exhibits trace the history of British discovery of foreign lands, and the rich cultural legacy brought about by Britain's membership in the Commonwealth.

Much of Bristol's waterfront has been now redeveloped for recreational use. @Bristol in Deanery Road, Harbourside is home to two unique attractions: Wildscreen, which brings visitors face to face with the natural world, and Explore, which explains the science behind the world around us and how it works. Part of a waterside redevelopment that promises to be a new cultural quarter for the city and a magnet for residents and visitors alike, it brings science, nature and art to life.

The **Bristol Industrial Museum** houses a fascinating record of the achievements of the city's industrial pioneers, including those with such household names as Harvey (wines and sherries), Fry (chocolate), Wills (tobacco) and McAdam (road building). Visitors can find out about Bristol's history as a port, view the aircraft and aero engines made in the city since 1910, and inspect some of the many famous motor vehicles which have borne the Bristol name since Victorian times. During the summer, the museum offers interesting working demonstrations of some of its more spectacular exhibits. These a giant crane, steam railway, printing workshop and a variety of motor vessels.

An excellent museum dedicated to the pioneering Victorian engineer, Isambard Kingdom Brunel, is located in the Great Train Shed at old Temple Meads station. The nearby **Exploratory** is a hands-on educational facility designed to put fun into everyday science. Situated in Gasferry Road on the southern side of the Floating Harbour, the **Maritime Heritage Centre** is an impressive visitor attraction which is dedicated to the history of Bristol shipbuilding. Among the increasing number of historic ships which line Bristol's wharves is Brunel's mighty *SS Great Britain*, the world's first iron-hulled, propeller-driven, ocean-going vessel which was built in the city in 1843. After a working life of 43 years, it was retired to the remote Falkland Islands where it was used as a storage hulk for over 70 years until 1970, when it was saved and brought back to the dry dock of its birth.

Brunel was also responsible for designing the **Clifton Suspension Bridge**, one of Bristol's most graceful landmarks which spans the Avon gorge a mile and a half to the west of the city centre. Opened five years after his death in 1864, it continues to carry an important route into the city. The bridge is suspended more than 200 feet above the river and offers drivers and pedestrians a magnificent view over the city and surrounding landscape.

The National Trust owned **Avon Gorge Nature Reserve** on the western side of the bridge offers some delightful walking through Leigh Woods to the summit of an Iron Age hill fort. A former snuff mill on the eastern side has been converted into an observatory whose attractions include a rare working example of a camera obscura. A nearby passage leads to the Giant's Cave, a subterranean chamber which opens onto a ledge high above the Avon.

Once a genteel suburb, modern Clifton is an attractive residential area whose elegant Georgian terraces are interspersed with stylish shops and restaurants. Clifton's **Goldney House**, now a university hall, is the location of a unique subterranean folly, **Goldney Grotto**, which dates from the 1730s.

A fantastic labyrinth filled with spectacular rock formations, foaming cascades and a marble statue of Neptune, its walls are covered with

Goldney Grotto

thousands of seashells and "Bristol diamonds", fragments of a rare quartz found in nearby Avon Gorge. The

205

grotto currently undergoing an ongoing programme of conservation and restoration, but is open most weekends between Easter and September. The renowned **Bristol Zoo Gardens** are located on the northwestern edge of Clifton in Clifton Down.

BURNHAM-ON-SEA

Burnham-on-Sea is a sizable seaside town with a wide sandy beach which at low tide seems to extend for miles. When mineral springs were discovered here in the late 18th century, an attempt was made to reinvent the resort as a spa town to rival Cheltenham and Bath. However, the efficacious effects of its waters were never properly demonstrated and in the end it had to fall back on its beach to attract visitors. The west tower of the part 14th-century parish church has a worrying lean owing to its sandy foundations. Inside, there is a remarkable Jacobean altarpiece which was originally made for Whitehall Palace; designed by Sir Christopher Wren, the carving has been attributed to Grinling Gibbons. The Low Lighthouse, the curious square structure raised above the beach on tall stilts, is perhaps Burnham's most distinctive landmark.

CAMELEY

An most exceptional church interior can be found in Cameley. The building was referred to by John Betjeman as "Rip Van Winkle's Church" because of the remarkable series of medieval wall paintings which lay undiscovered behind several centuries of whitewash until the 1960s. The murals are believed to have been painted between the 11th and 17th centuries and feature such diverse images as the foot of a giant St Christopher stepping through a fish and crab-infested river, a charming 14th century jester complete with harlequin costume and belled cap, and a rare coat of arms of Charles I.

The two large artificial lakes lying in the northern foothills of the Mendips to the west of Cameley form an area which is sometimes referred to as the region's lake district. Originally constructed to supply Bristol with fresh water, they also provide a first-rate recreational amenity. The smaller **Blagdon Lake** was completed in 1899 and the **Chew Valley Lake** in 1956. Together they have around 15 miles of shoreline and attract visitors from a wide area who come to fish, take part in watersports activities, or observe the wide variety of waterfowl and other birdlife which are attracted to this appealing habitat.

CHEDDAR

A spectacular ravine, the **Cheddar Gorge**, carries the B3371 southwestwards towards the Somerset Levels. One of the most famous and often-visited natural attractions in Britain, it is characterised by towering cliffs of weathered limestone and precariously-rooted bands of undergrowth. As well as being known for its gorge, the sprawling village of Cheddar is internationally-renowned for its caves and, of course, its cheese. Although much embellished by modern tourist paraphernalia, its two main show caverns, **Gough's Cave** and **Cox's Cave**, are worth seeing for their sheer scale and spectacular calcite formations. An almost complete skeleton dubbed "Cheddar Man" was discovered in Gough's Cave in 1903. This can now be seen in a nearby museum along with further evidence of human occupation of the caves, including flint and bone tools dating from the last Ice Age and artefacts from the Iron Age and the Romano-British period.

Starting from a little lower down the hill, the 322 steps of **Jacob's Ladder** lead up the side of the gorge to the site of **Pavey's Lookout Tower**, a novel vantage point which offers a spectacular view of the surrounding landscape. An unusual market cross stands at the centre of the old part of Cheddar village. Really two crosses in one, a hexagonal superstructure was added to the original 15th-century preaching cross around a century later.

The term Cheddar cheese refers to a recipe which was developed in the mid 19th century by Joseph Harding, a farmer and pioneer food scientist from near Bath who made the first scientific investigation into cheese-making. As the name refers to a recipe and not the place, the cheese can be made anywhere in the world; however, North Somerset is dotted with cheese manufacturers of various sizes, from single farmhouses to large-scale dairies. A number of these supplement their income by offering guided tours, craft demonstrations and catering facilities.

CLAVERTON

The ostentatious tomb of Ralph Allen, the quarry-owning co-founder of 18th-century Bath, lies in the churchyard at Claverton, a pleasant linear village. Six years before his death in 1764, Allen bought **Claverton Manor**, a 16th-century country mansion which was later demolished leaving only a series of overgrown terraces with impressive stonework balustrades. Some of the stone from the ruined house was used to construct the present manor on the hill above the village. The building was designed in elegant neoclassical style by Sir Jeffrey Wyatville, whose work is much in evidence at Windsor Castle, and is set in superb landscaped grounds.

Sir Winston Churchill is reputed to have made his first political speech at Claverton Manor in 1897; however, it is as the **American Museum and Gardens** that the building and grounds are now best known. This absorbing museum was founded in 1961 by Americans Dallas Pratt and John Judkyn and is the only

American Museum

establishment of its kind outside the United States. The rooms have been furnished to show the gradual changes in American living styles, from the arrival of the Pilgrim Fathers in 17th century New England to the Philadelphia and New York of the 18th and 19th centuries. The adobe walls and religious images in the New Mexico Living room give a flour of the life of the Spanish colonists. There is also a large section devoted to the history of Native Americans and a display dedicated to the Shakers. In the Folk Art Gallery, paintings, metalwork and wood carvings demonstrate the diversity and vibrancy of American Folk Art. The Mount Vernon Garden is a replica of George Washington's flower garden at his home in Mount Vernon, Virginia. Throughout the summer months the museum hosts a number of events including displays of Native American dancing and 18th century military drills.

CLEVEDON

The impressive National Trust-owned **Clevedon Court** lies near junction 20 on the M5. One of the earliest surviving country houses in Britain, the main part dates from the early 14th century, and the tower and great hall are even older, dating from the 12th and 13th centuries respectively. Once partly fortified, this imposing manor house has been the home of the

Clevedon Court

Elton family since 1709. Longstanding patrons of the arts, during the early 19th century they invited some of the finest poets and writers of their day to Clevedon Court, including Coleridge, Thackeray and Tennyson.

A few decades later, another member of the family invented a special technique for making the type of brightly coloured pottery which became known as Eltonware. Particularly popular in the United States, many fine examples are now on display at the house, along with a collection of rare glass from the works at Nailsea.

Clevedon Court is set within a delightful terraced garden which is known for its rare plants and shrubs. An attractive footpath leads up from here through nearby Clevedon Court Woods onto a ridge overlooking the Gordano valley. Clevedon Court is situated on the eastern edge of Clevedon, a genteel seaside town on the Severn estuary which has a population of around 20,000. A stylish holiday resort and residential centre since the late 18th century,

at one time it was larger and more popular than Weston-super-Mare. Its seafront is lined with bright stucco-fronted Regency and mid-Victorian houses in marked contrast to the grey limestone and brick of those further inland.

Although the town contains few of the popular attractions one would normally associate with a holiday resort, the exception is **Clevedon Pier**, a remarkably slim and elegant structure which was built in the 1860s from iron rails which were intended for Brunel's ill-considered South Wales railway. When part of the pier collapsed in the 1970s, its long-term future was placed in jeopardy. During the 1980s, however, a major programme of restoration was begun which took around ten years to complete. Throughout the summer the pier is used as a landing stage by large pleasure steamers such as the *Balmoral* and the *Waverley*, the only surviving seagoing paddle steamers in the world.

Among Clevedon's many fine old buildings is the **Market Hall** of 1869 which was built to provide a place for local market gardeners to sell their produce. The largely Norman parish church of St Andrew contains some poignant memorials to local parishioners, many of whom died young. The Poet's Walk, a flower-lined footpath said to be popular with Victorian bards, begins at Clevedon promenade and leads up around Church and Wain's hills. The latter is topped by the remains of an Iron Age coastal fort and offers some magnificent views over the Severn estuary, the Levels, and the town itself. Clevedon's appeal continues to be romantic rather than dramatic. Its geographical position and lack of railway access prevented the large-scale development which so transformed other seaside resorts, and as a consequence it has managed to retain an atmosphere of tranquil refinement which still has a certain charm.

EBBOR GORGE

The National Trust-owned **Ebbor Gorge** is a national nature reserve managed by English Nature. This dramatic landscape offers two scenic walks, the shorter of which takes around 30 minutes to complete and is suitable for wheelchair users accompanied by a strong pusher. The longer walks takes around an hour and a half and involves a certain amount of rock scrambling. The route climbs through woodland inhabited by badger and sparrowhawk, and passes close to caves which are home to greater and lesser horseshoe bats. From the top, buzzards can often be seen wheeling on the thermals above the gorge.

FROME

Standing beside the river from which it takes its name, the ancient settlement of Frome is the largest centre of population in northeast Somerset, and the fourth largest town in the county. The parish **church of St John the Baptist** was founded as a Saxon monastic house by St Aldhelm, Abbot of Malmesbury, in the 7th century. By the time of the Norman invasion, Frome was already a sizable market town which extended from the river to the church on the hill above.

The Frome valley became an important centre of the wool industry during the late Middle Ages when a series of weirs was constructed to regulate the flow of water to the many water-powered weaving and fulling mills which lined the riverbank. (Fulling was a process which softened and increased the volume of woven cloth by immersing it in water and feeding it through a series of mechanically-driven rollers.) However, the industry largely collapsed in the 18th century when textile production transferred to the industrial North, although one mill, A H Tucker's, continued in production right up until the 1960s.

The prolonged decline of the textile industry meant that little of central Frome was redeveloped during the 19th and early 20th centuries, and as a result, many of its narrow medieval streets and alleyways have survived intact. Some have wonderful names like Pudding Bag Lane and Twattle Alley, and others, such as Gentle Street, the steeply-sloping Catherine Hill, and Cheap Street with its water course running down the centre, are highly impressive in their own right. The bridge over the River Frome incorporates an 18th century lockup gaol, near to which can be seen the famous Bluecoat School and the restored **Blue House**, an elegant almshouse dating from 1726.

Best explored on foot, the centre of Frome is an attractive conservation area which contains an unusual number of interesting shops, cafes and residential buildings. Lively markets continue to be held in the town every day but Tuesday and Sunday, and for those interested in lo-

cal history, the excellent **Frome Museum** is open Wednesday to Saturday (it is advised you ring first to check times: 01373 467271). There is also an interesting arts complex, the **Black Swan Guild**, situated in Bridge Street, with workshops, gallery, craft shop and restaurant.

MELLS

Mells must be one of the loveliest villages in Somerset. Once the easternmost limit of the lands belonging to the mighty Glastonbury Abbey, Abbot Selwood drew up plans to rebuild the village in the shape of a St Anthony's cross (a cross with four arms of equal length) in the 15th century. Only one, **New Street**, was completed; this architectural gem can be seen to the south of St Andrew's parish church. The church itself is a magnificent example of Somerset Perpendicular, with a soaring 104 foot tower and spectacular pinnacled south porch. The interior contains a remarkable collection of monuments designed by some of the 20th century's most acclaimed artists, including Lutyens, Gill, Munnings and Burne-Jones. One is to Raymond Asquith, the eldest son of the Liberal Prime Minister, Herbert Asquith, who was killed during the First World War. A memorial to the pacifist and antiwar poet Siegfried Sassoon can be seen in the churchyard.

According to legend, the Abbot of Glastonbury, in an attempt to stave off Henry VIII's Dissolution of the Monasteries, dispatched his steward, John Horner, to London with a gift for the King consisting of a pie into which was baked the title deeds of 12 ecclesiastical manor houses. Far from persuading Henry, however, Horner returned to Somerset the rightful owner of three of the manors himself - Mells, Nunney and Leigh-upon-Mendip - for which he paid of total of £2000. This remarkable act of disloyalty is commemorated in the nursery rhyme Little Jack Horner which describes how Jack "put in his thumb and pulled out a plum", i.e. the deeds to the property. The manor house at Mells, which is not open to the public, remained in the hands of the Horner family until the early 20th century when it passed to the Asquiths by marriage.

Hidden in the lanes to the northwest of Mells, the 18th century country mansion **Babington House** stands at the end of a striking avenue of beech trees, a mile from the A362 Frome to Radstock road. Dating from around 1700, with a wing of 1790, the house and nearby church of St Margaret form an elegant composition. The church, with its original timber panelling and box pews, is a rarity in Somerset having been left virtually unchanged since it was constructed in 1750. These two buildings are the only evidence of the medieval hamlet of Babington, a settlement which suffered as a result the 18th century fashion for emparking - that is, removing the dwellings of the local inhabitants in order to create an uninterrupted view of the landscaped grounds from the big house.

SHEPTON MALLET

An important centre of communications since pre-Roman times, the old market town of Shepton Mallet lies on the River Sheppey, a little to the west of the **Fosse Way**, the old Roman route which at this point comprises a stretch of the modern A37. The settlement's Saxon name, which means simply "sheep town", reveals its main commercial activity during the pre-Norman and medieval periods, originally as a centre of wool production, and later as a weaving town. The industry reached its peak in the 15th century and it was then that Shepton Mallet's magnificent parish church was constructed. This striking building has one of the earliest Perpendicular towers in the county and a remarkable wagon roof with some 350 carved oak panels and around 300 bosses, each fashioned to a different design.

Perhaps Shepton Mallet's most characteristic structure, however, is its 50 foot **Market Cross**. Built around 1500 and restored in 1841, it has been the town's civic and commercial hub for almost 500 years. Indeed, a lively modern market continues to be held here every Friday. Several participants in the Duke of Monmouth's ill fated Pitchfork Rebellion were executed at the market cross in 1685 on the orders of the infamous Judge Jeffreys. The curious roofed structure standing nearby is a fixed market stall dating from the 15th century which is the only surviving remnant of Shepton's medieval butchers' market, or shambles. A lane running east off Town Street leads past the church to the old prison. Thought to be well away from the threat of enemy bombs, the Domesday Book was brought here for safe keeping during the Second World War.

Present-day Shepton Mallet is a prosperous light industrial town which has a good selection of shopping and leisure facilities. One of its largest industrial employers is Showerings, the makers of Babycham. For those with an interest in the town's social and industrial past, it is well worth visiting the district museum at the top of the High Street. Each year, Shepton Mallet plays host to two well-established agricultural shows: the **Mid-Somerset Show**, which is held in the town on a Saturday in August, and the **Royal Bath and West Show**, which is held over four days at the end of May on a permanent site beside the A371, a couple of miles to the south of the town centre.

In 1995, Bronze Age homesteads and pottery were found during excavations near **Cannards Grave**, to the south of the town. **Maesbury Ring**, the Iron Age hillfort which crowns the northern horizon of the town, 950 feet up on the Mendips, is the earliest visible trace.

STANTON DREW

The ancient settlement of Stanton Drew stands beside a series of stone circles over half a mile across which were constructed by the Bronze Age Beaker People between 2000 and 1600 BC. The complex of standing stones consists of three stone circles, a lone stone known as **Hauteville's Quoit**, and a large chambered burial tomb known as **The Cove**. The stones are composed of three different rock types - limestone, sandstone and conglomerate - and are thought to have been erected for religious, or perhaps astronomical, purposes.

In common with many stone circles in the west of Britain, the origin of those at Stanton Drew are steeped in legend. The most widespread account tells of a foolhardy wedding party who wanted to continue dancing into the Sabbath. At midnight, the piper refused to carry on, prompting the infuriated bride to declare that if she had to, she'd get a piper from hell. At that point, another piper stepped forward to volunteer his services and the party resumed. But then the music began to get louder and louder and the tempo faster and faster, until the dancers were gripped in a furious jig they were powerless to stop. They realised too late that the good natured piper was the Devil himself, and when his playing reached its terrifying climax, he turned them all to stone. To this day, this curious group of standing stones continues to be known as "The Wedding".

The village of Stanton Drew also contains a number of noteworthy old buildings, many of which are listed. Among them is the 15th century stone bridge over the River Chew, an unusual hexagonal thatched dwelling which later served as a turnpike tollhouse, and an assortment of handsome 17th and 18th century private residences.

A couple of miles to the north of Stanton Drew, the line of the ancient **Wansdyke** runs in a roughly east-west direction around the southern edge of Bristol. This great earthwork bank was built during the Dark Ages as a boundary line and defensive barrier against the Saxons. Although most evidence of its existence has long since disappeared, short sections can still be identified, for example along the ridge adjoining the Iron Age hill fort on Stantonbury Hill, east of Compton Dando, and at Maes Knoll, 4 miles west.

WELLS

The ancient ecclesiastical centre of Wells, with a population of under 10,000, is the smallest city in England. Were it not for its cathedral and neighbouring bishop's palace, it would be unlikely to be more than an attractive small market town. However, the magnificent **Cathedral of St Andrew**, the first entirely Gothic structure of its kind in Britain, and its adjacent cathedral close undoubtedly make this one of the gems of north Somerset.

Deriving its name from a line of springs which rises from the base of the Mendips, King Ine of the West Saxons is believed to have founded the first church at Wells around 700 AD. After a diocesan tussle with Bath, the present cathedral was begun in the 12th century and took over three centuries to complete. As a consequence, it demonstrates the three main styles of Gothic architecture - Early English, Decorated and Perpendicular. Its 13th century west front is generally considered to be its crowning glory: although defaced during the English Civil War, it incorporates over 100 larger-than-life-size statues of saints, angels and prophets who gaze down silently onto the cathedral lawn. The building's twin west towers were added a couple of centuries later; curious squat structures, they look as if they would benefit from the addition of spires. The cathedral's many superb internal features include the beau-

tiful and ingenious scissor arches which support the central tower, the great 14th century stained glass window over the high altar, the sweeping chapter house staircase with its elegant branching steps, and the great 14th century astronomical clock, one of the oldest working timepieces in the world. This shows the minutes, hours and phases of the moon on separate inner and outer dials, and marks the quarter hours with a lively mechanised knights' tournament.

The 52-acre cathedral close is a tranquil city within a city. Indeed for many centuries, Wells functioned as two distinct entities: the ecclesiastical city and civic city. At that time, the parishioners were not welcomed into the cathedral and instead had to listen to the choir through strategically placed holes in the cathedral walls. Similarly, the clergymen who died in the Black Death were buried under the cathedral green rather than in the town graveyard. The green itself is surrounded by a high wall which is breached at only three castellated entrance points. One of these sturdy gateways stands in the corner of the Market Place; known as **Penniless Porch**, it is where the bishop allowed the poor of the city to beg for alms from visitors entering the cathedral, a custom which appears to be back in fashion today.

The **Vicars' Close**, one of the oldest planned streets in Europe, lies on the northern side of the cathedral green. This remarkable cobbled thoroughfare was built in the mid 14th century, although the ornate chimneys were added

Vicars' Close

a century later. Originally intended for cathedral choristers, it is still occupied by officers of the cathedral. The close is connected to the cathedral by a bridge which leads directly from the Vicars' Hall to the chapter house stairs. Known as the **Chain Gate**, it was built so that the innocent cathedral clergymen could avoid having to run the gauntlet of temptation by having to cross one of the town streets. (In a similar vein, the name of a thoroughfare in the town's former red light district was changed by the easily-affronted Victorians from Grope Lane to Union Street.)

The fortified **Bishop's Palace** is situated in an adjoining site to the south of the cathedral cloisters. This remarkable medieval building is surrounded by a moat which is fed by the springs which give the city its name. The palace is enclosed within a high stone wall, and in order to gain access from the Market Place, it is necessary to pass under a 13th century arch known as the **Bishop's Eye** and then cross a drawbridge which was last raised for defensive purposes in 1831. Although still the official residence of the Bishop of Bath and Wells, several parts are open to visitors, including the bishop's chapel and Jocelin's hall. The wide palace moat is home to a family of swans which are renowned for their ability to ask for food by ringing a bell on the wall below the gatehouse window. The impressive **Bishop's Tithe Barn** is situated to the south of the Bishop's Palace; in its day, it has served as a billet for Cromwell's troops and it is now used for private functions.

For those keen to find out more about the history of the locality, **Wells Museum**, near the west front of the cathedral, contains an interesting collection of locally-found artefacts. The splendid Cathedral Library possesses a number of rare books and manuscripts, a selection of which are on open display. The Market Place still hosts a lively street market on Wednesdays and Saturdays, or for those wanting a view of the city from a distance, an attractive footpath starts from Moat Walk and leads up onto the summit of Tor Hill.

WESTON-SUPER-MARE

Weston-super-Mare is of course a popular seaside resort; in recent years it has also developed as a centre of light industry.

In 1811, the town was still just a fishing hamlet, with only 170 inhabitants; however, within the next 100 years it had grown to become the second largest town in Somerset. It now boasts a population of well over 50,000. Despite its relatively modern character, the locality has been inhabited since prehistoric times. The wooded promontory at the northern end of Weston Bay was the site of a sizable Iron Age hill settlement known as **Worlebury Camp**. In the 1st century AD, this was reputedly attacked and captured by the ancient Romans with great loss of life, an event confirmed by recent excavations which revealed a number of skeletons showing the effects of sword damage. A pleasant walk from the town now leads up through attractive woodland to the ancient hilltop site from where there is a magnificent view across the mouth of the Severn to Wales. Another spectacular view can be had from the clifftop site of the semi-ruined church at Uphill, a part-Norman structure which is situated at the southern end of Weston Bay, a couple of miles to the south.

The town's greatest resource is its long safe sandy beach which is ideal for paddling, sunbathing and ball games. However, its gentle incline means that swimmers have to wade out a long way to find water deep enough to take the plunge.

Weston's early tourist development took place in the 1830s around the Knightstone, an islet joined to the shore at the northern end of Weston Bay onto which was eventually built a large theatre and swimming baths. Following the arrival of the railway in 1841, the town began its most rapid period of development and in 1867, a pier was built on the headland below Worlebury Camp which connected offshore Birnbeck Island with the mainland. Intended mainly as a berth for steamer traffic, it was found to be slightly off the tourist track and in due course, a more impressive pier was built nearer the town centre which, prior to serious fires in the 1930s and during the Second World War, was approximately twice its present length.

Now, as then, the **Grand Pier** stands at the centre of an area crammed with souvenir shops, ice cream parlours, cafes and assorted attractions which are designed to appeal to the holidaymaker. Weston's indoor attractions include the **Winter Gardens** on the seafront, and the fascinating **Time Machine Museum** in Burlington Street.

The Museum Trail sponsored by the **Woodspring Museum**, also in Burlington Street, beings at the Tourist Information Centre on the seafront and offers visitors to take part in a "treasure hunt" for carved stones created by artist Michael Fairfax, which lead to the Museum itself. The **Weston Miniature Railway** leads from Marine Parade over half a mile around an 18 hole putting course and along the Beach Lawns overlooking the seafront.

The narrow coast road to the north of Weston-Super-Mare passes along the beach at Sand Bay before terminating at Middle Hope, a high ridge jutting out into the Severn Channel whose western end, **Sand Point**, provides another fine viewpoint. The ridge overlooks a lonely salt marsh which is home to a wide variety of wading birds, including shelduck and oystercatchers. To the east, a path leads down to the Landmark Trust-owned **Woodspring Priory**, a surprisingly intact medieval monastery which was founded around 1220 by a grandson of one of Thomas à Becket's murderers, William de Courtenay. The priory fell into disrepair following the Dissolution of the Monasteries of 1539 and its buildings were given over to agricultural use for many years. However, the church, tower, refectory and tithe barn have all survived, and the outline of the cloister can also be made out.

WESTWOOD

The **Peto Garden** at **Ilford Manor** is a Grade I listed Italian-style garden famed for its tranquil beauty. This unique hillside garden was the creation of architect and landscape gardener Harold Peto, who lived here from 1899 until 1933. Steps, terraces, sculpture and magnificent views characterise this superb garden.

The narrow river valley between Bath and Bradford on Avon is shared by the A36, the main railway line and the Kennet and Avon Canal. For around two centuries, water has been mechanically transferred to the canal from the River Avon at the impressive **Claverton Pumping Station**. A mile further south, the canal makes a spectacular diversion over both river and railway by way of the **Dundas Aqueduct**, an impressive Bath stone structure which is finished in characteristic neoclassical style.

Designed by the great engineer, John Rennie, the **Kennet and Avon Canal** was constructed between 1794 and 1810 to link the Thames with the Bristol Avon via Newbury and Devizes. A costly and ambitious project, much of its 75 mile length had to be cut through permeable rock which had to be lined with clay. The enterprise nevertheless succeeded in paying its investors a small dividend before the Great Western Railway arrived in 1841 to poach all its business.

In recent years, the Kennet and Avon Canal Trust has done much to restore this historic waterway, and it is now fully navigable between Bath and Caen Hill near Devizes. For those interested in joining a guided canal trip, narrowboats set out at regular intervals from Sydney Wharf and Bath's Top Lock. Alternatively, small electrically-powered self-drive boats are available from a variety of places including the Dundas Aqueduct.

WOOKEY HOLE

Wookey Hole is part of the rolling limestone upland in this part of the county, popular with walkers, cavers and motorised sightseers. Throughout the centuries, the carboniferous limestone core of the hills has been gradually dissolved by the small amount of carbonic acid in rainwater, an effect which has turned cracks into fissures, fissures into underground rivers and, on rare occasions, underground rivers into immense subterranean caverns such as these. During the Palaeolithic and subsequent eras, Wookey Hole was lived in by wild animals such as lions, bears and woolly mammoths. Evidence of their occupation is supported by the large cache of prehistoric mammals' bones which was discovered in a recess known as the **Hyena's Den**, many of them showing the animals' teeth marks. There is also evidence of human occupation during the Iron Age. In total, there are over 25 caverns, although only the largest half dozen are open to visitors. The **Great Cave** contains a rock formation known as the Witch of Wookey which casts a ghostly shadow and is associated with gruesome legends of child-eating.

The river emerging from Wookey Hole, the Axe, has been harnessed to provide power for industrial use since the 16th century. Originally constructed in the mid-1800s as a paper mill, the present building on the site was acquired in 1973 by **Madame Tussaud's** who have installed a number of popular visitor attractions. These include an exhibition on the history of waxworks, a museum of Victorian fairground equipment, and a workshop where paper continues to be produced by hand.

Butchers Arms | 213

Wick Road,
Bishop Sutton,
Somerset
Tel: 01275 332562
Fax: 01275 332562

Directions:

From junction 18 on the M4 take the A46 into Bath and then the A39 and A368 towards Weston-Super-Mare. The Butchers Arms can be found approximately 3 miles from the junction with the A37, close to Chew Valley Lake.

Dating back to the early 18th century, the **Butchers Arms** is an imposing stone built inn that stands beside the main Bath to Weston-Super-Mare road. Whilst offering excellent hospitality to travellers on this once busy route, the inn is also very much at the heart of the village of Bishop Sutton and, as such, it is well frequented by the locals who find it the ideal place to meet and catch up on local news. Much of this inn's success is due to its not only superb hospitality but also its relaxed and easy going atmosphere.

A traditional and popular country inn, that supports many local games teams, the two comfortable bars here serve a wealth of well kept beers, lagers and ciders as well as several real ales. The food here also makes a journey to the Butchers Arms worth while as the menus, which range from juicy freshly cut sandwiches and succulent steaks to full à la carte, represent the best of English country food. Taken in either the bar or in the more formal surroundings of the inn's attractive lounge/restaurant, eating here is a delicious experience. The house speciality is their traditional Sunday lunches, a treat not to be missed. There is also accommodation available with en suite facilities.

Opening Hours: Mon-Thurs 11.30 - 14.30 and 18.00-23.00; Fri-Sat 11.00-23.00; Sun 12.00-22.30

Food: Bar meals and snacks, À la carte, Traditional Sunday lunch

Credit Cards: None

Accommodation: En suite rooms

Facilities: Beer garden, Car parking, Late night supper licence to 00.30am if required

Entertainment: Live music every weekend, Karaoke Thursday evening

Local Places of Interest/Activities: Stone Circles at Stanton Drew 2 miles, Wells 9 miles, Cheddar Gorge 9 miles, Bath 10 miles, Walking, Cycling, Horse riding, Fishing

214 Drum and Monkey Inn

Kenn Road, Kenn,
near Clevedon,
Somerset BS21 6TJ
Tel: 01275 873433
Fax: 01275 873433

Directions:

From junction 20 on the M5 take the B3133 towards Congresbury then take the first left turn approximately 1 mile after the roundabout and The Drum and Monkey Inn can be found a short distance along the road.

A splendid old village pub, **The Drum and Monkey Inn** dates back to around the 1720s and it is a particularly eyecatching place during the summer when the hanging baskets and window boxes are at their most colourful. As befits a building as old as this, The Drum and Monkey has seen its fair share of personalities and none more so that Nellie No Change whose ghost can still be seen here from time to time. An very individual landlady who was known for miles around, Nellie acquired her unusual nickname after her habit of taking money from prosperous looking customers and saying "No change", assuming that they could afford to loose a few coppers. Today's landlord, Michael Beardshaw, whilst always returning the correct change, is also a well known local personality and it is his experience as a publican and his welcoming nature that draws many to this inviting inn.

With a mass of ceiling beams and exposed stone walls, the atmosphere inside the inn is very much that of a traditional English country pub. The pictures hanging on the walls are of local bird and wild fowl which reminds visitors that nearby wetlands of the Severn estuary are not far away. As well as the excellent range of drinks, including at least three real ales, served from the bar, The Drum and Monkey Inn has a fine reputation for the high standard of the homecooked dishes that are served here at both lunchtime and in the evening. From sandwiches and bar snacks through to the interesting à la carte menu, customers can enjoy a meal here in either the bar or the attractive and more formal restaurant.

Opening Hours: Mon-Fri 11.00-15.00, 18.00-23.00; Sat-Sun 11.00-23.00

Food: Bar meals and snacks, À la carte

Credit Cards: Visa, Access, Delta, Switch, Amex, Diners

Facilities: Car parking, Functions

Entertainment: Live music every Tuesday evening

Local Places of Interest/Activities: Clevedon 2 miles, Woodspring Priory 5 miles, Middle Hope Nature Reserve 5 miles, Bristol 11 miles, Severn Estuary 2 miles, Walking, Bird watching, Horse riding, Golf

The Eagle Inn

215

Highbury,
Coleford,
Somerset BA3 5NT
Tel: 01373 812440

Directions:

From junction 18 on the M4 take the A46 to Bath and then the A367 towards Shepton Mallet. At Stratton-on-the-Fosse, 3 miles From Radstock, take the road to the left signposted Holcombe. Follow for 2 miles and at Coleford that a left turn and The Eagle Inn can be found in the hamlet of Highbury.

The Eagle Inn is an attractive 300 year old building of local stone that stands solidly beside the road through Highbury. Very much a traditional place, and also the heart of the village, this is certainly the place to come to for genuine English pub hospitality. Managed by Mick and Chrissie Harrison, an experience couple, they have added much of their character to the place by displaying their large collections of tea pots and cigarette cards throughout the pub.

Those who enjoy a pint, or two, of real ale will certainly not be disappointed with the range of beers and ales served here and wine drinkers too will have plenty from which to choose. Up stairs, is the equally interestingly decorated and well furnished dining room where, customers can sample the delights of The Eagle Inn's menu - a delicious list that ranges from tasty sandwiches through to juicy steaks. All homemade and cooked to order, this is just the place for a lunchtime treat or a special meal out. During the time that they have been here, Mick and Chrissie have made the inn a centre for the local community and, from here, not only do they hold charity functions but also arrange outings and welcome a whole host of local sporting teams. A lively and welcoming pub - where no one is a stranger for long.

Opening Hours: Mon, Wed-Fri 12.00-23.00; Sat-Sun all day

Food: À la carte and bar snacks

Credit Cards: Visa, Access, Delta, Switch

Facilities: Function room, Car parking

Entertainment: Pool, Darts, Cribbage, Skittles

Local Places of Interest/Activities: Downside Abbey 3 miles, Bath 10 miles, Fishing, Walking, Horse racing

216

The Easton Inn

Sladebrook Road,
Easton,
near Wells,
Somerset BA5 1DU
Tel: 01749 870220
Fax: 01749 870220

Directions:

From junction 22 on the M5 take the A38 towards Bristol and then the A371 to Cheddar. Continue along the A371 towards Wells and The Easton Inn can be found on the road 4 miles from Cheddar.

The Easton Inn is not only well situated for the many local historic towns but it lies at the foot of the Mendip Hills overlooking the Somerset Levels. The pub is certainly not without character and charm and the stylish modern interior, open plan around the bar and with a separate dining room, has a light and airy feel that is markedly different from the more usual low ceilings and dark wood of older establishments. The addition of the rear patio area and new beer garden makes this an ideal pub for lazy summer afternoons and evenings.

An excellent place for a pint of real ale, Angus Bruce, the proprietor, places great emphasis on the food served here. Richard Hughes, formerly from the award winning Nantyffin in Crickhowell,not only provides traditional pub food, such as lunchtime sandwiches, baguettes and filled ciabattas, but also serves a superb à la carte menu. The menus change daily, depending on the seasons, with fresh fish and local meats featuring heavily. Special "Gastro evenings" throughout the year add an extra dimension to the exciting dishes that are prepared by Richard and his kitchen staff. Whether in the bar area or the dining room, a meal here is well worth savouring.

Opening Hours: Mon-Sun 12.00-15.00, 17.00-23.00; Summer 12.00-23.00

Food: Bar meals and snacks, à la carte, Sunday lunch

Credit Cards: Visa, Access, Delta, Switch

Facilities: Patio, garden, large car park

Entertainment: Special "Gastro" evenings

Local Places of Interest/Activities: Cheddar and Cheddar Gorge 4 miles, Wookey Hole Caves 1 mile, Wells 1½ miles, Walking, Bird watching, Glastonbury and Street 20 minutes drive.

The Full Moon

217

42 Southover,
Wells,
Somerset BA5 1UH
Tel: 01749 675792
Fax: 01749 671624

Directions:

From junction 21 on the M5 take the A370 towards Weston-Super-Mare and then the A371 to Wells. From Wells Cathedral travel down the High Street, turn left into Broad Street and then left again into St Johns Street. From here turn right into Southover and The Full Moon lies on the right. Cyclists follow NCN Route 3.

Found in a quiet area not far from the centre of this ancient ecclesiastical city **The Full Moon** is a delightful pub that sits in the middle of a terrace of attractive houses. Though its age is unknown, the inn is full of olde worlde charm and character, much of which is derived from the exposed beams, open stone fireplaces and gleaming decorative brass work. Experienced landlords, Robert and Carey Best moved here from Wiltshire and, not only have they quickly settled into life in Somerset, but they have also made their mark here by providing a pleasant and popular inn where customers can enjoy friendly, relaxed hospitality.

There is a fine choice of real ales served from the cask which, along with the usual beers, lagers and spirits and the good selection of wines, ensures that everyone can enjoy their favourite tipple. The food too is well chosen and includes a range of homemade specials that really make the mouth water. The traditional Sunday lunch is popular and along with the bar snacks and good selection of vegetarian food there really is something for everybody. Not only do Robert and Carey look after their customers food and drink needs but there is also live music here at the weekends, traditional pub games and a secluded rear beer garden in which to enjoy the sunshine.

Opening Hours: Mon-Sat 9.00-23.00; Sun 12.00-16.00, 19.00-22.30

Food: Bar meals, snacks and morning coffee from 9.00am, Traditional Sunday lunch 12.00-16.00

Credit Cards: Visa, Mastercard

Facilities: Beer garden, Street parking, Meetings/functions catered for

Entertainment: Regular live music, Satellite television, Pool, Darts, Cribbage, Dominoes

Local Places of Interest/Activities: Wells Cathedral, Bishop's Palace, Wookey Hole Caves 2 miles, Glastonbury 5 miles, Cheddar Gorge 8 miles, Walking, Cycling, Horse riding, Fishing

218 The Full Quart

Hewish,
nr Weston-Super-Mare,
Somerset BS24 6RT
Tel: 01934 833077
Fax: 01934 838396

Directions:

From junction 21 on the M5 take the A370 towards Congresbury. The Full Quart can be found approximately 2 miles along this road.

Situated beside the main road, **The Full Quart** is a large single storey inn that was built in the 19th century and is surrounded by large gardens and plenty of car parking. An attractive and inviting inn, although landlords Kate and John Tierney have only been here since spring 2000 they have put their years of experience in the trade to good use and have already made their mark here. Their aim to offer a high standard of service and cuisine has been realised and the popularity of this friendly pub is continuing to grow.

Very much a place for all the family, The Full Quart has a very traditional atmosphere that is helped along by the oak panelling and beams, fireplaces and antique furniture whilst, outside, there is not only a large beer garden with seating for adults but also swings and climbing frames for the children. Both food and drink are important here and, from the bar, there is an excellent choice of seven real ales, ciders, lagers and spirits whilst wine lovers have a fine selection from which to choose. The menu, for which the inn is becoming increasingly well known, is extensive and features many old favourites along with a range of house specialities, such as Mendip Chicken Casserole, Beef Bourguignon and Somerset Pork in Cider Sauce, that really tickle the tastebuds. Both children and vegetarians are well catered for and the range of West Country dairy ice creams is, surely, second to none. For a traditional country inn serving superb food and drink, The Full Quart is the place to visit.

Opening Hours: Mon-Sat 11.00-23.00; Sun 12.00-22.30

Food: Bar meals, À la carte, Traditional Sunday lunch

Credit Cards: Visa, Access, Delta, Switch, Amex, Diners

Facilities: Large beer garden, Children's play area, Car parking, Functions catered for

Local Places of Interest/Activities:
Weston-Super-Mare 5 miles, Middle Hope Nature Reserve 5 miles, Clevedon Court 5 miles, Bristol 14 miles, Walking, Cycling, Horse riding, Fishing, Bird watching

The Masons Arms | **219**

Marston Gate,
Frome,
Somerset BA11 4DJ
Tel: 01373 464537
Fax: 01373 455071

Directions:

From junction 18 on the M4 take the A36 around Bath to Frome. From the town, follow the A361 towards Glastonbury and The Masons Arms lies in the outskirts of Frome, just after Sainsburys supermarket.

Found on the road to Glastonbury, **The Masons Arms** is a particularly attractive inn that, apart from the inn signs, appears to be a row of cottages. In fact, it was originally three cottages, built in the 17th century, and its misleading appearance is gained from the three front doors which it still retains. The addition of colourful, flower filled hanging baskets further increases the homeliness of this delightful inn. Entering by any of the three doors, the interior of The Masons Arms is a labyrinth of small rooms and areas where the beams of the original cottages have been maintained and also their fireplaces.

In this cosy and inviting place customers are treated to an excellent selection of real ales, including those from Ushers of Trowbridge, beers and lagers as well as an extensive wine list. Landlord, Graham Mustow, also serves a delicious menu of tasty dishes, from the sumptuous grills served on the hot skillet to an à la carte list of pub favourites that are supplemented by a daily specials board. The traditional Sunday lunches too are popular and ideal for all the family. This is indeed a children friendly pub as not only are they welcomed but there is a play house for them in the beer garden and Graham also keeps some rare breed ducks which everyone is sure to find amusing.

Opening Hours: Mon-thu 11.00-15.00, 18.00-23.00; Fri-Sat 11.00-23.00; Sun 12.00-22.30

Food: Bar meals and snacks, À la carte, Traditional Sunday lunch, Themed evenings

Credit Cards: Visa, Access, Delta, Switch

Facilities: Beer garden, Car parking, Children's play area, Functions catered for

Entertainment: Darts

Local Places of Interest/Activities: Longleat House and Park 3 miles, Witham Friary 4 miles, East Somerset Railway 7 miles, Walking, Cycling, Horse riding, Fishing

220   The Old Down Inn

Emborough,
near Bath,
Somerset BA3 4SA
Tel: 01761 232398

Directions:
From junction 18 on the M5 take the A4 into Bristol and then the A37 for about 12 miles towards Shepton Mallet. After passing through Ston Easton The Old Down Inn can be found at the A37/B3139 junction. Turn left into large car park.

A splendid old stone coaching inn, **The Old Down Inn** stands on what was once the main route between Bath and Wells. Dating back to 1640, it was also a famous posting house which, as well as serving the needs of stage coaches, meant that it held its own post mark and received mail not only from Falmouth but also inland mail. Though this great coaching era has long since past, this wonderful old building is still offering exceptional hospitality to both locals and visitors. Landlords Bill and Sheila Filer began an extensive renovation programme in 1999 and now both the marvellous stone exterior and the comfortable and characterful interior show off The Old Down Inn at its best.

The large rear beer garden is ideal for summer barbecues whilst, inside, the extensive bar and restaurant areas are decorated with old local prints and photographs and are warmed by open fires. Here, not only is there an impressive array of real ales, wines and ciders served from the bar but customers can be treated to an excellent menu of delicious homecooked dishes. All prepared to order, whether it is a light sandwich lunch or a celebration à la carte dinner, The Old Down Inn is just the place. Bill is a local gentleman, who has worked in the building trade for most of his life before taking on the pub with Sheila, and his affinity with the locals is apparent. The inn is a meeting place for many local groups, including the Young Farmers and the Parish Council, who not only find this a convivial place to hold their meetings but are probably influenced by the inn's other claim to fame - it is the only inn in Somerset that has appeared in every edition of the Good Beer Guide.

Opening Hours: Mon-Sun 12.00-23.00

Food: Bar meals and snacks, À la carte

Credit Cards: Visa, Access, Delta, Switch, Diners, Amex

Accommodation: 3 double rooms all en suite

Facilities: Large beer garden, Car parking

Local Places of Interest/Activities:
Downside Abbey 3 miles, Wells 6 miles, Mendip Hills 4 miles, Walking, Fishing, Horse riding

The Old Mendip Inn | 221

Gurney Slade, nr Bath,
Somerset BA3 4UU
Tel/Fax: 01749 841234

Directions:

From junction 3 on the M32 continue to the centre of Bristol and then take the A37 towards Shepton Mallet. Gurney Slade is situated along this road and The Old Mendip Inn can be found opposite the B3135 to Cheddar road.

Originally a farm house that was built in the late 16th early 17th centuries, **The Old Mendip Inn** evolved into a coaching inn in the late 18th century as it lay on two ancient routes that joined Exeter and London and Bristol with the south coast. It is situated some 800 ft above sea level in the heart of the Mendip Hills. A delightful old building, this inn has fortunately maintained all its charm throughout the centuries and inside it is as pleasing as the exterior would suggest. Tastefully decorated and very much in keeping with the wealth of beams and Mendip stone that abound, this is a comfortable place that has been thoughtfully laid out to cater for diners, drinkers and families. Since being here the proprietors', Graham and Janet Symonds, carefully thought out improvements are certainly now paying dividends.

Food is an important part of life at the Mendip Inn and is a diner's paradise with a broad range of refreshments from tea and crumpets through to a full à la carte menu available. Very popular with locals; the extensive menu which changes all the time offers a tempting array of dishes freshly prepared to order by the resident chef from local ingredients. Best described as modern English cuisine, the house specialities include Whole Duck Breast Sizzler, Kaffir Lime Chicken in Tarragon, Fillet of Beef with Garlic and Herb Boursin Stuffing and a mouth watering selection of vegetarian dishes. In addition the pudding menu is a treat not to be missed and includes traditional English favourites such as rice pudding tasting like only 'Granny' made as well as the Inns homemade profiteroles and brandy snaps. A good choice of real ales and local ciders, a select wine list and a large choice of beers lagers and spirits served from the bar ensure that everyone will be able to enjoy their favourite tipple either in the cosy surroundings or outside in the well maintained beer garden. A superb country inn that is well worth finding and, you can always retire to one of the beautifully appointed rooms available.

Opening Hours: Mon-Sat 12.00-15.00, 17.30-23.00; Sun 12.00-15.00, 17.30-22.30

Food: Bar meals and snacks, À la carte, Children's menu

Credit Cards: Visa, Access, Delta, Switch

Accommodation: 4 double , 1 single room, all en suite

Facilities: Beer garden, Car parking, Children's play area, Functions catered for

Local Places of Interest/Activities: Mendip Hills 1 mile, Downside Abbey 2 miles, Wells 5 miles, Wookey Hole 6 miles, Cheddar Gorge 11 miles, Walking, Cycling, Horse riding, Fishing, Bird watching

Internet/Website:
gsymonds@compuserve.com

222   The Panborough Inn

Panborough,
near Wells,
Somerset BA5 1PN
Tel: 01934 712554
Fax: 01934 713900

Directions:

The pub lies on the B3139 between Wells and Wedmore, only 10 minutes form Wells, Glastonbury and Cheddar and only 20 minutes from the M5 junction 22 at Highbridge.

Dating back to the 17th century, **The Panborough Inn** is a traditional old coaching inn that, from its prominent raised position, overlooks the glorious Somerset countryside between the hamlet and Wells/Glastonbury. The pub is being completely refurbished, inside and out, by the proud owners Tom and Julie Lee. This country inn not only provides superb hospitality and service but it is also a pleasant and friendly place to visit.

A freehouse serving a range of real ales - from local brews to Scottish ales - there is also a comprehensive wine list that has been carefully chosen to provide a variety of wines for all occasions at reasonable prices. The comfortable bar area is the perfect setting for a quiet drink with friends and family, whilst, on Friday evenings, the mood changes when the regular live music begins. Tom and Julie have also taken great care in establishing an excellent reputation for the cuisine served at The Panborough Inn. The extensive menu, from light meals and snacks through to a full à la carte, is prepared by the resident team of chefs, with splendid dishes using local produce wherever possible. The large restaurant area is the ideal setting for a special meal and the menu, along with the Chef's seasonal specials, is well worth travelling to enjoy.

Opening Hours: Mon-Sun 12.00-15.00; 18.30-23.00/24.00

Food: Bar meals and snacks, à la carte, vegetarian, daily specials

Credit Cards: Visa, Access, Delta, Switch

Facilities: Skittle alley used also as function room, Large car park

Entertainment: Live music each Friday evening

Local Places of Interest/Activities: Wells 5 miles, Wookey Hole Caves 4 miles, Glastonbury 5 miles, Cheddar 6 miles, Walking, Cycling

The Plume of Feathers | 223

Rickford,
near Burrington,
Somerset BS40 7AH
Tel: 01761 462682

Directions:

From junction 19 on the M4 take the M32 into Bristol and then the A38 towards Bridgewater. At the Churchill traffic lights turn left on to the A368 and continue for approximately 3 miles. The Plume of Feathers lies the centre of the village.

A 300 year old traditional stone built inn, **The Plume of Feathers** is an attractive building that lies in the shadow of the Mendip Hills. To the rear of the inn there is an extensive beer garden that has a grassed play area that is sure to delight all children - there is a full size Wendy house - whilst adults will enjoy sitting under apple trees with a drink and watching the pet rare breed sheep. Inside, the scene is equally idyllic and this olde worlde inn is truly full of character, with low ceilings, half wood panelled walls and a mass of memorabilia - from porcelain pots to bank notes from around the world - hanging from the walls and beams. Cosy and very comfortable, this inviting inn is run by landlords Clare and Paul whose bubbly and welcoming personalities are sure to infect even the most disgruntled visitors.

Clare and Paul are also committed to customer care and the hospitality found here is second to none. The bar stocks all the usual drinks as well as an excellent range of real ales and ciders and the food here is a treat well worth travelling to find. The mouthwatering dishes are all homecooked and prepared from wonderful fresh local produce. Finally, the superb accommodation is of the same high standard as the rest of The Plume of Feathers and it makes a luxury base from which to explore the glorious Somerset countryside.

Opening Hours: Mon-Sat 11.30-14.30, 18.00-23.00; Sun 12.00-14.30, 18.00-22.30

Food: Bar meals and snacks, Barbecues in summer

Credit Cards: None

Accommodation: 1 double room, 1 Twin room, 1 Family room

Facilities: Beer garden, Car parking

Entertainment: Occasional live folk music

Local Places of Interest/Activities: Cheddar Gorge 5 miles, King John's Hunting Lodge 5 miles, Wells 10 miles, Bristol 10 miles, Weston-super-Mare 11 miles, Walking, Horse riding, Fishing

224   The Prince of Wales

Dunkerton Hill,
near Bath,
Somerset BA2 8PF
Tel: 01761 434262
Fax: 01761 431150

Directions:

From junction 18 on the M4 take the A46 into Bath and then the A367 towards Radstock. Turn right on to the first road after the junction with the B3115 and The Prince of Wales can be found a short distance away.

The Prince of Wales is a charming and attractive old inn that stands on the main road through the village of Dunkerton. Hard to miss, this 200 year old building is obviously well maintained and the black and white inn is bedecked by colourful hanging baskets and window boxes throughout the year. Inside, the story remains the same as this essentially open plan inn has a comfortable and relaxing atmosphere where customers will instantly feel at home. Although the decorations and furnishings are the same throughout, the different areas - bar, seating and dining - have subtly different colour schemes which shows just how much care and attention has been paid to detail.

The landladies of this excellent country inn are two local business women, Di and Maria, who, whilst having good business heads on their shoulders, also are bright, energetic and enthusiastic. A freehouse with a good selection of traditional ales and lagers, including examples from local breweries, The Prince of Wales is not only a well known place for a good pint but also has an enviable reputation for the high quality of its food. While Di is managing the front of house, Maria takes control of the catering and the splendid menus of homecooked dishes are both interesting and extensive. Ranging from light meals and snacks (served until 18.00) to a full and imaginative à la carte menu there is certainly something here to suit everyone's taste and pocket. With also superb en suite accommodation, The Prince of Wales is a place well worth seeking out that brings customers back time and time again.

Opening Hours: Mon-Fri 12.00-23.00; Sat 11.00-23.00; Sun 12.00-22.30 (Sun lunches 12.00-19.00)

Food: Bar meals and snacks, À la carte, Traditional Sunday lunch

Credit Cards: Visa, Access, Delta, Switch

Accommodation: 1 double room, 1 family room, 3 twin rooms, all en suite

Facilities: Beer garden, Car parking, Functions catered for

Entertainment: Live music every Sunday, Pool, Darts

Local Places of Interest/Activities: Bath 4 miles, Hinton Priory 4 miles, Bath Racecourse 6 miles, Walking, Cycling, Horse riding, Fishing

The Red Lion Inn

225

Wells Road,
Draycott,
near Cheddar,
Somerset BS27 3SN
Tel: 01934 743786
Fax: 01934 743786

Directions:

From junction 21 on the M5 take the A370 towards Weston-Super-Mare and then the A371 towards Wells. The Red Lion Inn lies on this road in the centre of Draycott.

Found in the heart of this pretty village set in the county's strawberry growing area, **The Red Lion Inn** dates back to 1640 when it was built as a cider house. A lovely old building with a vivid red tiled roof that sets off the sandstone walls, the inn is still a great meeting place for those who live in the area. With an attractive beer garden and a pretty patio that is a real sun trap, this is an ideal place to make for in the summer but, when the weather is less kind the interior of this charming old inn is both warm and inviting. Divided into two bars, the building's original beams are still visible and the gleam of the display brassware all adds to the olde worlde atmosphere here.

Though it is a long time since The Red Lion Inn was a cider house, visitors can still taste the real drink of Somerset as there are always three draught ciders served here. Along with the real ales, the extensive wine list and all the usual lagers, beers and spirits, the inn certainly does have everyone's favourite tipple. Landlords, John and Dawn Ayers, are also anxious that their customers don't go home hungry and, as a result, the inn serves a tasty range of traditional pub meals along with some special creations of their own. Definitely a treat worth trying, the delicious dishes are freshly prepared by Dawn whilst John is busy looking after customers' liquid refreshment.

Opening Hours: Mon-Sat 11.00-23.00; Sun 12.00-16.00; 19.00-22.30

Food: Bar meals and snacks, Traditional Sunday lunch

Credit Cards: None

Facilities: Beer garden, Car parking

Entertainment: Darts, Shove Ha'penny, Cribbage, Table skittles, Skittles

Local Places of Interest/Activities: Cheddar and Cheddar Gorge 2 miles, Wookey Hole 4 miles, Wells 6 miles, Beach 15 miles, Walking, Cycling, Horse riding, Fishing, Gliding, Go-karting, Pot-holing

226 The Ship at Oldford

Frome,
Oldford,
near Frome,
Somerset BA11 2ND
Tel: 01373 462043
Fax: 01373 462043

Directions:

From junction 18 on the M4 take the A46 towards Bath and then the A36 towards Frome. Approximately 2 miles before Frome, turn right on to the B3090 and The Ship at Oldford can be found in the centre of the village.

A delightful village inn, **The Ship at Oldford** dates back to the 18th century when it was built as a shipping - hence the name - station for sheep. A charming old stone building, with a large, well maintained beer garden, this is a lovely country inn that offers friendly hospitality to locals and visitors alike. The interior of The Ship is as full of character as its outward appearance would suggest and, along with the wood burning stove set in the feature stone fireplace which provides added warmth on cold nights, the skittle alley adjoining the bar is decorated with a mass of farming implements.

Although this is landlords Richard and Jill Pullen's first venture into the licensing trade they have certainly got hit just the right note. From the bar they serve a good range of real ales, along with all the usual beers, lagers and spirits, and there is also an extensive wine list. Food too is an important aspect of The Ship and the tempting menu of delicious dishes is all specially cooked to order from fresh ingredients. Finally, what makes The Ship so popular is the relaxed atmosphere where visitors can enter as strangers and leave as friends. There is always plenty going on here and whether it is just a quiet drink and good conversation or the entertaining live music or quiz evenings, all are welcome.

Opening Hours: Mon-Sat 11.00-23.00; Sun 12.00-22.30

Food: Bar meals and snacks

Credit Cards: Visa, Access, Delta, Switch, Diners

Facilities: Beer garden, Car parking, Functions catered for

Entertainment: Regular live music, Regular quiz nights, Skittles, Darts, Pool

Local Places of Interest/Activities: Frome 1 mile, Nunney Castle 4 miles, Longleat 4 miles, Witham Friary 6 miles, Walking, Cycling, Horse riding, Fishing

The Slab House Inn

West Horrington,
near Wells,
Somerset BA5 3EQ
Tel: 01749 840310
Fax: 01749 840358

Directions:

From Bristol take the A37 south towards Shepton Mallet. At Farrington Gurney turn right on to the A39 and follow the road to Green Ore. Turn left at the traffic lights on the B3135 and after 1 mile right at the B3139 to Wells. The Slab House is ¼ mile along on the left.

The Slab House Inn gained its curious name back in the medieval times when, during the Black Death, a three mile quarantine limit was imposed around the city of Wells. Cautious farmers and traders would then leave food and other produce on the large slab outside the inn for collection by the city folk who were under siege by the devastating plague. Fortunately, today's visitors to this splendid early 16th century inn need have no fear of developing some gruesome illness - they can, however, expect to receive exceptional hospitality at the hands of the inn's owners, Margaret and Alan Gripton.

Surrounded by its own delightful large beer garden and patio area, this attractive inn is a comfortable and well maintained property where care has been taken in displaying a mass of antiques to give the inn a sense of atmosphere and style. Well renowned locally for its excellent food, prepared by a team of four chefs, the choice varies from tasty bar snacks to a full à la carte menu in the restaurant. The bar snacks add an extra element of flair and imagination to a variety of traditional pub dishes and they can certainly not be seen as the poor relation to the restaurant dishes. However, the à la carte menu provides a delicious blend of traditional English cuisine with cosmopolitan sophistication that makes dining here a culinary treat. Vegetarians are also in for a surprise as, unusually, there is an equally impressive list of non meat dishes that are sure to tempt even the most hardened meat lover. Whilst The Slab House is, undoubtedly, a charming English country inn the level of hospitality, particularly the food, can only be second to the most chic of London establishments.

Opening Hours: Mon-Sat 11.00-15.00, 18.00-23.00; Sun 12.00-15.00, 19.00-22.30

Food: À la carte, bar meals and snacks (except Fri and Sat evenings and Sun lunchtime)

Credit Cards: Visa, Access, Delta, Switch

Facilities: Large beer garden and patio, Car parking

Local Places of Interest/Activities: Wells 2 miles, Wookey Hole 3 miles, Glastonbury 7 miles, Walking, Fishing, Clay pigeon shooting

228

The White Hart

Trudoxhill,
near Frome,
Somerset BA11 5DP
Tel: 01373 836324
Fax: 01373 836566

Directions:

From junction 18 on the M4
take the A46 south to Bath
then the A36 to Warminster.
Take the A361 around Frome
and, at the fifth roundabout,
take the road to Trudoxhill
and The White Hart lies 1
mile down the road.

One of Somerset's oldest inns, **The White Hart** dates back to the early 17th century when it first opened as a coaching inn. A splendid stone building, with a long frontage on the main road through the village, the inn retains many features of those far off days, not least the excellent hospitality it offers to weary travellers. Very much a family run inn, The new owners moved here from Leeds with Mrs Robsons parents and they have really made a success of the venture.

The centrally placed front door takes visitors right to the heart of inn, where the layout is open plan though the exposed stone walls, open fireplace and ceiling beams come from a very different age. Here, both visitors and locals can enjoy an excellent pint of real ale, including the product of the local brewery Ash Vine which started in the inn's converted smithy, as well as all the usual beers, lagers, wines and spirits. A delicious selection of bar snacks are also served here though, for more elegant dining the separate Stable Restaurant offers a mouthwatering à la carte menu of freshly prepared dishes that are worthy of the most special occasion. The White Hart is a popular place for everyone, particularly on the theme evenings when not only the menu changes but everyone here wears appropriate costumes.

Opening Hours: Mon-Sat all day; Sun 12.00-22.30

Food: Bar meals and snacks, à la carte in restaurant

Credit Cards: Visa, Access, Delta, Switch, Diners, Amex

Facilities: Large beer garden, Children's play area

Entertainment: Themed evenings

Local Places of Interest/Activities: Longleat 5 miles, Witham Friary 3 miles, Walking, Riding

The Woodborough Inn | 229

Sandford Road,
Winscombe,
Somerset BS25 1HD
Tel: 01934 844167

Directions:
From junction 21 on the M5 take the A370 towards Weston-Super-Mare and then the A371 towards Wells. One mile after Banwell take a right turn and follow the signs for Winscombe and The Woodborough Inn lies in the heart of the village.

As the only pub in the village, **The Woodborough Inn** is not only a friendly local but it also plays a part in village life as a central meeting place. An impressive and imposing modern building constructed along traditional lines, the inn is hard to miss in this quiet and picturesque place. When Philip Smith and his father first came here in 1997, the inn was in a very sorry state but, after much work, including a complete refurbishment, the inn is certainly one of the highlights of the area.

The interior is open plan, although small room dividers have been used to create intimate alcoves and hide aways, the high standard of the fixtures and fittings used have given the inn a traditional English country pub atmosphere. Not only is Philip an energetic and enthusiastic publican but he also has great experience in international catering and this has certainly been brought to good use in the pub's menu. An interesting and imaginative list of mouthwatering, freshly prepared dishes, the list includes everything from simple English pub fare to Middle and Far Eastern cuisine. Dining here is definitely an experience that can take customers to any corner of the globe they wish to go. Add to this the excellent selection of real ales served from the bar and the speciality coffees and Philip has certainly got a success on his hands.

Opening Hours: Mon-Thu 12.00-14.15, 18.00-21.30; Fri 12.00-14.15, 18.00-22.00; Sat 12.00-22.00; Sun 12.00-21.00

Food: Bar meals and snacks, À la carte restaurant

Credit Cards: Visa, Access, Delta, Switch, Amex, Diners

Facilities: Car parking

Local Places of Interest/Activities: King John's Hunting Lodge 1 mile, Cheddar Gorge 3 miles, Wells 11 miles, Beach 7 miles, Walking, Fishing, Sailing, Horse riding

This page is left intentionally blank

8 Dorset

PLACES OF INTEREST:

Abbotsbury   233
Beaminster   234
Blandford Forum   234
Bournemouth   234
Bridport   235
Cerne Abbas   235
Corfe Castle   236
Dorchester   237
Isle of Portland   239
Lyme Regis   239
Moreton   240
Osmington Mills   240

Poole   240
Shaftesbury   241
Sherborne   241
Swanage   243
Tolpuddle   243
Wareham   244
Weymouth   244
Whitchurch Canonicorum   245
Wimborne Minster   245
Winfrith Newburge   245

PUBS AND INNS:

The Albion Inn, Verwood   247
The Anchor Inn, Burton Bradstock   248
The Botany Bay Inn,
    Winterborne Zelston   249
The Brewers Arms, Martinstown   250
The Buffalo Inn, Wyke   251
The Clifton Hotel, The Grove   252
Eight Kings Inn, Portland   253
The Fox Inn, Ansty   254
The George Inn, Chideock   255
The Globe Inn, Swanage   256
The Griffins Head Inn,
    Nether Compton   257

The Halfway Inn, Norden   258
Ilchester Arms, Abbotsbury   259
Kings Arms, Wareham   260
The New Inn, Christchurch   261
The Piddle Inn Piddletrenthide   262
The Scott Arms, Kingston   263
The Smugglers Inn, Osmington Mills   264
The Talbot Arms, Benville   265
The Trooper Inn, Stourton Caundle   266
The White Horse, Stourpaine   267
The White Horse Inn, Swanage   268
The World's End Inn, Almer   269

The Hidden Inns of the West Country

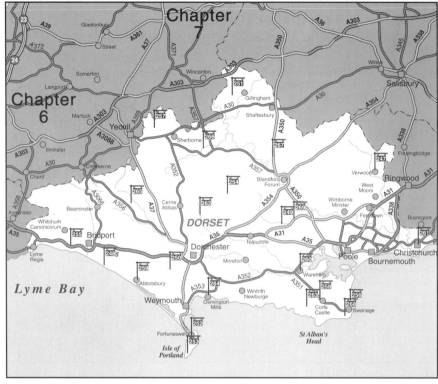

© MAPS IN MINUTES ™ (1998)

247 **The Albion Inn**, Verwood

248 **The Anchor Inn**, Burton Bradstock

249 **The Botany Bay Inn**, Winterborne Zelston

250 **The Brewers Arms**, Martinstown

251 **The Buffalo Inn**, Wyke

252 **The Clifton Hotel**, The Grove

253 **Eight Kings Inn**, Portland

254 **The Fox Inn**, Ansty

255 **The George Inn**, Chideock

256 **The Globe Inn**, Swanage

257 **The Griffins Head Inn**, Nether Compton

258 **The Halfway Inn**, Norden

259 **Ilchester Arms**, Abbotsbury

260 **Kings Arms**, Wareham

261 **The New Inn**, Christchurch

262 **The Piddle Inn** Piddletrenthide

263 **The Scott Arms**, Kingston

264 **The Smugglers Inn**, Osmington Mills

265 **The Talbot Arms**, Benville

266 **The Trooper Inn**, Stourton Caundle

267 **The White Horse**, Stourpaine

268 **The White Horse Inn**, Swanage

269 **The World's End Inn**, Almer

Please note all cross references refer to page numbers

Within a comparatively small area, Dorset provides an extraordinary variety of attractions. This county covers a land that encompasses the rolling chalk downs, the dark heathland beloved of Thomas Hardy, the long ridge of the Purbeck Hill sand the incomparable Dorset coast with its wealth of magnificent rock formations sculpted by

the sea. The county's two largest towns, Bournemouth and Poole (virtually one, nowadays), offer visitors one of the best beaches in Britain during the day, and first-class entertainments at night.

The magnificent ruins of Corfe Castle, set on a high hill above the charming village of the same name, is one of the grandest sights in southwest England and should not be missed. Inland, a string of villages along the River Piddle (delicately modified in Victorian times to 'Puddle') culminates in historic Tolpuddle, honoured in trades union history as the home of the Tolpuddle Martyrs. Largely agricultural, Dorset represents rural England at its most appealing. The north of the county, particularly, is a peaceful, unspoilt area embracing half a dozen small market towns and many attractive villages.

Dorset Coastline

This area's most glorious building is Sherborne Abbey; the same small town also contains Sir Walter Raleigh's Sherborne Old Castle as well as several other striking medieval houses. North Dorset is a place to explore for its enchanting countryside and beguiling little towns. To the south and west the county offers the attractive centres of Weymouth and Bridport, Lyme Regis and Abbotsbury. Nearly all of west Dorset's 417 square miles are designated an Area of Outstanding Natural Beauty. The coastline, which is part of the Dorset Heritage Coast, goes through dramatic changes from the spectacular Chesil Bank through the sandstone headland and west to fossil-encrusted cliffs.

PLACES OF INTEREST

ABBOTSBURY

Surrounded by hills, picturesque Abbotsbury is one of the county's most popular tourist spots and by any standards one of the loveliest villages in England. Its most striking feature as you approach is the 14th century **St Catherine's Chapel**, perched on the hill-top. Only 45 feet by 15 feet, it is solidly built to withstand the Channel gales with walls more than 4 foot thick. St Catherine was believed to be particularly helpful in finding husbands for the unmarried, and in medieval times spinsters would climb the hill to her chapel chanting a dialect

jingle which concludes with the words "Arn-a-one's better than Narn-a-one" - anyone is better than never a one.

Abbotsbury takes its name from the important **Benedictine Abbey** that once stood here but was comprehensively cannibalised after the Reformation, its stones used to build the attractive cottages that line the village streets. What has survived however is the magnificent **Great Abbey Barn**, 247 feet long and 31 feet wide, which was built in the 1300s to store the Abbey's tithes of wool, grain and other produce. With its thatched roof, stone walls and a might-

234

ily impressive entrance it is one of the largest and best-preserved barns in the country. It now houses a Terracotta Warriors exhibition and is surrounded by a Childrens Farm where youngsters can feed the animals. The Barn is open all year round.

About a mile south of the village is the famous **Abbotsbury Swannery**, established in Saxon times to provide food for the Abbey during the winter months. More than 600 free-flying swans have made their home here and visitor figures rocket from the end of May to the end of June - the baby swans' hatching season. There' s also a children's Ugly Duckling Trail and the oldest known duck decoy still working.

Just to the west of the village, **Abbotsbury Sub-Tropical Gardens** enjoy a particularly well-sheltered position and the 20 acres of grounds contain a huge variety of rare and exotic plants and trees. Other attractions include an 18th century walled garden, beautiful lily ponds and a children' s play area.

BEAMINSTER

In Hardy's novel, when Tess Durbeyville arrives in Beaminster ("Emminster" in the novel), she finds a delightful little market town. Outwardly, nothing much has changed: the 17th century almshouse, the majestic church tower in gold-tinted Hamstone, and the charming **Market Square** with its stone roofed market cross are

Beaminster Market Cross

all much the same as they were then. What have disappeared are the many small industries that thrived in those days - rope and sailcloth, embroidered buttons, shoes, wrought ironwork and clockmaking were just some of the artefacts produced here.

About as far west as you can get in Dorset, **Forde Abbey** enjoys a lovely setting beside the River Axe. Founded as a Cistercian monastery more than 800 years ago, it is now the home of the Roper family. The Abbey church has gone but the monks of those days would still recognise the chapter house, dormitories, kitchen and refectories. The Upper Refectory is particularly striking with its fine timbered roof and carved panelling. The gardens, extending to 30 acres with origins in the early 1700s, are landscaped around this enchanting house.

BLANDFORD FORUM

Blandford Forum, the administrative centre of North Dorset, is beautifully situated along the wooded valley of the River Stour. It's a handsome town, thanks mainly to suffering the trauma of a great fire in 1731. The gracious Georgian buildings erected after that conflagration, most of them designed by local architects John and William Bastard, provide the town with a quite unique and soothing sense of architectural harmony.

Three important ancient buildings escaped the fire of 1731: the **Ryves Almshouses** of 1682, the **Corn Exchange**, and the splendid 15th century **Old House in The Close**. The old parish church did not survive the fire, but its 18th century replacement, crowned by an unusual cupola, now dominates the market-place. It's well worth stepping inside the church to see the massive columns of Portland stone, and the elegant pulpit, designed by Sir Christopher Wren, removed here from St Antholin' s Church in the City of London.

BOURNEMOUTH

In 1998, no less a magazine than *Harpers & Queen* predicted that Bournemouth was on its way to becoming the "next coolest city on the planet", and another dubbed the town "Britain' s Baywatch", a reference to the comely young lifeguards who patrol the six miles of golden beaches. This cosmopolitan town has been voted the greenest and cleanest resort in the UK. (Even the town centre streets are washed and scrubbed every morning).

Two hundred years ago, the tiny village of Bourne was a mere satellite of the bustling port of Poole a few miles to the west. The empty coastline was ideal for smugglers, and Revenue men were posted to patrol the area. One of them, Louis Tregonwell, was enchanted by Bourne's glorious setting at the head of three deep valleys, or chines. He and his wife bought land here, built themselves a house and planted the valleys with the pines that give the present-day town its distinctive appearance. Throughout Victorian times, Bournemouth, as it became known, grew steadily and the prosperous new residents beautified their adopted town with wide boulevards, grand parks and public buildings, creating a Garden City by the Sea.

They also built a splendid **Pier** (1855) and, around the same time, **St Peter' s Church** which is much visited for its superb carved alabaster by Thomas Earp, and tomb in which Mary Shelley, the author of *Frankenstein*, is buried along with the heart of her poet-husband, Percy Bysshe Shelley. The **Casa Magni Shelley Museum**, in Shelley House where the poet' s son lived from 1849 to 1889, is the only one in the world devoted entirely to Shelley' s life and works. Other museums include the **Russell-Cotes Art Gallery & Museum**, based on the collection of the globe-trotting Sir Merton Russell-Cotes; the **Rothesay Museum** which follows a mainly nautical theme but also has a display of more than 300 vintage typewriters; the **Teddy Bear Museum** in the Expocentre and, north of the town, the **Aviation Heritage Museum** at Bournemouth International Airport, home to a collection of vintage jet aircraft which are flown on a regular basis.

As you might expect in such a popular resort, every conceivable kind of sport and recreation facility is available: anything from surfboarding to paragliding, from classical, pop and jazz concerts to international golf tournaments. And if you' re looking for a novel experience, and a really spectacular aerial view of the town and coastline, **Vistarama**, in the Lower Gardens near the Pier, offers day or night ascents in a tethered balloon which rises up to 650 feet.

BRIDPORT

With its broad streets (inherited from the days when they were used for making ropes), Bridport is an appealing little town surrounded by green hills and with a goodly number of 17th and 18th century buildings. Most notable amongst these are the medieval **Prior's House**, the stately Georgian **Town Hall**, and the pleasing collection of 17th century houses in the street running south from the Town Hall. If you visit the town on a Wednesday or Saturday you'll find its three main streets chock-a-block with dozens of stalls participating in the regular **Street Market**. The Town Council actively encourages local people who produce goods at home and not as part of their regular livelihood to join in. So there's an extraordinary range of artefacts on offer, anything from silk flowers to socks, fossils to fishing tackle. Another popular attraction is **Palmers Brewery** in West Bay Road. Established in 1794, part of the brewery is still thatched.During the season, visitors are welcomed on Tuesdays and Wednesdays for a tour of the historic brewery, the charge for which includes a commemorative Certificate and also a glass or two of beer. (More details on 01308 427500). **Bridport Museum** is good on local history and family records and also has an interesting collection of dolls. You can also learn about two distinguished visitors to the town. One was Joan of Navarre, who landed at Bridport in 1403 on her way to marry Henry IV; the other, Charles II, who arrived in the town after his defeat at the Battle of Worcester. He was fleeing to France, pretending to be the groom in a runaway marriage. As he attended his horses in the yard of an inn, an ostler approached him saying "Surely I know you, friend". The quick-thinking king-to-be asked where the ostler had been working before. When he replied "In Exeter", Charles responded "Aye, that is where we must have met,"excused himself and made a speedy departure from the town. If the ostler's memory for faces had been better, he could have claimed the £1,000 bounty for Charles' capture, and subsequent English history would have followed a very different course.

CERNE ABBAS

This pretty village beside the River Cerne takes its name from **Cerne Abbey**, formerly a major Benedictine monastery of which an imposing 15th century gatehouse, a tithe barn of the same period, and a holy well still survive, all well worth seeing. So too are the lofty, airy church with grotesque gargoyles and medieval statues adorning its west tower, and the old **Market House** on Long Street. In fact, there is much to see in this ancient village, from the remains of the Abbey, the Tithe

only have been authorised by the locally all-powerful Abbots of Cerne. What possible reason did those Christian advocates of chastity have for carefully preserving such a powerful pagan image of virility?

CORFE CASTLE

One of the grandest sights in the country is the impressive ruin of **Corfe Castle** (National Trust), standing high on a hill and dominating the attractive grey stone village below. Once the most impregnable fortress in the land, Corfe dates back to the days of William the Conqueror, with later additions by King John and Edward I. The dastardly John threw 22 French knights into the castle dungeons and left them

Abbots Porch, Cerne Abbas

Barn and 14th century houses to the **Cerne Abbas Giant** himself (National Trust), a colossal 180 foot high figure cut into the chalk hillside. He stands brandishing a club, naked and full-frontal, and there can be absolutely no doubt about his gender. An ancient tradition asserts that any woman wishing to become pregnant should sit - or preferably sleep the night - on the Giant's huge erect penis. The age of this extraordinary carving is hotly disputed, but a consensus is emerging that it was originally created by ancient Britons as a fertility symbol and that the Giant's club was added by the Romans. (There are clear similarities between the Giant and the representation of Hercules on a Roman pavement of AD 191, preserved at Sherborne Castle). As with all hill carvings, the best view is from a distance, in this case from a layby on the A352. A curious puzzle remains: the Giant's outlines in the chalk need a regular scouring to remove grass and weeds. Should this be neglected he would soon fade into the hillside. In medieval centuries, such a non-essential task of conservation could

Corfe Castle

to starve to death. Later, Edward II was imprisoned here before being sent to Berkeley Castle and his horrible murder.

Corfe remained important right up until the days of the Civil War, when it successfully withstood two sieges before it fell into Parliamentary hands through treachery. A month later, Parliament ordered the castle to be "slighted" - rendered militarily useless.

Although Corfe now stands in splendid ruin, you can see a smaller, intact version at the **Model Village** in West Street. This superbly accurate replica is built from the same Purbeck stone as the real thing and the details of the

237

miniature medieval folk going about their daily business are wonderful. Surrounded by lovely gardens, this intriguing display is well worth a visit.

DORCHESTER

One of England's most appealing county towns, Dorchester's known history goes back to AD 74 when the Romans established a settlement called Durnovaria at a respectful distance from the River Frome. At that time the river was much broader than it is now and prone to flooding. The town's Roman origins are clearly displayed in its street plan, in the beautiful tree-lined avenues known as **The Walks** which follow the course of the old Roman walls, at **Maumbury Rings**, an ancient stone circle which the Romans converted into an amphitheatre, and in the well-preserved **Roman Town House** behind County Hall in Colliton Park. As the town's most famous citizen put it, Dorchester "announced old Rome in every street, alley and precinct. It looked Roman, bespoke the art of Rome, concealed dead men of Rome". Thomas Hardy was in fact describing "Casterbridge" in his novel *The Mayor of Casterbridge*, but his fictional town is immediately recognisable as Dorchester. One place he describes in great detail is **Mayor Trenchard's House**, easily identified as what is now Barclays Bank in South Street which bears a plaque to that effect. Hardy made his home in Dorchester in 1883 and two years later moved in to Max Gate (National Trust) on the outskirts of the town, a strikingly unlovely "two up and two down" Victorian villa designed by Hardy himself and built by his brother at a total cost of £450. Here he would entertain a roll-call of great names - Robert Louis Stevenson, G.B. Shaw, Rudyard Kipling and H.G. Wells among many others - to tea at 4 o' clock.

For many visitors, the most accessible introduction to the town and the county will be found at the excellent **Dorset County Museum** in High Street West. Designated Best Social History Museum in the 1998 Museum of the Year Awards, the museum houses a comprehensive range of exhibits spanning the centuries, from a Roman sword to a 19th century cheese press, from dinosaur footprints to a stuffed Great Bustard which used to roam the chalk uplands of north Dorset but has been extinct in this country since 1810. Founded in 1846, the museum moved to its present site in 1883, into purpose-built galleries with lofty arches of fine

cast ironwork inspired by the Great Exhibition of 1851 at the Crystal Palace. The building was designed by G. R. Crickmay, the architect for whom Thomas Hardy worked in 1870, and the great poet and novelist is celebrated in a major exhibit which includes a fascinating reconstruction of his study at Max Gate, his Dorchester home. The room includes the original furnishings, books, pictures and fireplace. In the right-hand corner are his musical instruments, and the very pens with which he wrote *Tess of the d'Urbervilles*, *Jude the Obscure*, and his epic poem, the *Dynasts* are also here. More of his possessions are displayed in the Gallery outside - furniture, his watch, music books, and some of his notebooks. Also honoured in the Writers Gallery is William Barnes, the Dorset dialect poet, scholar and priest, who was also the first secretary of the Dorset Natural History and Archaeological Society which owns and runs the museum.

Other galleries display the rich and varied environment of Dorset in the past and present. There's a fossil tree, around 135 million years old, from Portland, skeletons of Iron Age warriors from Maiden Castle cemetery, part of a Roman mosaic from Dorchester, a 12th century ivory carving of a King found near Milborne St Andrew, a 19th century Dorset bow waggon, and much, much more. The museum also stages regularly changing temporary exhibitions on topics as varied as whales to sculpture, Dorset in wartime to abstract art.

Just outside the museum stands the Statue of William Barnes and, at the junction of High Street West and The Grove, is the Statue of Thomas Hardy. Opposite the Museum, the Antelope Hotel and the 17th century half-timbered

Judge Jeffries Lodgings

238

building beside it (now a tearoom) were where Judge Jeffreys (1648-89) tried 340 Dorset men for their part in Monmouth's Rebellion of 1685. As a result of this "Bloody Assize", 74 men suffered death by being hanged, drawn and quartered, and a further 175 were transported for life. Jeffreys' ferociousness has been attributed to the agony he suffered from gallstones for which doctors of the time could provide no relief. Ironically, when his patron James II was deposed, Jeffreys himself ended up in the Tower of London where he died. A century and a half after the "Bloody Assizes", another infamous trial took place in the Old Crown Court and Cells nearby. Here, 6 farm labourers who later became known as the Tolpuddle Martyrs were condemned to transportation for their part in organising a "Friendly Society" - the first agricultural trade union. The **Court and Cells** are now open to the public where they are invited to "stand in the dock and sit in the dimly-lit cells ... and experience four centuries of gruesome crime and punishment".

In High Street West is the **Tutankhamun Exhibition**, an impressive reconstruction of the young Pharaoh' s tomb and treasures, including his famous golden mask, with "sight, sound and smell combining to re-create the world's greatest discovery of ancient treasure". Close by, at the **Teddy Bear House**, visitors join Mr Edward Bear and his family of human-size bears as they relax around the house or busy themselves making teddies in the **Old Dorset Teddy Bear Factory**. Hundreds of the cuddly creatures are on sale in the exhibition's period shop.

The **Dinosaur Museum** was declared Dorset's Best Family Attraction in 1997. Actual fossils, skeletons and life-size reconstructions combine with audio-visual and hands-on displays to inform and entertain. Somewhat surprisingly, this is the only museum in Britain dedicated exclusively to these fascinating creatures. The museum is open daily throughout the year. Also well worth a visit is The **Keep Military Museum** housed in an interesting, renovated Grade II listed building. Audio technology and interactive computerised displays tell the remarkable story of those who have served in the regiments of Dorset and Devon. An additional bonus is the spectacular view from the battlements across the town and surrounding countryside.

There can be few churches in the country with such a bizarre history as that of **Our Lady, Queen of Martyrs & St Michael**. It was first erected in Wareham, in 1888, by a Roman Catholic sect who called themselves the Passionists, a name derived from their obsession with Christ's passion and death. When they found that few people in Wareham shared their fixation, they had the church moved in 1907, stone by stone to Dorchester where it was reassembled and then served the Catholic community for almost 70 years. By the mid-1970s the transplanted church had become too small for its burgeoning congregation. The Passionists moved out, ironically taking over an Anglican church whose communicants had become too few to sustain it. A decade later, their abandoned church was acquired by an organisation called World Heritage which has transformed its interior into a reconstruction of the tomb of Tutankhamun.With the help of a running commentary, visitors can follow the footsteps of the archaeologist Howard Carter who discovered the real tomb in 1922, a tour which ends beside a life-size facsimile of the youthful Pharaoh's mummy constructed from a genuine skeleton covered with organic-substitute flesh and animal skin.

Just a mile or so northeast of the town, **Kingston Maurward Gardens** are of such historical importance that they are listed on the English Heritage register of Gardens. The 35 acres of classical 18th century parkland and lawns sweep majestically down to the lake from the stately Georgian house. The Edwardian Gardens include a croquet lawn, rose garden, herbaceous borders and a large display of tender perennials, including the National Collection of Penstemons and Salvias. There' s also an Animal Park with an interesting collection of unusual breeds, nature trails, plant sales and the Old Coach House Restaurant serving morning coffee, lunches and teas.

Of even greater historical significance is **Maiden Castle**, a couple of miles southwest of Dorchester and one of the most impressive prehistoric sites in the country. This vast Iron Age fortification covering nearly 50 acres dates back some 4,000 years. Its steep earth ramparts, between 60 and 90 feet high, are nearly 2 miles round and, together with the inner walls, make a total of 5 miles of defences. The settlement flourished for 2,000 years until AD 44 when its people were defeated by a Roman army under Vespasian. Excavations here in 1937 unearthed a war cemetery containing some 40 bodies, one of which still had a Roman arrowhead embedded in its spine. The Romans occupied the site for some 30 years before moving closer to the River Frome and founding Durnovaria, modern Dorchester. Maiden Castle was never settled again and it is a rather forbidding, treeless place but the extensive views along the Winterborne valley by contrast are delightful.

ISLE OF PORTLAND

Portland is not really an island at all, but a 4½-mile long peninsula, well known to devotees of shipping forecasts and even more famous for the stone from its quarries. Numerous buildings in London are constructed of Portland stone, among them St. Paul's Cathedral and Buckingham Palace, and the stone was also favoured by sculptors such as Henry Moore. There are good cliff-top walks with grand views of **Chesil Beach**, a vast bank of pebbles worn smooth by the sea which stretches for some 10 miles to Abbotsbury. Inexplicably, the pebbles are graded in size from west to east. Fishermen reckon they can judge whereabouts on the beach they are landing by the size of the pebbles. In the west they are as small as peas; at Portland they have grown to the size of cooking apples! The area of water trapped behind the beach is known as **The Fleet**.

LYME REGIS

Known as "The Pearl of Dorset", this captivating little town enjoys a setting unrivalled in the county, an area of outstanding natural beauty where the rolling countryside of Dorset plunges to the sea. The town itself is a maze of narrow streets with many charming Georgian and Regency houses, and the picturesque harbour will be familiar to anyone who has seen the film *The French Lieutenant's Woman*, based on the novel by Lyme resident, John Fowles. The scene of a lone woman standing on the wave-lashed Cobb has become one of the cinema's most enduring images.

The Cobb, which protects the harbour and the sandy beach with its clear bathing water from south-westerly storms, was first recorded in 1294 but the town itself goes back at least another 500 years to Saxon times when there was a salt works here. A charter granted by Edward I allowed Lyme to add "Regis" to its name but during the Civil War the town was staunchly anti-royalist, routing the forces of Prince Maurice and killing more than 2,000 of them. Some 40 years later, James, Duke of Monmouth, chose Lyme as his landing place to start the ill-fated rebellion that would end with ferocious reprisals being meted out to the insurgents by Judge Jeffreys. Happier days arrived in the 18th century when Lyme became a fashionable resort, famed for its fresh, clean air. Jane Austen and her family visited in 1803 and part of her novel *Persuasion* is set in the town.

A few years later, a 12-year-old girl called Mary Anning was wandering along the shore when she noticed bones protruding from the cliffs. She had discovered the first ichthyosaur to be found in England. Later, as one of the first professional fossil collectors, she also unearthed locally a plesiosaur and a pterodactyl. The 6-mile stretch of coastline on either side of Lyme is world famous for its fossils and some fine specimens of local discoveries can be seen at the **Philpot Museum** in Bridge Street and at **Dinosaurland** in Coombe Street, which also runs guided "fossil walks" along the beach.

Just around the corner from Dinosaurland, in Mill Lane, you'll find one of the town's most interesting buildings. It was in January 1991 that a group of Lyme Regis residents got together in an effort to save the old **Town Mill** from destruction. There has been a mill on the River Lym in the centre of the town for many centuries, but most of the present buildings date back to the mid-17th century when the mill was rebuilt after being burned down during the Civil War siege of Lyme in 1644. Today, the restored Town Mill is one of Lyme's major attractions, housing two Art Galleries which stage a wide range of exhibitions, concerts, poetry readings and other live performances. There is also a stable building which houses craft workshops. No one who comes to Lyme Regis should leave without paying at least one visit to these exceptionally well-restored buildings set in such unique surroundings. The Town Mill site is open to the public most days between Easter and Christmas, from 10am to 5pm and admission is free.

Visitors to the Town Mill who enjoy walking will find a delightful riverside walk leading either to the inland village of Uplyme or back through the town to the harbour. The **South West Coast Path** also passes through Lyme: if

240

you follow it eastwards for about 5 miles it will bring you to **Golden Cap**, the highest point on the south coast with spectacular views from every vantage point. Or you can take a pleasant stroll along **Marine Parade**, a traffic-free promenade stretching for about a mile from The Cobb.

For its size, Lyme Regis has an extraordinary range of activities on offer, too many to list here although one must mention the famous week-long Regatta and Carnival held in August. Bands

Lyme Regis Town Crier

play on the Marine Parade, there are displays by Morris Men and folk dancers, and an annual Town Criers Open Championship. Lyme has maintained a Town Crier for over a thousand years without a break and the current incumbent in his colourful 18th century costume can be seen and heard throughout the town during the summer months.

MORETON

Thomas Hardy may be Dorset's most famous author, but in this small village it is another distinguished writer (also a scholar, archaeologist and military hero) who is remembered. In 1935 T.E. Lawrence - "Lawrence of Arabia"- left the RAF, where he was known simply as Aircraftsman T.E. Shaw, and retired to a spartan cottage he had bought ten years earlier. It stands

alone on the heath outside Moreton village and here Lawrence lived as a virtual recluse, without cooking facilities and with a sleeping bag as his bed. He was to enjoy this peaceful, if comfortless, retreat for only a few weeks. Lawrence loved speeding along the

Dorset lanes on his motor-cycle and one lovely spring day his adventurous driving led to a fatal collision with a young cyclist. The King of Iraq attended the hero's burial in the graveyard at Moreton, and the home Lawrence occupied for such a short time, **Cloud' s Hill** (National Trust), is now open to the public.

OSMINGTON MILLS

There are several "White Horses" carved into hillsides around the country, but the **White Horse** at Osmington, apart from being one of the largest (354 foot high and 279 foot wide), is the only one which also has a rider. Wearing a tall cocked hat and carrying a whip, the horseman represents George III. The king was a frequent visitor to nearby Weymouth and his royal patronage naturally attracted many free-spending courtiers to the town. The town fathers of Weymouth decided to express their appreciation by paying the local militia to scrape a hillside and form an unrecognisable, if undoubtedly loyal, tribute to His Majesty. Like all the other White Horses in England, it looks much better when seen from a few miles away.

POOLE

Once the largest settlement in Dorset, Poole is now a pleasant, bustling port. Its huge natural harbour, actually a drowned river valley, is the most extensive anchorage in Europe with a history going back well beyond Roman times. A 33 foot long Logboat, hollowed from a giant oak tree and dating back to around 295 BC, has been found off **Brownsea Island**, the largest of several islands dotting the harbour. **The Quay** is a great place to relax with a drink and watch people "just messing about in boats". Nearby is the **Waterfront Museum**, which celebrates 2,000 years of maritime heritage, and the internationally famed Poole Pottery which has been producing high-quality pottery for more than 125 years. Here visitors can watch a 12 minute video summarising two millennia of ceramic production, watch the age-old processes under way, and children can "have a go" themselves at this tricky craft. **The Pottery Shop** offers factory-direct prices and special savings on seconds, there are superb displays of the Pottery's distinctively designed creations, and a brasserie and bar overlooking the harbour. Close by, **The Aquarium Complex** brings you eyeball to eyeball with sharks, piranhas and crocodiles, although anyone with a horror of rattlesnakes, monster pythons, tarantulas or toads might be well-advised to have a stiff drink before paying a visit. Model train enthusiasts, on the other hand, will be delighted with the 3,000 feet of track of the **Great Scenic Model Railway**.

From the Quay there are regular ferries to **Brownsea Island** (National Trust), where there are quiet beaches with safe bathing and visitors can wander through 500 acres of heath and woodland which provide one of the few refuges for Britain's native red squirrel. Here, in 1907, General Robert Baden-Powell carried out an experiment to test his idea of teaching boys from all social classes the scouting skills he had refined during the Boer Wars. Just 20 boys attended that first camp: in its heyday during the 1930s, the world-wide Scouting Movement numbered some 16 million members in more than 120 countries.

SHAFTESBURY

Set on the side of a hill 700 feet high, Shaftesbury was officially founded in 880 AD by King Alfred who fortified the town and also built an Abbey of which his daughter was first Prioress. A hundred years later, the King Edward who had been murdered by his step-mother at Corfe Castle was buried here and the Abbey became a major centre of pilgrimage. Very little of **Shaftesbury Abbey** remains, but the associated **Museum** contains many interesting artefacts excavated from the site.

Gold Hill, Shaftesbury

Shaftesbury is a pleasant town to explore on foot. In fact, you have to walk if you want to see its most famous sight, Gold Hill, a steep, cobbled street, stepped in places and lined with 18th century cottages. Already well-known for its picturesque setting and grand views across the Vale of Blackmoor, **Gold Hill** became even more famous when it was featured in the classic television commercial for Hovis bread. Also located on Gold Hill is the Shaftesbury Local History Museum which vividly evokes the story of this ancient market town.

One of the liveliest arts centres in the country, the **Shaftesbury Arts Centre** is, remarkably, completely owned by its membership and administered entirely by volunteers. The results of their efforts are anything but amateur, however. From its beginnings as a Drama Club almost half a century ago, the organisation has evolved into an all-embracing Arts Centre, fully licensed for public performances. One of the most popular features of the Centre is its Gallery, which is open daily with a regularly changing variety of exhibitions - ranging from paintings, etchings and sculpture, to batiks, stained glass, embroideries and quilting.

About 3 miles northwest of Shaftesbury, **the Dorset Rare Breeds Centre** harbours the county's largest collection of rare and endangered farm animals. They range from knee-high Soay sheep to mighty Suffolk Punch horses weighing a ton or more. All of these native breeds are at great risk and the Centre hopes to alert animal lovers to the imminent threat.

SHERBORNE

One of the most beautiful towns in England, Sherborne beguiles the visitor with its serene atmosphere of a "Cathedral City", although it is not a city and its lovely **Abbey** no longer enjoys the status of a cathedral. Back in AD 705 though, when it was founded by St Aldhelm, the Abbey was the Mother Cathedral for the whole of southwest England. Of that original Saxon church only minimal traces remain: most of the present building dates back to the mid-1400s which, by happy chance, was the most glorious period in the history of English ecclesiastical architecture. The intricate tracery of the fan vaulting above the nave of the Abbey looks like the supreme culmination of a long-practised art: in fact, it is one of the earliest exam-

242 ples in England. There is much else to admire in this majestic church: 15th century misericords in the choir stalls which range from the sublime (Christ sitting in majesty on a rainbow) to the scandalous, (wives beating their husbands); a wealth of elaborate tombs amongst which is a lofty six-poster from Tudor times, a floridly baroque late-17th century memorial to the 3rd Earl of

Sherborne Castle

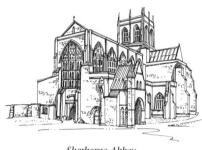

Sherborne Abbey

Bristol, and another embellished with horses' heads in a punning tribute to Sir John Horsey who lies below alongside his son.

As well as founding the Abbey, St Aldhelm is also credited with establishing **Sherborne School**, which numbered amongst its earliest pupils the two elder brothers of King Alfred, (and possibly Alfred himself), and in later times the Poet Laureate Cecil Day-Lewis and the writer David Cornwell, better known as John le Carré, author of *The Spy Who Came in from the Cold* and many other thrillers.

Perhaps the best-known resident of Sherborne, however, remains Sir Walter Raleigh. At a time when he enjoyed the indulgent favour of Elizabeth I he asked for, and was granted, the house and estate of **Sherborne Old Castle** (English Heritage). Sir Walter soon realised that the medieval pile with its starkly basic amenities was quite unsuitable for a courtier of his sophistication and ambition. He built a new castle alongside it, **Sherborne New Castle**, a strange three-storeyed, hexagonal structure which must rate, from the outside, as one of the most badly-designed, most unlikeable mansions to be erected in an age when other Elizabethan architects were creating some of the loveliest buildings in England. Inside Sir Walter's new castle, it is quite a different story: gracious rooms with elaborately-patterned ceilings, portraits of the man who single-handedly

began the creation of the British Empire, and huge windows which at the time Sir Walter ordered them proclaimed a clear message that its owner had the wealth to pay the enormous cost of glazing such vast expanses. After Sir Walter's execution, the castle was purchased in 1617 by Sir James Digby and it has remained with his descendants ever since. They added exquisite gardens designed by "Capability" Brown and in the late 1800s re-decorated the interior in Jacobean style. Amongst the castle's greatest treasures is the famous painting by Robert Peake depicting Elizabeth I on procession, being carried on a litter and surrounded by a sumptuously dressed retinue. The old cellar of the castle is now a museum housing an eclectic display of items, most gruesome of which is the skull of a Royalist soldier killed in the seige of 1645 with a bullet still lodged in his eye socket.

This appealing small town, with a population of around 8,500, has much else to interest the visitor. The **Almshouse of Saints John the Baptist** and **John the Evangelist**, near the Abbey, was founded in 1437 and the original buildings completed in 1448 are still in use as an almshouse, accepting both men and women. The almshouse chapel boasts one of the town's greatest treasures, a late-15th century Flemish altar tryptich which can be viewed on afternoons during the summer. Close by, the **Conduit House** is an attractive small hexagonal building from the early 1500s, originally used as a lavatorium, or washroom, for the Abbey monks' ablutions. It was moved here after the Reformation and has served variously as a public fountain and a police phone box. The Conduit House is specifically mentioned in Hardy's *The Woodlanders* as the place where Giles Winterborne, seeking work, stood here in the market place "as he always did at this season of the year, with his specimen apple tree". Another striking building is the former **Abbey Gatehouse** which frames the entrance to Church

Lane where the **Sherborne Museum** has a collection of more than 15,000 items of local history. Particularly notable are two major photographic collections recording events and people in the town since 1880.

SWANAGE

Picturesquely set beside a broad, gently curving bay with fine, clear sands and beautiful surrounding countryside, Swanage is understandably popular as a family holiday resort. A winner of 'Southern England in Bloom', the town takes great pride in the spectacular floral displays in its parks and gardens, and its other awards include the prestigious European 'Blue Flag' for its unpolluted waters, and the Tidy Britain Group's 'Seaside Award'. Swanage offers its visitors all the facilities necessary for a traditional seaside holiday, including boat-trips (with sightings of bottle-nosed dolphins if you're lucky), water-sports, sea angling and an attractive, old-fashioned pier. On the clifftops, **Durlston Country Park** covers some 260 acres of delightful countryside; on the front, the **Beach Gardens** offer tennis, bowls and putting, or you can just rent a beach hut or bungalow and relax. One attraction not to be missed is a ride on the **Swanage Railway**, along which magnificent steam locomotives of the old

Swanage Railway

Southern Railway transport passengers some 6 miles through lovely Dorset countryside to Norden, just north of Corfe Castle.

In the town itself, the **Town Hall** is worth seeing for its ornate façade, the work of Christopher Wren. Wren didn't build it for Swanage, however. It was originally part of Mercers Hall in Cheapside, London. When the Mercers Hall was being demolished, a Swanage man scavenged the fine frontage and rebuilt it here. He also brought the graceful little Clock Tower which stands near the pier. The tower used to adorn the Surrey end of London Bridge. No wonder older residents of the town refer to Swanage as "Little London".

Collectors of curiosities will want to make their way to **Tilly Whim Hill**, just south of Swanage, which is also well-known for its murky Caves. High above the Caves stands the **Great Globe**, a huge round stone, some 10 feet in diameter and weighing 40 tons, its surface sculpted with all the countries of the world. At its base, stone slabs are inscribed with quotations from the Old Testament Psalms, Shakespeare and other poets. They include moral injunctions such as "Let prudence direct you, temperance chasten you, fortitude support you", and the information that, "if a globe representing the sun were constructed on the same scale, it would measure some 1,090 feet across".

A couple of miles north of Swanage, **Studland Bay** offers a lovely 3-mile stretch of sandy beach, part of it clearly designated as an exclusive resort for nudists only.

TOLPUDDLE

The small village of Tolpuddle sits quietly just off the main road. In the early 19th century, Tolpuddle was a far sleepier place than it is now. Not the kind of place one would expect to foment a social revolution, but it was here that six ill-paid agricultural labourers helped to lay the foundations of the British Trade Union Movement. In 1833, they formed a "confederation" in an attempt to have their subsistence wages improved. The full rigour of the landowner-friendly law of the time was immediately invoked. Even the judge in their case was forced to say that it was not for anything they had done, or intended to do, that he passed the sentence of transportation to Australia, but "as an example to others". **The Martyrs' Museum** at Tolpuddle tells this inspiring story, but it's depressing to realise that the 7-shilling (35p) weekly payment to those farmworkers were protesting against actually had more buying power in the 1830s than the 1998 legally enforced minimum wage.

244

WAREHAM

Situated between the rivers Frome and Piddle, Wareham is an enchanting little town lying within the earthworks of a 10th century encircling wall. Standing close to an inlet of Poole Harbour, Wareham was an important port until the River Frome clogged its approaches with silt. Then, in 1726, a devastating fire consumed the town's timber buildings, a disaster which produced the happy result of a rebuilt town centre rich in handsome Georgian stone-built houses.

Wareham's history goes back much further than those days. It was Roman conquerors who laid out its street plan: a stern grid of roads which faithfully follows the points of the compass. Saxons and Normans helped build the **Church of St Mary**, medieval artists covered its walls with devotional paintings of remarkable quality. It was in the grounds surrounding the church that King Edward was buried in 879 AD after his stepmother, Queen Elfrida, contrived his murder at Corfe Castle. Elfrida added insult to injury by having the late King buried outside the churchyard, in unhallowed ground.

Tall Ship at Weymouth

WEYMOUTH

No wonder the good citizens of Weymouth erected a statue of George III to mark the 50th year of his reign in 1810. The troubled king had brought great kudos and prosperity to their little seaside resort by coming here to bathe in the sea water. George had been advised that sea-bathing would help cure his "nervous disorder" so, between 1789 and 1805, he and his royal retinue spent a total of 14 holidays in Weymouth. Fashionable society naturally followed in his wake. The imposing statue is unusual in being painted. Not far away, at the head of King Street, his grand-daughter Victoria's own 50th year as Queen is commemorated by a colourful Jubilee Clock erected in 1887. Nearby, the picturesque **Harbour** is always busy - fishing boats, paddle steamers, pleasure boats, catamarans servicing the Channel Islands and St Malo in France, and if you're lucky you may even see a Tall Ship or two.

One of the town's premier tourist venues is **Brewers Quay**, an imaginatively redeveloped Victorian brewery offering an enormous diversity of visitor attractions amidst a labyrinth of paved courtyards and cobbled streets. There are no fewer than 22 different establishments within the complex, ranging from craft shops and restaurants through a fully automated Ten Pin bowling alley to the "Timewalk Journey" which promises visitors that they will "See, Hear and Smell over 600 years of Weymouth's spectacular history."

From Brewers Quay, a path leads through Nothe Gardens to **Nothe Fort**, built between 1860 and 1872 as part of the defences of the new naval base being established on Portland. Ten huge guns face out to sea; two smaller ones are directed inland. The fort's 70 rooms on three levels now house the **Museum of Coastal Defence**, which has many interesting displays illustrating past service life in the fort, history as seen from the Nothe headland, and the part played by the people of Weymouth in the Second World War. Nothe Fort is owned and operated by the Weymouth Civic Society, which also takes care of **Tudor House**, just north of Brewers Quay. One of the town's few remaining Tudor buildings, the house originally stood on the edge of an inlet from the harbour and is thought to have been a merchant's house. It's now furnished in the style of an early-17th century middle class home and the guided tour gives some fascinating insights into life in those days.

WHITCHURCH CANONICORUM

Clinging to the steep hillside above the valley of the River Char, Whitchurch Canonicorum is notable for its enchanting setting and for its **Church of St Candida and Holy Cross**. This noble building with its Norman arches and an imposing tower built around 1400 is remarkable for being one of only two churches in England still possessing a shrine to a Saint. (The other is that of Edward the Confessor in Westminster Abbey). St Candida was a Saxon woman named Wite - the Anglo-Saxon word for White, which in Latin is Candida. She lived as a hermit but was murdered by a Viking raiding party in AD 831. During the Middle Ages a major cult grew up around her memory. A large shrine was built of golden Purbeck stone, its lower level pierced by three large ovals into which the sick and maimed thrust their limbs, their head or even their whole body, in the hope of being cured. The cult of St Wite thrived until the Reformation when all such "monuments of feigned miracles" were swept away. That might have been the end of the story of St Wite but during the winter of 1899-1900 the foundations of the church settled and cracked open a 13th century tomb chest. Inside was a lead casket with a Latin inscription stating that "Here rest the relics of St Wite," and inside the casket the bones of a small woman about 40 years old. The shrine still attracts pilgrims today, the donations they leave in the openings beneath the tomb now being devoted to causes which aid health and healing.

WIMBORNE MINSTER

Happily, the A31 now by-passes this beguiling old market town set amongst meadows beside the rivers Stour and Allen. The glory of the town is **Wimborne Minster**, a distinctive building of multi-coloured stone boasting some of the finest Norman architecture in the county. The Minster is also notable for its 14th century astronomical clock, and the 'Quarterjack', a life-sized figure of a grenadier from the Napoleonic wars, which strikes the quarter hours on his bells. Inside, the unique Chained Library, founded in 1686, contains more than 240 books, amongst them a 14th century manuscript on vellum.

In the High Street, the **Priest's House** is a lovely Elizabethan house set amidst beautiful gardens. It houses the **Museum of East Dorset Life** which recreates 400 years of history in a series of rooms where the decoration and furnishings follow the changing fashions between Jacobean and Victorian times. There's also an archaeology gallery with hands-on activities and a recently opened Gallery of Childhood.

In King Street you can see Wimborne as it was in the early 1950s - but at one tenth the size. **Wimborne Model Town** presents a meticulous miniature version of the town, complete with an Old English fair and a working small scale model railway.

A mile or so northwest of Wimborne, **Kingston Lacy** (National Trust) is an imposing 17th century mansion and an irresistible attraction for anyone who loves the paintings of such Old Masters as Brueghel, Rubens and Van Dyck. Apart from those owned by the Queen, the pictures on display here are generally acknowledged by experts as the finest private collection in the country. Kingston Lacy's fabulous gilded-leather Spanish Room and elegant Grand Saloon, both with lavishly decorated ceilings, and a fascinating exhibit of Egyptian artefacts dating back to 3000 BC, all add to the interest of a visit. Outside, you can wander through 250 acres of wooded parkland, home to a herd of splendid Red Devon cattle, collect souvenirs from the gift shop, or enjoy refreshments in the restaurant.

WINFRITH NEWBURGE

This charming little village stands on a minor road that leads to one of the county's best-known beauty spots, **Lulworth Cove**. An almost perfectly circular bay, the Cove is surrounded by towering 440-foot cliffs. Over the centuries, the sea has gnawed away at a weak point in the limestone here, inadvertently creating a breathtakingly beautiful scene. Best to visit out of season, however, as parking places nearby are limited.

About a mile to the west of Lulworth Cove stands another remarkable natural feature which has been sculpted by the sea. **Durdle Door** is a magnificent archway carved from the coastal limestone. There's no road to the coast at this point, but you can reach it easily by following the **South West Coast Path** from Lulworth Cove. Along the way, you will also see another strange outcrop, a forest of tree-stumps which have become fossilised over the centuries.

246

A couple of miles inland, Lulworth Castle (English Heritage) looks enormously impressive from a distance: close-up, you can see how a disastrous fire in 1929 destroyed most of it. Amongst the re-

sensibilities by looking like a church. It doesn't, and that's a great part of its appeal.

Durdle Door

mains, though, is a curious circular building dating from 1786: the first Roman Catholic church to be established in Britain since Henry VIII' s defiance of the Pope in 1534. Sir Thomas Weld was given permission to build this unique church by George III. The King cautiously added the proviso that Sir Thomas' new place of worship should not offend Anglican

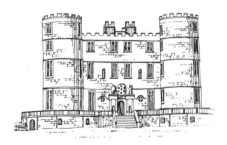

Lulworth Castle

The Albion Inn

Station Road,
Verwood,
Dorset BH31 7LB
Tel: 01202 825267
Fax: 01202 820623

Directions:
From junction 1 on the M27 take the A31 towards Poole. Just after Ringwood, turn right on to the B3081 towards Verwood. Pass through the village and The Albion Inn is last building on the right.

A symetrical, cream painted inn that stands back from the main road through Verwood, **The Albion Inn** was built in 1866 as a hotel adjoining Verwood railway station. Although the station has long since gone, the bridge over the line still exists and can be seen in one of the inn's two gardens - one for adults and the other with a children's play area. A charming and typical Victorian building, the inn is as quaint and welcoming inside as the attractive exterior would suggest. There are two bars, each with a mass of beams, brassware and open fireplaces and, naturally, both house a wealth of railway memorabilia.

However, it is not just railway enthusiasts who will enjoy stopping at this inviting little inn but real ale drinkers also. The Albion Inn is well known for the high standard of the real ales served here - they are usually local brews - and was, in 1997, CAMRA pub of the year. This reputation is one that today's landlord, Rex Neville, who has been here since late 1998, is keen to maintain and he is certainly succeeding. As well as beers, lagers and ales, Rex also has a good selection of wines here which complement perfectly the inn's menu of traditional pub food. Whether it is a juicy sandwich, a freshly filled baguette, ham and eggs, steak and kidney pudding or lasagne, all the dishes on the menu are homecooked and, thanks to the freshest ingredients, a delicious treat. For excellent ale, good homecooking and an interesting history, The Albion Inn is hard to beat.

Opening Hours: Mon-Sat 11.00-23.00; Sun 12.00-22.30

Food: Bar meals and snacks

Credit Cards: Visa, Access, Delta, Switch

Facilities: Beer garden, Car parking, Children's play area, Functions catered for

Entertainment: Quiz nights, Darts

Local Places of Interest/Activities:
Edmondsham House Gardens 2 miles, Moors Valley Country Park 3 miles, Ringwood 5 miles, Priest's House, Wimborne Minster 8 miles, Kingston Lacy 9 miles, Walking, Cycling, Horse riding, Fishing, Golf

248

The Anchor Inn

High Street,
Burton Bradstock,
near Bridport,
Dorset DT6 4QF
Tel/Fax: 01308 897228

Directions:

From Bridport follow the B3157 towards Weymouth for 2 miles and The Anchor Inn can be found along the first road on the right.

It's well worth seeking out the tiny village of Burton Bradstock just to visit **The Anchor Inn,** an interesting old pub going back some 300 years though the battlemented extension and the intricate metal windows give no clues to the building's age. Inside, the inn has a cosy and intimate atmosphere and all the rooms - there are two bars and two restaurant areas - have been decorated and furnished in a pleasant manner that is both comfortable and but maintains the pub's maritime theme. However, the true force behind the recent success of The Anchor is the landlord, John Plunkett. A welcoming host, John, a Scotsman, has worked in catering all his life, including a long spell travelling the world as a chef on board cruise ships. With many interesting stories to tell, John, along with his partner Tracey, settled at The Anchor in 1996 and have not looked back since.

Fish and seafood is very much a speciality of the house and the fresh produce is bought in Bridport by John. However, fine ingredients are not all that is required to reach the high standards of the dishes served here and John's culinary skills have been an essential part in putting The Anchor on Dorset's eating map. In the last two years, the pub has been winner and runner up in the Ushers Best Pub Food Competition and, with interest aroused, it is essential to book.

Opening Hours: Mon-Sat 11.00-15.00, 18.00-23.00; Suns 12.00-15.00, 19.00-22.30

Food: Bar and Restaurant Meals available all day

Credit Cards: Mastercard, Visa, Switch

Facilities: Patio seating to front, large car park

Entertainment: Skittles, Bar billiards, Darts, Cribbage, Live country music occasionally

Local Places of Interest/Activities: Beach under a mile away, Walking, Golf, West Bay (famous for the TV series Harbour Lights) 2 miles

The Botany Bay Inn 249

Winterborne Zelston,
nr Wimborne,
Dorset DT11 9LS
Tel: 01929 459227

Directions:

From Poole take the A350 towards Blandford Forum. After approximately 6 miles turn left on to the A31 towards Dorchester. The Botany Bay Inn can be found in the village, along this road.

Situated on the outskirts of the village, which takes part of its name, like other villages in the area, after the river that meanders erratically across East Dorset, **The Botany Bay Inn** is a splendid post war inn that is said to have been built in memory of General Allenby. Though relatively modern, this inn certainly does not lack character and charm and, in summer, the abundance of colourful flower filled window boxes and hanging baskets soften the lines of the building. Inside, The Botany Bay Inn is equally charming and the large bar area is divided by stained glass panels which add subtle shades to the interior lighting.

Landlords, Deborah and David Schroetter have been here since 1996 and, in that time, these qualified chefs have certainly put the inn on the culinary map of East Dorset. Their experience and expertise is apparent in the wide range of interesting and tasty dishes on the menu and visitors can rest assured that the dishes are as mouth-watering as their tempting descriptions suggest. Whether it is a light meal or snack or dinner after a busy day, anyone eating here will not be surprised to hear that The Botany Bay Inn is many people's first choice when planning a celebration meal out. Amongst the house specialities are huge steaks and a gourmet platter for two which, as the menu warns, should only be tried 'on your own, if you dare!' However, it would be wise, also, to remember that the dessert menu is equally splendid and, as with the rest of the inn, is a treat not to be missed.

Opening Hours: Mon-Sun 11.00-14.30, 17.30-23.30

Food: Bar meals and snacks, À la carte, Children's menu

Credit Cards: Visa, Access, Mastercard

Facilities: Beer garden, Car parking

Local Places of Interest/Activities: Kingston Lacy 5 miles, Poole 8 miles, Bloxworth Heath 3 miles, Coast 6 miles, Walking, Sailing, Bird watching

250   The Brewers Arms

Martinstown,
Dorset DT2 9LU
Tel: 01305 889361
Fax: 01305 889788

Directions:

Take the A35 from Dorchester towards Bridport, at the Monkey Julip roundabout take the road to the left signposted Martinstown and The Brewers Arms lies in the centre of the village.

This charming village, which was, for centuries called Winterbourne St Martin after the local river and its parish church, is also the home of **The Brewers Arms**. A striking turn of the century black and white building, the inn has been serving the needs of locals ever since it first opened. Today's landlords, Glen and Kerry Shaw are continuing the tradition and, though they have only been at the pub since September 1999, they have lived in Martinstown nearly 20 years and are very much part of the local community.

This is a friendly place, where the superb atmosphere of a real village inn goes hand in hand with the excellent hospitality on offer. Though many come here to enjoy a pint or two from the range of real ales, draught beers, ciders and wines served from the bar it is for its tasty menu of homemade sandwiches, filled jacket potatoes and serve yourself salad bar that keeps many coming back time and time again. In the evening the mood and menu change as the intimate restaurant area fills with diners looking forward to a meal from the interesting and popular list of evening dishes. Whilst the interior of The Brewers Arms is both a pleasant and comfortable place in which to pass the time, during the summer the attractive and secluded courtyard becomes an extension of the bar as customers settle down with a drink, some delicious food and good conversation - warm summer evenings, however, cannot be guaranteed!

Opening Hours: Mon-Thur 11.00-15.00, 18.00-23.00; all day Fri-Sun

Food: Bar meals at lunchtime, dinner menu in the evening

Credit Cards: Visa, Mastercard, Switch

Facilities: Patio garden, Summer barbecues

Entertainment: Skittles, Pool, Occasional live music

Local Places of Interest/Activities: Hardy's Monument 2 miles, Maiden Castle Iron Age hill fort 1 mile, Weymouth 6 miles, Walking, Birdwatching

The Buffalo Inn

Lydfords Lane,
Wyke,
Gillingham,
Dorset SP8 4NJ
Tel: 01747 823759

Directions:

From Wincanton take the A303 towards Mere, then, after 3 miles, the B3081 to Gillingham and The Buffalo Inn is signposted just off the road through the village of Wyke.

Once in the village, **The Buffalo Inn** is hard to miss, especially in the autumn, as the front of this attractive pub is covered in Virginian creeper which turns a splendid red in the latter part of the year. Underneath all this foliage is a late Victorian building but only the slate roof has been left uncovered by vegetation. The interior of the inn is equally charming and homely. There are two cosy bar areas both of which have retained a character and charm that befits an old country pub and the exposed stone walls have been decorated with old walking sticks, jugs and mugs as well as an old photograph of Mathews Brewery that was once also to be found in Wyke.

Well known for serving an excellent pint of real ale, as well as stocking a good selection of keg beers, lagers, ciders and wines, the landlady, Carole Savin also takes great pride in the high standard of the pub meals here. English homecooked pub fare at its very best, though the menu is small everything is prepared to order and served to customers with style. The perfect country inn, in every respect, The Buffalo Inn is certainly the place for people to meet, relax and enjoy good conversation and hospitality in a very pleasant atmosphere.

Opening Hours: Mon-Sat 12.00-14.30; Mon-Fri 17.30-23.00; Sat 19.00-23.00; Sun 12.00-15.00, 19.00-22.30

Food: Bar meals for lunch and dinner except Sunday evenings

Credit Cards: None

Facilities: Beer garden, Patio area, Children welcome

Entertainment: Cribbage, Quizzes

Local Places of Interest/Activities: Wincanton 7 miles, Stourhead Gardens 6 miles, Walking

252 The Clifton Hotel

50 Grove Road,
The Grove,
Portland,
Dorset DT5 1DA
Tel: 01305 820473

Directions:

From Weymouth take the A354 to Easton and turn left into Grove Road. The Clifton Hotel lies 1 mile along the road on the right.

The Clifton Hotel, a low stone building, has been offering customers food, drink and shelter in this delightful setting for over 150 years. Situated on the eastern shore of the Isle of Portland, the hotel provides splendid vistas across the sea to the Sussex coastline from both its windows and the large, attractive beer garden. Though Derek and Annette Frankton have been at the hotel for a number of years, they became the proud owners in 1998 and, though this now takes up all their time, this charming couple have spent much time and effort in ensuring that all who come here receive the best possible hospitality as well as a warm and friendly welcome.

Real ales and keg lagers are the order of the day in the hotel's large, open bar which, like the rest of The Clifton, has been extensively refurbished by Derek and Annette. Highlighting many of the building's original features, care has also been taken to provide a comfortable and relaxing atmosphere that will please all. The excellent home-cooked bar food and traditional Sunday lunches are prepared by Annette and, along with the superb family accommodation, goes to make the hotel a much sought after retreat in this attractive area.

Opening Hours: Mon-Fri 12.00-14.00, 19.00-23.00; All day Sat (until 23.00) and Sun (until 22.30)

Food: Bar Meals available all day, Traditional Sunday lunches

Credit Cards: None

Accommodation: 3 double rooms all ensuite

Facilities: Garden, Functions catered for

Entertainment: Darts, Skittles, Pool, Quizzes

Local Places of Interest/Activities: Hang gliding, Fishing, Beach, Portland Bill 2 miles, Portland Castle and Museum 1 mile

Eight Kings Inn

40 Southwell,
Portland,
Dorset DT5 2DP
Tel: 01305 821276

Directions:

From Weymouth take the A354 through Fortuneswell and continue to towards Portland Bill. The Eight Kings Inn lies on the far south of Portland Isle.

Right in the heart of Southwell, Dorset's most southerly village, the **Eight Kings Inn** is a lively village pub that plays an important part in the life of the local community. Originally two old cottages, the building has seen several alterations over the 200 years of its existence and, built of Portland stone, it is sure to be standing for another 200 years. Apart from being the only Eight Kings Inn in the country, the pub is also unique, and lucky, in having Kathryn and Jim as landlady and landlord. An interesting and very active couple, with many years experience in the trade, they have certainly stamped their personalities on the pub since they arrived here in 1996.

Well known locally for Kathryn's excellent home-cooked meals, and in particular the great value Sunday lunches, this an ideal place for a both a relaxing drink in the spacious bar or a tasty meal in the cosy and atmospheric restaurant area. The couple's keen interest in music - Jim plays the guitar - is reflected in the weekly live music evenings to which all are invited to come and join in.

Opening Hours: Mon-Fri 12.00-15.00, 19.00-23.00; Sat 12.00-16.00, 19.00-23.00; Sun 12.00-14.00, 19.00-22.30

Food: Bar Meals available all day, Traditional Sunday lunches

Credit Cards: Cheques with bankers card only

Facilities: Private parties catered for

Entertainment: Darts, Quiz league, Live music every Saturday

Local Places of Interest/Activities: Bird watching, Climbing, Fishing all year round, Walking, Bill of Portland 1 mile, Weymouth 5 miles.

254

The Fox Inn

Ansty,
near Dorchester,
Dorset DT2 7PN
Tel: 01258 880328
Fax: 01258 881440

Directions:

Take the A35 from Dorchester to Bere Regis, exit at the Northbrook junction and take the road to Piddlehinton. After 450 yards turn right onto the Cheselbourne road and continue for 5 miles and The Fox Inn is on the right.

Set in the rolling countryside of Thomas Hardy's Wessex, **The Fox Inn** has an idyllic location which makes it the ideal base for a driving, cycling or walking holiday. The surrounding area is also rich in history and interest - there are picturesque hamlets, ancient houses and spectacular viewpoints. However, those who find The Fox Inn will also be tempted to stay put. The house dates back more than 200 years and it was once the home of the brewery family, Woodhouse, who opened their brewery here in 1777. This lovely old house became an inn in 1915 and, today, it is an impressive hotel, restaurant and bar owned and personally run by Philip and Shirley Scott.

The popular family bar is a great meeting place for both locals and those out exploring the countryside and, as well as the excellent range of real ales, beers and lagers on offer, visitors can quell their hunger from the bar menu. For more formal dining, The Woodhouse Restaurant provides guests with the opportunity to dine in comfort and style from a superb à la carte menu and also accompany their delicious meal with a bottle of wine from the extensive list. Above all, though, The Fox Inn is a place for relaxation where the pace of modern living can be forgotten.

Opening Hours: All day, every day

Food: Bar Meals available all day, À la carte restaurant

Credit Cards: Mastercard, Visa, Amex, Delta, Switch

Accommodation: 14 double rooms ensuite, Honeymoon suite

Facilities: Gardens, Function room

Local Places of Interest/Activities: Milton Abbey 2 miles, Bulbarrow Hill 1 mile, Walking, Cycling, Horse riding, Fishing, Clay pigeon shooting

The George Inn 255

Chideock,
Dorset DT6 6JD
Tel: 01297 489419

Directions:
From Dorchester take the A35 towards Honiton. Four miles from Bridport lies the village of Chideock and The George Inn.

Set amongst steep hills just a short walk from the coast, this pleasant village of thatched cottages and local stone houses is also the home of **The George Inn**. A splendid, traditional Dorset inn that is over 350 years old and still has its thatched roof, this is a relaxed and easy going place. As is typical of a building of this age, The George Inn is a place with character and charm and, inside, it is divided into several small and intimate areas which provide a cosy atmosphere. The delightful landscaped patio and garden to the rear are natural sun traps and a must on long summer afternoons and evenings.

Today, The George is run by Mike Gooderham, an experienced publican who, before joining the industry 25 years ago, served in the Royal Navy. Helped by his daughter, Amy, Mike, and his team, are justly very proud of this marvellous, traditional pub and, judging by the popularity of the inn, their style is certainly appreciated both by the locals and by visitors. There are always at least three real ales available and, for those not wanting a strong drink teas and coffee can be served in the garden. However, it is for their delicious menu of homecooked bar snacks and meals that many frequent the inn. A tantalising mix of traditional and more exotic dishes, there are splendid homemade pies, fresh fish - Mike will only buy from local fishermen - and a range of vegetarian meals. The emphasis here is very much on serving good food and, as each dish is prepared to order, those in a hurry will find they have little time to appreciate the superb meal.

Opening Hours: Mon-Fri 11.00-14.30, 17.00-23.00; Sat 11.00-23.00; Sun 12.00-22.30; Food Mon-Sun 12.00-14.00, 18.00-21.00

Food: Bar meals and snacks

Credit Cards: Visa, Access, Delta, Switch

Accommodation: Can be arranged

Facilities: Car parking, Beer garden, Children and dogs welcome

Local Places of Interest/Activities: Heritage Coast, Golden Cap 1 mile, Walking, Sailing

Internet/Website: george.inn@virgin.net

256   The Globe Inn

3 Bell Street,
Swanage,
Dorset BH19 2RY
Tel: 01929 423515

Directions:

From junction 1 on the M27 take the A31 to Poole and then the A351 through Wareham to Swanage. Pass the Welcome to Swanage sign and, after 500 yards, turn right into Bell Street and The Globe Inn lies on the left.

An attractive and very picturesque building, **The Globe Inn** dates back to the 16th century when it was originally built as a house with a mortuary attached. Situated in a row of similarly constructed houses, in a quiet part of this popular holiday resort, visitors will be surprised to find that there is a charming and secluded rear garden, complete with children's play area, makes a very peaceful haven. The interior of this ancient inn is as delightful as the outside would suggest and, with flagstone floors, open fireplaces, old beams and a mass of gleaming brassware, there is still plenty of olde worlde character. As might also be expected, this was after all a mortuary, there is a resident ghost but he is seen rarely and does not seem to upset the tropical fish in the large display tank.

Paul and Donna Thompson have been the licensees here since October 1999 but their relationship with the inn goes back further as they have worked here for some time. Well liked by the locals who continue to give their support, the couple offer a warm welcome as well as friendly hospitality to anyone who ventures in. As well as the real ales and all the usual beers, ales, lagers and spirits served here there is also a menu of traditional English pub food. Though not extensive, the steaks, gammon and lighter snacks such as sandwiches, are not only well prepared but come as a welcome change from more exotic fare.

Opening Hours: Mon-Fri 12.00-14.30, 18.00-23.00; Sat 12.00-15.00, 18.00-23.00; Sun 12.00-15.00, 19.00-22.30

Food: Bar meals and snacks

Credit Cards: None

Facilities: Beer garden, Car parking, Children's play area

Entertainment: Pool, Darts

Local Places of Interest/Activities: Durlston Head Visitors Centre 1 mile, Beach 1 mile, Corfe Castle 5 miles, Lulworth Castle 10 miles, Walking, Cycling, Horse riding, Fishing, Sailing, Bird watching

The Griffins Head Inn 257

Nether Compton,
Sherbourne,
Dorset DT9 4QE
Tel: 01935 812523

Directions:

From Sherbourne take
the A30 towards Yoevil
then the first road on
the right to Nether
Compton and The Grif-
fins Head Inn lies 3
miles down the road.

Found in the heart of the village, **The Griffins Head Inn** is an attractive stone building that dates from 1599 and sits right on the roadside. A place full of character and charm, this old inn has retained many of its original features and the two main bars, each with an inglenook fireplace, have been decorated in a pleasing sympathetic style. The games room too matches the age of the inn though the oak wood ceiling is taken from a 16th century ship. Throughout, and very much adding to the cosy air, the walls are adorned with all manner of memorabilia including old pictures and photographs.

Raymond, Ross and Derek Read, the hosts, have been here at The Griffins Head for many years and, whilst they have found time to pursue their own hobbies, they have also created a popular and friendly environment for both locals visitors to meet and enjoy conversation. As well as serving an excellent range of real ales and other drinks from the bar, they have also put the inn on the culinary map of north Dorset. The menu, a mix of old favourites, light snacks and interesting variations on well known themes, is created and homecooked by Ross. The traditional Sunday roast lunches are also a must and, as the word has spread far and wide, booking is essential.

Opening Hours: Mon-Sat 12.00-14.30, 19.00-23.00; Sun 12.00-14.30, 19.00-22.30

Food: Bar meals available all day, Traditional Sunday lunches

Credit Cards: None

Facilities: Beer garden, Skittle alley used for functions, Large car park

Local Places of Interest/Activities:
Sherbourne 3 miles, Horse riding, Walking.

258   The Halfway Inn

Norden,
near Corfe Castle,
Wareham,
Dorset BH20 5DU
Tel: 01929 480402
Fax: 01929 481208

Directions:

From Poole take the A351 towards Swanage. The Halfway Inn can be found along this road, 3 miles from the last Wareham roundabout.

The attractive hamlet of Norden, surrounded by pine trees and heathland, is home to the equally delightful **Halfway Inn**. A charming, thatched cob building, parts of which date back to the 16th century, the inn is ideally placed for those visiting Corfe Castle and the Isle of Purbeck. Welcoming and inviting, this popular inn is run by the experience team of Rod and Claire Darroll-Brough who are helped by their very capable daughters, Amanda (their assistant manager) and Emma along with an enthusiastic staff. Inside, the panelled ceilings and old beams, the many nooks and crannies and the fireplaces all add to the appealing ambience that is suggested by the well maintained and eyecatching exterior. Not surprisingly, as with many buildings of antiquity, The Halfway Inn has a resident ghost - an amiable làdy who has often been seen by guests in the lounge.

However, whilst they might be spirits, of the drinking variety, in the bar, there is certainly nothing insubstantial about the food on offer here. The menu of homemade dishes includes many pub favourites as well as catering for more cosmopolitan tastes with such delights as seared tuna and Cajun chicken. The various hearty salads are the speciality and, with the addition of a specials board, children's menu and vegetarian options, there is plenty for the whole family to enjoy. For those who enjoy wine with their meal, The Halfway Inn's list is extensive and some are available as half bottles.

Opening Hours: Mon-Thu 11.00-23.00 (Food 12.00-21.00); Fri and Sat 11.00-23.00; Sun 12.00-22.30

Food: Bar meals and snacks, Children's menu

Credit Cards: Visa, Mastercard, Amex, Diners

Facilities: Beer garden, Car parking

Local Places of Interest/Activities: Corfe Castle 2 miles, Swanage Railway 4 miles, Durlston Head 7 miles, Coast 4 miles, Walking, Sailing, Fishing, Bird watching

Ilchester Arms | 259

9 Market Street,
Abbotsbury,
Dorset DT3 4JR
Tel: 01305 871243
Fax: 01305 871225

Directions:

From Weymouth take the B3157 coast road towards Bridport and the Ilchester Arms can be found in Abbotsury, 8 miles from Weymouth.

Found right in the heart of one of Dorset's prettiest villages, the impressive **Ilchester Arms** was formerly an 18th century coaching inn though its is believed to have been built as the Old Abbotsbury Gaol. An attractive stone building, with a mellow stone façade and still displaying a coat of arms, the inn has very successfully managed to maintain its character and charm whilst also providing customers with superb late 20th century accommodation. Stepping inside the Ilchester Arms is stepping back in time - although the delightful ground floor bar areas have been completely refurbished, many of the original features remain - including the flag stone floors, the mass of ceilings beams and a large inglenook fireplace.

Managed by two Hughs (McGill and Williams) since 1997, this amiable couple are both committed to customer service and quality - and it shows. The friendly, relaxed atmosphere of the inn, the loyal and welcoming staff and the excellent reputation the Ilchester Arms has gained far and wide are all testament to their belief that their patrons come first. The high standard of hospitality is not only evident in the extensive range of well kept real ales, beers, ciders and well chosen wine cellar but also in the menus. From sandwiches, light meals and traditional pub food menus served at lunchtime to the mouthwatering à la carte menu and specials board dining here in the very pleasant Conservatory Restaurant is a treat to be savoured.

Opening Hours: Summer - Mon-Sat 11.00-23.00; Sun 12.00-22.30; Winter - Mon-Thur 11.00-15.00, 18.00-23.00; Fri-Sun all day (closes 22.30 Sun)

Food: Bar meals and full menu served at lunchtime and in the evening

Credit Cards: Visa, Mastercard, Amex, Diners, Switch, Delta

Accommodation: Honeymoon suite, 6 double rooms ensuite, 2 family rooms ensuite, 2 twin rooms ensuite

Facilities: Beer garden and patio, Conservatory restaurant, Car parking,

Entertainment: Live music (usually guitarist) once a month, Darts, Sky TV

Local Places of Interest/Activities: Abbotsbury Sub-tropical gardens, Abbotsbury Swannery, Chesil Beach ½ mile, Hardy Monument 2 miles, Walking, Fishing, Bird watching

260 Kings Arms

41 North Street,
Wareham,
Dorset BH20 4AD
Tel: 01929 552503

Directions:

From junction 1 on the M27 take the A31 and then the A348 to Poole and then the A351 to Wareham. The Kings Arms lies in the centre of the town.

The **Kings Arms** is a splendid old white painted inn that dates from 1550 when it was originally built as cottages. Converted into an inn in 1680, today it is only one of four buildings in the town that still has a thatched roof - all the others were destroyed in a great fire in 1786. Very attractive and picturesque from the street, the interior of this delightful old place is just as pretty. The flagstone floors and old ceiling beams have withstood the test of time and, along with the two open fires, create a charming and traditional inn atmosphere. Meanwhile, to the rear of the building is a lovely beer garden with a heated patio area which makes an ideal place to sit out and enjoy the peace and quiet even when the sun has set.

A friendly and relaxed inn, which hosts regularly live folk music on alternate Tuesday evenings, this is an excellent place to come to for traditional English inn hospitality. Landlords Mike and Judy Brown, who have been here since late 1998, ensure that both locals and visitors are treated to the very best in food and drink. From the bar there are always three real ales, one of which is a local brew, and as well as the usual lagers, beers and spirits, there is a well chosen mini wine cellar. For a light meal or snack, the bar menu is ideal and includes a whole host of tempting sandwiches and a superb all day breakfast. In the separate, more formal, restaurant, the extensive menu covers a wide range of tastes and includes such delights as Thai curries, homemade steak and kidney pie and Moules Marinieres. A lovely place that offers the very best to both locals and visitors alike.

Opening Hours: Mon-Wed 11.30-14.30, 17.30-23.00; Thu-Sat 11.30-23.00; Sun 11.30-22.30

Food: Bar meals and snacks, À la carte, Traditional Sunday lunch

Credit Cards: None

Facilities: Beer garden, Car parking, Functions catered for

Entertainment: Regular live music, Darts, Cribbage, Dominoes

Local Places of Interest/Activities: Poole Harbour 2 miles, Hartland Moor Nature Reserve 3 miles, Corfe Castle 4 miles, Beaches 8 miles, Walking, Cycling, Horse riding, Fishing, Sailing, Bird watching, Golf

The New Inn

Fairmile Road,
Christchurch,
Dorset BH23 2LJ
Tel: 01202 485348
Fax: 01202 485348

Directions:

From junction 1 on the M271 take the A35 to Christchurch. From the town centre follow the B3073 towards Hurn and Bournemouth Airport and The New Inn can be found on the left, ½ mile along the road.

Found on one of the main roads out of Christchurch, **The New Inn** is an eyecatching place that is hard to miss. Set back off the road, with a large forecourt car park, this brick building is painted bright blue and is a typical 1930s style. Although a relatively recent inn, The New Inn was constructed on the site of an older pub - hence its name. However, what is special about this inn is the warm and friendly welcome extended to all by landlords, Tim and Claire Unwin. As well as the tastefully decorated and comfortable open plan bar area and separate restaurant, the couple also have a charming and well maintained rear beer garden that is ideal in the summer.

An excellent place to come to for a pint of real ale or, for wine lovers, there is a list taking in wines from all over the world, this is a popular and busy pub where many come to enjoy good conversation, perhaps a game of pétanque and a sociable drink. However, Tim and Claire are fast getting an enviable reputation for the high standard of cuisine on offer. There is always a roast available, not just on Sundays, and as well as the usual steaks, fish and lobster, the list of daily specials changes regularly. One look at the mouthwatering desserts and it is easy to see why many are also coming here to dine.

Opening Hours: Mon-Sat 12.00-23.00; Sun 12.00-22.30

Food: Bar meals and snacks, Traditional Sunday lunch throughout the week

Credit Cards: Visa, Access, Delta, Switch

Facilities: Beer garden, Car parking, Functions catered for

Entertainment: Pétanque, Darts, Pool, Quiz nights

Local Places of Interest/Activities:
Christchurch Priory and Harbour, Russell-Cotes Art Gallery and Museum, Bournemouth 4 miles, New Forest 6 miles, Walking, Cycling, Horse riding, Fishing, Sailing, Golf

Internet/Website: claire@tim-claire.com

262   The Piddle Inn

Piddletrenthide,
Dorset DT2 7QF
Tel: 01300 348468
Fax: 01300 348102

Directions:

From the A35 Poole to Dorchester road take the B3142 then the B3143 5 miles north through the Piddle Valley and The Piddle Inn is in the centre of the village.

Found very much at the heart of this attractive village, **The Piddle Inn** has been at the centre of village life here since it was built in the late 1700s and it remains so today. A delightful old stone building, with many Georgian features, the addition of a recent extension - which uses aged materials in a sympathetic manner - has enlarged the inn's accommodation without changing its character - no mean achievement! This work, along with the superb interior design, was the idea of owners Bill and Liz Bishop, who took over here in 1998, and since then they have transformed The Piddle Inn from an ordinary village pub into a splendid country inn.

Very much dedicated to serving excellent food and drink, those looking for something special should certainly take the time to find The Piddle Inn. Surrounded by pictures taken in the local countryside, guests can enjoy a wide selection of wines, lagers and ciders as well as an interesting and unusual range of real ales, many from micro breweries. Whilst Liz is busy ensuring that everything is running smoothly behind the bar and in the inn's two restaurants, Bill, the chef of the partnership, is in kitchen creating a mouthwatering array of modern dishes that make up both the à la carte and daily set menu.

Opening Hours: Mon-Sat 11.00-14.30, 18.00-23.00; Sun 12.00-15.00, 18.30-22.30

Food: Bar snacks and Restaurant

Credit Cards: Mastercard, Visa

Accommodation: 3 double rooms all en-suite

Facilities: Riverside patio, Parking

Entertainment: Darts, Pool, Cribbage

Local Places of Interest/Activities: The Giant at Cerne Abbas 3miles, Dorchester 7 miles, Walking.

The Scott Arms | 263

West Street,
Kingston,
Dorset BH20 5LH
Tel: 01929 480270
Fax: 01929 481570

Directions:
From Poole take the A35 then the A351 towards Swanage, after passing through Corfe Castle, take the B3069 to Kingston and The Scott Arms lies in the heart of the village.

Dating back to the 18th century, **The Scott Arms** is a picturesque old inn that is clad in a mass of Virginia creeper. Very much a traditional country inn, the interior is full of character and charm - there are two cosy bars and three intimate restaurant rooms, each with open fireplaces, low beamed ceilings and an interesting array of local memorabilia hanging from the walls. Comfortable and with a wonderful relaxed atmosphere, the beer garden is a must (even if only for a few minutes in the winter) as not only is this a delightful place to sit in the sunshine, there are magnificent views over the rolling Dorset countryside to Corfe Castle.

A popular place for many years - in fact, it is one of the areas best kept secrets - The Scott Arms is well known for the superb dishes that are served here both a lunchtime and in the evening. The bar menu of well filled sandwiches and tasty snacks is ideal for a lunchtime while the extensive à la carte menu, accompanied by the everchanging specials board, offers customers a mouthwatering choice of traditional pub favourites as well as dishes that combine flavours from around the world with the very best of local fresh produce. To complement any meal taken here there is a well stocked bar offering well kept traditional ales, beers and ciders as well as fine wines and spirits.

Opening Hours: Mon-Sat 11.00-15.00, 18.00-23.00; Sun 12.00-15.00, 18.00-22.30 (Food 12.00-14.00, 18.30-21.00)

Food: Bar meals and snacks, full restaurant

Credit Cards: Visa, Mastercard, Amex, Switch, Delta

Accommodation: 2 double rooms ensuite, each with four-poster bed

Facilities: Beer garden and patio

Local Places of Interest/Activities: Corfe Castle 2 miles, Swanage Railway 4 miles, Durlston Country Park 4 miles, Tilly Whim Caves 5 miles, Dorset Coastal Path, Walking, Beach.

264   The Smugglers Inn

Osmington Mills,
Weymouth,
Dorset DT3 6HF
Tel: 01305 833125
Fax: 01305 832219

Directions:

From Poole take the A35, the A351 and then the A352 towards Dorchester. Just over a mile after Owermoigne turn left on to the A353 towards Weymouth and, after 2 miles, turn left and The Smugglers Inn can be found on the coast.

It is not surprising, given the secluded location and nearby beach which provides safe landing, that the village was once a haunt of smugglers and the aptly named **Smugglers Inn** was at the centre of the illegal trade. Dating back to the 13th century, this former fisherman's cottage has had many landlords over the years but not more infamous that Emmanuel Carless. During the early 1800s, Carless, along with his French partner, Pierre Latour, ran a thriving business importing thousands of galleons of brandy each year. However, the brandy was of inferior quality and, as the inn's locals refused to drink it, Carless and Latour carried the spirit inland, disguised as luggage on a regular stagecoach run, where it was distilled further.

Today's landlords at The Smugglers Inn, Jacqui and David Southward, have no such problems with their drinks and they serve an excellent choice of real ales, beers and lagers - and they are all legal! Being so close to the sea, the inn's enticing à la carte menu features an abundance of fresh fish and seafood and the house speciality, and certainly a treat not to be missed, is fresh Weymouth Bay lobster. Those who prefer meat, poultry or vegetarian dishes will also find a superb choice of delicious homecooked meals on offer - and children, too, have their own specially prepared menu. A cosy and characterful place in winter when the log burner is roaring away, outside, there is a large beer garden overlooking Weymouth Bay and Portland Bill.

Opening Hours: Winter; Mon-Fri 11.00-14.30, 18.00-23.00; Sat and Sun 11.00-23.00. Summer; All day every day 11.00-23.00

Food: Bar meals, À la carte, Children's menu

Credit Cards: Visa, Access, Delta, Switch, Amex, Diners

Accommodation: 2 double rooms, 1 twin room, 1 bunk room all en suite

Facilities: Large, scenic beer garden, Car parking

Entertainment: During the summer

Local Places of Interest/Activities: White Horse 2 miles, Weymouth 5 miles, Lulworth Cove 7 miles, Walking, Fishing, Sailing

The Talbot Arms

Benville,
near Corscombe,
Dorset DT2 ONN
Tel: 01935 83381

Directions:

From junction 1 on the M27 take the A31 round Bournemouth and Poole and then the A35 to Dorchester. Leave the town on the A37 and then the A356 towards Crewkerne. At Toller Down Gate turn right on to a minor road towards Evershot and The Talbot Arms can be found on the left.

Dating back to the 17th century, **The Talbot Arms** is a delightful and typical English country inn that is run by landlady Cheryl Moulsdale along with her son Richard. Although they have only been at the inn since spring 1999, Cheryl and Richard have lived in the area since 1980 and so have not only excellent knowledge of the surrounding area but also a great understanding of the needs of their regular customers. What mother and son have created here is a place where the local people can meet up for good conversation and perhaps a game or two of table football and their success is easily measured by the popularity of The Talbot Arms.

However, providing a comfortable and relaxed meeting place is not enough and the choice of drinks here, including four real ales and some excellent wine, will certainly help to lubricate the vocal chords. Food too is on offer throughout the day and ranges, literally, from a slice of toast to the interesting and imaginative à la carte. Both children and dogs are welcome here and anyone arriving by horse will find that there is a hitching rail out in the car park. Whilst the interior of the inn is a warm and particularly cosy place in winter, during the summer, customers can make excellent use of the inn's well maintained beer garden where, whilst the adults have a drink the children can play on the swings and slide in their own specially constructed area or watch the farm animals.

Opening Hours: Mon-Sat 09.00-23.00; Sun 09.00-22.30

Food: Bar meals and snacks, À la carte

Credit Cards: Visa, Access, Delta, Switch, Amex, Diners

Facilities: Beer garden, Car parking, Children's play area, Functions catered for

Entertainment: Occasional live music, Table football

Local Places of Interest/Activities: Mapperton Gardens 3 miles, Sutton Bingham Reservoir 4 miles, Parnham House 5 miles, Bridport 8 miles, Beach 11 miles, Walking, Cycling, Horse riding, Fishing, Sailing, Bird watching, Golf

266 The Trooper Inn

Stourton Caundle,
near Sturminster Newton,
Dorset DT10 2JW
Tel: 01963 362405

Directions:

From junction 8 on the M3 take the A303 beyond Andover to Wincanton. From the town take the A357 towards Blandford Forum and at Stalbridge turn right and follow the signs for Stourton Caundle. The Trooper Inn lies in the heart of the village.

Found in the heart of this charming village is an equally delightful inn - **The Trooper Inn**. Dating back to 1760 and formerly called The Catherine Wheel, the inn changed its name in the early 19th century after soldiers gathered outside it before going off to fight in the Battle of Waterloo. With a beer garden and children's play area outside, the interior of this lovely old inn is also well worth investigating. Full of olde worlde charm and character, the first thing that visitors to the inn will notice are the extraordinary wealth of artefacts that can be found inside - there is a collection of over 80 horse bits in the bar alone. However, this is just the tip of the iceberg when it comes to landlord Larry Skeats' collection. At the rear of the pub is Larry's own personal museum of countryside bygones, a fascinating collection of agricultural and domestic implements and appliances that range from milk churns to root pulpers and much more. A shepherd before he came to the pub with his wife, Sue, Larry acquired the items during a 40 year career and such is his knowledge that he has become a well known television country life expert.

Larry's museum is certainly well worth a visit and, to add to this, the inn itself has an excellent reputation for the high standard of food and drink served here. Real ales and draught ciders can be drunk in these splendid surroundings and there is also a tempting menu of light meals and snacks served at lunchtime. In the summer, whilst Larry turns his hands to making walking sticks, cream teas are served.

Opening Hours: Mon 19.00-23.00; Tue-Sat 12.00-14.30, 19.00-23.00; Sun 12.00-14.30, 19.00-22.30

Food: Bar meals and snacks, Cream teas

Credit Cards: None

Facilities: Beer garden, Car parking, Children's play area, Functions catered for

Entertainment: Countryside museum, Skittles, Darts, Cribbage

Local Places of Interest/Activities: Sherbourne 4 miles, Fiddleford Manor 6 miles, The Giant 9 miles, Walking, Cycling, Horse riding, Fishing, Bird watching

The White Horse 267

Sharston Road,
Stourpaine,
Blandford Forum,
Dorset DT11 8TA
Tel/Fax: 01258 453535

Directions:
From Blandford Forum take the A350 towards Shaftesbury and The White Horse lies in the heart of the village of Stourpaine.

Originally three separate buildings, **The White Horse** is an attractive mix of architectural styles that date from between the 16th and 18th centuries. Although it was not designed to be an inn, this now large establishment has a variety of cosy and intimate areas that, along with the low ceilings and original beams, give The White Horse a real country inn atmosphere. Hosts, Malcolm and Pru Collins, have been here since 1998 and, as well as becoming very much part life in the village they have also built up an excellent reputation for the food and hospitality on offer at their inn.

The public bar and the comfortable lounge bar are both ideal for enjoying a pint or two from the inn's range of traditional real ales, keg beers and ciders as well as satisfying any hunger pains with one of the tastiest bar snacks around. The menu, full of traditional dishes 'just the way grannie used to make' is a joy in itself. More formally, there is also a dining room and family room where, again, there is a magnificent menu of delicious dishes all cooked by Pru, with the help of son Ben, from locally supplied organic ingredients. Their chilli is reputed to be the hottest in Dorset - beware! Finally, The White Horse also offers charming family accommodation where guests can also make use of the family sitting room and, possibly, meet the resident ghost - a young bride jilted at the altar.

Opening Hours: Mon-Sat 11.00-14.30, 18.00-23.00; Sun 12.00-16.00, 19.00-22.30

Food: Bar meals and restaurant for lunch and dinner

Credit Cards: Mastercard, Visa, Switch

Accommodation: 1 double room, 1 twin room.

Facilities: Enclosed patio area at front of pub, Children and pets welcome

Entertainment: Theme nights, Darts, Pool, Shove h'penny, Cribbage, Quizzes

Local Places of Interest/Activities: Blandford Forum 2 miles, Hod Hill Iron Age settlement, Walking

Website: Pru@whitehorse48.freeserve.co.uk

268   The White Horse Inn

11 The High Street, Swanage,
Dorset BH19 2LP
Tel: 01929 422469

Directions:

From junction 1 on the M27 take the A31 to Poole and then the A351 through Wareham to Swanage. Continue to Swanage seafront and then turn right into the High Street, The White Horse Inn lies on the right.

Situated right in the heart of this popular holiday resort, **The White Horse Inn** is a striking stone building that was dates back to the early 19th century. With elegant, large windows and a wrought iron balcony on the first floor, a style that is mirrored by the other buildings down this street, the inn has a charming and pleasing appearance. Inside, the story is the same and the large, stylish open plan bar area is decorated with a mass of interesting memorabilia that ranges from a collection of 1950s radios and musical instruments to old clocks and sports equipment. A busy and bustling place during the summer when the town too is alive with visitors, during the quieter winter months the place changes character and becomes the haunt, almost exclusively, of locals looking for a relaxing lunchtime or evening out.

Although this is licensees, Diane and Ross Shakespeare's first venture into the trade, the time that they have spent here, since 1996, has proved that they have a flair for the business. Well known for the high standard of real ales, wines and other drinks served here, The White Horse Inn has a well earned reputation for its tasty menu of homecooked food. Not surprisingly, with the sea so close, fish and sea food is the house speciality and is well worth making the effort to try here when the season is right. Add to this the superb accommodation in this elegant building and the high standards of service and customer care and The White Horse Inn is one place not to overlook in Swanage.

Opening Hours: Mon-Sat 11.00-23.00; Sun 12.00-22.30, Late licence, Sat & Thurs night

Food: Bar meals and restaurant

Credit Cards: Visa, Access, Delta, Switch

Accommodation: 6 double and twin rooms, all en suite

Facilities: Car parking, Children welcome,

Functions catered for

Entertainment: Regular live music, Darts, Pool

Local Places of Interest/Activities: Durlston Head Visitors Centre 1 mile, Steam Railway, Beach 1 mile, Corfe Castle 5 miles, Lulworth Castle 10 miles, Walking, Cycling, Horse riding, Fishing, Sailing, Bird watching

The World's End Inn

Almer,
near Blandford Forum,
Dorset DT11 9EW
Tel: 01929 459671
Fax: 01929 459125

Directions:

From Poole take the A350 towards Blandford Forum. After approximately 6 miles turn left on to the A31 towards Dorchester. The World's End Inn can be found just over 2 miles along this road.

Situated on the main Wimborne to Bere Regis road, **The World's End Inn** got its interesting name as all the parishes once ended here. That was back in the 16th century and, though much has changed over the years, this old inn has retained much of its character and charm. This is despite the fact that, in 1992 it suffered severe fire damage but, fortunately, the building has been completely and faithfully rebuilt and the thatched roof, panelling and open fires look much has they would have done many years ago.

In 1965, when the travel writer Ralph Wightman was passing through he came upon The World's End Inn and noted then that cars and motorcoaches were flocking here. Earlier, the World War II commander General Montgomery came here whilst planning the D-Day landings and, today, and the inn is still a popular place that offers visitors a chance to experience some excellent country hospitality. Managers, Lisa and Adam Walkey, continue the fine traditions of this delightful hostelry and, as well as serving some well conditioned ales, they also provide a menu that is both extensive and imaginative. Homecooked food is very much order of the day and, under Lisa's careful and experienced eye, a mouthwatering range of wholesome dishes are produced to satisfy even the hungriest diner. Whether it is an old pub favourite such as ham and eggs or a rich creamy curry, the menu here is well worth browsing through. There is also a well chosen and reasonably priced list of both European and New World wines to complement any meal.

Opening Hours: Mon-Sat 10.30-23.00; Sun 11.00-22.30; Food from 11.30

Food: Bar meals, snacks and à la carte

Credit Cards: Visa, Access, Delta, Switch, Amex

Facilities: Beer garden, Car parking

Local Places of Interest/Activities: Kingston Lacy 4 miles, Wimborne Minster 6 miles, Poole 8 miles, Coast 7 miles, Walking, Sailing, Fishing

This page is left intentionally blank

Alphabetic List of Pubs and Inns

A

Admiral Benbow, The	Penzance, nr Penzance, Cornwall	17
Albion Inn, The	Verwood, Dorset	247
Anchor Inn, The	Burton Bradstock, nr Bridport, Dorset	248
Anchor Inn, The	Ugborough, Devon	109
Angarrack Inn, The	Angarrack, nr Hayle, Cornwall	18
Artful Dodger, The	St Davids, nr Exeter, Devon	145
Ashcott Inn, The	Ashcott, nr Street, Somerset	185
Awliscombe Inn, The	Awliscombe, nr Honiton, Devon	146

B

Barley Sheaf, The	Gorran Churchtown, nr Mevagissey, Cornwall	19
Bell Inn, The	Bovey Tracey, Devon	110
Bell Inn, The	Evercreech, Somerset	186
Black Venus Inn, The	Challacombe, nr Barnstaple, Devon	83
Blacksmiths Arms, The	Lamerton, nr Tavistock, Devon	111
Blacksmiths Arms, The	Plymtree, nr Cullompton, Devon	147
Blue Anchor Inn, The	Helston, Cornwall	20
Boscawen Hotel, The	St Dennis, nr St Austell, Cornwall	21
Botany Bay Inn, The	Winterborne Zelston, nr Wimborne, Dorset	249
Bowd Inn, The	Bowd Cross, nr Sidmouth, Devon	148
Brewers Arms, The	Martinstown, Dorset	250
Bridford Inn	Bridford, nr Exeter, Devon	112
Buffalo Inn, The	Wyke, nr Gillingham, Dorset	251
Bullers Arms	Chagford, nr Newton Abbot, Devon	113
Butchers Arms	Bishop Sutton, Somerset	213
Butterleigh Inn, The	Cullompton, Devon	149

C

Cable Station Inn	Porthcurno, nr Penzance, Cornwall	22
Candlelight Inn, The	Bishopswood, nr Chard, Somerset	187
Carpenters Arms, The	Lower Metherell, nr Callington, Cornwall	53
Castle Inn, The	Lydford, nr Okehampton, Devon	114
Chip Shop Inn, The	Chipshop, nr Tavistock, Devon	115
Church House Inn	Linkhorne, nr Callington, Cornwall	54
Church House Inn, The	Churchstow, nr Kingsbridge, Devon	116
Church House Inn, The	Rattery, nr Totnes, Devon	117
Church House Inn, The	Stokeinteignhead, nr Newton Abbot, Devon	118
Clifton Hotel, The	The Grove, nr Portland, Dorset	252
Coach and Horses, The	Horns Cross, nr Bideford, Devon	84
Coombe Barton Inn, The	Crackington Haven, nr Bude, Cornwall	55
Cornish Arms, The	Pendoggett, nr Port Isaac, Cornwall	56
Cornish Arms, The	St Blazey, Cornwall	23
Cornish Inn, The	Gunnislake, Cornwall	57
Countryman, The	North Petherwin, nr Launceston, Cornwall	58
Crabshell Inn, The	Kingsbridge, Devon	119

Crow's Nest, The	Port Isaac, Cornwall	59
Crown and Sceptre, The	Newton St Cyres, nr Exeter, Devon	150
Crown Inn, The	St Ewe, nr St Austell, Cornwall	24

D

Darlington Inn, The	Camelford, Cornwall	60
Dartmoor Railway Inn	Crediton, Devon	151
Dolphin Inn, The	Kenton, Devon	120
Drum and Monkey Inn	Kenn, nr Clevedon, Somerset	214

E

Eagle Inn, The	Highbury, nr Coleford, Somerset	215
Earl of Chatham, The	Lostwithiel, Cornwall	61
Easton Inn, The	Easton, nr Wells, Somerset	216
Ebrington Arms	Knowle, nr Braunton, Devon	85
Eight Kings Inn	Portland, Dorset	253

F

Farmers Arms, The	St Merryn, nr Padstow, Cornwall	25
Ferry Boat Inn, The	Helford Passage, nr Falmouth, Cornwall	26
Fishponds House	Luppitt, nr Honiton, Devon	152
Fountain Inn, The	Newbridge, nr Penzance, Cornwall	27
Fox Inn, The	Ansty, nr Dorchester, Dorset	254
Foxhunters Inn	West Down, nr Ilfracombe, Devon	86
Full Moon, The	Wells, Somerset	217
Full Quart, The	Hewish, nr Weston-Super-Mare, Somerset	218

G

George and Dragon, The	Bodmin, Cornwall	28
George Inn, The	Buckfastleigh, Devon	121
George Inn, The	Chideock, Dorset	255
Globe Inn, The	Frogmore, nr Kingsbridge, Devon	122
Globe Inn, The	Milverton, Somerset	188
Globe Inn, The	Swanage, Dorset	256
Globe, The	Somerton, Somerset	189
Golden Inn, The	Highampton, nr Beaworthy, Devon	87
Greyhound Inn, The	Stogursey, nr Bridgwater, Somerset	190
Griffins Head Inn, The	Nether Compton, nr Sherbourne, Dorset	257

H

Half Moon Inn, The	Sheepwash, nr Hatherleigh, Devon	88
Halfway House Inn, The	Twowatersfoot, nr Liskeard, Cornwall	62
Halfway Inn, The	Norden, nr Corfe Castle, Dorset	258
Harbour Moon, The	West Looe, Cornwall	63
Hunters Lodge Inn, The	Leigh Common, nr Wincanton, Somerset	191
Hunters' Inn, The	Heddons Valley, nr Parracombe, Devon	89

I

Ilchester Arms	Abbotsbury, Dorset	259

J

Journey's End Inn, The	Ringmore, nr Kingsbridge, Devon	123
Jubilee Inn, The	Pelynt, nr Looe, Cornwall	64

K

Kings Arms	Wareham, Dorset	260
Kings Arms, The	Paul, nr Penzance, Cornwall	29
Kings Arms, The	St Just, Cornwall	30
Kings Arms, The	St Stephen, nr St Austell, Cornwall	31

L

Lamb Inn, The	Silverton, Devon	153
Ley Arms, The	Kenn, nr Exeter, Devon	124
Live and Let Live Inn, The	Landscove, nr Ashburton, Devon	125
London Inn, The	Horrabridge, nr Yelverton, Devon	126
London Inn, The	Kilkhampton, nr Bude, Cornwall	65
London Inn, The	Padstow, Cornwall	32
London Inn, The	South Brent, Devon	127

M

Maltsters Arms, The	Chapel Amble, nr Wadebridge, Cornwall	66
Masons Arms, The	Frome, Somerset	219
Molesworth Arms, The	Pyworthy, nr Holsworthy, Devon	90

N

Napoleon Inn, The	Boscastle, Cornwall	67
New Fountain Inn	Whimple, nr Exeter, Devon	154
New Inn, The	Christchurch, Dorset	261
North Inn, The	Pendeen, nr Penzance, Cornwall	33

O

Old Court House, The	Chulmleigh, Devon	155
Old Down Inn, The	Emborough, nr Bath, Somerset	220
Old Inn, The	Kilmington, nr Axminster, Devon	156
Old Inn, The	St Breward, nr Bodmin Moor, Cornwall	68
Old Mendip Inn, The	Gurney Slade, nr Bath, Somerset	221
Old Union Inn, The	Stibbs Cross, nr Torrington, Devon	91

P

Panborough Inn, The	Panborough, nr Wells, Somerset	222
Passage House Inn, The	Topsham, nr Exeter, Devon	157
Pendarves Arms, The	Gwithian, nr Hayle, Cornwall	34
Piddle Inn, The	Piddletrenthide, Dorset	262
Pilgrims' Rest Inn, The	Lovington, nr Castle Cary, Somerset	192
Plough Inn, The	Ipplepen, Devon	128
Plume of Feathers, The	Rickford, nr Burrington, Somerset	223
Port Light Inn	Bolberry Down, nr Salcombe, Devon	129
Post Inn, The	Whiddon Down, nr Okehampton, Devon	130
Prince of Wales, The	Dunkerton Hill, nr Bath, Somerset	224
Prospect Inn, The	Exeter, Devon	158

Q

Queens Arms, The	St Just, nr Penzance, Cornwall	35

R

Red Lion Inn, The	Draycott, nr Cheddar, Somerset	225
Ring O' Bells, The	West Alvington, nr Kingsbridge, Devon	131
Rose and Crown, The	Yealmpton, nr Plymouth, Devon	132
Royal Oak Country Inn	Dolton, Devon	92
Royal Oak, The	Chawleigh, nr Chulmleigh, Devon	159
Royal Standard Inn, The	Gerrans, nr Truro, Cornwall	36

S

Sawles Arms, The	Carthew, nr St Austell, Cornwall	37
Scott Arms, The	Kingston, Dorset	263
Seven Stars, The	Winkleigh, Devon	160
Ship at Oldford, The	Oldford, nr Frome, Somerset	226
Ship Inn, The	Polmear, nr Par, Cornwall	38
Ship Inn, The	Portloe, Cornwall	39
Ship Inn, The	Wellington, nr Somerset, Somerset	193
Sir Walter Raleigh, The	East Budleigh, Devon	161
Slab House Inn, The	West Horrington, nr Wells, Somerset	227
Smugglers Inn, The	Cawsand, nr Torpoint, Cornwall	69
Smugglers Inn, The	Osmington Mills, nr Weymouth, Dorset	264
Snooty Fox, The	Morval, nr Looe, Cornwall	70
Stag Hunters Hotel, The	Brendon, nr Lynton, Devon	93
Swan at Kingston, The	Kingston St Mary, nr Taunton, Somerset	194

T

Talbot Arms, The	Benville, nr Corscombe, Dorset	265
Thatched Inn, The	Abbotsham, nr Bideford, Devon	94
Three Horseshoes, The	Batcombe, nr Shepton Mallet, Somerset	195
Three Tuns Inn, The	Silverton, nr Exeter, Devon	162
Toby Jug Inn, The	Bickington, nr Newton Abbot, Devon	133
Tolcarne Inn, The	Newlyn, nr Penzance, Cornwall	40
Travellers Rest, The	East Pennard, nr Shepton Mallet, Somerset	196
Tree Inn, The	Stratton, Cornwall	71
Trooper Inn, The	Stourton Caundle, nr Sturminster Newton, Dorset	266
Two Mile Oak	Abbotskerswell, Devon	134

W

White Hart Inn, The	Woodbury, Devon	163
White Hart, The	Trudoxhill, nr Frome, Somerset	228
White Horse, The	Stourpaine, nr Blandford Forum, Dorset	267
White Horse Inn, The	Swanage, Dorset	268
White Lion Inn, The	Bradninch, nr Exeter, Devon	164
White Thorn Inn	Shaugh Prior, nr Plymouth, Devon	135
Windsor Arms, The	Bradiford, nr Barnstaple, Devon	95
Woodborough Inn, The	Winscombe, Somerset	229
World's End Inn, The	Almer, nr Blandford Forum, Dorset	269
Wrey Arms, The	Sticklepath, nr Barnstaple, Devon	96
Wyndham Arms, The	Kentisbeare, nr Cullompton, Devon	165

Special Interest Lists

ACCOMMODATION

WEST CORNWALL

Angarrack Inn, The	Angarrack, nr Hayle, Cornwall	18
Blue Anchor Inn, The	Helston, Cornwall	20
Boscawen Hotel, The	St Dennis, nr St Austell, Cornwall	21
Cable Station Inn	Porthcurno, nr Penzance, Cornwall	22
Cornish Arms, The	St Blazey, Cornwall	23
Farmers Arms, The	St Merryn, nr Padstow, Cornwall	25
Fountain Inn, The	Newbridge, nr Penzance, Cornwall	27
George and Dragon, The	Bodmin, Cornwall	28
Kings Arms, The	Paul, nr Penzance, Cornwall	29
Kings Arms, The	St Stephen, nr St Austell, Cornwall	31
London Inn, The	Padstow, Cornwall	32
North Inn, The	Pendeen, nr Penzance, Cornwall	33
Royal Standard Inn, The	Gerrans, nr Truro, Cornwall	36
Ship Inn, The	Polmear, nr Par, Cornwall	38
Ship Inn, The	Portloe, Cornwall	39

EAST CORNWALL

Carpenters Arms, The	Lower Metherell, nr Callington, Cornwall	53
Coombe Barton Inn, The	Crackington Haven, nr Bude, Cornwall	55
Cornish Arms, The	Pendoggett, nr Port Isaac, Cornwall	56
Cornish Inn, The	Gunnislake, Cornwall	57
Countryman, The	North Petherwin, nr Launceston, Cornwall	58
Crow's Nest, The	Port Isaac, Cornwall	59
Darlington Inn, The	Camelford, Cornwall	60
Earl of Chatham, The	Lostwithiel, Cornwall	61
Harbour Moon, The	West Looe, Cornwall	63
Jubilee Inn, The	Pelynt, nr Looe, Cornwall	64
London Inn, The	Kilkhampton, nr Bude, Cornwall	65
Snooty Fox, The	Morval, nr Looe, Cornwall	70
Tree Inn, The	Stratton, Cornwall	71

NORTH DEVON

Coach and Horses, The	Horns Cross, nr Bideford, Devon	84
Foxhunters Inn	West Down, nr Ilfracombe, Devon	86
Half Moon Inn, The	Sheepwash, nr Hatherleigh, Devon	88
Hunters' Inn, The	Heddons Valley, nr Parracombe, Devon	89
Old Union Inn, The	Stibbs Cross, nr Torrington, Devon	91
Royal Oak Country Inn	Dolton, Devon	92
Stag Hunters Hotel, The	Brendon, nr Lynton, Devon	93
Thatched Inn, The	Abbotsham, nr Bideford, Devon	94
Wrey Arms, The	Sticklepath, nr Barnstaple, Devon	9

SOUTH DEVON

Anchor Inn, The	Ugborough, Devon	109
Bell Inn, The	Bovey Tracey, Devon	110
Bullers Arms	Chagford, nr Newton Abbot, Devon	113
Castle Inn, The	Lydford, nr Okehampton, Devon	114
Church House Inn, The	Churchstow, nr Kingsbridge, Devon	116
George Inn, The	Buckfastleigh, Devon	121
Globe Inn, The	Frogmore, nr Kingsbridge, Devon	122
Journey's End Inn, The	Ringmore, nr Kingsbridge, Devon	123
London Inn, The	South Brent, Devon	127
Port Light Inn	Bolberry Down, nr Salcombe, Devon	129
Ring O' Bells, The	West Alvington, nr Kingsbridge, Devon	131
Rose and Crown, The	Yealmpton, nr Plymouth, Devon	132

EAST DEVON

Awliscombe Inn, The	Awliscombe, nr Honiton, Devon	146
Dartmoor Railway Inn	Crediton, Devon	151
Fishponds House	Luppitt, nr Honiton, Devon	152
Old Court House, The	Chulmleigh, Devon	155
Royal Oak, The	Chawleigh, nr Chulmleigh, Devon	159
Three Tuns Inn, The	Silverton, nr Exeter, Devon	162
White Lion Inn, The	Bradninch, nr Exeter, Devon	164

SOUTH AND WEST SOMERSET

Bell Inn, The	Evercreech, Somerset	186
Globe Inn, The	Milverton, Somerset	188
Ship Inn, The	Wellington, nr Somerset, Somerset	193

NORTH AND EAST SOMERSET

Butchers Arms	Bishop Sutton, Somerset	213
Old Down Inn, The	Emborough, nr Bath, Somerset	220
Old Mendip Inn, The	Gurney Slade, nr Bath, Somerset	221
Plume of Feathers, The	Rickford, nr Burrington, Somerset	223
Prince of Wales, The	Dunkerton Hill, nr Bath, Somerset	224

DORSET

Clifton Hotel, The	The Grove, nr Portland, Dorset	252
Fox Inn, The	Ansty, nr Dorchester, Dorset	254
Ilchester Arms	Abbotsbury, Dorset	259
Piddle Inn, The	Piddletrenthide, Dorset	262
Scott Arms, The	Kingston, Dorset	263
White Horse Inn, The	Swanage, Dorset	267
White Horse, The	Stourpaine, nr Blandford Forum, Dorset	266

ALL DAY OPENING

WEST CORNWALL

Blue Anchor Inn, The	Helston, Cornwall	20
Boscawen Hotel, The	St Dennis, nr St Austell, Cornwall	21
Cable Station Inn	Porthcurno, nr Penzance, Cornwall	22
Crown Inn, The	St Ewe, nr St Austell, Cornwall	24
Farmers Arms, The	St Merryn, nr Padstow, Cornwall	25
Ferry Boat Inn, The	Helford Passage, nr Falmouth, Cornwall	26
Fountain Inn, The	Newbridge, nr Penzance, Cornwall	27
George and Dragon, The	Bodmin, Cornwall	28
Kings Arms, The	Paul, nr Penzance, Cornwall	29
Kings Arms, The	St Just, Cornwall	30
Kings Arms, The	St Stephen, nr St Austell, Cornwall	31
London Inn, The	Padstow, Cornwall	32
North Inn, The	Pendeen, nr Penzance, Cornwall	33
Queens Arms, The	St Just, nr Penzance, Cornwall	35
Sawles Arms, The	Carthew, nr St Austell, Cornwall	37
Ship Inn, The	Polmear, nr Par, Cornwall	38
Ship Inn, The	Portloe, Cornwall	39

EAST CORNWALL

Cornish Arms, The	Pendoggett, nr Port Isaac, Cornwall	56
Cornish Inn, The	Gunnislake, Cornwall	57
Countryman, The	North Petherwin, nr Launceston, Cornwall	58
Crow's Nest, The	Port Isaac, Cornwall	59
Earl of Chatham, The	Lostwithiel, Cornwall	61
Harbour Moon, The	West Looe, Cornwall	63
Snooty Fox, The	Morval, nr Looe, Cornwall	70
Tree Inn, The	Stratton, Cornwall	71

NORTH DEVON

Black Venus Inn, The	Challacombe, nr Barnstaple, Devon	83
Coach and Horses, The	Horns Cross, nr Bideford, Devon	84
Foxhunters Inn	West Down, nr Ilfracombe, Devon	86
Hunters' Inn, The	Heddons Valley, nr Parracombe, Devon	89
Old Union Inn, The	Stibbs Cross, nr Torrington, Devon	91
Stag Hunters Hotel, The	Brendon, nr Lynton, Devon	93
Thatched Inn, The	Abbotsham, nr Bideford, Devon	94
Wrey Arms, The	Sticklepath, nr Barnstaple, Devon	96

SOUTH DEVON

Crabshell Inn, The	Kingsbridge, Devon	119
Dolphin Inn, The	Kenton, Devon	120
London Inn, The	Horrabridge, nr Yelverton, Devon	126
London Inn, The	South Brent, Devon	127
Plough Inn, The	Ipplepen, Devon	128
Post Inn, The	Whiddon Down, nr Okehampton, Devon	130
Two Mile Oak, The	Abbotskerswell, Devon	134

ALL DAY OPENING

EAST DEVON

Artful Dodger, The	St Davids, nr Exeter, Devon	145
Bowd Inn, The	Bowd Cross, nr Sidmouth, Devon	148
Old Court House, The	Chulmleigh, Devon	155
Old Inn, The	Kilmington, nr Axminster, Devon	156
Passage House Inn, The	Topsham, nr Exeter, Devon	157
Prospect Inn, The	Exeter, Devon	158
Seven Stars, The	Winkleigh, Devon	160

South and West Somerset

Bell Inn, The	Evercreech, Somerset	186
Hunters Lodge Inn, The	Leigh Common, nr Wincanton, Somerset	191

North and East Somerset

Eagle Inn, The	Highbury, nr Coleford, Somerset	215
Full Moon, The	Wells, Somerset	217
Full Quart, The	Hewish, nr Weston-Super-Mare, Somerset	218
Old Down Inn, The	Emborough, nr Bath, Somerset	220
Red Lion Inn, The	Draycott, nr Cheddar, Somerset	225
Ship at Oldford, The	Oldford, nr Frome, Somerset	226
White Hart, The	Trudoxhill, nr Frome, Somerset	228

DORSET

Albion Inn, The	Verwood, Dorset	247
Fox Inn, The	Ansty, nr Dorchester, Dorset	254
New Inn, The	Christchurch, Dorset	261
Talbot Arms, The	Benville, nr Corscombe, Dorset	264
White Horse Inn, The	Swanage, Dorset	267
World's End Inn, The	Almer, nr Blandford Forum, Dorset	268

CHILDREN WELCOME/CHILDREN'S FACILITIES | 279

WEST CORNWALL

Angarrack Inn, The	Angarrack, nr Hayle, Cornwall	18
Cable Station Inn	Porthcurno, nr Penzance, Cornwall	22
Farmers Arms, The	St Merryn, nr Padstow, Cornwall	25
George and Dragon, The	Bodmin, Cornwall	28
Kings Arms, The	Paul, nr Penzance, Cornwall	29
Kings Arms, The	St Just, Cornwall	30
Pendarves Arms, The	Gwithian, nr Hayle, Cornwall	34
Ship Inn, The	Polmear, nr Par, Cornwall	38

EAST CORNWALL

Church House Inn	Linkhorne, nr Callington, Cornwall	54
Coombe Barton Inn, The	Crackington Haven, nr Bude, Cornwall	55
Cornish Inn, The	Gunnislake, Cornwall	57
Countryman, The	North Petherwin, nr Launceston, Cornwall	58
Earl of Chatham, The	Lostwithiel, Cornwall	61
Halfway House Inn, The	Twowatersfoot, nr Liskeard, Cornwall	62
Harbour Moon, The	West Looe, Cornwall	63
Jubilee Inn, The	Pelynt, nr Looe, Cornwall	64
London Inn, The	Kilkhampton, nr Bude, Cornwall	65
Snooty Fox, The	Morval, nr Looe, Cornwall	70

NORTH DEVON

Coach and Horses, The	Horns Cross, nr Bideford, Devon	84
Ebrington Arms	Knowle, nr Braunton, Devon	85
Half Moon Inn, The	Sheepwash, nr Hatherleigh, Devon	88
Hunters' Inn, The	Heddons Valley, nr Parracombe, Devon	89
Old Union Inn, The	Stibbs Cross, nr Torrington, Devon	91
Royal Oak Country Inn	Dolton, Devon	92
Windsor Arms, The	Bradiford, nr Barnstaple, Devon	95

SOUTH DEVON

Blacksmiths Arms, The	Lamerton, nr Tavistock, Devon	111
Bullers Arms	Chagford, nr Newton Abbot, Devon	113
Chip Shop Inn, The	Chipshop, nr Tavistock, Devon	115
Church House Inn, The	Churchstow, nr Kingsbridge, Devon	116
Church House Inn, The	Rattery, nr Totnes, Devon	117
Crabshell Inn, The	Kingsbridge, Devon	119
George Inn, The	Buckfastleigh, Devon	121
Globe Inn, The	Frogmore, nr Kingsbridge, Devon	122
Journey's End Inn, The	Ringmore, nr Kingsbridge, Devon	123
Port Light Inn	Bolberry Down, nr Salcombe, Devon	129
Post Inn, The	Whiddon Down, nr Okehampton, Devon	130
Ring O' Bells, The	West Alvington, nr Kingsbridge, Devon	131
Rose and Crown, The	Yealmpton, nr Plymouth, Devon	132
Toby Jug Inn, The	Bickington, nr Newton Abbot, Devon	133
White Thorn Inn	Shaugh Prior, nr Plymouth, Devon	135

280   CHILDREN WELCOME/CHILDREN'S FACILITIES

EAST DEVON

Bowd Inn, The	Bowd Cross, nr Sidmouth, Devon	148
Butterleigh Inn, The	Cullompton, Devon	149
Crown and Sceptre, The	Newton St Cyres, nr Exeter, Devon	150
Old Court House, The	Chulmleigh, Devon	155
White Lion Inn, The	Bradninch, nr Exeter, Devon	164
Wyndham Arms, The	Kentisbeare, nr Cullompton, Devon	165

SOUTH AND WEST SOMERSET

Ashcott Inn, The	Ashcott, nr Street, Somerset	185
Candlelight Inn, The	Bishopswood, nr Chard, Somerset	187
Globe, The	Somerton, Somerset	189
Greyhound Inn, The	Stogursey, nr Bridgwater, Somerset	190
Hunters Lodge Inn, The	Leigh Common, nr Wincanton, Somerset	191
Ship Inn, The	Wellington, nr Somerset, Somerset	193
Travellers Rest, The	East Pennard, nr Shepton Mallet, Somerset	196

NORTH AND EAST SOMERSET

Full Quart, The	Hewish, nr Weston-Super-Mare, Somerset	218
Masons Arms, The	Frome, Somerset	219
Old Mendip Inn, The	Gurney Slade, nr Bath, Somerset	221
White Hart, The	Trudoxhill, nr Frome, Somerset	228

Dorset

Albion Inn, The	Verwood, Dorset	247
Buffalo Inn, The	Wyke, nr Gillingham, Dorset	251
George Inn, The	Chideock, Dorset	255
Globe Inn, The	Swanage, Dorset	256
Talbot Arms, The	Benville, nr Corscombe, Dorset	264
Trooper Inn, The	Stourton Caundle, nr Sturminster Newton, Dorset	265
White Horse Inn, The	Swanage, Dorset	267
White Horse, The	Stourpaine, nr Blandford Forum, Dorset	266

CREDIT CARDS ACCEPTED ·

WEST CORNWALL

Admiral Benbow, The	Penzance	17
Barley Sheaf, The	Gorran Churchtown, nr Mevagissey, Cornwall	19
Cornish Arms, The	St Blazey, Cornwall	23
Crown Inn, The	St Ewe, nr St Austell, Cornwall	24
Farmers Arms, The	St Merryn, nr Padstow, Cornwall	25
Ferry Boat Inn, The	Helford Passage, nr Falmouth, Cornwall	26
Kings Arms, The	Paul, nr Penzance, Cornwall	29
Kings Arms, The	St Just, Cornwall	30
North Inn, The	Pendeen, nr Penzance, Cornwall	33
Royal Standard Inn, The	Gerrans, nr Truro, Cornwall	36
Ship Inn, The	Polmear, nr Par, Cornwall	38
Ship Inn, The	Portloe, Cornwall	39
Tolcarne Inn, The	Newlyn, nr Penzance, Cornwall	40

EAST CORNWALL

Carpenters Arms, The	Lower Metherell, nr Callington, Cornwall	53
Church House Inn	Linkhorne, nr Callington, Cornwall	54
Coombe Barton Inn, The	Crackington Haven, nr Bude, Cornwall	55
Cornish Arms, The	Pendoggett, nr Port Isaac, Cornwall	56
Countryman, The	North Petherwin, nr Launceston, Cornwall	58
Darlington Inn, The	Camelford, Cornwall	60
Earl of Chatham, The	Lostwithiel, Cornwall	61
Halfway House Inn, The	Twowatersfoot, nr Liskeard, Cornwall	62
Harbour Moon, The	West Looe, Cornwall	63
Jubilee Inn, The	Pelynt, nr Looe, Cornwall	64
London Inn, The	Kilkhampton, nr Bude, Cornwall	65
Maltsters Arms, The	Chapel Amble, nr Wadebridge, Cornwall	66
Napoleon Inn, The	Boscastle, Cornwall	67
Old Inn, The	St Breward, nr Bodmin Moor, Cornwall	68
Smugglers Inn, The	Cawsand, nr Torpoint, Cornwall	69
Snooty Fox, The	Morval, nr Looe, Cornwall	70
Tree Inn, The	Stratton, Cornwall	71

NORTH DEVON

Black Venus Inn, The	Challacombe, nr Barnstaple, Devon	83
Ebrington Arms	Knowle, nr Braunton, Devon	85
Foxhunters Inn	West Down, nr Ilfracombe, Devon	86
Half Moon Inn, The	Sheepwash, nr Hatherleigh, Devon	88
Hunters' Inn, The	Heddons Valley, nr Parracombe, Devon	89
Molesworth Arms, The	Pyworthy, nr Holsworthy, Devon	90
Royal Oak Country Inn	Dolton, Devon	92
Stag Hunters Hotel, The	Brendon, nr Lynton, Devon	93
Thatched Inn, The	Abbotsham, nr Bideford, Devon	94
Windsor Arms, The	Bradiford, nr Barnstaple, Devon	95
Wrey Arms, The	Sticklepath, nr Barnstaple, Devon	96

CREDIT CARDS ACCEPTED

SOUTH DEVON

Blacksmiths Arms, The	Lamerton, nr Tavistock, Devon	111
Bridford Inn	Bridford, nr Exeter, Devon	112
Bullers Arms	Chagford, nr Newton Abbot, Devon	113
Castle Inn, The	Lydford, nr Okehampton, Devon	114
Church House Inn, The	Churchstow, nr Kingsbridge, Devon	116
Church House Inn, The	Stokeinteignhead, nr Newton Abbot, Devon	118
Crabshell Inn, The	Kingsbridge, Devon	119
Dolphin Inn, The	Kenton, Devon	120
George Inn, The	Buckfastleigh, Devon	121
Globe Inn, The	Frogmore, nr Kingsbridge, Devon	122
Journey's End Inn, The	Ringmore, nr Kingsbridge, Devon	123
Ley Arms, The	Kenn, nr Exeter, Devon	124
Live and Let Live Inn, The	Landscove, nr Ashburton, Devon	125
London Inn, The	Horrabridge, nr Yelverton, Devon	126
London Inn, The	South Brent, Devon	127
Port Light Inn	Bolberry Down, nr Salcombe, Devon	129
Post Inn, The	Whiddon Down, nr Okehampton, Devon	130
Ring O' Bells, The	West Alvington, nr Kingsbridge, Devon	131
Rose and Crown, The	Yealmpton, nr Plymouth, Devon	132
Toby Jug Inn, The	Bickington, nr Newton Abbot, Devon	133
Two Mile Oak, The	Abbotskerswell, Devon	134

EAST DEVON

Awliscombe Inn, The	Awliscombe, nr Honiton, Devon	146
Bowd Inn, The	Bowd Cross, nr Sidmouth, Devon	148
Butterleigh Inn, The	Cullompton, Devon	149
Crown and Sceptre, The	Newton St Cyres, nr Exeter, Devon	150
Dartmoor Railway Inn	Crediton, Devon	151
Fishponds House	Luppitt, nr Honiton, Devon	152
Lamb Inn, The	Silverton, Devon	153
New Fountain Inn	Whimple, nr Exeter, Devon	154
Old Court House, The	Chulmleigh, Devon	155
Old Inn, The	Kilmington, nr Axminster, Devon	156
Passage House Inn, The	Topsham, nr Exeter, Devon	157
Prospect Inn, The	Exeter, Devon	158
Royal Oak, The	Chawleigh, nr Chulmleigh, Devon	159
Seven Stars, The	Winkleigh, Devon	160
Sir Walter Raleigh, The	East Budleigh, Devon	161
Three Tuns Inn, The	Silverton, nr Exeter, Devon	162
White Hart Inn, The	Woodbury, Devon	163
White Lion Inn, The	Bradninch, nr Exeter, Devon	164
Wyndham Arms, The	Kentisbeare, nr Cullompton, Devon	165

CREDIT CARDS ACCEPTED

SOUTH AND WEST SOMERSET

Ashcott Inn, The	Ashcott, nr Street, Somerset	185
Bell Inn, The	Evercreech, Somerset	**186**
Candlelight Inn, The	Bishopswood, nr Chard, Somerset	187
Globe, The	Somerton, Somerset	189
Hunters Lodge Inn, The	Leigh Common, nr Wincanton, Somerset	191
Pilgrims' Rest Inn, The	Lovington, nr Castle Cary, Somerset	192
Three Horseshoes, The	Batcombe, nr Shepton Mallet, Somerset	195

NORTH AND EAST SOMERSET

Drum and Monkey Inn	Kenn, nr Clevedon, Somerset	214
Eagle Inn, The	Highbury, nr Coleford, Somerset	215
Easton Inn, The	Easton, nr Wells, Somerset	216
Full Moon, The	Wells, Somerset	217
Full Quart, The	Hewish, nr Weston-Super-Mare, Somerset	218
Masons Arms, The	Frome, Somerset	219
Old Down Inn, The	Emborough, nr Bath, Somerset	220
Old Mendip Inn, The	Gurney Slade, nr Bath, Somerset	221
Panborough Inn, The	Panborough, nr Wells, Somerset	222
Prince of Wales, The	Dunkerton Hill, nr Bath, Somerset	224
Ship at Oldford, The	Oldford, nr Frome, Somerset	226
Slab House Inn, The	West Horrington, nr Wells, Somerset	227
White Hart, The	Trudoxhill, nr Frome, Somerset	228
Woodborough Inn, The	Winscombe, Somerset	229

DORSET

Albion Inn, The	Verwood, Dorset	247
Anchor Inn, The	Burton Bradstock, nr Bridport, Dorset	248
Botany Bay Inn, The	Winterborne Zelston, nr Wimborne, Dorset	249
Brewers Arms, The	Martinstown, Dorset	250
Fox Inn, The	Ansty, nr Dorchester, Dorset	254
George Inn, The	Chideock, Dorset	255
Halfway Inn, The	Norden, nr Corfe Castle, Dorset	258
Ilchester Arms	Abbotsbury, Dorset	259
New Inn, The	Christchurch, Dorset	261
Piddle Inn, The	Piddletrenthide, Dorset	262
Scott Arms, The	Kingston, Dorset	263
Smugglers Inn, The	Osmington Mills, nr Weymouth, Dorset	263
Talbot Arms, The	Benville, nr Corscombe, Dorset	264
White Horse Inn, The	Swanage, Dorset	267
White Horse, The	Stourpaine, nr Blandford Forum, Dorset	266
World's End Inn, The	Almer, nr Blandford Forum, Dorset	268

WEST CORNWALL

Angarrack Inn, The	Angarrack, nr Hayle, Cornwall	18
Barley Sheaf, The	Gorran Churchtown, nr Mevagissey, Cornwall	19
Cable Station Inn	Porthcurno, nr Penzance, Cornwall	22
Crown Inn, The	St Ewe, nr St Austell, Cornwall	24
Farmers Arms, The	St Merryn, nr Padstow, Cornwall	25
Ferry Boat Inn, The	Helford Passage, nr Falmouth, Cornwall	26
Fountain Inn, The	Newbridge, nr Penzance, Cornwall	27
George and Dragon, The	Bodmin, Cornwall	28
Kings Arms, The	Paul, nr Penzance, Cornwall	29
North Inn, The	Pendeen, nr Penzance, Cornwall	33
Pendarves Arms, The	Gwithian, nr Hayle, Cornwall	34
Queens Arms, The	St Just, nr Penzance, Cornwall	35
Royal Standard Inn, The	Gerrans, nr Truro, Cornwall	36
Sawles Arms, The	Carthew, nr St Austell, Cornwall	37
Ship Inn, The	Polmear, nr Par, Cornwall	38
Ship Inn, The	Portloe, Cornwall	39
Tolcarne Inn, The	Newlyn, nr Penzance, Cornwall	40

EAST CORNWALL

Carpenters Arms, The	Lower Metherell, nr Callington, Cornwall	53
Cornish Arms, The	Pendoggett, nr Port Isaac, Cornwall	56
Countryman, The	North Petherwin, nr Launceston, Cornwall	58
Crow's Nest, The	Port Isaac, Cornwall	59
Earl of Chatham, The	Lostwithiel, Cornwall	61
Halfway House Inn, The	Twowatersfoot, nr Liskeard, Cornwall	62
Jubilee Inn, The	Pelynt, nr Looe, Cornwall	64
London Inn, The	Kilkhampton, nr Bude, Cornwall	65
Napoleon Inn, The	Boscastle, Cornwall	67
Old Inn, The	St Breward, nr Bodmin Moor, Cornwall	68
Snooty Fox, The	Morval, nr Looe, Cornwall	70
Tree Inn, The	Stratton, Cornwall	71

NORTH DEVON

Black Venus Inn, The	Challacombe, nr Barnstaple, Devon	83
Foxhunters Inn	West Down, nr Ilfracombe, Devon	86
Golden Inn, The	Highampton, nr Beaworthy, Devon	87
Hunters' Inn, The	Heddons Valley, nr Parracombe, Devon	89
Molesworth Arms, The	Pyworthy, nr Holsworthy, Devon	90
Old Union Inn, The	Stibbs Cross, nr Torrington, Devon	91
Royal Oak Country Inn	Dolton, Devon	92
Stag Hunters Hotel, The	Brendon, nr Lynton, Devon	93
Thatched Inn, The	Abbotsham, nr Bideford, Devon	94
Windsor Arms, The	Bradiford, nr Barnstaple, Devon	95
Wrey Arms, The	Sticklepath, nr Barnstaple, Devon	96

Garden, Patio or Terrace

SOUTH DEVON

Blacksmiths Arms, The	Lamerton, nr Tavistock, Devon	111
Bridford Inn	Bridford, nr Exeter, Devon	112
Bullers Arms	Chagford, nr Newton Abbot, Devon	113
Castle Inn, The	Lydford, nr Okehampton, Devon	114
Chip Shop Inn, The	Chipshop, nr Tavistock, Devon	115
Church House Inn, The	Churchstow, nr Kingsbridge, Devon	116
Church House Inn, The	Stokeinteignhead, nr Newton Abbot, Devon	118
Church House Inn, The	Rattery, nr Totnes, Devon	117
Crabshell Inn, The	Kingsbridge, Devon	119
Dolphin Inn, The	Kenton, Devon	120
Globe Inn, The	Frogmore, nr Kingsbridge, Devon	122
Journey's End Inn, The	Ringmore, nr Kingsbridge, Devon	123
Live and Let Live Inn, The	Landscove, nr Ashburton, Devon	125
London Inn, The	Horrabridge, nr Yelverton, Devon	126
London Inn, The	South Brent, Devon	127
Plough Inn, The	Ipplepen, Devon	128
Port Light Inn	Bolberry Down, nr Salcombe, Devon	129
Post Inn, The	Whiddon Down, nr Okehampton, Devon	130
Ring O' Bells, The	West Alvington, nr Kingsbridge, Devon	131
Rose and Crown, The	Yealmpton, nr Plymouth, Devon	132
Toby Jug Inn, The	Bickington, nr Newton Abbot, Devon	133
Two Mile Oak, The	Abbotskerswell, Devon	134
White Thorn Inn	Shaugh Prior, nr Plymouth, Devon	135

EAST DEVON

Artful Dodger, The	St Davids, nr Exeter, Devon	145
Awliscombe Inn, The	Awliscombe, nr Honiton, Devon	146
Blacksmiths Arms, The	Plymtree, nr Cullompton, Devon	147
Bowd Inn, The	Bowd Cross, nr Sidmouth, Devon	148
Butterleigh Inn, The	Cullompton, Devon	149
Crown and Sceptre, The	Newton St Cyres, nr Exeter, Devon	150
Dartmoor Railway Inn	Crediton, Devon	151
Fishponds House	Luppitt, nr Honiton, Devon	152
New Fountain Inn	Whimple, nr Exeter, Devon	154
Old Court House, The	Chulmleigh, Devon	155
Old Inn, The	Kilmington, nr Axminster, Devon	156
Passage House Inn, The	Topsham, nr Exeter, Devon	157
Royal Oak, The	Chawleigh, nr Chulmleigh, Devon	159
Seven Stars, The	Winkleigh, Devon	160
Sir Walter Raleigh, The	East Budleigh, Devon	161
Three Tuns Inn, The	Silverton, nr Exeter, Devon	162
White Hart Inn, The	Woodbury, Devon	163
White Lion Inn, The	Bradninch, nr Exeter, Devon	164
Wyndham Arms, The	Kentisbeare, nr Cullompton, Devon	165

SOUTH AND WEST SOMERSET

Ashcott Inn, The	Ashcott, nr Street, Somerset	185
Bell Inn, The	Evercreech, Somerset	186
Candlelight Inn, The	Bishopswood, nr Chard, Somerset	187
Globe Inn, The	Milverton, Somerset	188
Globe, The	Somerton, Somerset	189
Greyhound Inn, The	Stogursey, nr Bridgwater, Somerset	190
Hunters Lodge Inn, The	Leigh Common, nr Wincanton, Somerset	191
Pilgrims' Rest Inn, The	Lovington, nr Castle Cary, Somerset	192
Ship Inn, The	Wellington, nr Somerset, Somerset	193
Travellers Rest, The	East Pennard, nr Shepton Mallet, Somerset	196

NORTH AND EAST SOMERSET

Butchers Arms	Bishop Sutton, Somerset	213
Easton Inn, The	Easton, nr Wells, Somerset	216
Full Moon, The	Wells, Somerset	217
Full Quart, The	Hewish, nr Weston-Super-Mare, Somerset	218
Masons Arms, The	Frome, Somerset	219
Old Down Inn, The	Emborough, nr Bath, Somerset	220
Old Mendip Inn, The	Gurney Slade, nr Bath, Somerset	221
Plume of Feathers, The	Rickford, nr Burrington, Somerset	223
Prince of Wales, The	Dunkerton Hill, nr Bath, Somerset	224
Red Lion Inn, The	Draycott, nr Cheddar, Somerset	225
Ship at Oldford, The	Oldford, nr Frome, Somerset	226
Slab House Inn, The	West Horrington, nr Wells, Somerset	227
White Hart, The	Trudoxhill, nr Frome, Somerset	228

DORSET

Albion Inn, The	Verwood, Dorset	247
Anchor Inn, The	Burton Bradstock, nr Bridport, Dorset	248
Botany Bay Inn, The	Winterborne Zelston, nr Wimborne, Dorset	249
Brewers Arms, The	Martinstown, Dorset	250
Buffalo Inn, The	Wyke, nr Gillingham, Dorset	251
Clifton Hotel, The	The Grove, nr Portland, Dorset	252
Fox Inn, The	Ansty, nr Dorchester, Dorset	254
George Inn, The	Chideock, Dorset	255
Globe Inn, The	Swanage, Dorset	256
Griffins Head Inn, The	Nether Compton, nr Sherbourne, Dorset	257
Halfway Inn, The	Norden, nr Corfe Castle, Dorset	258
Ilchester Arms	Abbotsbury, Dorset	259
Kings Arms	Wareham, Dorset	260
New Inn, The	Christchurch, Dorset	261
Piddle Inn, The	Piddletrenthide, Dorset	262
Scott Arms, The	Kingston, Dorset	263
Smugglers Inn, The	Osmington Mills, nr Weymouth, Dorset	263
Talbot Arms, The	Benville, nr Corscombe, Dorset	264
Trooper Inn, The	Stourton Caundle, nr Sturminster Newton, Dorset	265
White Horse, The	Stourpaine, nr Blandford Forum, Dorset	266
World's End Inn, The	Almer, nr Blandford Forum, Dorset	268

OCCASIONAL/REGULAR LIVE ENTERTAINMENT | 287

WEST CORNWALL

Barley Sheaf, The	Gorran Churchtown, nr Mevagissey, Cornwall	19
Boscawen Hotel, The	St Dennis, nr St Austell, Cornwall	21
Cable Station Inn	Porthcurno, nr Penzance, Cornwall	22
Cornish Arms, The	St Blazey, Cornwall	23
Farmers Arms, The	St Merryn, nr Padstow, Cornwall	25
Fountain Inn, The	Newbridge, nr Penzance, Cornwall	27
Kings Arms, The	Paul, nr Penzance, Cornwall	29
London Inn, The	Padstow, Cornwall	32
North Inn, The	Pendeen, nr Penzance, Cornwall	33
Queens Arms, The	St Just, nr Penzance, Cornwall	35
Sawles Arms, The	Carthew, nr St Austell, Cornwall	37
Ship Inn, The	Polmear, nr Par, Cornwall	38
Tolcarne Inn, The	Newlyn, nr Penzance, Cornwall	40

EAST CORNWALL

Cornish Inn, The	Gunnislake, Cornwall	57
Countryman, The	North Petherwin, nr Launceston, Cornwall	58
Crow's Nest, The	Port Isaac, Cornwall	59
Darlington Inn, The	Camelford, Cornwall	60
Earl of Chatham, The	Lostwithiel, Cornwall	61
Harbour Moon, The	West Looe, Cornwall	63
Napoleon Inn, The	Boscastle, Cornwall	67
Old Inn, The	St Breward, nr Bodmin Moor, Cornwall	68
Smugglers Inn, The	Cawsand, nr Torpoint, Cornwall	69
Tree Inn, The	Stratton, Cornwall	71

NORTH DEVON

Foxhunters Inn	West Down, nr Ilfracombe, Devon	86
Royal Oak Country Inn	Dolton, Devon	92
Stag Hunters Hotel, The	Brendon, nr Lynton, Devon	93
Wrey Arms, The	Sticklepath, nr Barnstaple, Devon	96

SOUTH DEVON

Anchor Inn, The	Ugborough, Devon	109
Bridford Inn	Bridford, nr Exeter, Devon	112
Castle Inn, The	Lydford, nr Okehampton, Devon	114
Chip Shop Inn, The	Chipshop, nr Tavistock, Devon	115
Crabshell Inn, The	Kingsbridge, Devon	119
George Inn, The	Buckfastleigh, Devon	121
Globe Inn, The	Frogmore, nr Kingsbridge, Devon	122
Journey's End Inn, The	Ringmore, nr Kingsbridge, Devon	123
Live and Let Live Inn, The	Landscove, nr Ashburton, Devon	125
London Inn, The	South Brent, Devon	127
Plough Inn, The	Ipplepen, Devon	128
Post Inn, The	Whiddon Down, nr Okehampton, Devon	130
Toby Jug Inn, The	Bickington, nr Newton Abbot, Devon	133
Two Mile Oak, The	Abbotskerswell, Devon	134

EAST DEVON

Artful Dodger, The	St Davids, nr Exeter, Devon	145
Blacksmiths Arms, The	Plymtree, nr Cullompton, Devon	147
Bowd Inn, The	Bowd Cross, nr Sidmouth, Devon	148
Crown and Sceptre, The	Newton St Cyres, nr Exeter, Devon	150
New Fountain Inn	Whimple, nr Exeter, Devon	154
Prospect Inn, The	Exeter, Devon	158
Seven Stars, The	Winkleigh, Devon	160
Three Tuns Inn, The	Silverton, nr Exeter, Devon	162
White Hart Inn, The	Woodbury, Devon	163
White Lion Inn, The	Bradninch, nr Exeter, Devon	164
Wyndham Arms, The	Kentisbeare, nr Cullompton, Devon	165

SOUTH AND WEST SOMERSET

Bell Inn, The	Evercreech, Somerset	186
Globe Inn, The	Milverton, Somerset	188
Greyhound Inn, The	Stogursey, nr Bridgwater, Somerset	190
Ship Inn, The	Wellington, nr Somerset, Somerset	193
Travellers Rest, The	East Pennard, nr Shepton Mallet, Somerset	196

NORTH AND EAST SOMERSET

Butchers Arms	Bishop Sutton, Somerset	213
Drum and Monkey Inn	Kenn, nr Clevedon, Somerset	214
Full Moon, The	Wells, Somerset	217
Panborough Inn, The	Panborough, nr Wells, Somerset	222
Plume of Feathers, The	Rickford, nr Burrington, Somerset	223
Prince of Wales, The	Dunkerton Hill, nr Bath, Somerset	224
Ship at Oldford, The	Oldford, nr Frome, Somerset	226

DORSET

Anchor Inn, The	Burton Bradstock, nr Bridport, Dorset	248
Brewers Arms, The	Martinstown, Dorset	250
Eight Kings Inn	Portland, Dorset	253
Ilchester Arms	Abbotsbury, Dorset	259
Kings Arms	Wareham, Dorset	260
Smugglers Inn, The	Osmington Mills, nr Weymouth, Dorset	263
Talbot Arms, The	Benville, nr Corscombe, Dorset	264
White Horse Inn, The	Swanage, Dorset	267
White Horse, The	Stourpaine, nr Blandford Forum, Dorset	266

PETS WELCOME

WEST CORNWALL

Cable Station Inn	Porthcurno, nr Penzance, Cornwall	22
Kings Arms, The	Paul, nr Penzance, Cornwall	29

EAST CORNWALL

Earl of Chatham, The	Lostwithiel, Cornwall	61

NORTH DEVON

Half Moon Inn, The	Sheepwash, nr Hatherleigh, Devon	88
Old Union Inn, The	Stibbs Cross, nr Torrington, Devon	91
Stag Hunters Hotel, The	Brendon, nr Lynton, Devon	93

SOUTH DEVON

Bullers Arms	Chagford, nr Newton Abbot, Devon	113
Chip Shop Inn, The	Chipshop, nr Tavistock, Devon	115
Church House Inn, The	Churchstow, nr Kingsbridge, Devon	116
Church House Inn, The	Rattery, nr Totnes, Devon	117
George Inn, The	Buckfastleigh, Devon	121
Journey's End Inn, The	Ringmore, nr Kingsbridge, Devon	123
Port Light Inn	Bolberry Down, nr Salcombe, Devon	129
Post Inn, The	Whiddon Down, nr Okehampton, Devon	130
Toby Jug Inn, The	Bickington, nr Newton Abbot, Devon	133

EAST DEVON

Butterleigh Inn, The	Cullompton, Devon	149
Fishponds House	Luppitt, nr Honiton, Devon	152
Old Court House, The	Chulmleigh, Devon	155

DORSET

George Inn, The	Chideock, Dorset	255
White Horse, The	Stourpaine, nr Blandford Forum, Dorset	266

WEST CORNWALL

Admiral Benbow, The	Penzance	17
Barley Sheaf, The	Gorran Churchtown, nr Mevagissey, Cornwall	19
Cornish Arms, The	St Blazey, Cornwall	23
London Inn, The	Padstow, Cornwall	32
Pendarves Arms, The	Gwithian, nr Hayle, Cornwall	34
Ship Inn, The	Polmear, nr Par, Cornwall	38

EAST CORNWALL

Church House Inn	Linkhorne, nr Callington, Cornwall	54
Cornish Arms, The	Pendoggett, nr Port Isaac, Cornwall	56
Cornish Inn, The	Gunnislake, Cornwall	57
Crow's Nest, The	Port Isaac, Cornwall	59
Halfway House Inn, The	Twowatersfoot, nr Liskeard, Cornwall	62
Harbour Moon, The	West Looe, Cornwall	63
Jubilee Inn, The	Pelynt, nr Looe, Cornwall	64
London Inn, The	Kilkhampton, nr Bude, Cornwall	65
Maltsters Arms, The	Chapel Amble, nr Wadebridge, Cornwall	66
Napoleon Inn, The	Boscastle, Cornwall	67
Old Inn, The	St Breward, nr Bodmin Moor, Cornwall	68
Smugglers Inn, The	Cawsand, nr Torpoint, Cornwall	69
Snooty Fox, The	Morval, nr Looe, Cornwall	70
Tree Inn, The	Stratton, Cornwall	71

NORTH DEVON

Black Venus Inn, The	Challacombe, nr Barnstaple, Devon	83
Ebrington Arms	Knowle, nr Braunton, Devon	85
Golden Inn, The	Highampton, nr Beaworthy, Devon	87
Half Moon Inn, The	Sheepwash, nr Hatherleigh, Devon	88
Hunters' Inn, The	Heddons Valley, nr Parracombe, Devon	89
Molesworth Arms, The	Pyworthy, nr Holsworthy, Devon	90
Royal Oak Country Inn	Dolton, Devon	92
Stag Hunters Hotel, The	Brendon, nr Lynton, Devon	93
Thatched Inn, The	Abbotsham, nr Bideford, Devon	94

SOUTH DEVON

Anchor Inn, The	Ugborough, Devon	109
Blacksmiths Arms, The	Lamerton, nr Tavistock, Devon	111
Bridford Inn	Bridford, nr Exeter, Devon	112
Castle Inn, The	Lydford, nr Okehampton, Devon	114
Church House Inn, The	Rattery, nr Totnes, Devon	117
Crabshell Inn, The	Kingsbridge, Devon	119
Dolphin Inn, The	Kenton, Devon	120
George Inn, The	Buckfastleigh, Devon	121
Globe Inn, The	Frogmore, nr Kingsbridge, Devon	122
Live and Let Live Inn, The	Landscove, nr Ashburton, Devon	125
London Inn, The	South Brent, Devon	127
London Inn, The	Horrabridge, nr Yelverton, Devon	126
Port Light Inn	Bolberry Down, nr Salcombe, Devon	129
Post Inn, The	Whiddon Down, nr Okehampton, Devon	130
Ring O' Bells, The	West Alvington, nr Kingsbridge, Devon	131
Rose and Crown, The	Yealmpton, nr Plymouth, Devon	132
Toby Jug Inn, The	Bickington, nr Newton Abbot, Devon	133

SEPARATE RESTAURANT/DINING AREA

EAST DEVON

Awliscombe Inn, The	Awliscombe, nr Honiton, Devon	146
Bowd Inn, The	Bowd Cross, nr Sidmouth, Devon	148
Crown and Sceptre, The	Newton St Cyres, nr Exeter, Devon	150
Fishponds House	Luppitt, nr Honiton, Devon	152
Lamb Inn, The	Silverton, Devon	153
New Fountain Inn	Whimple, nr Exeter, Devon	154
Royal Oak, The	Chawleigh, nr Chulmleigh, Devon	159
Three Tuns Inn, The	Silverton, nr Exeter, Devon	162
Wyndham Arms, The	Kentisbeare, nr Cullompton, Devon	165

SOUTH AND WEST SOMERSET

Ashcott Inn, The	Ashcott, nr Street, Somerset	185
Bell Inn, The	Evercreech, Somerset	186
Globe Inn, The	Milverton, Somerset	188
Globe, The	Somerton, Somerset	189
Hunters Lodge Inn, The	Leigh Common, nr Wincanton, Somerset	191
Pilgrims' Rest Inn, The	Lovington, nr Castle Cary, Somerset	192
Three Horseshoes, The	Batcombe, nr Shepton Mallet, Somerset	195
Travellers Rest, The	East Pennard, nr Shepton Mallet, Somerset	196

NORTH AND EAST SOMERSET

Butchers Arms	Bishop Sutton, Somerset	213
Drum and Monkey Inn	Kenn, nr Clevedon, Somerset	214
Eagle Inn, The	Highbury, nr Coleford, Somerset	215
Easton Inn, The	Easton, nr Wells, Somerset	216
Old Down Inn, The	Emborough, nr Bath, Somerset	220
Old Mendip Inn, The	Gurney Slade, nr Bath, Somerset	221
Panborough Inn, The	Panborough, nr Wells, Somerset	222
Prince of Wales, The	Dunkerton Hill, nr Bath, Somerset	224
Slab House Inn, The	West Horrington, nr Wells, Somerset	227
Woodborough Inn, The	Winscombe, Somerset	229

DORSET

Anchor Inn, The	Burton Bradstock, nr Bridport, Dorset	248
Brewers Arms, The	Martinstown, Dorset	250
Eight Kings Inn	Portland, Dorset	253
Fox Inn, The	Ansty, nr Dorchester, Dorset	254
Ilchester Arms	Abbotsbury, Dorset	259
Kings Arms	Wareham, Dorset	260
New Inn, The	Christchurch, Dorset	261
Piddle Inn, The	Piddletrenthide, Dorset	262
Scott Arms, The	Kingston, Dorset	263
White Horse, The	Swanage, Dorset	268

This page is left intentionally blank

Index of Towns and Villages

A

Abbotsbury 233
Allerford 169
Altarnun 43
Arlington 75
Ashburton 100
Ashton 43
Axminster 139

B

Barnstaple 76
Barrington 169
Bath 199
Beaminster 234
Belstone 77
Bideford 77
Bishops Lydeard 170
Blandford Forum 234
Bodmin 3
Bodmin Moor 44
Boscastle 45
Bournemouth 234
Bovey Tracey 100
Braunton 78
Bridgwater 170
Bridport 235
Bristol 202
Brixham 100
Buckfastleigh 101
Bude 45
Budleigh Salterton 139
Burnham-on-Sea 205
Burrow Bridge 171

C

Cadbury Castle 171
Cameley 205
Camelford 45
Castle Drogo 101
Cerne Abbas 235
Chard 172
Charlestown 4
Cheddar 206
Cheddon Fitzpaine 172
Clapton 172
Claverton 206
Clevedon 207
Clovelly 78
Colyton 140
Come to Good 4
Corfe Castle 236
Creed 4
Crewkerne 172

D

Dalwood 140
Dartmouth 101
Dawlish 102
Dawlish Warren 102
Dobwalls 46
Dorchester 237
Dunster 173

E

East Lambrook 174
Ebbor Gorge 207
Exeter 140
Exmoor 174
Exmouth 142

F

Falmouth 4
Fowey 46
Frome 208

G

Glastonbury 174
Godolphin Cross 5
Great Torrington 78
Gweek 6

H

Hartland 79
Hayle 6
Helford 6
Helston 7
Honiton 142

I

Ilfracombe 79
Ilminster 177
Isle of Portland 239

K

Kestle Mill 7
Kingsbridge 102
Kingsdon 177

L

Land's End 7
Langport 177
Launceston 46
Liskeard 47
Lizard Peninsula 8
Loddiswell 103

Looe 47
Lostwithiel 48
Lyme Regis 239
Lynmouth 79

M

Martock 178
Mawnan Smith 8
Mells 208
Mevagissey 8
Minehead 178
Minions 49
Monksilver 179
Montacute 179
Moreton 240
Moretonhampstead 103
Muchelney 180
Muddiford 80
Murrayton 50

N

Newquay 9
Newton Abbot 103
North Bovey 103
North Tawton 80

O

Okehampton 80
Osmington Mills 240
Otterton 143
Ottery St Mary 143

P

Padstow 10
Paignton 103
Penzance 10
Plymouth 104
Polperro 50
Poole 240
Porlock 180
Port Isaac 50
Porthcurno 11
Portquin 50
Postbridge 105

R

Redruth 11

S

Salcombe 106
Saltash 51
Seaton 143

Selworthy 180
Shaftesbury 241
Shepton Mallet 209
Sherborne 241
Shute 144
Sidmouth 144
Somerton 181
St Agnes 12
St Austell 12
St Cleer 51
St Columb Major 13
St Endellion 51
St Ives 13
St Just in Roseland 15
St Keyne 51
St Michael's Mount 15
Stanton Drew 209
Stoke 81
Stoke-sub-Hamdon 181
Swanage 243

T

Taunton 181
Tavistock 106
Teignmouth 106
Thorne St Margaret 182
Tintagel 52
Tintinhull 182
Tolland 183
Tolpuddle 243
Torpoint 52
Torquay 107
Totnes 107
Treborough 183
Truro 15

W

Wareham 244
Washaway 16
Washford 183
Watchet 183
Wells 210
Wembury 108
Weston-super-Mare 211
Westward Ho! 81
Westwood 212
Weymouth 244
Whitchurch Canonicorum 245
Whitsand Bay 52
Williton 184
Wimborne Minster 245
Wincanton 184
Winfrith Newburge 245
Wookey Hole 212
Woolacombe 81

Y

Yeovil 184

Hidden Inns
Reader Reaction

The *Hidden Inns* research team would like to receive reader's comments on any visitor attractions or places reviewed in the book and also recommendations for suitable entries to be included in the next edition. This will help ensure that the *Hidden Inns* series continues to provide its readers with useful information on the more interesting, unusual or unique features of each attraction or place ensuring that their stay in the local area is an enjoyable and stimulating experience.

To provide your comments or recommendations would you please complete the forms below and overleaf as indicated and send to:The Research Department, Travel Publishing Ltd., 7a Apollo House, Calleva Park, Aldermaston, Reading, RG7 8TN.

Your Name:

Your Address:

Your Telephone Number:

Please tick as appropriate: Comments ☐   Recommendation ☐

Name of *"Hidden Inn"*:

Address:

Telephone Number:

Name of Contact:

Hidden Inns
Reader Reaction

Comment or Reason for Recommendation:

....

....

....

....

....

....

....

....

....

....

....

....

Order Form

To order any of our publications just fill in the payment details below and complete the order form *overleaf*. For orders of less than 4 copies please add £1 per book for postage and packing. Orders over 4 copies are P & P free.

Please Complete Either:

I enclose a cheque for £ .... made payable to Travel Publishing Ltd

Or:

Card No: ☐☐☐☐ ☐☐☐☐ ☐☐☐☐ ☐☐☐☐

Expiry Date: ☐☐ ☐☐

Signature: ....

NAME: ....

ADDRESS: ....

                ....

                ....

POSTCODE:..

TEL NO: ....

Please either send or telephone your order to:

Travel Publishing Ltd   Tel: 0118 981 7777
7a Apollo House   Fax: 0118 982 0077
Calleva Park
Aldermaston
Berks, RG7 8TN

	Price	Quantity	Value
Hidden Places Regional Titles			
Cambridgeshire & Lincolnshire	£7.99	....	....
Channel Islands	£6.99	....	....
Cheshire	£7.99	....	....
Chilterns	£7.99	....	....
Cornwall	£7.99	....	....
Derbyshire	£7.99	....	....
Devon	£7.99	....	....
Dorset, Hants & Isle of Wight	£7.99	....	....
Essex	£7.99	....	....
Gloucestershire & Wiltshire	£7.99	....	....
Heart of England	£7.99	....	....
Hereford, Worcs & Shropshire	£7.99	....	....
Highlands & Islands	£7.99	....	....
Kent	£7.99	....	....
Lake District & Cumbria	£7.99	....	....
Lancashire	£7.99	....	....
Norfolk	£7.99	....	....
Northeast Yorkshire	£6.99	....	....
Northumberland & Durham	£6.99	....	....
North Wales	£7.99	....	....
Nottinghamshire	£6.99	....	....
Potteries	£6.99	....	....
Somerset	£7.99	....	....
South Wales	£7.99	....	....
Suffolk	£7.99	....	....
Surrey	£6.99	....	....
Sussex	£7.99	....	....
Thames Valley	£7.99	....	....
Warwickshire & West Midlands	£6.99	....	....
Yorkshire	£7.99	....	....
Hidden Places National Titles			
England	£9.99	....	....
Ireland	£9.99	....	....
Scotland	£9.99	....	....
Wales	£8.99	....	....
Hidden Inns Titles			
West Country	£5.99	....	....
South East	£5.99	....	....
South	£5.99	....	....
Wales	£5.99	....	....
		_____	_____
		_____	_____

*For orders of less than 4 copies please add £1 per book for postage &
packing. Orders over 4 copies P & P free.*